Imaginary Friends
and the People
Who Create Them

Imaginary Friends and the People Who Create Them

Second Edition

Marjorie Taylor
Naomi R. Aguiar

OXFORD
UNIVERSITY PRESS

Oxford University Press is a department of the University of Oxford.
It furthers the University's objective of excellence in research, scholarship,
and education by publishing worldwide. Oxford is a registered trade mark of
Oxford University Press in the UK and in certain other countries.

Published in the United States of America by Oxford University Press
198 Madison Avenue, New York, NY 10016, United States of America

© Oxford University Press 2024

First Edition published in 1999
Second Edition published in 2024

All rights reserved. No part of this publication may be reproduced, stored in a retrieval system,
or transmitted, used for text and data mining, or used for training artificial intelligence, in any form or
by any means, without the prior permission in writing of Oxford University Press, or as expressly
permitted by law, by licence or under terms agreed with the appropriate reprographics rights
organization. Inquiries concerning reproduction outside the scope of the above should be sent
to the Rights Department, Oxford University Press, at the address above

You must not circulate this work in any other form
and you must impose this same condition on any acquirer.

CIP data is on file at the Library of Congress.

ISBN 9780190888886

DOI: 10.1093/9780190888916.001.0001

Printed by Integrated Books International, United States of America

For Amber, Anna, Sarah, and Isabelle

and all the children who told us about their imaginary friends

Contents

Note on Second Edition   viii
Acknowledgments   x
Permissions   xii

1. What Is an Imaginary Friend and How Many Children Have Them?   1
2. Imaginary Friends Who Are Invisible   15
3. Imaginary Friends Who Are Personified Objects   30
4. Children Who Create Imaginary Friends: Individual Characteristics   47
5. Children Who Create Imaginary Friends: The Influence of Family and Culture   70
6. Why Do Children Create Imaginary Friends?   92
7. Do Imaginary Friends Help Children Cope with Adversity?   110
8. Do Children Think Their Imaginary Friends Are Real?   128
9. What Happens to the Imaginary Friends Created in Early Childhood?   148
10. Paracosms: The Imaginary Worlds of Middle Childhood   163
11. Parasocial Relationships with Celebrities and Media Characters   179
12. The Imaginary Friends of Adults   197
13. Adult Fiction Writers and Their Characters   213
14. Final Thoughts: Fantasy in the Lives of Children and Adults   234

References   244
Index   264

Note on Second Edition

This book is an updated and expanded edition of *Imaginary Companions and the Children Who Create Them*, originally published in 1999. A lot has happened in the 25 years since this book first appeared. To cover the new work, this edition has 14 chapters compared with 8 chapters in the first edition. Describing all the progress that has been made in the field and incorporating the findings of 21st-century researchers have been exciting for us. In particular, Tracy Gleason of Wellesley College has made extensive contributions to our understanding of the functions that imaginary friends serve and their connections to social development. Among the many other researchers whose work was conducted after 1999, we want to note the important contributions of Yusuke Moriguchi (Joetsu University of Education, Japan), Qiyi Lin (Huaiyin Normal University, People's Republic of China), Brad Wigger (Louisville Seminary, United States), Paula Bouldin (La Trobe University, Australia), Paige Davis (University of Leeds, United Kingdom), and Charles Fernyhough (Durham University, United Kingdom).

For this edition, we changed our title from *Imaginary Companions and the Children Who Create Them* to *Imaginary Friends and the People Who Create Them*. We changed "Children" to "People" because there is much more discussion here than in the first edition of imaginary characters in the lives of adolescents and adults, including three new chapters. The harder decision was whether to keep "imaginary companions." A variety of other terms have been suggested, including Adams, Stanford, and Singh's use of "invisible companion,"[1] and Klausen and Passman's use of "pretend companion."[2] Some of the objections to "imaginary companion" focus on the "imaginary" part because this word reflects the Euro-Western perspective assuming all invisible beings are imaginary. We do not comment on whether there are categories of invisible entities that have a basis in reality, but we acknowledge that our use of "imaginary" would exclude them. We do not see this as a problem because, although we include some discussion of other types of invisible entities, almost all of the research described here is with children who *themselves* report that their friends are "just pretend." The book is not meant to be an exhaustive survey of all the possible categories of invisible entities (e.g., fairies, ghosts, God, angels). We believe "imaginary" is the best descriptive term for the phenomenon that is the subject of this book.

In the end, it was "companion" that gave us the most trouble. In 1999, Marjorie chose "companion" because children have different types of relationships with their imaginary creations, including being its parent and being protected by it, as well as treating it as a friend. "Companion" does not apply perfectly for all types of relationships but is more inclusive than "friend." However, while in 1999 "imaginary friend" and "imaginary companion" were used somewhat interchangeably, times have changed. "Imaginary companion" is common in academic circles, but the term in popular culture is overwhelmingly "imaginary friend." In fact, Kastenbaum and Fox reported that the adult participants in their research "preferred to speak of imaginary friends as distinguished from imaginary companions, the term most often used in the literature."[3] Our book was written for parents, teachers, and other interested adults as well as researchers, so we opted for the term that would reach them. At the same time, we remind our readers that the beauty of an imagined relationship is that it can take whatever form its creator would like.

Notes

1. Adams, K., Stanford, E., & Singh, H. (2022). Reconceptualizing imaginary friends: Interdisciplinary approaches for understanding invisible companions. *Journal of Childhood Studies, 47,* 32–49.
2. Klausen, E., & Passman, R. H. (2007). Pretend companions (imaginary playmates): The emergence of a field. *The Journal of Genetic Psychology, 167,* 349–364.
3. Kastenbaum, R., & Fox, L. (2008). Do imaginary companions die? An exploratory study. *OMEGA -Journal of Death and Dying, 56*(2), 123–152.

Acknowledgments

Our work on imaginary friends began in the 1990s with a series of studies by Marjorie and Stephanie Carlson that were inspired by Paul Harris' work on imagination. Three decades later, the creativity in children's inventions still amazes us. Over the years we have been supported, inspired, encouraged, mentored, edited, and taught by so many people. We are very grateful for the help we have received from friends and colleagues and wish we could list all of you.

First, we want to thank Tracy Gleason for her thought-provoking research, editorial brilliance, and unsurpassed sense of humor. She has been correcting our grammar, making fun of our mistakes, and improving our writing for years. In Marjorie's case, decades. Tracy was at the very beginning of her career when the first edition of this book was written in 1999. But in this edition, Tracy has her rightful place as one of the most important voices and prolific researchers on imaginary *companions* (she officially objects to our switch to imaginary *friends*). We are very grateful for Tracy's extensive comments on the final-until-Tracy draft of the manuscript for this book.

Our research has been guided and challenged by the theories and research findings of Stephanie Carlson, Suzanne Gaskins, Tracy Gleason, Alison Gopnik, Paul Harris, Angeline Lillard, Michele Root-Bernstein, Jacqueline Woolley, Dorothy and Jerome Singer, Jennifer Mauro, and Jeremy Baillenson, among others. We have greatly benefited from the wisdom of wonderful colleagues, coauthors, and mentors, a group that includes John Flavell, Dare Baldwin, Sara Hodges, Susan Gelman, Robert Kavanaugh, Ulrich Mayr, Lou Moses, Sandra Calvert, Phil Fisher, Mike Posner, and Elaine Reese. We also want to thank all the friends and colleagues who have assisted us in so many ways personally and professionally: sending literary and scholarly references to imaginary friends, children's books about them, cartoons featuring them, stories about their own imaginary friends or imaginary friends in their families, as well as lots of encouragement, enthusiasm, companionship, and love. This supportive group of people includes Taiya Barss, Marcia Barss, Louise Bishop, Jenny Ellis, Ellie Flavell, Lew Goldberg, Jim Hardman, Mary Jaeger, Sue Jurasin, Deborah Legoretta, Christina Martin, Reema Mendoza, Caitlin Monroe, Elizabeth Monroe, Mose Mosley, Marisa Putnam, Catrin Rode, JJ, Nickolas, and Julia Scheri, Anne Simons, Chris Simpson, and Seth Wilson. Anna Harbaugh read the first very rough draft of our manuscript, and her enthusiasm was the boost we needed to keep going.

Over the years we have been very fortunate to work with many talented graduate students who have made huge contributions to our research and to the literature, as well as to our personal lives. Alison Sachet and Candee Mottweiler were our partners extraordinaire in developing ideas and launching studies. We are very grateful to

Bridget Cartwright, Michele Grimes, Annemarie Hulette, Adele Kohanyi, Jacob Levernier, Gretchen Lussier, Anne Mannering, Bayta Maring, Emilee Naylor, Adrienne Samuels, Lynn Smith, Caryn Stoess, and Deniz Tahiroglu for all their work. Many undergraduate research assistants have worked on our studies of imagination—providing feedback, critique, suggesting ideas, running participants, entering data, and completing a million other tasks to keep our research moving along. We thank all of them, but in particular we want to acknowledge the important contributions of Sara Amini, Ariann Bolton, Carolyn Charlie, Mirjam Harrison, Vicki Luu, Andrea Minton-Edison, Beth Shawber, Molly Biedermann, Montana Boone, Marie Frolich, Angella Liu, and Charlotte Wright.

We are grateful for the generous support of the National Science Foundation, the John Templeton Foundation, and the University of Oregon. We thank Hayley Singer (senior associate editor) and Kayley Gilbert (project editor) at Oxford University Press for their work on this book. Most of the first edition was written while Marjorie was an Erskine Fellow at the University of Canterbury in Christchurch, New Zealand. Thanks to Gill Rhodes and Ian McLean who were friends and hosts in New Zealand and were very supportive of this work.

Three imaginary friends in our own families have been influential in shaping our ideas about children's imagination. Amber's stories about her imaginary friend, Michael Rose, were a big part of what initially motivated Marjorie to begin her research. Later on, Marjorie's cousin Joshua Barss-Donham documented and videotaped his daughter Rosa's years-long friendship with an invisible white cat, providing the kinds of intriguing details, commentary, and insight that are not always possible in a laboratory setting or with a single interview. For Naomi, Isabelle has been her most important teacher. Isabelle's devotion to Ellie the Elephant has been a constant reminder of the power and importance of imagination. Along with Amber, Rosa, and Isabelle, over a thousand children, parents, and other adults have shared their imaginary friends with us. We are forever grateful.

Finally, our love and thanks to our families for all the countless and steadfast ways they have encouraged and supported us. Particular thanks is due to Naomi's parents, James Aguiar and Randi Burke-Aguiar, for their loving support through all the twists and turns of a dancer-turned-academic career, and Isabelle, who delighted in hearing sections of chapters read aloud. Doug (Marjorie's brother) filled her studio with the music from his radio show. Amber, Sarah, Anna, and Taiya always wanted to know how the writing was going. Marjorie's husband Bill kept the printers printing, the Internet connecting, and the fire burning at their home on Orcas Island.

Permissions

Winnie-the-Pooh and friends. Printed by permission from Children's Center at 42nd Street, ©The New York Public Library.

"The Two Fridas" by Frida Kahlo.

© 2024 Banco de México Diego Rivera Museums Trust, Mexico, D.F. /Artists Rights Society (ARS), New York.

Photo Credit: Schalkwijk / Art Resource, New York.

Artist: Kahlo, Frida (1907–1954) ©ARS, New York 2024.

Description: The Two Fridas (Las Dos Fridas). 1939. Oil on canvas, 173 × 173 cm (5' 8 1/2' × 5' 8 1/2').

Location: Museo Nacional de Arte Moderno, Mexico City, Mexico.

Image of tiny book by Charlotte Brontë printed by permission of Clark Hodgin, photographer.

Program for Paul Taylor Dance Company. Used by permission. All rights reserved, Playbill Inc.

Excerpts from *Private Domain: An Autobiography* by Paul Taylor printed by permission from The Paul Taylor Dance Company.

Excerpts from *Agatha Christie: An Autobiography* reprinted by permission of HarperCollins Publishers Ltd, ©1977, Agatha Christie.

Images of research stimuli printed in Chapter 11 by permission of Shutterstock and Oslund Design Inc.

Cover art by Amanda Blake: "She was surrounded by traces of lives that might've been," 2023, oil painting on birch panel.

Chapter 1
What Is an Imaginary Friend and How Many Children Have Them?

> He kind of looks like me... we like to play sword fighting... we pretend to play Lego Star Wars. He's super funny... nice, generous, crazy sometimes. He tells me jokes... shares his snacks with me.... When I'm upset he makes me talk sometimes; he makes me feel a little bit better. He's really good at doing things... helping me with my homework. He can run super fast. He's super nice... a good friend.
> (9-year-old boy's description of his friend "Bob")

Bob sounds like a wonderful friend. In fact, the child's description includes many of the features that have been identified as signaling high quality in a friendship—a combination of recreation, guidance, validation, and intimate exchange.[1] The support and companionship of such friends are important to our happiness and psychological health throughout life, and in childhood, they are connected to social competence and resilience. Thus, having a friend like Bob might seem to be obviously a good thing—but there is a caveat. Does it matter that Bob is imaginary? That he eats bugs, can read a 150-page book in a minute, and likes to shapeshift into animals or trees?

The creation of an imaginary friend is only one of many forms that fantasy production takes during the preschool years, but we think it is special. Children as young as 2 or 3 talk to their imaginary friends and listen to what they have to say, showing that the capacity to love and derive comfort from an imaginary other does not require a lengthy history or extensive experience with social interactions. However, adult observers often do not know what to make of this type of behavior. While they might admire or be amused by the creativity in children's extravagant descriptions, they quickly become concerned if children seem too caught up in the fantasy. On the other hand, some parents express concern if their child does *not* have an imaginary friend. They wonder if this is a negative sign regarding their child's intellectual or creative potential.

What does having an imaginary friend mean? Is it an early marker of special intelligence or the first sign of mental illness? What is the likelihood of a child who is engrossed in an imaginary world losing touch with reality? Can an imaginary friend be a source of resilience by providing support and love that is experienced as real?

Imaginary Friends and the People Who Create Them. Second Edition. Marjorie Taylor and Naomi R. Aguiar, Oxford University Press. © Oxford University Press (2024). DOI: 10.1093/9780190888916.003.0001

These are some of the questions addressed in this book. The answers come from an analysis of psychological research with young children. It turns out that creating an imaginary friend is a normal and healthy activity that is surprisingly common. Exactly how common depends upon what is counted as an imaginary friend and the source of information about them (children, parents, or adults who are asked about childhood imaginary friends).

What Is an Imaginary Friend?

"Bob," the bug-eating, joke-telling shapeshifter, is clearly an imaginary friend, but it is not that straightforward to come up with a concise definition that covers all the different types of entities that children imagine. Imaginary friends are a diverse and multifaceted lot. Many researchers still fall back on a definition Margaret Svenson came up with in 1934:

> ... an invisible character, named and referred to in conversation with other persons or played with directly for a period of time, at least several months, having an air of reality for the child but no apparent objective basis. This excludes that type of imaginative play in which an object is personified, or in which the child himself assumes the role of some person in his environment.[2]

But there are some problems with this definition. First of all, there are sometimes good reasons to include toys or other objects as imaginary friends. Plus, the part about the activity lasting "at least several months" is arbitrary and difficult to document. Preschoolers are notoriously idiosyncratic in their estimations of time (e.g., using "yesterday" to refer to any amount of time in the past),[3] and parents are often not initially aware of an invisible friend or might not realize exactly when a comfort toy evolved into a personal friend. In our research, we defined an imaginary friend as "a character created by a child that is interacted with and/or talked about on a regular basis." This definition does not spell out everything that needs to be considered when categorizing children's fantasy activities, but it is more inclusive and more appropriately vague than Svenson's definition. It is a place to start.

How Many Children Have Imaginary Friends?

The answer to this question depends on not only the definition, but also the source of the information. Who are the best informants about imaginary friends—the parents or the children themselves? What about retrospective reports—the memories of adults for the imaginary characters they created as young children? Each source of information has drawbacks, as well as advantages.

Sources of Information about Imaginary Friends

Interviews with Children

We think children are the best source of information about imaginary friends. They are the experts. But that doesn't mean that there are no problems interpreting what they have to say. Sometimes children are not completely sure what you mean by "pretend friend." They might say yes and then describe a real friend. Or they have their own way of referring to their friend (e.g., "fake friend," "ghost sister," or "friends who live in my house") and thus say no when asked about a "pretend friend." Other children might say yes and then describe a stuffed animal that actually spends most of its time in the toy box.

An even trickier problem is that some children make up imaginary friends in response to questions about them. A pretend friend? What a good idea! And they invent one on the spot. For example, one child described a wonderful giant penguin who tended to get into trouble for knocking over lampposts. (His mother, who was watching from behind a one-way mirror, was absolutely transfixed!) A week later, he said he didn't have an imaginary friend and drew a blank when asked about the penguin. We suspect that the penguin made a cameo appearance in the child's fantasy life on the day that we brought up the topic of imaginary friends.

Even when children clearly are describing an imaginary friend that they play with on a regular basis, there are often inconsistencies in their accounts, suggesting that the children are making up some details as they go along. When Marjorie first started interviewing children, the discrepancies and spontaneously created details bothered her. Were these descriptions revealing anything meaningful about children's fantasy lives? Now we view the dynamic character of children's reports as part of the phenomenon and something to be expected. After all, although the adult's goal is to find out about the imaginary friend, from the point of view of the child, the interview might be just another opportunity to pretend. Probably every time children think about their imaginary friends, they invent new details or change existing ones. These sorts of inconsistencies do not make the child's report any less interesting and should not be taken as evidence that there is nothing substantive in what the child has to say. And typically, the basic description and fundamental characteristics of imaginary friends last for months or even years.[4]

Interviews with Parents

Given the challenges in interviewing young children, it is reassuring when the child's report is corroborated by the parent. Parents can also sometimes provide very helpful additional information. They might recall the content of overheard conversations between the child and the friend, describe events in the child's life when the imaginary friend first appeared, or help the researcher determine if a beloved toy functions as an imaginary friend.

However, in general, parents are not particularly good primary sources. Some studies have found consistency in the reports of parents and young children for whether or not the child has an imaginary friend,[5] but when it comes to what the imaginary friend is like, parents' reports can be hit or miss. Gleason has had some success with parents' descriptions being similar to their children's (particularly for invisible friends),[6] but we have often found large discrepancies in what the parent and child have to say. It is easy for parents to make incorrect assumptions. For example, one parent told Marjorie that her son had an imaginary friend named Nobby, a little invisible boy who functioned as a playmate. The child also named Nobby but when asked how often he played with him, the child scowled and replied, "I don't *play* with him." The child explained that Nobby was a 160-year-old businessman who visited him between business trips to Portland and Seattle, whenever the child wanted to "talk things over."

The parents of another boy got a surprise when they saw the drawing their son made of his invisible friend, The Butcher Shop Guy (see Figure 1.1). They thought they were well acquainted with The Butcher Shop Guy, who had been part of their family for two years, but they had not realized he was a green-skinned Cyclops. The boy described his friend as a very friendly person and world traveler—who had never worked in a butcher's shop. When asked why he was called The Butcher Shop Guy, the boy said he didn't know ("That's just his name."). In another study, a parent described her daughter's invisible friend Olympia as a naughty invisible girl who was responsible for damage in the child's room, whereas the child described Olympia as an invisible giraffe who turned different colors when she danced.[7]

Sometimes parents don't know many details about the imaginary friend because they are reluctant to ask. They report that although they are comfortable with their children having pretend friends, they don't want to actively encourage this type of play. They allow their children to "do their thing," but they don't press for details or participate in the pretense. Especially as they get older, children are quite sensitive to this sort of ambivalence. One 6-year-old girl told us all about her imaginary friend, but when the researcher was leaving the interview room, she asked her not to repeat anything she had said to her mother. In fact, it is not unusual for parents to be completely unaware that their children have imaginary friends. In research with 6- and 7-year-olds, Taylor and Carlson[8] found that parents were aware of only 7 of 32 imaginary friends created after the age of 4. Even with younger children, parents sometimes learn about their children's imaginary friends for the first time when the children participate in our research.

When parents do not know about their children's imaginary friends, it is not necessarily because they are uninvolved in their children's lives or harbor negative feelings about imaginary friends. Sometimes pretend friends have commonplace names that the child mentions, in passing, along with the names of real children at the local day care or in the neighborhood. When Marjorie's daughter was 3, she sometimes

Figure 1.1 Drawing of "The Butcher Shop Guy" by 8-year-old boy.

referred to a person named Michael Rose. Amber seemed to enjoy her time with Michael Rose, and Marjorie became curious about him. But when the preschool teachers were asked to point him out, they had no idea who he was. Subsequently Amber was asked for more details and she reported, among other things, that he had a barn full of giraffes. Michael Rose lived only in Amber's imagination.

Adult Memories of Imaginary Friends

Another way to find out about imaginary friends is to ask adults about their own childhoods. Adults often provide interesting and thoughtful accounts. The insight gained from maturity allows them to speculate about why they created the imaginary friend, and they can sometimes provide information about how long the fantasy friends lasted and why they happened to disappear. Here is a description of two childhood imaginary friends provided by a man in his 40s that exemplifies the rich detail that adults are sometimes able to report:

> Sometime before my sixth birthday, possibly when I was three or four, I began to have two imaginary companions. These two folks were named Digger and Dewgy. They were with me for several years and I remember them mostly as play mates, more specifically playing with me in the backyard, enough so that I would consider from this perspective of time and space, that they lived in the backyard. I don't remember them ever coming into the house, though I don't think it was forbidden or anything, it's just that I mostly remember going into the backyard to find them, like you would go to the neighborhood playground to meet your friends.
>
> Digger was my twin. He looked like me and spoke in pretty much the same voice. The major difference was that he was more serious. He was the leader, the person who initiated the games, designed the roads in the sandbox, tempted me to stay when my mother called me home. He was very smart and knew many answers to complex questions like: why are there trees? or, where do you really come out if you dig straight down? I say he was my twin, but he was also bigger and stronger than me. We never fought. He was there to protect me from the unknowns of the woods. He was very brave and sometimes even daring. He looked out for the rest of us. He had a dog that wasn't really a dog. The dog's name was Dewgy.
>
> Dewgy was more than a mere dog. He was sort of a superdog. He was at least half human. He could talk and he liked to make jokes. He laughed a lot. Sometimes when Digger got too serious, Dewgy and I would smile at each other and nod knowingly. Dewgy walked mostly on his hind legs. He reminds me most closely of a cartoon character, maybe modelled after Goofy, only he wasn't clumsy or stupid. Dewgy was black with short hair and he smelled like a dog only I don't remember him having dog breath. Sometimes Dewgy and I would rumble together, play tag, fall asleep next to each other in a thicket of red cedar. I was much more physical with Dewgy than I ever was with Digger. Dewgy and I loved each other freely and openly like a boy loves a dog. Digger and I were on more of an intellectual plane. Digger was the thinker and doer. Dewgy liked to play for the sheer joy of playing. He laughed for the joy of laughing. On the other hand, you always got the feeling that Dewgy would be there growling if there was ever any real danger. Together Dewgy and Digger watched the woods for you, they made it safe to go up the hill into the Kaschel's farm with the Big Rock and all the scary dairy cows.

The problem with relying on retrospective reports is that many children forget about their imaginary friends once they no longer play with them. Even a few months later, children sometimes do not remember the friends they used to enjoy so much.[9] Consequently, memories for a large number of imaginary friends likely do not survive into adulthood. As a result, estimates of the incidence of imaginary friends based on adult memories are likely too low. Another issue with retrospective reports is that the source of the memory is not clear. Many adults report that they don't remember firsthand having had an imaginary friend, but their parents tell them they did and have the anecdotes to prove it. Thus, adult answers to questions about their childhood imaginary friends are sometimes based on family stories, rather than actual memories of interacting with a pretend friend.

Multiple Sources and Follow-Up Interviews

In the Taylor Imagination Lab, our main method has been to conduct interviews with children and parents in separate rooms, compare their responses, and then resolve discrepancies by conducting second follow-up interviews.[10] Two or three members of the lab later read all the information that was collected from the children and their parents and decide if the child should be categorized as having an imaginary friend.[11]

This method is not foolproof, but it avoids a few common pitfalls. Some children say they don't have an imaginary friend, but their parents provide descriptions of one. In the follow-up with the child, we ask about the one described by the parent by name (e.g., "Who is Baintor?"). These follow-up questions have been uniformly successful in eliciting descriptions from the children. Maybe these children simply had not understood our original question. The information from the parents gathered at the first interview can also help to clear up any source of confusion (e.g., in the child follow-up, we use the child's own term to ask about an imaginary friend).

We also use the information provided by the child in our follow-up with the parent. If the child named an imaginary friend that was not mentioned by the parent, we ask the parent if the child's description corresponds to any real friend or if they have any idea who the child was talking about. If the child mentions a stuffed animal or doll at the first interview, the parent is asked questions about the extent of the child's interaction and play with the named toy.

Based on this method, our estimate is that 28% of preschool children create imaginary friends. This number might be a little low, reflecting our conservative approach to identifying children who have them. For example, we give special weight to the child's report, so we don't include children whose parents described imaginary friends if the children did not corroborate those descriptions. However, some of these children might not have wanted to share their private fantasies with us, or might have forgotten about an imaginary friend, even though at one time it was important to them. Some of the toys that we rejected as imaginary friends on the basis of the parent interview might also have played a more significant role in the children's fantasy lives than the parents realized.

Despite these caveats, we think that 28% is a reasonable estimate for the incidence of imaginary friends for children up to 4 years of age, the age that is commonly mentioned as the peak time for imaginary friend production, the "high season" of imaginative play.[12] However, in a study with 6- and 7-year olds,[13] a surprisingly large number of children had created imaginary friends after age 4 (32 of the 69 children with imaginary friends, 46%). The majority of these later-developing imaginary friends were invisible and included a variety of interesting and exotic individuals, including our first cases of an imaginary friend with a pierced ear, an invisible snowman, an invisible elephant, and an invisible squirrel. If we consider all cases of imaginary friends created by children any time up to the age of 7, the percentage of children who has ever had one is 65%. If you want to include only invisible friends—excluding the ones based on toys—the number is 43%. Although the numbers decline, children also create imaginary friends after the age of 7. In a large study in which 1,800 children aged 5–12 years were asked if they "talked to a friend that no one else can see," 19% of 10-year-olds, 14% of 11-year-olds, and 9% of 12-year-olds answered yes (the overall prevalence is this study was 46.2%).[14]

Our preferred method of interviewing both children and parents and then crosschecking their responses with follow-up interviews is laborious and not always feasible for other researchers or even for us. But the results of the many different types of studies in the current literature add up to a fairly consistent picture of the real world of imaginary friends. Our goal with this book was to integrate these research findings to present what is known and what is speculated. Here are brief summaries of the topics we address.

Overview of Chapters

Parents, teachers, psychologists, and other adult observers express a range of reactions to imaginary friends—delight, amusement, indifference, flickers of worry, serious concern, and alarm. Adults often wonder why children have imaginary friends, and we believe that imaginary friends have been one of the most misunderstood types of childhood behavior. We hope this book will illuminate the role played by such fantasies in cognitive, social, and emotional development; help explain some of the reasons for misconceptions; and suggest what children's creation of imaginary friends can tell us about human creativity and imagination.

Chapter 2: Imaginary Friends Who Are Invisible

Invisible friends are fascinating because they are designed by the children themselves rather being based on a toy designed by someone else. Invisible friends include a wild assortment of species that vary in appearance, personality, ability, behavior, age, and size. In this chapter, we describe some of this diversity and discuss why we think the category of imaginary "friends" should include the invisible characters that are sometimes mean, disobedient, uncooperative, or scary. But while we do not require that an imagined character be consistently well behaved and agreeable to be counted as an imaginary friend, it is necessary that the child have a relationship with the character. Thus, we exclude cases in which children pretend to *be* the imagined animal or another person. We do not consider such "pretend identities" as a type of imaginary friend because children are taking on the character themselves rather than pretending to have a relationship with an entity that is separate from themselves.

Chapter 3: Imaginary Friends Who Are Personified Objects

Does the friend have to be invisible to count as an imaginary friend, or are children's teddy bears and other toys also candidates? Many children develop sustained interactive relationships with toys or other objects that are a source of support and companionship. Most current researchers include such objects as potential imaginary friends depending on the extent to which the child imagines its thoughts, actions, and/or emotions. This chapter provides examples of imaginary friends based on objects and how these "personified objects" differ from invisible imaginary friends.

Chapter 4: Children Who Create Imaginary Friends: Individual Characteristics

How accurate is the stereotype of children with imaginary friends as lonely children who are too shy to make real friends and maybe are a little lost in a fantasy world? Not at all. The older studies that painted this negative picture had methodological problems, and more reliable information collected in recent years indicates that the creation of an imaginary friend is healthy and relatively common. In general, the similarities between the children who have imaginary friends and children who do not have imaginary friends are more striking than their differences. When differences are found, they tend to turn the stereotype on its head. Children who create pretend friends tend to be outgoing and creative individuals who enjoy interacting with others.

Chapter 5: Children Who Create Imaginary Friends: The Influence of Family and Culture

Although American parents sometimes worry about imaginary friends, in general they tend to promote children's pretend play, and our culture provides a wealth of fantasy material that is often incorporated into children's private fantasy creations. However, not all children are encouraged to engage in pretend play, and substantial cultural differences emerge in parental reaction to and interpretation of imaginary friends. In this chapter, we review the influence of family structure, parental attitudes, religion, and culture.

Chapter 6: Why Do Children Create Imaginary Friends?

An imaginary friend can serve a variety of functions, but the primary ones are entertainment, love, and companionship. Imaginary friends also provide a vehicle for storytelling, communicating and bargaining with parents, and developing self-esteem. They help children process ongoing events in their lives and deal with a variety of concerns, fears, and problems, including actual or perceived restrictions. They might serve some of these needs simultaneously or evolve as children's interests and lived experiences change.

Chapter 7: Do Imaginary Friends Help Children Cope with Adversity?

Imaginary friends serve as safe recipients for sharing things children might not tell others about the trials and tribulations of everyday life. They also might help with more serious life events and chronic stressors—the death of a parent, chaotic home environments, ongoing neglect and/or abuse, and protracted regional violence. In this chapter, we explore the possibility that imaginary friends can provide the comfort, companionship, and security that are associated with resilience in the face of such adversity.

Chapter 8: Do Children Think Their Imaginary Friends Are Real?

Some adults worry that children think their imaginary friends are real, but responding to this concern requires a broader discussion of the general distinction between fantasy and reality. The topics covered in this chapter include children's beliefs in fantasy characters such as Santa Claus; their understanding of fantasy material on television, movies and online; and their comprehension of joint pretend play with others, as well as their beliefs about their imaginary friends. Sometimes the boundary between fantasy and reality is not entirely clear to children, but when it comes to pretend friends, children know exactly what is going on.

Chapter 9: What Happens to the Imaginary Friends Created in Early Childhood?

In most cases, there are no well-marked events associated with the imaginary friend's disappearance—it simply fades away. But imaginary friends also die, sometimes violently. Many parents report that children abandon their imaginary friends at about 6 years of age when they start school, but we question this commonly held assumption. Some pretend friends are retained much longer, and sometimes imaginary friends first appear when the children are well beyond the preschool years.

Chapter 10: Paracosms: The Imaginary Worlds of Middle Childhood

As children reach middle childhood and beyond, they sometimes create entire imaginary worlds, referred to as "paracosms," for their imaginary friends to inhabit.[15] In other cases, paracosms are created by children who never had imaginary friends, or the paracosms are not related in content to current or former imaginary friends. The creation of artifacts is often part of this activity. Thus, many paracosms come equipped with documents, maps, cultures, religions, histories, public transportation systems, currency, national anthems, magazines, and/or languages specified by the child. In this chapter, we review what is known about this type of fantasy and how children use paracosms for storytelling and to explore real-life interests.

Chapter 11: Parasocial Relationships with Celebrities and Media Characters

Research on parasocial relationships began with investigations of adults who formed emotional bonds with real people they would never actually meet (e.g., celebrities) and imaginary characters in books, films, and TV shows. Children also develop bonds with favorite characters, artificially intelligent robots, and other agents. What exactly are "parasocial relationships"? Are they really all that different from imaginary friends? This chapter explores what is currently known about child and adult parasocial relationships, including ambiguities in how they these relationships are defined, how these bonds are formed, and their functions in people's lives.

Chapter 12: The Imaginary Friends of Adults

We might assume that imaginary friends are created early in life and are given up as children mature, but the capacity to contemplate fictional worlds and gain comfort, companionship, and insight from imaginary others is lifelong. Some imaginary friends continue into adulthood as cherished memories, but in other cases, adults continue to interact with their imaginary friends. In this chapter we discuss long-lasting and late-appearing imaginary friends, with detailed examples from the autobiographies of Agatha Christie and choreographer Paul Taylor.

Chapter 13: Adult Fiction Writers and Their Characters

Like children who regularly imagine the exploits of pretend friends, adult fiction writers create characters and the invented worlds they inhabit. In this chapter, we take a closer look at the relationships between writers and their characters. Like children with imaginary friends, authors sometimes report that their characters are experienced as having their own thoughts and feelings, a phenomenon we call "the illusion of independent agency." We describe this illusion as it occurs in various contexts and report the results of interviews with 50 adults who enjoy writing fiction and five accomplished authors who are true experts on what happens when you spend years thinking and writing about a character.

Chapter 14: Final Thoughts: Fantasy in the Lives of Children and Adults

This chapter summarizes some of the major themes that have emerged from the decades of research on children's imaginary friends and related phenomena. The bottom line is that although imaginary friends have sometimes been interpreted as signs of emotional disturbance, a break with reality, or even the emergence of multiple personalities, they really are just a variation on the theme of all the pretend play that is going on in the preschool years. In addition, we see a connection between the creation of imaginary friends and adult imaginative activities such as storytelling, a universal and lifelong activity that is believed to contribute to empathy and extend our experience beyond personal circumstance. We hope this book will clarify the important roles played by such fantasies in cognitive, social, and emotional development and help explain some of the reasons for misconceptions about imaginary friends.

Summary

The creation of imaginary friends is an elaborate type of imaginative activity that is relatively common. If both children and parents are consulted and their responses are cross-checked, by age 7 as many as 65% of children have interacted with imaginary friends at some point in their lives. This estimate includes imaginary friends that are based on special toys as well as ones that are invisible. Invisible friends are particularly diverse, including imaginary versions of real people, fictional characters from books, and many types of invented people and animals that are custom designed to meet the whims and needs of their creators. In the next chapter, we take a deeper dive into the idiosyncratic world of imaginary friends that only the children can see.

Notes

1. Bagwell, C. L., & Schmidt, M. E. (2013). *Friendships in childhood and adolescence.* Guilford Press.
   Parker, J. G., & Asher, S. R. (1993). Friendship and friendship quality in middle childhood: Links with peer group acceptance and feelings of loneliness and social dissatisfaction. *Developmental Psychology, 29,* 611–621.
2. Svendsen, M. (1934). Children's imaginary companions. *Archives of Neurology and Psychiatry, 2,* 985–999, see p. 988.
3. Harner, L. (1975). Yesterday and tomorrow: Development of early understanding of the terms. *Developmental Psychology, 11*(6), 864–865.
4. Taylor, M., Cartwright, B. S., & Carlson, S. M. (1993). A developmental investigation of children's imaginary companions. *Developmental Psychology, 29*(2), 276–285.
   Taylor, M., Carlson, S. M., Maring, B. L., Gerow, L., & Charley, C. (2004). The characteristics and correlates of high fantasy in school-aged children: Imaginary companions, impersonation and social understanding. *Developmental Psychology, 40,* 1173–1187.
5. Bouldin, P., & Pratt, C. (2001). The ability of children with imaginary companions to differentiate between fantasy and reality. *British Journal of Developmental Psychology, 19,* 99–114.
6. Gleason, T. R. (2004). Imaginary companions: An evaluation of parents as reporters. *Infant and Child Development: An International Journal of Research and Practice, 13*(3), 199–215.
7. Mannering, A. M., & Taylor, M. (2009). Cross-modality correlations in the imagery of adults and 5-year-old children. *Imagination, Cognition, and Personality, 28,* 207–238.
8. Taylor, M., & Carlson, S. M. (1997). The relation between individual differences in fantasy and theory of mind. *Child Development, 68,* 436–455.
9. Taylor, M., Cartwright, B. S., & Carlson, S. M. (1993). A developmental investigation of children's imaginary companions. *Developmental Psychology.*
10. At the time of the first meeting, we ask the child about imaginary friends in the following way: "Now I'm going to ask you some questions about friends. Some friends are real like the kids who live on your street, the ones you play with. And some friends are pretend friends. Pretend friends are ones that are make-believe, that you pretend are real. Do you have a pretend friend?"
    If the child answers "yes," we ask a series of questions about the friend, including questions about its name, whether it was a toy or completely pretend, its gender, age, physical appearance, what the child liked and did not like about the friend, and where the friend lived and slept.
    Here is the way we ask parents about imaginary friends at the time of the first interview: "An imaginary companion is a very vivid imaginary character (person, animal) with which a child interacts during his/her play and daily activities. Sometimes the companion is entirely invisible; sometimes the companion takes the form of a stuffed animal or doll. An example of an imaginary companion based on a stuffed animal is Hobbes in the popular comic strip 'Calvin and Hobbes.' Does your child have an imaginary companion?"

11. Taylor, M., & Carlson, S. M. (1997). The relation between individual differences in fantasy and theory of mind.
12. Singer, D. G., & Singer, J. L. (1990). *The house of make-believe: Children's play and developing imagination.* Harvard University Press.
13. Taylor, M., Carlson, S. M., Maring, B. L., Gerow, L., & Charley, C. (2004). The characteristics and correlates of high fantasy in school-aged children: Imaginary companions, impersonation and social understanding. *Developmental Psychology.*
14. Pearson, D., Rouse, H., Doswell, S., Ainsworth. C., Dawson, O., Simms, K., Edwards, L., & Falconbridge, J. (2001). Prevalence of imaginary companions in a normal child population. *Child: Care, Health and Development, 27,* 12–22.
15. Cohen, D., & MacKeith, S. A. (1991). *The development of imagination: The private worlds of childhood.* Routledge.

Chapter 2
Imaginary Friends Who Are Invisible

"You can't see her. Only I can see her. She's invisible for everyone except for me!"

(4-year-old girl describing an invisible friend named "Sethrophina")[1]

One 4-year-old who participated in our research told us about two invisible birds named Nutsy and Nutsy (a male and a female) who lived in a tree outside her bedroom window. According to the child, the two "Nutsies" had brightly colored feathers, were about 12 inches tall, and talked too much. Sometimes the little girl was irritated by the clumsy and generally raucous behavior of these birds, but usually their silliness made her laugh. The child's parents were well aware of the Nutsies; they regularly observed their daughter talking and playing with them, and they were frequently informed about the Nutsies' opinions and activities. Nutsy and Nutsy were almost like part of the family. They went along on outings by riding on top of the car, they had their own places set at the dinner table, and their antics were enjoyed by all. Marjorie met the Nutsies herself when they accompanied the little girl to her lab. She provided a chair for them, and the little girl laughed at how funny the Nutsies looked as they stood on tiptoe to peer over the table. Two years later, Nutsy and Nutsy had moved on, but the child remembered them, and her mother reported that she and her daughter sometimes reminisced about their exploits.

Elaborate and well-documented invisible creatures like Nutsy and Nutsy who are played with for an extended period of time and are described consistently by both the child and her parents would fit almost anyone's definition of an imaginary friend. However, there are many variations on the theme. The people and animals who populate children's fantasy lives differ in their vividness, longevity, personality development, and the extent to which they have some basis in the real world. Some children create entirely unique imaginary beings like Nutsy and Nutsy, but others have an imaginary version of a real friend or adopt a character from a movie or book as an imaginary friend (e.g., Moana from the Disney movie *Moana*). Other children form sustained and elaborate relationships with a special stuffed animal or toy, like Christopher Robin and Winnie-the-Pooh, the inspiration for the books of A. A. Milne.[2] We believe that toys and other objects can be imaginary friends, but they are different enough from invisible friends that we have given them their own chapter (see Chapter 3). In this chapter we focus on the invisible variety.

Invisible friends vary in the length of time they inhabit children's imaginations. Sometimes they are stable, long-lived, and played with regularly. They might even be passed down from one child to the next in a family, like outgrown but still serviceable clothes. Others have a more transitory existence, drifting in and out of the child's fantasy life. In our research, we have encountered children whose lives were crowded with invisible friends, none of whom lingered for substantial periods of time. Other children had only one or two at a time, but they updated their friends frequently, for example, trading in a blue-eyed blond boy named Tompy for a mischievous female mouse named Gadget. Sometimes invisible friends come in groups—a herd of invisible cows,[3] an army of Martians, or a host of lizards—rather than a well-defined individual. In the face of all this richness and diversity, parents are often unsure how to categorize their own child's activities.

What Are Invisible Friends Like?

When a child looks into the face of a teddy bear, its face provides perceptual support for the experience of a friend, but what about the child who looks into the space occupied by an invisible friend? Similarly, when a child holds and talks to a stuffed bear, the softness of its fur provides perceptual support for deriving comfort, but the comfort derived from an invisible friend is more unambiguously cerebral. What exactly are children experiencing when they look at and interact with their invisible friends?

With some exceptions ("I don't know what he looks like because he is invisible"; "It doesn't look like anything!"), children seem to have clear mental images of their friends. The majority of children with invisible friends promptly provide physical descriptions upon request ("she has red hair and a blue coat and orange pants and green eyes and yellow shoes and pink socks and purple pants and a sweatshirt that is orange"), often complete with idiosyncratic details (e.g., brown toenails, purple hair, glasses). They also are happy to draw pictures of them (see Figure 2.1). In one study, children who were reinterviewed seven months after the initial interview provided descriptions of the invisible friends that were as stable as their descriptions of real friends.[4] In some cases, the child's sense of what the invisible friend looks like can be retained for years. For example, one 4-year-old girl who described and drew her invisible friend Elfie Welfie as a tiny person with tie-dye-colored hair described and drew Elfie Welfie with the same characteristics when she was seven years old (see Figure 2.2).

In addition to describing visual appearances, many children mention other types of sensory experiences (e.g., "Sometimes I tap her on the shoulder and she pops up like a horse"; "I don't like him to take up too much space in my bed"; "I like the way Pajama Sam talks"; "One day I touched him and he said, 'Hey don't touch me';

Figure 2.1 Drawings of invisible imaginary friends.

I said, 'What are you and what's your name?'"). Moreover, when asked explicitly about whether they can see, hear, and/or touch their imaginary friends, the majority of children say "yes."[5]

What do children say when asked to describe the personalities and behaviors of their invisible friends? Many are quite prosaic—just regular everyday sorts of imaginary children who function as good playmates. Some are based on real-life people—the children themselves ("He looks like the whole self of me") or favorite relatives and friends. For example, one child told us about MacKenzie, an invisible version of her favorite cousin who lived in another state. Fake Rachel was an invisible girl who was originally based on a real friend named Rachel. The child enjoyed playing with Rachel at her preschool, so when she went home, she continued the play via

18   Imaginary Friends and the People Who Create Them

Figure 2.2 Drawings of Elfie Welfie at age 4 years (left) and age 7 (right).

Fake Rachel. For a time, this child had fake versions for all her friends. Three years after we first interviewed this child, we found that Fake Rachel was still going strong; real Rachel, not so much. Tracy Gleason describes interviewing a boy who had created an invisible version of a little girl at his school named Anna. He pretended to marry the invisible Anna but not the real Anna, so to distinguish the two Annas Tracy ended up conducting the entire interview referring to "your wife."

Some invisible friends have characteristics that take them out of the realm of what might be expected of a real child playmate. They have special capabilities, such as being able to fly, fight crocodiles, perform magic, or transform their shapes. Some have unusual physical attributes (e.g., "Baintor," a tiny invisible boy who is completely white and lives in the white light of a lamp; "Belly," "the biggest hugest person in the whole entire world"). They also vary in age. Although many are about the same age as the child, some are infants and have to be cared for (e.g., "Cream," a tiny invisible baby who lives on the child's hand) and some are old (e.g., "Dandel," an old invisible man who lives on the beach by himself). The oldest imaginary friend we have encountered was a 1,500-year-old vampire. They communicate with the child by talking ("I can hear her like I hear you"), telepathy ("I can hear him in my head and I can read his mind"), sign language ("She can't talk; she has to do sign language"), lip reading ("she can't hear so she looks at my lips so she knows what I'm saying"), the child talking for them ("I make him talk myself"), and some don't talk ("He doesn't talk but I can understand him"). Sometimes they simply appear when they are wanted (and sometimes when they aren't); otherwise children contact them in a variety of ways (e.g., saying the magic words "hoodie, goodie, goodie"; pressing a secret button).

Invisible friends are not always human. Many are animals, including a wide variety of species (e.g., cows, dogs, tigers, turtles, beavers, dinosaurs, mice, cats, giraffes, horses, ponies, lions, elephants, squirrels, alligators, beavers, octopuses, monkeys, dolphins, bears, fleas, moths, worms, flies, ducks, opossums, panthers, and rats). Invisible animals tend to have characteristics that would not be found in the real-life versions (e.g., they talk, walk upright, and wear clothing). Many have special powers (e.g., a dog who barks so loud it makes everybody faint) or other distinctive attributes (e.g., superior intelligence). In addition to people and animals, our research included ghosts, elves, monsters, vampires, aliens, fairies, dragons, unicorns, angels, a Cyclops, and unique creatures that we categorized as "other" (e.g., "Humpty Dumpty's mother," an invisible talking egg with spiky hair, a big round egglike head, and a human body; Alice, who "looks like dust but she is not made of dust; she looks like sunlight when it shines on the wall"). You will meet many of the invisible friends from our research throughout this book, but to underline the point about their diversity, we have provided more examples in Table 2.1.

A minority of children's imaginary friends are based on fictional characters from books, television, and movies. For example, in a recent study conducted by Ruben and colleagues,[6] only 56 (12%) of 435 preschool-aged children's descriptions of

Table 2.1 Examples of invisible friends

Randy Trouble-free (created by 3-year-old boy): A little brother with yellow hair, but very big (bigger than parents and too big for child's bed); goes to his own school, lives in Grandpa-land, Alaska; likes fruit salad, can read and play on swings, takes good photographs.

Rainbow (created by 3-year-old girl): A tall, playful, invisible 5-year-old girl. She has long black hair, colorful clothing, and lots of money. She has a dog named Polo and a baby sister named Applepie. She likes to draw tattoos on her body. She can drive a car and ride a pony. When she is not with the child, she goes to Disneyland.

Ashlin (created by 5-year-old girl): 9-year-old invisible girl with rainbow eyes and wings. She only comes out at night when other people are not around. She lives up in the clouds—that is where the child saw her one day. "I have a magic ball of light. Only me can touch it. She comes out when I call her in the light and say her name twice." Child likes her "cause she can do a lot of stuff and she can do cool things in the water with her wings."

Angelina (created by 5-year-old girl): 79-year-old angel/ghost, but not "old." She is the same size as the child, has long blonde hair and a dress with hearts. Angelina can fly and "shrink into a parrot and go into my head." She has a boyfriend named Jeff. Angelina is always with child; she "sneaks around with her" and "hang[s] onto my hand so she won't get lost." Child whispers "Angelina, come to me" when she wants to see her. When child's brother is there, "she turns me invisible too."

continued

Table 2.1 *continued*

Freddie and RD (5-year-old boy): Invisible vampires who live in Monsterland; they look like real vampires but they are twins with different colored vampire coats; they eat cat food, mosquitos, and food that is red, travel in a vampire helicopter; child met them when he was wearing his x-ray eyes (at the time of the interview he was wearing his regular eyes). "Sometimes I fight when they pretend to suck people's blood. It really is not appropriate."

Invisible Brother (created by 5-year-old boy): Child says magic words to get IB to show up ("Hoodie, goodie, goodie") and then holds thumb in the air and IB appears. IB was "born out of my mom's tummy." They play Star Wars and like to write words. When he sleeps, he curls up into a little ball. "We are friends because we're good brothers and we live together and I like living together. I just love, love, love it."

Hermione (created by 4-year-old girl): Invisible white kitten. Hermione likes to live in places that are white (e.g., the Moon, Antarctic). She mostly eats onions so the child asks family members to get onions on the side for Hermione when they go to a restaurant. Her mother often finds raw onions in the child's pockets. Hermione also gets food from her vending machine. Child likes to push Hermione on a swing at the playground.

Clover (created by 5-year-old boy): a little astronaut alien with a clover on his head. He is really smart. He is brownish with blue legs, a yellow head and purple hands. "He can fly and he can jump and he can shoot out anything (e.g., dinner). They play pirate and sometimes Clover is defeated. "I always sneak up behind him and push him into the water." "He just stays next to me everywhere."

Simoney (created by 4-year-old girl): A small multi-colored alligator ("he has lots of colors, all of the colors") who is a wise instructor, lives in a tiny green house and likes to ride on child's shoulders or in her pockets. They color, play puzzles, and watch over child's dog who is "in heaven." They like to argue ("it's fun arguing"). "I had him for a long time. I didn't meet him at all. God gave him to me."

Bunsen (created by 4-year-old girl): 10' tall child with gray hair and glasses; Bunsen has a family—Peechop (mom), Petreep (Dad), Cinnarole (sister), Bowie (younger sister), and Pum-Pum (dog); Bunsen likes to sit on the lap of whoever is driving the family car.

Wind (created by 8-year-old girl): She fell from her breeze territory house; When Wind is mad she turns into a dark cloud; her sister is Rain, but not Pour. "We like to have races—she flies, I run; she can do her special wind dance that we can do together; we hold hands and fly together"; "She's my friend because she's her. I don't want someone who pretends to be someone else."

Squinch (created by 5-year-old girl): Squinch is very, very small and has a point on her head like a little horn; she does handstands, likes to play Monopoly and to travel in her tiny car; she has a computer in her car that lets her know when the child wants her to come; "I don't like her when we are fighting, one time when she was playing with one of my princess dolls."

Invisible (5-year-old boy): Large 6-year-old creature who likes to swim, box, and play tricks on people. He has a pet ghost. He was born at the child's house. Child and Invisible go to the beach and hide in caves. When child is away, Invisible turns into a fish and plays with a fish named Fishy. When child drew Invisible, he held the pen above the paper and drew in the air. "He has a drum set just like me and we can play our drum sets together... except I have a little one and he has a big one."

Jackson (4-year-old boy): a ghost giraffe that can turn into an elephant or zombie. He has a blue sweatshirt, blue pants, light-up Spiderman shoes and a Batman shirt with sunglasses in the pocket. He has a "huge fat tummy" and a "huge head." He can do magic and make toys disappear and appear. When he is not with child, "Jackson goes to the ice cream department." "He shows up by himself when he wants to."

---

imaginary friends had any connections to a media character. And of these 56 descriptions, most of the connections to media were based on the imaginary friend's name and physical appearance only. Sometimes the idea for the imaginary friend comes from a media source, but children make the character their own. According to his mother, Marshall Mathers (aka rap musician Eminem) did not watch Casper the Friendly Ghost much on TV but had an imaginary friend named Casper who could walk through walls and was his best friend for several years.[7] One 3-year-old we know started talking about Woset after she read *There's a Wocket in My Pocket*, Dr. Seuss' story about invisible creatures.[8] Echoing one of the lines, she would fearfully say, "Mommy, there's a woset in the closet." However, when Woset eventually came out of the closet, the little girl discovered that he was really nice and lots of fun—not scary at all. She enjoyed showing him new things, finding out what he liked to eat, and playing games with him so much that she invented several more invisible friends. In the end, she had enough for her very own "circle time." Her mother reported that scarcely an hour went by without the child playing with one or more of her invisible friends or referring to them in some way.

Invisible "Friends" That are Mean, Disobedient, Uncooperative or Scary

> Sammy is a little bit mean. Sometimes he is a little bit nice, but he kinda hurts people and he kinda bited people. He bited me one time and he bited me right here (points to self) and it hurt really bad, but I didn't cry.[9]

What should you do if a 4-year-old tells you about a preschool bully like Sammy? Some sort of intervention might seem appropriate, but there is a complication. Sammy is the little boy's invisible friend.

When adults think about the attractions of having an imaginary friend, they tend to focus on the joys of having a friend who is always supportive and helpful and consistently loving—one who agrees with you, does what you want, keeps your secrets, and provides good company (e.g., "we always know what the other one is going to say."). Assuming that a made-up friend would not suffer from the moodiness, stubbornness, or other flaws of real friends seems reasonable. But while most imaginary friends are supportive and agreeable, a substantial number (almost a third) misbehave and have to be disciplined.[10]

Children in our research have described imaginary friends who punch, bite, steal, swear, talk too loudly, do not share, and tell lies. They can be greedy ("she takes all my stuff"), destructive ("the first time I tried to make him turn a page, he ripped the page off"), arrogant ("he thinks he knows everything"), overbearing ("she's a really mean friend, really bossy"), lazy ("she leaves when we make a mess; she thinks I am a slave"), and/or aggressive ("she hits me on the head and puts yogurt in my hair"). They have to be monitored ("when he is bad, I just lock the door") and admonished ("Eric, I created you. You can't boss me around. I'm the boss of you. Don't forget that."). Table 2.2 provides excerpts of interviews with a child describing a badly behaved imaginary friend and a child describing a well-behaved one.

A few might more accurately be called "imaginary enemies." Singer and Singer[11] speculated that Samuel Clements' (aka Mark Twain's) childhood imaginary "friend" was a devil because: (1) Clements often included material from his childhood in his novels; (2) in *The Mysterious Stranger*, Satan is an invisible character that communicates with young boys; and (3) Clements' mother referred to Satan frequently in the home. Other imaginary friends, if not downright evil, can be scary. For example, a 14-year-old boy who was in bed recovering from a long illness imagined that a picture facing him showed a giant that sometimes stepped out from the wall intent on cutting off his hands.[12] Similarly, Russian psychologist Eugene Subbotsky[13] described a 4-year-old who developed a fear of a "bamzeli," a monster who came to the child when he was alone in his bed at night. The child developed a ritual for freeing himself from the bamzeli by holding a rolled-up blanket in his hands, which allowed him to sleep peaceably. According to the mother of a 4-year-old in

Table 2.2 Example of a badly behaved and a well-behaved imaginary friend

---

"Boo," a noncompliant badly behaved invisible ghost
  Researcher: How did you meet Boo?
  Child: He came to my house and I said, "Please don't eat my Daddy."
  Researcher: When you want to play with Boo, how do you get him to come?
  Child: He usually takes something and eats it and I get really mad.
  Researcher: Does Boo ever surprise you with the things he says or does?
  Child: He turns on music and it sucks him in.
  Researcher: Does Boo do whatever you say?
  Child: Yes, I vacuum him up because he is naughty.
  Researcher: What is special about Boo?
  Child: He goes under the table and bites my foot.

"Sally," a compliant well-behaved invisible girl
  Child: Sally is my best friend. She zooms everywhere I go.
  Researcher: Where does Sally go when she is not with you?
  Child: She always wants to be with me.
  Researcher: Do you ever have fights or argue with Sally?
  Child: No, never.
  Researcher: Does Sally ever try to boss you around or make you do things that you
          don't want to do?
  Child: No, never.
  Researcher: Does Sally always play what you want to play?
  Child: Yes, she always shares.
  Researcher: Does Sally ever help you do things?
  Child: Yes, she helps me, sweep, mop and rake.
  Researcher: Does Sally ever help you feel better?
  Child: Yes, when I am feeling sad, she makes me feel happy because she gives me
          things.

---

research by Newson and Newson, the child imagined monkeys who "live in the cellar, and that's why he won't go down the cellar, because they might get him; and if there's something wrong, it's always a monkey that comes up from the cellar and done it."[14]

In many of these accounts the imagined creatures are not fully elaborated and do not have much interaction with the children beyond scaring them, so we would not consider them to be imaginary friends. However, sometimes imagined characters who are frightening serve other functions as well. Frances Wickes reported a case in which an ominous being appeared to help a child overcome her fear of the dark or the unknown:

> She deliberately let this figure go with her. She walked into the dark places where she believed it was and faced it. She let it walk with her on the street, she deliberately took it as her companion until she found that not only had it lost its terrifying power but that also her unreasoned fears of dark places and of being alone were dropping from her.[15]

Imaginary beings who have other characteristics associated with imaginary friends (e.g., a relatively stable personality) but who are *primarily* disliked or feared are rare. Almost all the naughty imaginary friends also have some redeeming qualities. Melissa McInnis and her colleagues[16] found that a third of the children in their sample of 3-to-8-year-olds described their imaginary friends as "mean" and provided details about the friends' bad behavior. One 6-year-old described Violet, an invisible 6-year-old girl with dark brown hair, a peach face, a pink shirt, brown shoes, and striped mittens who lived in the child's braid. The child and Violet "sometimes hit and push each other, ignore each other when they are mad, and tell each other that they aren't friends."[17] But McInnis and her colleagues described this relationship and others as mixed rather than negative because all the children also had positive things to say and reported that they could make their friends be "nice."

We have also found that many children are frustrated or angered by the behavior of imaginary friends who, in most respects, serve as good companions. Imaginary friends who are mean and naughty can also be loyal and fun. Freddy French Fries, although mischievous and annoying, cheers up the child and makes him laugh. A child who described the argumentative Elfie Welfie as "kind of like a terrorist" also enjoyed long chats on the phone with her about Elfie Welfie's preference for tie-dye clothes and her job as a veterinarian.

Some complaints are particularly bewildering—for example, imaginary friends who are too busy to play. Adam Gopnik charmed the readers of the *New Yorker* with an essay featuring Charlie Ravioli, the invention of his 3-year-old daughter Olivia.[18] Charlie Ravioli was clearly an interesting and friendly fellow. Olivia described him as pursuing a career in show business, reading books, and occasionally catching up with her over coffee—but mostly he was too busy to play. From Gopnik's parental perspective, Ravioli's tendency to cancel lunches, run off after a too brief chat with his daughter, or simply not be available to schedule a playdate made him an "oddly discouraging" imaginary friend.

We have also encountered imaginary friends who, like Charlie Ravioli, were strangely unavailable to their child creators—coming and going on their own schedule rather than according to the child's wishes. For example, Bing, a very smart and superior type of imaginary friend, was experienced as having a mind and life of his own and was often too busy to play. The boy solved the problem by inventing a second imaginary friend named Hood to keep him company while he was sitting around wondering what Bing was doing and if he would show up to play. Gopnik's daughter Olivia also created a second imaginary friend: Laura, Ravioli's assistant, who answered when Olivia used her play cell phone to try to reach Ravioli at his office. This development disturbed Olivia's mother, who asserted that

> An imaginary playmate shouldn't have an assistant. An imaginary playmate shouldn't have an agent. An imaginary playmate shouldn't have a publicist or a personal trainer or a caterer—an imaginary playmate shouldn't have ... *people*. An imaginary playmate should just *play*. With the child who imagined it.

Most of the time, the failure of the imaginary friend to show up when wanted is an occasional problem rather than a prominent feature. A parent in one study described a trying situation that arose one afternoon when she took her 3-year-old daughter to a horse show. The child loved horses, but the outing was ruined because the child's imaginary pony was not there. The child was sure he would be with all the other horses, but a thorough search of the grounds indicated that the invisible pony must have had other plans for the day. The child's frustration seemed entirely genuine—the episode did not seem to be a manipulative ploy on the child's part to spend the afternoon some other way. The situation was exasperating for the mother who saw a seemingly obvious solution to the problem. Why couldn't her daughter just pretend the pony was there? For some reason, the imaginary pony did not seem to be at the beck and call of the child, and the mother was unable to do anything about it.

We should mention, though, that most imaginary friends do show up to play, sometimes to a fault. So it is not surprising that we have encountered them in our lab:

> CHILD: He's right beside me everyday, all the time.
> RESEARCHER: Is he beside you right now?
> CHILD: Yeah, he's right there in an invisible chair (points to space beside child).

We have observed a number of face-to-face interactions during the interview when children consulted with the invisible friends, asked them questions, or reprimanded them ("Will you stop it! How many times have I told you not to do that?"). Some children enjoy having a constant companion ("I like her because she goes wherever

I go"), but other children complain about the ever-present nature of their invisible imaginary friend ("she was a little annoying because she followed me around everywhere").

Why would a child create a pretend friend who was disobedient, scary, bossy, argumentative, annoying, unpredictable, too busy, aggressive, or overly clingy? According to developmental psychologists and child clinicians, notably Vivian Paley, Inge Bretherton, Dorothy Singer, and Jerome Singer,[19] pretend play can be important in the exploration of real-life themes and challenges, such as exploring their feelings about a parent who is sometimes too busy to play. It's a child's way of mulling things over. An unruly imaginary friend is not fundamentally different from a loyal and compliant one; both reflect the child's thoughts about behavior. By interacting with a badly behaved imaginary friend, they can explore what it means to be disobedient and think through the consequences. For example, in the case of the imaginary friend who bites, the child might have observed this behavior at preschool or elsewhere. Asking if there is someone the imaginary friend wants to bite, or if there is anyone at preschool who bites the imaginary friend, might be informative. Or perhaps having contact with a disobedient, mischievous creature who gets into trouble and has to be chastised and disciplined is simply exciting. The child can play the role of disciplinarian or explore what it is like for a parent in that situation. This type of friend also allows children to think of themselves as being brave in the face of adversity (e.g., not crying even though one has been bitten by a nasty pretend friend).

Pretend Characters That Are Identities, Not Imaginary Friends

> "Hallo Rabbit," said Pooh. "Is that you?"
> "Let's pretend it isn't," said Rabbit, "and see what happens."
> (Milne, 1926)[20]

Many children pretend to *be* an animal or another person on a regular basis; they take on the imaginary character and act it out, rather than pretend it is a separate entity from themselves. Is this type of pretend play fundamentally different from having an imaginary friend? According to Paul Harris,[21] role play activities in which the child imagines the thoughts, actions, and emotions of a person or creature are conceptually related. Within role play, Harris makes distinctions based on the vehicle for the imagined character: (1) an object as the vehicle (i.e., a personified stuffed animal, doll, action figure), (2) nothing as the vehicle (i.e., an invisible friend), or (3) the self as the vehicle (i.e., a pretend identity). There are similarities in the characteristics of children who have invisible friends, personified objects, and pretend identities,[22] but which of these activities should be counted as imaginary friends? We count invisible friends and personified objects as imaginary friends. We don't count pretend identities—when children create an imaginary personality or character that they act out themselves—but we want to say a bit more about them.

Most children act out a variety of roles in their pretend play. On any given day, one child might be the firefighter, another the monster, and so on.[23] But for some children, a particular role is more enduring (e.g., a child who pretends to be Superman every day for months). The completeness of the identification and the persistence with which the impersonated identity is maintained distinguishes "pretend identities" from other role playing. For example, one child we originally thought had an imaginary friend named Applejack (based on her mother's report), turned out to have an imagined character that she impersonated, rather than one she interacted with as a separate individual. The child corrected the researcher over the course of the interview by responding to questions such as "How much do you play with Applejack?" by saying, "No, I *am* Applejack."

Ames and Learned[24] considered the creation of an imaginary character that is acted out rather than treated as a separate person as an activity that is closely related to playing with an imaginary friend. Their data include some fascinating descriptions of pretend identities as well as imaginary friends, including cases of children who engaged interchangeably in play involving invisible imaginary friends, companions based on props, and the impersonation of imagined characters. Of the 210 children who participated in their study, 17 were observed or described by parents as habitually impersonating animals or people. Four were described as carrying out the pretense extensively: "... going around on all fours, saying 'woof woof' or 'meow' instead of talking, lapping up food from a dish on the floor, chasing automobiles, even urinating in animal fashion by standing on one leg."[25] Given this description, it is unsurprising that some parents in this study reported that pretend identities were more troublesome than other kinds of imaginative play.

We have also found that regular impersonation of an imaginary character can be vexing. One mother told us that when company was expected, she and her husband worried about whether their sons would be children or cats during the evening. The cat possibility was undesirable because the boys would meow instead of talk, try to eat directly from a plate instead of using silverware, and rub against the legs of the guests in feline fashion. One of the frustrations is that animals do not understand English and do not talk. When asked to do something (e.g., "It's time to pick up your things and go to bed"), the animal-child is apt to bark or look quizzically at the parent rather than comply. One evening Marjorie took her 4-year-old to the home of two clinical psychologists for dinner. As soon as Amber saw their dog, she immediately became one herself. Marjorie's requests for her to stop being a dog became pleas, and finally whispered threats. Amber responded to all of the above with whimpering dog sounds and licks. Marjorie ended up smiling foolishly, while her friends politely tried to ignore the behavior.

A few children take on the identities of machines (e.g., a vacuum cleaner) rather than animate beings. In his autobiography, Sir Peter Ustinov, the British actor, playwright, and director, recalls this type of childhood activity:

I was a motor-car, to the dismay of my parents. Psychiatry was in its infancy then, both expensive and centered in Vienna. There was no one yet qualified to exorcise an internal combustion engine from a small boy . . . I switched on in the morning, and only stopped being a car at night when I reversed into bed, and cut the ignition.[26]

Parents who put up with this sort of behavior might be helped by the advice Ustinov's grandfather gave to his mother: "don't think of it as the sound of an automobile, but rather as the sound of his imagination developing, and then you will see, it will become bearable."[27]

Impersonating an individual that has positive characteristics might have some benefits. In a series of studies, Rachel White and her colleagues[28] asked preschool children to complete a repetitive task that required self-control and perseverance. In one condition, children dressed up as a character who was described as "really good at working hard" (i.e., Batman, Bob the Builder, Rapunzel, or Dora the Explorer) and pretended to be that character while performing the task. Children in character worked harder and longer than children in the other conditions. White and her colleagues called this the "Batman Effect." This result raises the question of how more sustained impersonation of a character might have an impact on a child's behavior.

In our work, we have found that determining if a child's impersonation is extensive enough to be called a pretend identity is challenging. Almost all children report that they pretend to be a person or an animal. To identify children who impersonated an imagined character on a regular basis, we had to rely on their parents' reports. Children were categorized as having a pretend identity if the parent reported that their child pretended to be an animal or person every day for a period of at least one month. Nineteen percent (29 of 152 children) were categorized as having pretend identities, including unique characters (e.g., Mr. Electricity, Flashman of the World) as well as more mundane ones (e.g., cats). Over 40% of these children also had imaginary friends.[29] The overlap we found in imaginary friends and pretend identities substantiates our belief that these kinds of fantasy play can be related. However, pretending to be a character is not the same as having a *relationship* with a character. When children pretend to be characters, they take on those identities, whereas when they have imaginary friends, their individual identities are preserved, and the focus is on the imagined interactions with the characters. Pretend identities seem different enough that we do not count them as a type of imaginary friend.

Summary

When Marjorie first started doing research on imagination in the early 1990s, one of her objectives was to identify the characteristics of the "typical" pretend friend. However, she quickly discovered that this goal was not going to be straightforward to achieve because of the amazing (and wonderful) originality in so many of the descriptions. After a few more studies, she abandoned it altogether. The typical imaginary friend does not exist. Variability is the name of the game. Marjorie has been talking to children, parents, and other adults about imaginary friends for over three decades and has collected over a thousand descriptions, but she is still hearing about new ones. When a child says, "Yes! I have a pretend friend," you don't know what is coming next.

All this diversity in the products of children's imaginations can pose challenges when deciding if a particular type of pretend play should be categorized as having an imaginary friend. The clearest example of imaginary friends are the ones that are invisible. We include the ones who are sometimes badly behaved. After all, our real friends can be provocative, neglectful, or infuriating, as well as provide companionship, love, and support. Imaginary friends are not so very different. Sometimes children act out a character rather than treating it as a separate entity. This behavior is not the same as having an imaginary friend, although having a pretend identity is a related and interesting type of pretend play.

In summary, children talk about, interact with, and develop friendships with an astonishing range of imaginary friends. In this chapter we have focused on the ones that are invisible, but imaginary friendships involving the animation of objects can also be elaborate, vivid, and important to children. We include personified objects in our definition of an imaginary friend and they are the topic of the next chapter.

Notes

1. This quote is from a video provided by Stephanie Carlson.
2. Milne, A. A. (1926). *Winnie-the-Pooh*. Methuen & Co.
3. Gleason, T. R., Sebanc, A. M., & Hartup, W. W. (2000). Imaginary companions of preschool children. *Developmental Psychology, 36*, 419–428.
4. Taylor, M., Cartwright, B. S., & Carlson, S. M. (1993). A developmental investigation of children's imaginary companions. *Developmental Psychology, 29*, 276–285.
5. Ibid.
6. Ruben, E., French, J., Lee, H. J., Aguiar, N. R., Richert, R., & Gleason, T. (2023, March). *Let it go: Media influences on imaginary companions in early childhood* [Poster presentation]. Biennial Meeting of the Society for Research in Child Development, Salt Lake City, UT.
7. Nelson, D. (2008). *My son Marshall, my son Eminem*. Phoenix Books, Inc.
8. Seuss, Dr. (1974). *There's a wocket in my pocket*. Random House.
9. From interview with preschool child. Taylor Imagination Lab, University of Oregon.
10. Taylor, M., Carlson, S. M., & Shawber, A. B. (2007). Autonomy and control in children's interactions with imaginary companions. In I. Roth (Ed.), *Imaginative minds* (pp. 81–100). British Academy and Oxford University Press.
11. Singer, D. G., & Singer, J. L. (1990). *The house of make-believe: Children's play and developing imagination*. Harvard University Press.
12. Harriman, P. L. (1937). Some imaginary companions of older subjects. *The American Journal of Orthopsychiatry, 7*, 368–370.

13. Subbotsky, E. V. (1993). *Foundations of the mind: Children's understanding of reality.* Harvard University Press.
14. Newson, J., & Newson, E. (1968). *Four years old in an urban community.* George Allen & Unwin Ltd., p. 184.
15. Wickes, F. G. (1927). *The inner world of childhood.* D. Appleton, p. 206.
16. McInnis, M. A., Pierucci, J. M., & Gilpin, A. T. (2013). Investigating valence and autonomy in children's relationships with imaginary companions. *International Journal of Developmental Science, 7,* 151–159. https://doi.org/10.3233/DEV-130123
17. Ibid., p. 155.
18. Gopnik, A. (2002, September 30). Bumping into Mr. Ravioli. *The New Yorker.* https://www.newyorker.com/magazine/2002/09/30/bumping-into-mr-ravioli
19. Bretherton, I. (1989). Pretense: The form and function of make-believe play. *Developmental Review, 9,* 383–401.
    Paley, V. G. (2004). *A child's work: The importance of fantasy play.* Chicago: University of Chicago Press.
    Singer, D. G., & Singer, J. L. (1990). *The house of make-believe: Children's play and developing imagination.* Harvard University Press.
20. Milne, A. A. (1926). *Winnie-the-Pooh.* Methuen & Co.
21. Harris, P. L. (2000). *The work of the imagination.* Basil Blackwell.
22. Taylor, M., & Carlson, S. M. (1997). The relation between individual differences in fantasy and theory of mind. *Child Development, 68,* 436–455.
23. Paley, V. G. (2004). *A child's work: The importance of fantasy play.* University of Chicago Press.
24. Ames, L. B., & Learned, J. (1946). Imaginary companions and related phenomena. *Journal of Genetic Psychology, 69,* 147–167.
25. Marjorie doesn't know how many children actually urinate like an animal when pretending to be one, but a colleague told her that his 6-year-old daughter pretended to urinate like a male dog on their living room furniture, a practice which surely elicited some interesting reactions from visitors to the household.
26. Ustinov, P. (1977). *Dear me.* Penguin, p. 72.
27. Ibid., p. 74.
28. White, R. E., Prager, E. O., Schaefer, C., Kross, E., Duckworth, A. L., & Carlson, S. M. (2017). The "Batman Effect": Improving perseverance in young children. *Child Development, 88,* 1563–1571.
29. Taylor, M., & Carlson, S. M. (1997). The relation between individual differences in fantasy and theory of mind. *Child Development, 68,* 436–455.

Chapter 3
Imaginary Friends Who Are Personified Objects

Mom, can't you hear Ellie's heart beating?
No, I can't.
Mom, can you *pretend* that you can hear the heartbeat?
Yes, I can do that.
        (Naomi and her child talking about Ellie, a stuffed elephant)

Many young children endow a stuffed animal, doll, or other toy with a stable personality and treat it as if it were real—talking to it, making a special voice for it, and listening to what it has to say. Children often describe these toys as autonomous agents capable of thinking, feeling, and acting (e.g., a stuffed dog that likes to ride in cars and go camping but is afraid of the dark).

Experts on childhood fantasy differ in their opinions about whether such toys and other objects should be called imaginary friends. In one of the first widely read articles on the subject, Svendsen[1] explicitly excluded this type of play, but Professors Dorothy and Jerome Singer (authors of *The House of Make-Believe*) included stuffed animals and dolls when children endowed them with human qualities and treated them as companions.[2] Even researchers who have used Svendsen's more stringent definition have had to relent in some cases. According to John and Elizabeth Newson, "It was clearly necessary to admit a character to the fantasy category because, although having a 'real' origin, so extensive a saga had been built upon this foundation that fantasy had long since out-stripped reality."[3] Newson and Newson's own daughter had such elaborate fantasies about her doll Susanna that her parents decided to interview the child about her 4-year-old daughter (the doll) in the same way as they interviewed real parents about their children. The transcript—a 4-year-old's opinions on the upbringing of her 4-year-old child (the doll)—is published as an appendix at the end of Newson and Newson's book *Four Years Old in an Urban Community*.

One argument for excluding stuffed animals is that they have an existence and physical appearance that is independent of the child's imagination. Perhaps a companion is only truly imaginary when it exists solely in the mind's eye of the child and none of the details are specified by the environment. The trouble with this reasoning is that when it comes to how much imagination is involved, play involving

Imaginary Friends and the People Who Create Them. Second Edition. Marjorie Taylor and Naomi R. Aguiar,
Oxford University Press. © Oxford University Press (2024). DOI: 10.1093/9780190888916.003.0003

stuffed animals is not always as different as one might think from play with invisible imaginary friends. Children use imagination to embellish the appearance of toys, so in the child's mind eye, the imaginary friend might look quite different from the way the toy appears to an impartial observer. The mother sees a scruffy little stuffed dog that she would like to whisk away for a quick cycle through the washing machine, whereas the child sees a large, fluffy dog. This insight was captured in Bill Watterson's technique of drawing the stuffed tiger in his comic strip differently, depending on whether the reader was seeing Hobbes as he appeared to Calvin (i.e., a large, expressive, and lifelike beast) or as he appeared to Calvin's parents (i.e., a small inert toy).[4] Ronald Benson and David Pryor[5] described this kind of discrepancy in perspective when they asked a 16-year-old girl to show them the stuffed dog that had previously served as her companion. When she located the dog in the back of her closet, she was shocked to see how tattered and worn it was. She felt she was seeing the toy for the first time as it appeared to other people.

One of the biggest advocates for including personified objects as imaginary friends is Tracy Gleason, professor of psychology at Wellesley College. Marjorie discovered why when she read Tracy's essay in Sherry Turkle's book *Evocative Objects*.[6] It's because of Murray, a stuffed bunny that belonged to Tracy's much younger sister:

> He developed Boing-de-Boing Eyes that allowed him to see through barriers of all kinds, around corners and across miles. He could see what Shayna was doing no matter where she was, and he always knew when she was coming for him. His Boing-de-Boing ears allowed him to hear Shayna speaking no matter how far apart they were. He could fly, magically transporting himself through space and time to be by her side—in spirit, if not in body. . . . When Shayna began kindergarten Murray developed new competencies. He and Shayna began communicating in the Bunny Language, thus elevating their discussions beyond the comprehension of our parents. In order to keep them informed, Shayna gave Bunny language lessons, complete with tape recordings of vocabulary and worksheets for grammar.[7]

Tracy's front row seat for observing Shayna's everyday interactions with Murray must have contributed to her view that one should not underestimate children's capacity to create friends out of stuffed animals and other toys and the potential of these imagined relationships to provide companionship. Although the consideration of personified objects as potential imaginary friends can be tricky, we agree that it is a mistake to categorically exclude them.

Distinguishing Personified Objects from Other Toys

In our view, there is more continuity between play with personified objects and everyday play behaviors than there is for interactions with invisible friends. Most children have favorite toys, dolls, and stuffed animals that they talk to and animate (e.g., having a tea party with dolls). A toy that is played with from time to time but that spends most of its time on the shelf would not warrant the label "imaginary friend." Some toys are special, but not in the same way as an imaginary friend. For example, some children have a teddy bear that they habitually cling to, sleep with, and use for comfort. Toys, blankets, and other items used in this way by young children are referred to as "transitional objects."[8] Transitional objects are of interest to psychologists because they are believed to help some children work out the distinction between self and other, but enjoying the comfort of a soft toy is not the same as creating a distinct personality for it.

We think the capacity to give objects personal and emotional significance is fascinating in its own right, but at what point does this type of play become elaborate and consistent enough to be referred to as having an imaginary friend? This is a challenging issue that confronts all researchers in this area. After all, identifying a child as having an imaginary friend begins to lose any meaning when every teddy bear is considered to be one. The inclusion of personified objects is one reason why estimates for the prevalence of imaginary friends in the United States are as high as 65%.[9]

Where do you draw the line? Our strategy is to collect as much information as we can about how the child plays with the toy, including questions for parents whose child tells us about a toy: "Does your child treat the toy primarily as a comfort object (e.g., she or he carries it around and/or sleeps with it), or does she or he treat it as if it were another person (e.g., talks to it, listens to what it says, describes its life to others)?" Then it comes down to a judgment call by three research assistants who are assigned the job of reading the transcripts of interviews with children and their parents and deciding if a relationship with a toy is sustained, interactive, and special enough for it to be categorized as an imaginary friend.

One of the child's toys usually emerges as the primary imaginary friend, with the other toys playing supporting roles, but some children have two or more toys that are treated as personified objects. Less frequently, children create an extensive network of highly elaborate social relationships involving a large number of stuffed animals, as described by a former graduate student:

> I attributed various personality traits to each animal and treated them according to my beliefs about each one. For example, one of the animals was a stuffed bear who was far older and considerably more tattered than my other animals. I worried that he would think I liked the other animals better because of their more attractive appearance, so I made a special effort to reassure him that I loved him just as much as the others. I also had concerns about the larger animals bullying the smaller ones. I remember telling these larger animals to remember to be extra kind and gentle to the littler ones.
>
> Occasionally, conflict arose in my relationships with the animals. The conflicts usually centered around one of two events: my receiving a new stuffed animal or toy, and times when I left home on a trip and had to choose which animal would travel with me. In the case where I was given a new stuffed animal for Christmas

or my birthday, I reassured the other animals that I still loved them as much as I always had, and that an "addition to the family" would have no impact on my relationships with them. I would then engage in an elaborate procedure of introducing the new animal to each of the older ones. I presumed that the new animal would be shy in his new home, and reassured him that we would all get along with each other.

When I traveled away from home with my family, I was allowed to take only one animal. I remember agonizing over the decision, not wanting to hurt anyone's feelings. I eventually developed a rotating system that allowed each animal to essentially go on the same number of trips as any other animal. Before each trip, I carefully selected the animal who would accompany me, and then proceeded to have a "meeting" with all of the animals together. I would tell them to the best of my ability where I was going, how long I would be gone, and what I expected to do on the trip. I reassured the animals who were staying behind that I would take them all if I could, but due to parental constraints I had been forced to choose one of them. I tried to make it clear to all of them that I was doing my best to be fair, and that they would all eventually go on a trip with me. In addition to this elaborate clarification of my motives for choosing the animal that I had, I felt the need to protect the animal who was going with me from possible retaliation from the other animals upon our return. I pleaded with the other animals to be kind to the one who had been selected. I also advised the animal who had been selected to refrain from bragging about how much fun the trip had been, as this would only provoke the other animals.

This child's relationship with a menagerie of stuffed animals is similar to the way some children have many invisible friends (e.g., a family of invisible hamsters). However, Gleason and her colleagues found that multiple friends are actually more common for invisible friends than for personified objects.[10]

Descriptions of Personified Objects

The objects that become props for children's invention of imaginary friends go well beyond teddy bears. We have interviewed children who made friends out of toy rabbits, frogs, dogs, monkeys, muppets, kangaroos, dinosaurs, hedgehogs, opossums, cows, tigers, elephants, horses, dolphins, smurfs, Tasmanian devils, cats, donkeys, squirrels, and moose. Less often, children develop fantasies about imaginary others based on other types of props, such as reflections in a mirror, a chest of drawers, or the leaves on a tree. Ames and Learned described a child who used her fingers to represent her imaginary friends:

> She animated her hands and had the fingers talk to each other, before she herself could talk well. Outdoors she used sticks as imaginary people. Later when she

could talk, she called her hands "hand-duds" when they were acting as imaginary companions. She dressed up her hands with ribbons between the fingers for hair.[11]

Table 3.1 provides some more examples of personified objects from our research.

Table 3.1 Examples of personified objects

Josie (character created by 6-year-old girl): Josie is a paper doll based on a girl in child's class. "I make her out of paper ... she's on a piece of paper." Josie is really nice and can walk on her head. The child can hear Josie in her mind. They play games and pretend that child is the teacher. Josie gets mad and cries when child leaves.

Ellie (character as described by 10-year-old child): Ellie is a stuffed elephant that the child became friends with as a toddler. Ellie started as a comfort object and evolved into a friend. Ellie is not a "he, she or they; Ellie is just Ellie." Ellie is left-handed, funny, and goes with the child everywhere. Ellie is part of the family.

Fred Bear (character created by 4-year-old boy): He likes to play with the child but doesn't like some foods that the child likes. Child gets mad when Fred Bear calls people names. He takes naps, gets hungry, had birthday parties, flies and jumps up to the ceiling. "Sometimes I have to jump out of an airplane with him." "I'm his daddy and my sister's his mother."

Max (character created by 4-year-old girl): Maxie is an 8-year-old pink stuffed dog that has two puppies. The child talks "doggy talk" and barks with Max. Max does tricks and goes for walks. The child doesn't like it when Max throws up on her bed.

Plum (character created by 4-year-old girl): Plum is a purple stuffed bear who is 5 years old. She plays hide and seek with the child and Plum's two brothers. When she is not with child "she pretends she's real by herself and with her parents and her brothers and with her pet."

Nuni (character created by 5-year-old girl): Nuni is a large, stuffed, purple unicorn as big as the child that can "almost fly" and likes to play checkers. There's nothing about Nuni that the child doesn't like.

Froggy (character created by 4-year-old boy): Froggy is a stuffed green and white frog that likes to play the guitar, watch television, and likes to be fed fly soup. The child doesn't like it when "he's a bad boy."

Rainbow (character created by 5-year-old girl): Rainbow is a stuffed poodle with long eyelashes that child likes to play with. "She likes to spend time with me alone and her likes to go on walks with me when nobody's around." "Well, her is just really nice and I really like her a lot."

Clover (character created by 5-year-old boy): Clover is a green stuffed bear with a clover on its tummy. "I can hear him the way I hear you." "I can play with him any time except I don't know what he is doing right now." The child doesn't like that Clover sometimes is mean and punches him in the face."

Polka Dot (character created by 8-year-old boy): Polka Dot is a stuffed Dalmatian dog who is playful, friendly, and likes to do what the child likes to do. The child carried him around, made homes for him, and liked that Polka Dot "is a dog and it's nice." "I always remembered him as sometimes tricky." "I used to play with him a lot, a lot, a lot."

Ouchie Piggy (character created by 5-year-old girl): Ouchie Piggy is a stuffed pig that is child's daughter. Ouchie Piggy does and feels whatever the child is doing or feeling (e.g., pretending to fly, feeling happy, hungry, etc.). "I like everything ... I didn't like it when I threw up on her."

One of our most unusual personified objects involved the floor protectors that fit on the bottom of furniture legs. An adult participant recalled that as a child he had worn a couch caster on his thumb and called it "Johann":

> It was male and human. Even though its outward visible form was a caster, I still thought of it as human. I would talk to it when alone, and telepathically to it in the company of others. It didn't speak to me as much as it spoke to other people. I felt secure when thinking about or actually in the company of Johann. Everyone knew about Johann. There were even several kidnapping attempts made on Johann.

In one study, Gleason, Sebanc, and Hartup found differences in the way mothers described children's relationships with personified objects versus invisible friends.[12] Many children tended to assume a parent-like role in their relationships with personified objects, providing care, guidance, and praise for their personified object's good behavior. Children with invisible friends were more likely to describe the relationship as egalitarian.[13] However, subsequent research has not replicated this finding, suggesting more variability in the roles of both personified objects and invisible friends (see Chapter 6).[14] Sometimes the personified object is the caretaker, as described by a 13-year-old girl who described how her stuffed pony would do what a "mom would do . . . try and calm someone down."[15] For other personified objects there are multiple and/or changing roles; children report taking turns with caretaking, whereby sometimes the child cares for the personified object, and other times, the personified object takes care of the child. In our research, we have found examples of both invisible friends and personified objects who are described as individuals in need of caretaking, individuals who provide supportive caretaking, egalitarian friends who are like peers, and friends who are like protective superheroes.

The examples we provided show that almost any sort of object can serve as a prop for a personified object and children can be inventive in the way they envision their appearances, behaviors, and personalities. However, personified objects are rated by adults as less creative than invisible friends.[16] We also believe that, overall, they tend to be less idiosyncratic or diverse than invisible imaginary friends. This hypothesized difference makes sense, given that the starting point for an invisible friend is open-ended, whereas characteristics of the bear, doll, or other toy constrain to some degree the way the child conceptualizes the personified object.

Another difference between invisible friends and personified objects is that parents often have more of a scaffolding role for imaginary friends based on toys. Not only are parents the ones who often provide the toys, they also often model the animation of the toy and/or encourage children to treat it as sentient.

> PARENT TO SON WHO IS HOLDING A NEW STUFFED RABBIT: What is the rabbit's name?
> CHILD: I don't know.
> PARENT: Why don't you ask him and see what he says?

Parents also sometimes encourage children to adopt a personified object version of an imaginary friend that started out as invisible. One adult recalled that her mother asked her lots of questions about the imaginary friend she had as a small child (an invisible "Mouse-Mouse") and then made a stuffed animal to her daughter's specifications, complete with blue-flowered superhero cape. More commonly, parents simply buy toys that correspond to the type of animals their children are imagining in their play. They interpret their child's account of an invisible friend as an expression of interest in a particular kind of individual and supply the child with a toy version of it. One 5-year-old in our research began her fantasies about dolphins when she was 2 years old. Her father reported that she used to pretend to hold tiny imaginary dolphins in her hands and to give them to family members. Because of her interest in dolphins, the parents gave her a stuffed dolphin that became the prop for an imaginary friend named Dipper, an invisible flying dolphin who lived on a star, never slept, and was "very very very very fast." When asked to describe Dipper, the child did not describe the physical attributes of her toy (a small gray dolphin) but instead reported that Dipper was "the size of a door" and had sparkles and stripes (unlike "a regular dolphin"). These details were repeated when the child was interviewed a year later. In her pretend play about dolphins, this child moved flexibly between interacting with an entirely invisible friend and using a toy as a prop in her play. There are also cases in which the child first used a toy as an imaginary friend and later invented an invisible version.

There are some disadvantages to having a personified object as your imaginary friend. Unlike invisible friends, personified objects wear out, get dirty, break, lose their stuffing, and can be lost. Parents sometimes buy duplicates of the treasured toy as a backup plan for avoiding the drama that ensues when the original is misplaced. But children vary in how tolerant they are about the mending, washing, and replacing of a personified object. When Ellie the Elephant was washed and restuffed, Isabelle rejoiced over Ellie being clean and once again being able to sit up straight when they played checkers. However, a little girl name Caitlin had a different reaction when her mother tried to do something about the sad state of Ernie, the Muppet doll who was Caitlin's constant companion. No matter how smelly and dirty Ernie became, Caitlin refused to let him be washed, and replacement with a new identical doll was completely out of the question (see Figure 3.1).

A former graduate student recalled that when she was 7 years old, her bear Homer was lost and she was devastated. She wrote a letter to Homer and threw it into the wind, but "the wind didn't take it far and my mom retrieved it from the front yard" (see Figure 3.2). Her aunt and uncle were able to provide a new bear that was identical except that it was not worn out like the original Homer. She played with it some, thinking of him as Homer's identical twin. Still, she "somehow couldn't quite imagine the same personality, vividness, attachment, and personal history . . . and it somehow felt fake to try to do so."

Neuroscientist Michael Graziano recalled his distress when a beloved personified object named Mubbiton (an action figure he had made out of pipe cleaners)

Imaginary Friends Who Are Personified Objects 37

Figure 3.1 An Ernie doll who served many years as a personified object type of imaginary friend.

was accidentally thrown away. Graziano's first solution was to make a duplicate toy, but it just didn't seem to be his friend. However, this story has a happier ending than Homer's because Graziano then came up with an elaborate backstory that made it possible for him to install the original essence of Mubbiton into a duplicate body.

I decided that Mubbiton, before he died, had invented a machine for storing his brain waves. The machine had to do with an old clock that I had disassembled

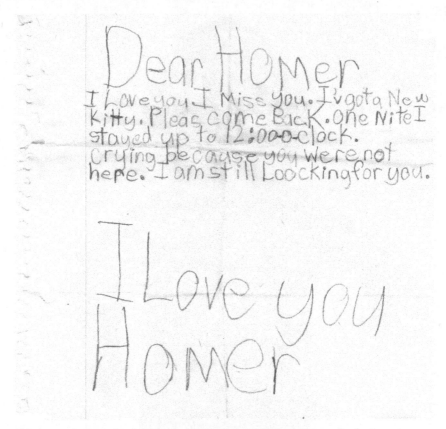

Figure 3.2 Letter written by 7-year-old after her beloved Homer was lost.

and some pieces of dried spaghetti. Anyway, using the machine, I successfully transplanted Mubbiton's brain waves into the new body. And presto, my friend was back. He was surprised to find himself in a new body, but overall delighted that his pipe cleaners were fresh and not so rusty.[17]

In the absence of a machine for storing brainwaves, most children in this situation are left with a replacement toy that Graziano described as lacking the soul of the original.[18] Hood and Bloom explored this phenomenon in a study in which they convinced children aged 3–6 years that they had a machine that could perfectly duplicate an object placed inside.[19] About half the children brought a toy they liked a lot to the lab, and the other half of the children brought an "attachment object" (identified by parents' ratings of how distressed their child would become if the toy was lost, how possessive their child was toward the toy, and how emotionally attached to the toy their child was). The distinction between personified versus transitional objects is not addressed in this study, but many of the "attachment objects" would probably have been considered imaginary friends. In any case, the results showed a clear difference between the two groups of children in their reactions to having their toys duplicated by the machine. All children with nonattachment toys allowed their toy to be copied, and 62% chose the duplicate when asked which one they would want to keep. In contrast, a few children flat out refused to allow the experimenter to copy their attachment toy in the machine, and of those that allowed the copying procedure to proceed, only 28% said they would keep the duplicate.

Why would children want only the original toy? And why that particular toy? One of the mysteries about personified objects is why one toy is chosen to become a trusted companion and others are passed over. What was it about Ellie, a stuffed elephant, that caused Isabelle to select Ellie as a beloved companion, of much greater importance than any of Isabelle's many other toys? Sometimes there is a plausible explanation based on who gave the toy to the child or the timing of the gift (e.g., when a sibling was born). Sometimes the child provides a simple answer. According to Tracy Gleason, Murray won out over Shayna's other toys because he could sit without falling over. For Caitlin, Ernie was special because of her interest in tags (i.e., the small pieces of fabric attached to toys that identifies their makers). Ernie had a particularly long, soft tag.

Mostly we don't know why a child selects a particular toy to be a best friend. But while we don't always know why one toy is chosen over all the others, we have noticed a type of toy that seems *not* to be chosen. Social robots (i.e., toys like Furby or robotic pets that are programmed to express needs and solicit caregiving) have not shown up as imaginary friends in any of our studies. It's an absence that is interesting and potentially informative. Maybe some speculation is in order.

Social Robots

Research on children's concepts of social robots does not suggest any obvious reason for their exclusion from the ranks of imaginary friends. It is not because children can't see them as thinking and feeling entities. When introduced to a social robot, children attempt to engage them in social interactions and believe that friendship is possible.[20] Children understand that social robots are not alive[21] but attribute psychological and perceptual properties to them. For example, when a humanoid robot named Robovie protested against being put away in a closet by an experimenter, the majority of the children (9-, 12-, and 15-year-olds) attributed mental states to it (i.e., the ability to have feelings and experience sadness). Many also reported that the experimenter had done something wrong by making Robovie go into the closet against its wishes: "... it kind of made me feel bad how it hurt his feelings going into the closet so maybe he could have been out somewhere else 'cause he said he was scared of the closet."[22]

In other work, Kahn and his colleagues focused on how children think about and interact with a sophisticated Sony robotic dog named AIBO.[23] AIBO has an impressive ability to initiate interactions and respond to children's behaviors, but children did not prefer AIBO over a stuffed dog when they were asked about the possibility of friendship. Turkle and colleagues[24] gave social robots to children and found that some children formed friendship-like relationships with them; however, the robots were removed after a few weeks, so we don't know if the relationship would last after the novelty wore off and adults were no longer carefully attending to the children's interactions with the robots. We suspect that the potential for longevity in a relationship with a robot that generates its own behaviors does not compare with the staying power of a simple stuffed toy.

Updated versions of social robots provide increasingly realistic cues to mimic intentionality and emotions; greater capacities for voice, facial, and emotional recognition; and enhanced ability to respond to tactile input that discourages or reinforces certain behaviors.[25] Thus, children play a role in shaping the robot's behavior and "personality," although there are limitations due to the context and the level of programming sophistication. Efforts to improve the technology might help with some of the goals for social robots (e.g., education), but will they enhance the relationships that children develop with them? Will there be other consequences? Ever since a talking Barbie in 1992 complained that "math class is tough," there has been some discomfort about toys with built-in behaviors.[26] It's a theme that filmmakers exploit in horror movies from *Child's Play* (1988), featuring Chucky, a doll with the soul of a serial killer, to *Megan* (2023), about a doll robot that is programmed to be a child's caregiver, with violent consequences. Sherry Turkle and her colleagues are troubled even when a robot says something like "I love you" because they believe it is not authentic. "Do we want robots saying things that they could not possibly mean?"[27]

Interactions with a social robot are shaped, at least in part, by the ideas, goals, and values of the programmer. It is possible that creating a toy that has immediate appeal in order to increase sales is not completely compatible with creating a toy that will have a sustained presence in children's lives. And to the extent that the programmed behaviors constrain children's creative control over interactions, perhaps they ultimately make social robots less attractive partners for the exchange and affection that characterize friendship. Is that why there are no robotic toys in our research on imaginary friends? On the other hand, perhaps social robots are not represented in research on imaginary friends because not that many children have them—yet. Children's relationships with robots and other artificially intelligent agents, as well as the possible dampening effects of programmed behaviors, will be revisited when we discuss children's parasocial relationships in Chapter 11.

While we do not think that social robots will overtake stuffed animals as potential best friends, there is no doubt that children readily attribute thoughts and feelings to them. But such responses are to be expected. Anthropomorphism—the attribution of human personality, emotions, beliefs, desires, and intentions to inanimate objects[28]—is a common lifelong tendency that has been documented as early as the first year of life.[29] Even adults readily attribute any manner of humanlike traits to inanimate objects—talking to their cars; attributing agency to plants; and personifying computers, boats, and musical instruments. A general tendency to anthropomorphize sets the stage for the transformation of stuffed toys and other objects into imaginary friends.

Anthropomorphism in Children and Adults

Sophisticated technology is not required to induce children or adults to attribute humanlike traits to inanimate objects. Consider the relationship between a lonely man and an imaginary other (a volleyball named Wilson) depicted in the movie *Cast Away*.[30] Chuck Noland (played by Tom Hanks) is marooned on an uninhabited island after he survives the crash of his FedEx plane. Among the many packages from the plane that wash up on the island's beach, one contains a volleyball. In the absence of human companionship, Chuck develops an imaginary relationship with "Wilson," and this friendship sustains him during four long years of isolation. Chuck's attachment to Wilson is so strong that he risks his life trying to retrieve the volleyball when a wave sweeps it from the raft during Chuck's escape from the island. We understand that Wilson is much more than a volleyball to Chuck. In fact, after less than 90 minutes of vicarious acquaintance, Wilson was more than a volleyball to the many audience members who were moved to tears by his fate.

In a series of studies, Epley, Waytz, and Cacioppo[31] examined the contexts in which adults anthropomorphize and found that some situations trigger anthropomorphism more than others. For example, adults are more likely to anthropomorphize when the nonhuman agent is similar to a human in some respect (face, body, or motion). However, the tendency to anthropomorphize is not restricted to objects that have faces or humanlike characteristics. In a classic psychology experiment, Heider and Simmel[32] found that the self-propelled and contingent movement of even simple faceless geometric shapes (a large triangle, small triangle, and small circle) in a short film was enough to elicit anthropomorphic interpretations from adults (e.g., bullying behavior attributed to the large triangle, and fear to the small circle and triangle).

Starting with Jean Piaget in 1929,[33] several researchers have studied anthropomorphism in young children.[34] In a study by Deniz Tahiroglu and Marjorie,[35] 5-year-old children were asked to describe what was happening in a movie similar to the one used by Heider and Simmel. Our movie starred a pentagon, triangle, square, and circle. There were no faces and no sound—just simple 2-D geometric shapes moving around the screen—but children readily interpreted the movements of the shapes as depicting a story of someone (the pentagon) being excluded from play and then making a new friend. Children who had imaginary friends were particularly impressive in their use of anthropomorphism. Here is one example:

Triangle and square don't want pentagon to play with them. Because they are playing their own game. Pentagon came up and said "Please" and they said "No." Triangle and square scared him. They don't want him because they thought he would be really annoying. They wanted to move him away so that they could play by themselves. Pentagon tried to sneak away. . . . Ball wanted to play with him. They wanted to play together. Ball thought the pentagon would not be annoying. They played together forever. Liked each other and played.

The capacity and inclination to anthropomorphize is a first step in the creation of a personified object. For many objects, it ends there; the child plays house with her dolls and then puts them away. But for the special object that captures the heart of a child, there is much more frequent and sustained animation, moving from everyday anthropomorphism to the development of the toy into a companion that the child loves and feels loved by in return.

Personified objects tend to participate in daily routines more often and are more widely known among family and friends than invisible friends.[36] For the adult observer, objects that a child has loved that much acquire a certain magic. Parents become attached. Children eventually move on to other pursuits, but many parents keep the personified object as a treasured keepsake instead of throwing it away like other worn-out toys. It's been 20 years since Ernie was Caitlin's imaginary friend, but when Marjorie asked Caitlin's mother (with no preamble), "Where's Ernie?," she immediately knew the answer: "On top of a dresser in a guest bedroom." When asked how she felt about the grubby little guy, without hesitation she answered, "I love Ernie."

Celebrities in the world of personified objects sometimes get special attention. The stuffed parrot belonging to Gustave Flaubert, author of *Madame Bovary*, is said to reside in a museum in Rouen, France.[37] Wilson, the volleyball prop from *Cast Away* (technically a fictional personified object) was sold at auction for over $85,000.[38] One of the most extreme examples is that of the original Winnie-the-Pooh, Tigger, Eeyore, Piglet, and Kanga, who reside in a climate-controlled display case in the New York Public Library (see Figure 3.3). In 1998, Gwyneth Dunwoody, a member of the British Parliament, attempted to get them returned to British soil. "I saw them recently, and they looked very unhappy indeed," she said. "I am not surprised, considering they have been incarcerated in a glass case in a foreign country for all these years."[39] Several prominent politicians got involved in the dispute over Pooh and his friends: Governor George Pataki, Rep. Nita Lowey, Tony Blair, and Mayor Rudolph Giuliani (who "vowed to do anything we can to keep them here"). The White House issued the following statement: "We do not expect this to be on the formal agenda of the meeting between President Clinton and Prime Minister Blair, although we would not exclude that it could come up in discussion." Ultimately, the position of the British government was to allow the stuffed animals to remain in New York. Note, however, that the tiny kangaroo named Roo is still in the United Kingdom because Christopher Robin lost Roo long ago in a Surrey apple orchard.

Figure 3.3 Winnie-the-Pooh and friends on display in New York City.
Printed by permission from Children's Center at 42nd Street, ©The New York Public Library.

Summary

Today, most researchers include beloved toys and other objects as potentially imaginary friends, depending on the extent to which the child imagines its thoughts, actions, and/or emotions. Nevertheless, invisible friends and personified objects differ in several ways. Overall, we think there is less diversity in children's descriptions of personified objects and that parents have a greater role in their creation. Some types of objects are more likely than others to be transformed into imaginary friends. Stuffed animals and dolls are common choices. In our studies, we have not observed interactive social robots to be among the toys that become long-lasting imaginary friends. Our speculation is that although children might be initially fascinated by the programmed responses of social robots, ultimately they like to have creative control over what an imaginary friend says and does. Finally, we noted that the creation of sustained relationships with personified objects is an extension of anthropomorphism, a natural and common tendency in adults as well as children to treat objects as if they had humanlike thoughts and feelings.

Thus far, we have focused on describing different types of imaginary friends, but who are the children who create them? In what ways and to what extent are they different from other children? We address these questions in our next chapter.

Notes

1. Svendsen, M. (1934). Children's imaginary companions. *Archives of Neurology and Psychiatry, 2*, 985–999.
2. Singer, D. G., & Singer, J. L. (1990). *The house of make-believe: Children's play and developing imagination*. Harvard University Press. See p. 100.
3. Newson, J., & Newson, E. (1968). *Four years old in an urban community*. George Allen & Unwin Ltd.
4. Watterson, B. (1995). *The Calvin and Hobbes tenth anniversary book*. Andrews and McMeel.
5. Benson, R. M., & Pryor, D. B. (1973). When friends fall out: Developmental interference with the function of some imaginary companions. *Journal of the American Psychoanalytic Association, 21*, 457–468.
6. Gleason, T. (2007). Murray: The stuffed bunny. In Turkle, S. (Ed.), *Evocative objects: Things we think with* (pp. 171–177). The MIT Press.
7. Ibid., p. 174.
8. Winnicott, D. W. (1953). Transitional objects and transitional phenomena. *International Journal of Psychoanalysis, 34*, 89–97.
9. Singer, D. G., & Singer, J. L. (1990). *The house of make-believe: Children's play and developing imagination*.
   Taylor, M., Carlson, S. M., Maring, B. L., Gerow, L., & Charley, C. (2004). The characteristics and correlates of high fantasy in school-aged children: Imaginary companions, impersonation and social understanding. *Developmental Psychology, 40*, 1173–1187.
10. Gleason, T. R., Sebanc, A. M., & Hartup, W. W. (2000). Imaginary companions of preschool children. *Developmental Psychology, 36*, 419–428.
11. Ames, L. B., & Learned, J. (1946). Imaginary companions and related phenomena. *Journal of Genetic Psychology, 69*, 147–167, see p. 156.
12. Gleason, T. R., Sebanc, A. M., & Hartup, W. W. (2000). Imaginary companions of preschool children. *Developmental Psychology. 36*, 419–428.
13. It is possible that parents and children differ in their perspective of how personified objects function. For example, there are probably differences in how mothers describe relationships with personified objects versus invisible friends because children's interactions with personified objects are easier for parents to observe.
14. Gleason, T. R., & Kalpidou, M. (2014). Imaginary companions and young children's coping and competence. *Social Development, 23*(4), 820–839.
    Gleason, T. R. (2002). Social provisions of real and imaginary relationships in early childhood. *Developmental Psychology, 38*, 979–992.
    Lin, Q., Fu, H., Wan, Y., Zhou, N., & Xu, H. (2018). Chinese children's imaginary companions: Relations with peer relationships and social competence. *International Journal of Psychology, 53*(5), 388–396.
15. Aguiar, N. R., Mottweiler, C. M., Taylor, M., & Fisher, P. (2017). The imaginary companions created by children who have lived in foster care. *Imagination, Cognition and Personality, 36*(4), 340–355.
16. Mottweiler, C. M., & Taylor, M. (2014). Elaborated role play and creativity in preschool age children. *Journal of Aesthetics, Creativity and the Arts, 8*, 277–286.
17. Graziano, M. S. A. (2010). *God, soul, mind, brain*. Leapfrog Press, p. 37.

18. Naomi and her child Isabelle once lost Ellie the Elephant for 24 hours. Because Naomi had foreseen this as a possibility, she had already purchased an identical (albeit new) stuffed elephant that could take Ellie's place. Naomi proceeded with an elaborate "soul transfer" ceremony to place Ellie's soul into the body of the new stuffed elephant. Isabelle and the new "Ellie" were adjusting to this change when the original Ellie was found. Tears of joy and relief ensued, and the new stuffed animal was quickly dismissed as the original Ellie took their rightful place at Isabelle's side.
19. Hood, B. M., & Bloom, P. (2008). Children prefer certain individuals over perfect duplicates. *Cognition, 106*, 455–462.
20. Kahn, P. H., Jr., Friedman, B., Perez-Granados, D. N., & Freier, N. G. (2006). Robotic pets in the lives of preschool children. *Interaction Studies, 7*, 405–436.
21. Jipson, J. L., & Gelman, S. A. (2007). Robots and rodents: Children's inferences about living and nonliving kinds. *Child Development, 78*(6), 1675–1688.
22. Kahn, P. H., Jr., Gary, H. E., & Shen, S. (2013). Children's social relationships with current and near-future robots. *Child Development Perspectives, 7*(1), 32–37, see p. 34.
23. Friedman, B., Kahn Jr, P. H., & Hagman, J. (2003). Hardware companions? What online AIBO discussion forums reveal about the human-robotic relationship. In Cockton, G., & Korhonen, P. (Eds.), *CHI '03: Proceedings of the SIGCHI Conference on Human Factors in Computing Systems*, Association for Computing Machinery, (pp. 273–280). DOI: https://doi.org/10.1145/642611.642660.
24. Turkle, S. Taggart, W., Kidd, C. D., & Dasté, O. (2006). Relational artifacts with children and elders: The complexities of cybercompanionship. *Connection Science, 18*, 347–361, https://doi.org/10.1080/09540090600868912
25. Kahn Jr., P., Gary, H. E., & Shen, S. (2013). Children's social relationships with current and near-future robots. *Child Development Perspectives, 7*, 32–37.
26. Mattel says it erred: Teen talk Barbie turn silent on math. (1992, October 21). *The New York Times*, Section D, p. 4. https://www.nytimes.com/1992/10/21/business/company-news-mattel-says-it-erred-teen-talk-barbie-turns-silent-on-math.html
27. Turkle, S., Taggart, W., Kidd, C. D., & Dasté, O. (2006). Relational artifacts with children and elders: The complexities of cybercompanionship. *Connection Science, 18*(4), 347–361, p. 360.
28. Waytz, A., Epley, N., & Cacioppo, J. T. (2010). Social cognition unbound: Insights into anthropomorphism and dehumanization. *Current Directions in Psychological Science, 19*, 58–62.
29. Hamlin, J. K., Wynn, K., & Bloom, P. (2007). Social evaluation by preverbal infants. *Nature, 450*, 557–560.
30. Zemeckis, R. (Director). (2000). *Cast away* [Film]. 20th Century Fox.
31. Ibid.
32. Heider, F., & Simmel, M. (1944). An experimental study of apparent behavior. *American Journal of Psychology, 57*, 243–259.
33. Piaget, J. (1929). *The child's conception of the world*. Routledge and Kegan Paul.
34. Hamlin, J. K., Wynn, K., & Bloom, P. (2007). Social evaluation by preverbal infants. *Nature, 450*, 557–560.
    Hamlin, J. K., Wynn, K., & Bloom, P. (2010). Three-month-olds show a negativity bias in their social evaluations. *Developmental Science, 13*, 923–929.

35. Tahiroglu, D., & Taylor, M. (2019). Anthropomorphism, social understanding, and imaginary companions. *British Journal of Developmental Psychology, 37*, 284–299. https://doi.org/10.1111/bjdp.12272
36. Gleason, T. R., Sebanc, A. M., & Hartup, W. W. (2000). Imaginary companions of preschool children. *Developmental Psychology, 36*, 419–428.
37. Barnes, J. (1985). *Flaubert's parrot.* Alfred A. Knopf.
38. Montanez, A. (2022, November 4). *Wilson, the volleyball that kept Tom Hanks company in"Castaway,"just sold for over $85,000.* Robb Report. https://robbreport.com/lifestyle/news/wilson-volleyball-auction-1234769064/
39. Barry, D. (1998, February 6). Briton demands Pooh bear's release. *New York Times*, Section B, p. 3. https://www.nytimes.com/1998/02/06/nyregion/pooh-cornered-blair-cedes-bear.html

Chapter 4
Children Who Create Imaginary Friends
Individual Characteristics

> She was a very creative child who loved to make up stories that she dictated to me.
> **(Mother describing a child who had an invisible friend at age 4)**

Not all children create imaginary friends. Who are the ones that do? Are they especially bright and creative? Are they too shy or socially awkward to develop friendships with real children? What about the Hollywood portrayal of such children as emotionally damaged or lacking a firm grasp of reality?

One of the earliest papers on the subject described the children who created imaginary friends as tending to have a "nervous temperament."[1] Other researchers have generated longer lists of the shortcomings and problems that they believed to characterize these children. In 1934, Margaret Svendsen[2] reported that 35 of the 40 children (aged 3–16 years) who she identified as having imaginary friends were described by their parents as having some type of personality problem, including "timidity in the presence of other children; a domineering manner with other children, fear in physical activity, sensitivity; an undemonstrative manner and reserved demeanor; evasiveness and irresponsibility; eagerness for being in the limelight and fear of being outdone."[3]

In another commonly cited (but dated) article, Ames and Learned[4] asserted that all children with imaginary friends must have personality defects, with the type of imaginary friend indicative of the particular problem they faced. They were especially negative about the children whose imaginary friends were animals and provided a long list of behavior problems that they considered to be characteristics of these children.[5]

One might be convinced by these reports that children with imaginary friends have a lot of issues, but there is a fundamental flaw with this conclusion. What these early studies share, in addition to negativity, is a failure to compare the characteristics of children who have imaginary friends with those of children who do not. How many of these personality characteristics and behavior problems might be generated by the parents of children who do not have imaginary friends? This piece of missing information is crucial. We are not interested in whether children with imaginary friends have problems, but whether problems are more common for children with imaginary friends than for other children. Any group of parents—the parents of musical children, red-headed children, or children who live in New York, as well as the parents of children with imaginary friends—could probably generate a list of less-than-desirable attributes of their offspring. However, such lists provide no information about whether these problems are uniquely associated with being musical, having red hair, living in New York, or having an imaginary friend. The lack of an appropriate comparison or control group makes a list of problems generated by a single group of parents impossible to interpret.

One might argue that although a control group would be nice, the negativity in these descriptions is striking and unlikely to be found to the same extent in descriptions of other children. But there is a second problem with the early research. Researchers tended to study children who were particularly likely to have emotional or behavioral problems. For example, the children in the Ames and Learned study were enrolled in a guidance nursery at the Yale Clinic of Child Development or recruited from the private practice of a mental health professional. In another early study, the children were patients on the Children's Ward of Bellevue Psychiatric Hospital.[6]

When a nonclinical random sample of children is recruited (instead of the outpatients of a clinic or some other biased group), and the children who have imaginary friends are compared with other children, a much more positive picture emerges. For example, the two groups of children do not seem to differ in the incidence of a wide range of behavior problems,[7] and some positive behaviors are more common among children with imaginary friends.[8] However, while current research debunks the negative stereotype of children with imaginary friends, an overly glowing portrait of these children as dramatically superior to other children is also misguided. When differences are found, they tend to be positive ones, but these differences usually are small and often do not show up in every study. In many studies and for many characteristics, children with imaginary friends are not very different from other children. For example, children (aged 6 and 7 years) with and without imaginary friends do not differ on any of the five major factors that are used to describe personality[9] and do not differ in how many friends they have.[10] So keeping this in mind and treading lightly, here are some of the differences that research with control groups has revealed.

Children with Imaginary Friends Are Less Shy

In a comprehensive study by Jennifer Mauro,[11] children with imaginary friends and their parents were interviewed three times over a period of three years, beginning when the children were about 4 years old. Their responses were compared with those of children who were similar in age, gender, and socioeconomic background, but who did not have imaginary friends. The two groups of children were very similar in most respects.[12] However, 4-year-old children with imaginary friends were rated as *less* shy than children who did not have imaginary friends.[13] For example, parents of children who had imaginary friends were less likely to report that their children preferred watching rather than joining in play or that they were embarrassed by a stranger's attention. This result is the opposite of what many people would predict because imaginary friends are often thought to be created by children who are too shy to make real friends.

Although Mauro's results might seem surprising, Marjorie and her colleagues[14] also found that parents rated their children with imaginary friends as *less* shy than parents of other children. In addition, other results suggest that children with imaginary friends are socially skilled and interact easily with others. Jerome and Dorothy Singer[15] observed 111 children playing at their day cares over the course of a year and found that children who were identified as having imaginary friends were less fearful and anxious in their play and as smiling and laughing more than other children. In another study, college students who remembered having imaginary friends in childhood were less neurotic, less introverted, and more dominant in face-to-face situations; possessed more self-confidence; and were more sociable than college students who did not remember any childhood pretend friends.[16]

Differences in shyness do not show up in every study. Martin Manosevitz and his colleagues[17] found that preschool children with imaginary friends were rated as being more adept at talking and interacting with adults, but there were no differences between the two groups in the extent to which parents described their children as shy. However, we do not know of any studies in which children with imaginary friends were found to be *more* shy than other children. Based on the evidence to date, the stereotype of children with imaginary friends as especially shy is wrong.

Children with Imaginary Friends Have Advanced Social Understanding (Theory of Mind)

The term "theory of mind" is used in developmental research to refer to children's developing knowledge about their own mental life and that of others. Between the ages of 2 and 5, there is considerable development in this kind of knowledge as children become aware of mental states such as belief and desire and begin to use their understanding of these mental states to explain and predict human behavior.[18]

The importance of a theory of mind becomes apparent when we observe the perspective-taking errors that are routinely made by children under 5 years of age. They tend to assume that a person's understanding of a situation—their mental representation of it—always corresponds to reality. In one classic task, children are shown a box that typically contains objects that are familiar to young children, such as a Band-Aid box.[19] When children open the box, they discover that it has crayons inside instead of Band-Aids. Once young children learn that the Band-Aid box contains crayons, they predict that another person will know there are crayons in the box even before the person looks inside. The children's responses suggest that they have difficulty appreciating that it is possible for someone else to have a belief about the world that is wrong (e.g., a belief that there are Band-Aids in a box that actually contains crayons). Similarly, the typical 3-year-old will predict that a person looking for some candy will search for it where the child knows the candy to be, even in cases in which the searcher last saw the candy in a different place.[20] By 5 years of age, most children understand that someone would think there were Band-Aids in the box and would not be able to find the candy.

Does having an imaginary friend facilitate these types of insights about mental life? After all, imaginary friends frequently take part in family life—joining the family at the dinner table, joining the children at bath time and story time, and going along on family excursions. On these occasions, only the child knows what the imaginary friend is thinking, and others have to depend upon the child to report on the contents of the imaginary friend's mind. According to Harris,[21] the practice in simulation that occurs as children explore the perspectives of others in role play (e.g., interacting with an imaginary friend) enhances their ability to do so in real life, contributing to theory-of-mind development. Once children master the distinction in pretend play between an entity or event in the real world and their internal mental representation of it, they might be better equipped to think about similar distinctions in other situations or contexts. In other words, they might have an advanced understanding of mental life. Marjorie and Stephanie Carlson[22] investigated this idea by giving preschool children with and without imaginary friends a series of tasks assessing theory of mind, which all required the insight that mental representations may not constitute an accurate reflection of the external world (e.g., the Band-Aid box example). We found that children who had imaginary friends did better than the other children on these tasks.

The differences on theory-of-mind tasks between children with and without imaginary friends tend to be small and not every study finds them,[23] but in a large-scale study by Angeline Lillard and Robert Kavanaugh that followed children from age 2½ to 5 years, one of the variables related to performance on theory-of-mind tasks was having an imaginary friend.[24] In addition, Marta Giménez-Dasí and her colleagues found that children aged 4–6 years who had imaginary friends scored higher than children without imaginary friends on comprehensive assessments of both theory of mind and emotional understanding.[25] Several other studies have found supporting evidence linking imaginary friends with advanced social understanding. For example, children with imaginary friends scored higher on a task in which they had to take the perspective of another person than children who did not have imaginary friends,[26] and in a Chinese sample[27] children with imaginary friends scored higher on a type of advanced theory-of-mind task (i.e., second-order false belief)[28] than children without imaginary friends. In addition, children with imaginary friends are more aware that other people do not have access to the children's own private thoughts[29] and are better able to identify emotions and understand their impact on behavior.[30]

Thinking about the thoughts and feelings of an imaginary friend might enhance a child's ability or inclination to do the same with real people, but the inverse might also be true: being particularly adept at understanding other people might be what inspires children to create and enjoy interacting with an imaginary friend. Yuko Motoshima and colleagues explored this latter hypothesis by identifying theory-of-mind-related experiences or behaviors in infancy and determining the extent to which they were associated with the later creation of an imaginary friend.[31] They found that the infants whose parents tended to talk to them about thoughts and feelings (e.g., "You want this toy") were more likely to have imaginary friends when they were 3½ years old.[32] In another study, babies who responded to the movement of a mechanical claw as if the claw had an intentional goal were more likely to have an imaginary friend at age 4.[33] This result is consistent with the finding that children with imaginary friends are more likely than other children to attribute biological attributes (e.g., agency) to a geometric shape moving randomly in a video (see Chapter 3).[34] Overall, the literature suggests that children with imaginary friends have an early developing inclination and ability to attribute mental life (thought, emotions, beliefs, goals) to inanimate objects as well as to other people.[35]

Girls Are *Somewhat* More Likely to Have Imaginary Friends than Boys

Many studies have found that girls are more likely to have imaginary friends than boys.[36] For example, in a study of 1,795 children aged 5–12 years, 52.2% of the girls reported having imaginary friends compared with 47.8% of the boys. Although some studies find no difference between boys and girls,[37] we have not seen a single study in which the number of boys with imaginary friends was greater than the number of girls. Why would girls be more likely than boys to have imaginary friends? Is it because more girls play with dolls, which are sometimes included as imaginary friends? This explanation seems unlikely because studies with varying definitions (e.g., including or excluding dolls) have found gender differences, and boys seem to have as many imaginary friends based on toys as girls.[38]

We believe at least part of the reason for the reported gender difference is that most of the research on this topic has been conducted with preschool children. We have found that preschool boys are just as interested in creating imaginary characters as their female counterparts, but preschool boys often impersonate the characters that they create rather than treat them as separate entities. For example, instead of pretending that Batman is a friend, a preschool boy might be more likely to pretend that he *is* Batman (see Chapter 2). While more girls than boys have imaginary friends in early childhood, this difference tends to disappear as the children get older. At least that is what Marjorie and her colleagues found when children were followed up to age 7.[39] Thus, boys might be underrepresented in imaginary friend groups in research with preschoolers because they haven't created them yet.

What about studies in which adults are asked whether they had imaginary friends when they were children? In a large study of 675 young adults,[40] women (34%) were twice as likely as men (17%) to recall having had imaginary friends. This result is not consistent with the idea that boys might create imaginary friends at older ages compared with girls, but there is a complication. Men are more likely than women to forget the imaginary friends they had as children.[41] Thus, accounts collected from men likely underestimate the incidence of childhood imaginary friends. When men do remember their childhood imaginary friends, they report having created them at older ages than women.[42]

Despite the interpretive issues raised by the tendency for preschool boys to impersonate imagined characters (rather than treating them as friends) and for adult males to forget their imaginary friends, we still think that girls are somewhat more likely than boys to have imaginary friends. This gender difference keeps cropping up in our own research, as well as research conducted in other labs, and is consistent with broader research on gender differences, including research studies showing that girls engage in more pretend play scenarios involving people than boys.[43]

Children with Imaginary Friends Are Generally More Interested in Fantasy

Children differ considerably in how much they enjoy and engage in fantasy play. One child who is fascinated by vacuum cleaners, for example, might create a pretend game in which the vacuum cleaner is a monster that has to be tamed, whereas another child might manifest an interest in vacuum cleaners by taking them apart to see how they work. To what extent does a general predisposition to engage in fantasy characterize children who have imaginary friends?

In a large study of 478 parents, Bouldin and Pratt[44] found that children with imaginary friends (17% of the 3- to 9-year-olds in this sample) were scored by their parents as higher on "imaginativeness." These children were reported to make up stories about mythical beings (not the imaginary friend), to incorporate mythical beings into their pretend play, and to explain events as magical more than other children. This study relied on parent report, but in a subsequent study, Bouldin[45] interviewed the children themselves (aged 3–9 years) and found a similar result. In addition, these results are consistent with other work suggesting that children with imaginary friends are particularly inclined to engage in fantasy. When Linda Acredolo and her colleagues[46] studied the play behavior of a group of children from infancy through the preschool years, they found that children who created imaginary friends at age 4 showed signs of being more interested in fantasy play than their peers even as infants. The infants who would later develop imaginary friends enjoyed playing with toy phones and dolls (which are props in pretend play), but were less interested in toys such as a shape sorter and busy box, which focus the child's attention on the real properties of objects and are less likely to elicit pretense.

Marjorie and her colleagues[47] also found a difference in the willingness of children with and without imaginary friends to engage in pretend play in the lab. They provided children with a toy phone and asked them to pretend to call one of their *real* friends. We wondered if children who regularly talk to an imaginary friend would find it easier to generate an imaginary conversation, even if it was to one of their real-life peers. Children with imaginary friends had no difficulty pretending to talk on the phone (e.g., "Hi. Do you want to come to my birthday party?") and in some cases carried on lively conversations for several minutes. In contrast, many of the children without imaginary friends seemed uncomfortable with this task. Some said "hello" and then hung up or reported that nobody was home to answer the phone. Overall, the evidence suggests that the creation of an imaginary friend is part of a more general tendency to enjoy and engage in fantasy.

Given their greater interest and involvement in fantasy, do children with imaginary friends clearly understand the difference between fantasy and reality? This question is more fully addressed in Chapter 8, but briefly, the evidence suggests that children with imaginary friends do not have a problem with this distinction. A few studies show that children with imaginary friends might be quicker to engage with fantasy scenarios introduced by adults,[48] but Sharon and Woolley found that high-fantasy children were *better* at categorizing real and fantastical entities than other children.[49] Research using other methods (e.g., reporting whether events could happen in real life) have found no differences between high- and low-fantasy children on the ability to distinguish reality and fantasy.[50]

Children with Imaginary Friends Are Particularly Able to Focus Their Attention

The development of executive function—the cognitive processes involved in the control of thought, action, and emotion—is one of the most important achievements of early childhood.[51] Although executive function includes several components (e.g., working memory, goal-directed planning, flexible thinking), inhibitory control—the capacity to focus one's attention and inhibit distractions—has received the most attention in relation to having imaginary friends. A variety of findings suggest that children with imaginary friends might be particularly able to stay focused on a task and not be distracted from their goals.

In some of this research, preschool children with imaginary friends were described by their mothers as being better able to focus their attention than other children.[52] For example, mothers described items such as "when picking up toys, usually keeps at the task until it's done" as true of their child and items such as "has a hard time concentrating on an activity when there are distracting noises" as not true of their child. In behavioral research, Jerome and Dorothy Singer[53] assessed the possibility that imaginative children, who presumably have a rich inner life, would be able to sit quietly doing nothing for longer periods of time than other children. (Being imaginative is not the same as having an imaginary friend, but the two are closely related in the context of this research because the question "Do you have a make-believe friend?" was one of four questions used to identify children as high in imaginative predisposition.) Children between the ages of 6 and 9 years were asked to pretend to be spacemen by sitting quietly in a "space capsule" (a cardboard box) for as long as possible. As predicted, the children who had been categorized as highly imaginative were able to sit quietly for longer than the other children. Singer and Singer interpreted this result as suggesting that children who enjoy fantasy play are better equipped to entertain themselves mentally when faced with delays or situations in which external stimulation is minimal.

Not every study has found a difference in inhibitory control between children with and without imaginary friends. Manosevitz and his colleagues[54] assessed waiting ability by seating children (average age was 5 years, 9 months) on the floor surrounded by a heavy cardboard box. The child was instructed that to be a "good driver, you have to sit real still, watch the road, and not talk or turn around." The researcher said "go" and then recorded the number of seconds children remained seated without moving or speaking. Although children with imaginary friends were able to sit still a little longer than children without imaginary friends (215.4 seconds compared with 171.3 seconds), this difference was not statistically significant (i.e., this difference could simply be due to chance).[55]

Stephanie Carlson and Angela Davis[56] used a battery of other methods to assess inhibitory control and found that, in general, children with imaginary friends had enhanced abilities. For example, children with imaginary friends did better on tasks in which they had to inhibit a prepotent response (e.g., to say "day" when shown a picture of a moon and "night" when shown a picture of the sun). However, there was an intriguing exception to this result. As discussed in Chapter 2, imaginary friends vary in the extent to which they are well behaved. Children who reported having imaginary friends that were noncompliant—almost as if the child could not control the imaginary friend—had more difficulty with inhibitory control tasks than other children. This result is consistent with Healy's[57] study of children who were rated as highly creative. She found that some of these children had the characteristics of attention deficit disorder. More generally, the literature on the relation between inhibitory control and creativity suggests that, although in many studies creativity is related to an enhanced ability to focus attention, there is also some evidence for the opposite result (e.g., focused attention interfering with creative problem-solving because inhibition is associated with less access to unusual ideas).[58]

The contradictory research findings indicate that there is much to learn about the complex relation between inhibition and creative behavior. According to Alison Gopnik, children's general uninhibitedness (as compared with adults) is one of their greatest strengths, allowing for their free wide-ranging exploration of the actual and possible worlds.[59] She describes early childhood as the research and development phase of life, followed by a phase when the knowledge that has been gathered is put to use. In her view, "uninhibited useless pretense turns out to be among the most deeply functional human activities."[60]

Children with Imaginary Friends Are Not Necessarily More Intelligent but They Have Elevated Verbal Skills

Although the personalities of children with imaginary friends were maligned in early research, their intellects were viewed in a more positive light. Early research linked the creation of an imaginary friend with superior intelligence, reporting that children with imaginary friends tended to score above what is considered average in the population.[61] When children with imaginary friends are compared more directly with a control group of other children, some studies report small but significant differences in intelligence.[62] Despite these results, the evidence for an association between imaginary friends and superior intelligence is weak. While some of the older studies reported higher levels of intelligence for children with imaginary friends, others did not,[63] and one of the most carefully conducted studies showed no difference.[64] Moreover, some children on the ability/disability spectrum (e.g., children with Down syndrome) have been reported to talk to imaginary friends.[65] Why are the results inconsistent? The answer probably has to do with variability in the assessment of intelligence, as well as in the criteria used to categorize children as having imaginary friends.

For typically developing children, the link between having an imaginary friend and doing well on intelligence tests might be limited specifically to tests of verbal abilities. For example, Mauro found that children with imaginary friends scored significantly higher on the Vocabulary subtest of the Wechsler Intelligence Scale for Children—Revised (WISC-R), a comprehensive test of intelligence designed for use with young children, but no difference emerged in scores on the Block Design subtest, which assesses spatial abilities.[66] Marjorie and Stephanie Carlson found a similar difference in verbal intelligence between children with and without imaginary friends, as assessed by the Peabody Picture Vocabulary Test, a widely used test of verbal intelligence in which the child's task is to point to the picture considered to illustrate best the meaning of a word presented orally by the experimenter.[67] Again, even for tests of verbal intelligence, a link with imaginary friends is not found in every study;[68] however, other work suggests that children with imaginary friends tend to have advanced language skills.[69] According to Bouldin, Bavin, and Pratt,[70] the language used by children with imaginary friends is qualitatively different from that of other children. More specifically, in their comprehensive study, children with imaginary friends (mostly invisible friends) aged 4–8 years demonstrated more complex syntax in their speech, with higher rates of adverbial and relative clauses, compared with children without imaginary friends. These types of clauses are particularly important in helping a listener understand what is being communicated by providing information about the time, location, manner, cause, result, or context of the main event. Bouldin and colleagues interpreted the differences in language use as reflecting the children's more advanced ability to take the perspective of another person.

Some Children with Autism Have Imaginary Friends

Autism spectrum disorder is described as involving marked deficits in pretend play (as well as deficits in communication and socialization).[71] Children with autism tend not to engage spontaneously in pretend play, and when they do, it occurs later in development and is more repetitive and stereotyped than the pretend play of other children. However, when Paige Davis and her colleagues[72] asked the parents of children with autism about imaginary friends, they found that 16.2% of the children had them. In a second study,[73] an even higher percentage (49.2%) of children with autism were reported by their parents to have created imaginary friends between one and 11 years of age. Compared with typically developing children, children with autism had fewer imaginary friends, their imaginary friends were created at older ages, and more of them were personified objects, but the descriptions and functions of the imaginary friends were similar in most respects. In addition, the beneficial association between theory of mind and imaginary friends was found for the children who had autism as well as for the typically developing children.[74]

Although some authors have argued for a positive view of the imaginative potential of people with autism,[75] the creation of imaginary friends by children with a disorder so strongly associated with deficits in pretend play is surprising. However, the view of imagination and pretend play deficits in autism is also at odds with first-person accounts written by people with autism. Imagination and visual imagery are central to Temple Grandin's description of her experiences as a person with autism.[76] Other memoirs include specific references to imaginary friends. In *Pretending to Be Normal*, Willey[77] attributes her difficulty in interacting successfully with peers and being accepted by them as the motivation for creating private imaginary friends. She writes, "When I think of my earliest years, I recall an overwhelming desire to be away from my peers. I much preferred the company of my imaginary friends. Penny and her brother Johnny were my best friends, though no one saw them but me."[78] Other case studies and firsthand accounts also mention the creation of imaginary friends as a way to address the desire to have a friend.[79] Daniel Tammet[80] (a savant with autism) describes how "Anne," a very tall and thin ancient invisible woman who was grateful for his company, helped him with cope with his difference from other children.[81] Perhaps new insights might result from research investigating how interactions with imaginary friends for some individuals fit into the overall difficulties that are evident in other imaginative behaviors for people with autism.

Children with Imaginary Friends Are More Creative in Storytelling but Not on Most Other Tests of Creativity

The invention of an imaginary friend is an impressive act of the imagination, but are children who have imaginary friends generally more creative than other children? One might expect that children who have imaginary friends would score higher than other children on creativity tasks, either because the practice of interacting with an imaginary friend might have a training effect or, alternately, because creative children might be the ones who find this type of pretend play particularly enjoyable. Evidence for this hypothesis comes mostly from research with older children and adults. For example, Eva Hoff found that 10-year-old children with imaginary friends engaged in more creative activities and hobbies (e.g., drawing, writing stories) and had higher scores on the Unusual Uses Test,[82] a commonly used creativity test in which children are asked to generate as many possible uses they can think of for a common object (e.g., a paperclip, coat hanger).[83] In a study of 800 high school students by Charles Schaefer, the adolescents who were identified as having achieved distinction in creative writing were more likely to report having had imaginary friends in childhood.[84] In addition, adults who reported having a childhood imaginary friend produced more creative responses on a task in which they were asked to imagine themselves in a scene (standing by a small stream deep in a forest) and then to describe the experience in detail.[85]

Despite the differences found in older children and adults, most standard creativity tests show no difference between young children with and without imaginary friends.[86] Part of the problem might be that devising suitable methods for measuring creativity in young children is challenging. For example, the Unusual Uses Test requires children to give multiple answers to the same question, often with the repeated requests ("Can you think of any other ways?"). Candice Mottweiler and Marjorie[87] point out that being asked to generate new answers to the same question is potentially confusing for young children. Another standard way of assessing creativity is to show children a series of abstract patterns and ask them to report what they see in the patterns (Abstract Patterns Task). On these tests, young children with and without imaginary friends do not differ.[88] Other tasks in which children respond to a series of pictures (Torrance's Thinking Creatively with Pictures, Penguin Picture Stories) also show no differences in creativity between young children with and without imaginary friends.[89]

One type of creativity does distinguish children with and without imaginary friends: the ability to tell a good story. In research by Gabe Trionfi and Elaine Reese,[90] a researcher read a story to the child and then asked the child to retell the story (from "beginning to end") to a puppet. In another task, the researcher asked the child to tell a story about a unique event that had happened to them in the past. (The researcher had earlier collected information about past events from the child's mother.) On both tasks, the children who currently or previously had imaginary friends produced narratives that were richer and more detailed than the narratives produced by other children. Trionfi and Reese speculated that having an imaginary friend might facilitate children's narrative ability because of the practice they have creating stories about their friend that they tell to their parents and other family members.

Candice Mottweiler and Marjorie[91] investigated creativity in storytelling by beginning a story and asking children aged 4–6 years to finish it. The researcher placed a felt path and a small key on the table and walked two small dolls (female dolls for girls and male dolls for boys) down the path. "Susan and Jane / George and Bob are going for a walk outside when they see a key. Susan/George says, 'What's this on the ground?' Jane/Bob says, 'It's a key. I wonder if it's magic.'" Then the experimenter asked, "Can you show me and tell me what happens now?" Three adults independently rated the creativity of how children finished the story (see Table 4.1 for examples). Children with invisible friends produced endings to the story that were rated as more creative than other children.

Young children with imaginary friends also tend to be more creative than other children in some types of drawing tasks. Imafuku and Seto[92] found that children with imaginary friends used more colors than other children when asked to draw a self-portrait, a dog, and a bird and tended to include more features (e.g., ears, neck, shoulders) in the self-portraits. The authors interpreted the use of more colors and features as evidence that the children with imaginary friends were more creative than other children. Candice Mottweiler and Marjorie used a different drawing task that was adapted from work by Karmiloff-Smith on representational change in drawing.[93] They asked 4- and 5-year-olds to draw a person, then to draw a "pretend person, a person that couldn't exist, a person that is made up," and finally to describe what they had drawn.[94] Children with invisible friends (particularly the children whose imaginary friends were rated as highly inventive) provided the most creative solutions to drawing a pretend person, perhaps because inventing an invisible friend has some

Table 4.1 Examples of Children's Story Stem Completions

"Then they tried to open a door with the key and it opened and it had fake scary stuff, like fake scary xxx and costumes or Frankenstein costumes or mummies or pumpkin ones. Then they went out and locked the door. Then they went and then they went into jungle and with the key and they rode in the front until a board that came by and it took the key out of Bob's hand. And then it, then it put it down the chimney. And inside the chimney was on fire. It dropped the key and it fell in the fire."

(Creativity rating: 4.5 out of 5)

"She picks the key up and then they find something to unlock, like maybe, like that lock over there. It doesn't work. And then they pick up the key and then they found a lock and they put the key in it and they unlock it and the door opens. And then they say, 'Mom, Mom, a door opens!' And then they said, 'Come on' and then they went inside. And then they went and they set the key back where it was and she put it back there and they went home. Because they were supposed to be right here."

(Creativity rating: 2.5 out of 5)

similarity to the task of drawing a person who could not exist. We also suspect that the children's verbal descriptions of the pretend person, in addition to the drawings, might have influenced the creativity ratings. Many of the children had a lot to say about the pretend person they had drawn—which added a storytelling component to this task.

In summary, not all highly creative children have imaginary friends, and not having one should not be interpreted as a negative sign regarding a child's creative potential. However, children with imaginary friends are able to tell a good story. Maybe they just have a lot of practice. According to Gleason,[95] one of the functions of imaginary friends is providing a vehicle for telling stories about the imaginary friend's lives, family, pets, homes, and adventures to their parents, siblings, friends, and even to researchers who are listening carefully and writing it all down.

Children with Invisible Friends *Might* Have More Vivid Mental Imagery

Having an imaginary friend seems indicative of a rich, inner fantasy life, and researchers have wondered over the years whether children with imaginary friends experience particularly vivid mental imagery. The evidence for this idea is mixed and depends, in part, on the method used to assess mental imagery. Many studies rely on self-report. When children are simply asked to describe their imagery, children with imaginary friends are more likely to report experiencing vivid visual images and to report that their images sometimes seem so real that they could almost see or hear them.[96] In addition, adults who recall having imaginary friends as children report more colorful night dreams and more daily use of imagery.[97] However, the method of asking children and adults to describe their own mental imagery is not completely convincing and does not always yield differences between children with and without imaginary friends.[98] In addition, a number of studies have failed to find any relation between what people say about their imagery and their performance on tasks that require them to use visual[99] or auditory imagery.[100]

Anne Mannering and Marjorie took a different approach by investigating children's use of visual imagery on a series of behavioral tasks.[101] For example, in one task children were asked to form visual images of two animals and report which one was larger. In this type of task, people are assumed to be using visual imagery if they take longer to make their decision when the animals are similar in size (e.g., cat vs. dog) than when the animals are very different in size (e.g., cat vs. mouse).[102] The idea is that when the size difference is small, one has to inspect one's mental images more carefully, which takes more time than when the difference in size is large. Overall, children's reaction times indicated that they were comparing visual images of the two animals, but individual differences were not related to having an imaginary friend.[103]

In a follow-up study, Deniz Tahiroglu, Anne Mannering, and Marjorie[104] discovered that the use of visual imagery on this task was associated with having a particular type of imaginary friend. As discussed in Chapter 2 and elsewhere, imaginary friends—particularly invisible ones—are a diverse group. There is variability in every characteristic of imaginary friends, including the extent that they involve visual imagery. In this study, children gave a variety of responses when asked if their friend was "easy to see" (e.g., "yes, I just picture him in my mind"; "no, 'cause you can't see him, 'cause he's invisible"). Children who had invisible friends that they claimed were "easy to see" showed the reaction time pattern associated with visual imagery more often than children with invisible friends that were "not easy to see," children with personified objects, or children with no imaginary friends.

Some evidence suggests differences in auditory imagery. In two studies using a "Jumbled Speech Task," children listened to a meaningless sample of speech sounds and wrote down or told the experimenter any words that they heard. Fernyhough and colleagues[105] tested 212 children aged 9–11 years and found that the 20 children with imaginary friends reported hearing words in the speech sounds more often than other children. (The authors did not specify whether the imaginary friends were invisible or also included personified objects.) Fernynough and his colleagues[106] replicated this result with a younger sample of 80 children aged 4–8 years, including 37 children who reported having imaginary friends (78% were invisible friends). The authors suggested that interacting with an imaginary friend might be similar in some respects to having an auditory hallucination. (This interpretation is related to Fernyhough's broader theory about the fuzzy boundaries between the varieties of experiences in which people hear voices in their heads.)[107] However, the Jumbled Speech task is an unusual type of task that is unlike everyday auditory experience, and it is uncertain if the difference in performance for children with imaginary friends was linked to their practice of imagining the voices of imaginary friends or if there is some other explanation (e.g., differences in suggestibility). Note that, as is the case for visual imagery, children differ in their responses to questions about whether their imaginary friends are "easy to hear" (e.g., "yeah, I listen to him in my mind"; "no, I just say it and pretend she is saying it").[108]

Children with Imaginary Friends Watch Less Digital Media

To date, research on the extent to which children with imaginary friends differ from other children in their consumption of digital media is limited. Much of the current research has focused instead on the extent to which children's digital media can enhance or degrade creativity more generally.[109] The media research that specifically addresses a link with imaginary friends is dated and focuses on television. For example, in the 1990s, two studies found that children with imaginary friends spent less time watching television than other children.[110] Given the pace of technological change, these studies might no longer seem relevant, but current reports of American children's digital media consumption indicate that young children (ages 0–8 years) still spend much of their time watching television and/or videos.[111] A 2019 survey conducted with 1,000 parents in the United Kingdom suggests that the findings of American research from the 1990s might still hold. British children aged 1–4 years old whose daily screen time was less than one hour per day were 3.5 times more likely to have an imaginary friend compared with children whose daily screen time was two or more hours daily.[112]

The relation between having an imaginary friend and watching less television is not surprising for a couple of reasons. First, when children are asked why they watch television, their answers reveal that television serves some of the same functions as imaginary friends—both are entertaining and can provide distraction from real-life concerns. A child who is bored or wants relief from worries can turn on the television. Another solution would be to create a pretend friend. Second, some of the impulses toward imaginative play might be displaced by television watching. Television programs (and other digital media) provide an externally generated fantasy world that might substitute for one of the child's own invention.[113] Third, children who watch a lot of television simply might not have time for imaginative play.

According to Singer and Singer,[114] watching television is not a bad thing, in and of itself, but the time it takes away from other kinds of activities could be an issue. In order to develop imaginative kinds of play, children need unstructured time, but often children (and adults, for that matter) are tempted to turn to screens whenever they have nothing to do. For some children, this dependence on visual media turns into a regular habit of screen time for several hours a day—hours that could be spent in imaginative play. Although digital media can be an enjoyable way to pass the time, children who complain of having nothing to do are likely to eventually develop imaginative ways of entertaining themselves.

Summary

In this chapter we have described some of the individual characteristics of children who have the inclination to invent and become attached to an imaginary friend. Children with imaginary friends might be somewhat advanced in their social understanding, better at storytelling, and at some ages a little less shy and more able to focus their attention We also suspect that children with imaginary friends, particularly invisible ones, might tend to have more vivid visual imagery than other children or a greater tendency to use imagery habitually, but the evidence is not strong. Girls tend to be more likely to have imaginary friends than boys, but caution is needed to not overstate this gender difference. Some of the results might be due to the timetable for creating imaginary friends, with boys tending to create them at older ages than girls. At the younger ages, there might be differences in how boys and girls play with imaginary characters, rather than a more general difference in their interest in fantasy play. Caution is also warranted in interpreting the findings of research investigating individual differences in intelligence. It is not true that all (or only) highly intelligent children create imaginary friends and when differences are found, they tend to be small and/or pertain only to verbal intelligence.

Overall, the similarities in the individual characteristics of children with and without imaginary friends are more striking than differences. In the next chapter, we broaden our investigation to explore how the social context of children's family and culture affect the extent to which they create imaginary friends.

Notes

1. Vostrovsky, C. (1895). A study of imaginary companions. *Education, 15,* 383–398.
2. Svendsen, M. (1934). Children's imaginary companions. *Archives of Neurology and Psychiatry, 2,* 985–999.
3. Ibid., p. 991.
4. Ames, L. B., & Learned, J. (1946). Imaginary companions and related phenomena. *The Journal of Genetic Psychology, 69,* 147–167.
5. Ibid. Ames and Learned provided the following descriptions of children who had imaginary animals as playmates: "gets along badly with children"; "very fearful of new people"; "dependent on mother and aversion to children, slow to adjust to a group and plays quietly by herself"; "dictatorial, plays poorly with contemporaries"; "moody, negative, explosive, slightly dependent"; "a very dependent child, a lone wolf in school"; "negative, strong tendency to react by opposites, slow to adjust to new people," p. 162.
6. Bender, L., & Vogel, B. F. (1941). Imaginary companions of children. *American Journal of Orthopsychiatry, 11,* 56–65.
7. Manosevitz, M., Prentice, N. M., & Wilson, F. (1973). Individual and family correlates of imaginary companions in preschool children. *Developmental Psychology, 8,* 72–79
8. Singer, D. G., & Singer, J. L. (1990). *The house of make-believe: Children's play and developing imagination.* Harvard University Press.
Taylor, M., & Carlson, S., M. (1997). The relation between individual differences in fantasy and theory of mind. *Child Development, 68,* 436–455.
9. Taylor, M., Carlson, S. M., Maring, B. L., Gerow, L., & Charley, C. (2004). The characteristics and correlates of high fantasy in school-aged children: Imaginary companions, impersonation and social understanding. *Developmental Psychology, 40,* 1173–1187.
In this study parents provided information about their children's extraversion, agreeableness, conscientiousness, neuroticism, and openness.
10. Gleason, T. R. (2004). Imaginary companions and peer acceptance. *International Journal of Behavioral Development, 28,* 204–209.
11. Mauro, J. (1991). *The friend that only I can see: A longitudinal investigation of children's imaginary companions* [Doctoral dissertation]. University of Oregon.
12. The parents of both groups of parents filled a questionnaire that includes assessments of 15 different aspects of temperament. More specifically, there were no differences on the following dimensions: activity (rate and extent of locomotion), anger (amount of negative affect related to the interruption of ongoing tasks or goal blocking), approach

(amount of excitement and positive anticipation for expected pleasurable activities), discomfort (amount of negative affect related to sensory qualities of stimulation), soothability (rate of recovery from peak distress, excitement, or general arousal), fear (amount of negative affect related to anticipated pain or distress and/or potentially threatening situations), high-intensity pleasure (amount of pleasure or enjoyment related to situations involving high stimulus intensity, rate, complexity, novelty, and incongruity), impulsivity (speed of response initiation), inhibition (the capacity to plan and to suppress inappropriate approach responses under instructions or in novel or uncertain situations), low-intensity pleasure (amount of pleasure or enjoyment related to situations involving low stimulus intensity, rate, complexity, novelty, and incongruity), perceptual sensitivity (amount of detection of slight, low-intensity stimuli from the external environment), sadness (amount of negative affect and lowered mood and energy related to exposure to suffering, disappointment, and object loss), and smile/laughter (amount of positive affect in response to changes in stimulus intensity, rate, complexity, and incongruity).

13. Shyness was defined as the slow or inhibited approach in situations involving novelty or uncertainty.
14. Taylor, M., Sachet, A. B., Mannering, A. M., & Maring, B. L. (2013). The assessment of elaborated role-play in young children: Invisible friends, personified objects and pretend identities. *Social Development, 22*, 75–93.
15. Singer, J. L., & Singer, D. G. (1981). *Television, imagination, and aggression: A study of preschoolers.* Erlbaum.
16. Wingfield, R. C. (1948). Bernreuter personality ratings of college students who recall having imaginary companions during childhood. *Journal of Child Psychiatry, 1*, 190–194.
17. Manosevitz, M., Prentice, N. M., & Wilson, F. (1973). Individual and family correlates of imaginary companions in preschool children. *Developmental Psychology, 8*, 72–79.
18. Wellman, H. M., Cross, D., & Watson, J. (2001). Meta-analysis of theory of mind development: The truth about false belief. *Child Development, 72*, 655–684. https:/doi.org/10.1111/1467-8624.00304
19. Wimmer, H., & Perner, J. (1983). Beliefs about beliefs: Representation and constraining function of wrong beliefs in young children's understanding of deception. *Cognition, 13*, 103–128.
20. Perner, J., Leekam, S. R., & Wimmer, H. (1987). Three-year-olds' difficulty understanding false beliefs: Representational limitation, lack of knowledge or pragmatic misunderstanding. *British Journal of Developmental Psychology, 5*, 125–137.
21. Harris, P. L. (2000). *The work of the imagination.* Basil Blackwell.
22. Taylor, M., & Carlson, S. M. (1997). The relation between individual differences in fantasy and theory of mind. *Child Development, 68*, 436–455.
23. Davis, P. E., Meins, E., & Fernyhough, C. (2011). Self-knowledge in childhood: Relations with children's imaginary companions and understanding of mind. *British Journal of Developmental Psychology, 29*(3), 680–686.
    Fernyhough, C., Bland, K., Meins, E., & Coltheart, M. (2007). Imaginary companions and young children's responses to ambiguous auditory stimuli: Implications for typical and atypical development. *Journal of Child Psychology and Psychiatry, 48*(11), 1094–1101.
24. Lillard, A. S., & Kavanaugh, R. D. (2014). The contribution of symbolic skills to the development of an explicit theory of mind. *Child Development, 85*(4), 1535–1551.

25. Giménez-Dasí, M., Pons, F., & Bender, P. K. (2016). Imaginary companions, theory of mind and emotion understanding in young children. *European Early Childhood Education Research Journal, 24*(2), 186–197.
26. Roby, A. C., & Kidd, E. (2008). The referential communication skills of children with imaginary companions. *Developmental Science, 11*, 531–540.
27. Lin, Q., Zhou, N., Wan, Y., & Fu, H. (2020). Relationship between Chinese children's imaginary companions and their understanding of second-order false beliefs and emotions. *International Journal of Psychology, 55*(1), 98–105.
28. Second-order false belief refers to the insight that it is possible for a person to have an incorrect belief about another person's belief. The child is asked to predict what one character believes about another character's beliefs.
29. Motoshima, Y., Shinohara, I., Todo, N., & Moriguchi, Y. (2014). Parental behaviour and children's creation of imaginary companions: A longitudinal study. *European Journal of Developmental Psychology, 11*(6), 716–727.
  Zhang, Y. Q., Pei, M. J., Chen, X. L., & Zhang, W. R (2014). The impact of imaginary companions on 5 to 6 years old children's emotion understanding. *Journal of Tongling Vocational College, 9*, 66–69.
30. Ibid.
31. Motoshima, Y., Shinohara, I., Todo, N., & Moriguchi, Y. (2014). Parental behaviour and children's creation of imaginary companions: A longitudinal study. *European Journal of Developmental Psychology, 11*(6), 71–727.
32. In addition, having an imaginary friend at 3½ was associated with mothers who were less intrusive in their interactions with their babies at six months (i.e., they did not interfere with or overcontrol the baby's behavior).
33. Moriguchi, Y., Shinohara, I., & Ishibashi, M. (2016). Agent perception in children with and without imaginary companions. *Infant and Child Development, 25*(6), 550–564.
34. Ibid.
35. It's important to note here that correlational research suggests a link between imaginary friends and theory of mind, rather than specifying that interacting with an imaginary friend causes an understanding of mind. The infancy research suggests that it is also possible that children who are advanced in theory of mind are better equipped for interacting with an imaginary friend.
36. Bouldin, P., & Pratt, C. (1999). Characteristics of preschool and school-age children with imaginary companions. *The Journal of Genetic Psychology, 160*, 397–410.
  Hoff, E. (2005b). Imaginary companions, creativity, and self-image in middle childhood. *Creativity Research Journal, 17*, 167–180.
  Taylor, M., & Carlson, S. M. (1997). The relation between individual differences in fantasy and theory of mind. *Child Development.*
37. Trionfi, G., & Reese, E. (2009). A good story: Children with imaginary companions create richer narratives. *Child Development, 80*, 1301–1313.
38. Bouldin, P. (2006). An investigation of the fantasy predisposition and fantasy style of children with imaginary companions. *The Journal of Genetic Psychology, 167*, 17–29.
  Taylor, M., & Carlson, S., M. (1997). The relation between individual differences in fantasy and theory of mind. *Child Development.*

39. Taylor, M., Carlson, S. M., Maring, B. L., Gerow, L., & Charley, C. (2004). The characteristics and correlates of high fantasy in school-aged children: Imaginary companions, impersonation and social understanding. *Developmental Psychology, 40*, 1173–1187.
40. Brinhthaupt, T. M., & Dove, C. T. (2012). Differences in self-talk frequency as a function of age, only-child, and imaginary companion status, *Journal of Research in Personality, 46*, 326–333.
41. McAnally, H. M., Forsyth, B. J., Taylor, M., & Reese, E. (2020). Imaginary companions in childhood: What can prospective longitudinal research tell us about their fate by adolescence? *The Journal of Creative Behavior, 55*, 276–283. https://doi.org/10.1002/jocb.468
42. Hurlock, E. B., & Bernstein, M. (1932). The imaginary playmate: A questionnaire study. *Journal of Genetic Psychology, 41*, 380–391.
43. Field, T., De Stephano, L. & Koewler, J. H. (1982). Fantasy play of toddlers and preschoolers., *Developmental Psychology, 18*, 503–508.
44. Bouldin, P., & Pratt, C. (1999). Characteristics of preschool and school-age children with imaginary companions. *The Journal of Genetic Psychology, 160*, 397–410.
45. Bouldin, P. (2006). An investigation of the fantasy predisposition and fantasy style of children with imaginary companions. *The Journal of Genetic Psychology, 167*, 17–29.
46. Acredolo, L. P., Goodwyn, S. W., & Fulmer, A. H. (1995). *Why some children create imaginary companions: Clues from infant and toddler play preferences* [Paper presentation]. Biennial Meeting of the Society for Research in Child Development, Indianapolis, IN.
47. Taylor, M., Carlson, S. M., Maring, B. L., Gerow, L., & Charley, C. (2004). The characteristics and correlates of high fantasy in school-aged children: Imaginary companions, impersonation and social understanding. *Developmental Psychology*.
48. Bouldin, P., & Pratt, C. (1999). Characteristics of preschool and school-age children with imaginary companions. *The Journal of Genetic Psychology*.
    Woolley, J. D., Boerger, E. A., Markman, A. B. (2004). A visit from the Candy Witch: Factors influencing young children's belief in a novel fantastical being. *Developmental Science, 7*, 456–468.
49. Sharon, T., & Woolley, J. D. (2004). Do monsters dream? Young children's understanding of the fantasy/reality distinction. *British Journal of Developmental Psychology, 22*(2), 293–310.
50. Taylor, M., Cartwright, B. S., & Carlson, S. M. (1993). A developmental investigation of children's imaginary companions. *Developmental Psychology, 29*, 276–285.
51. For a review see Carlson, S. M., Zelazo, P. D., & Faja, S. (2013). Executive function. In P. Zelazo (Ed.), *The Oxford handbook of developmental psychology: Vol. 1. Body and mind* (pp. 706–743). Oxford University Press.
52. Mauro, J. (1991). *The friend that only I can see: A longitudinal investigation of children's imaginary companions* [Unpublished doctoral dissertation]. University of Oregon.
53. Singer, J. L. (1961). Imagination and waiting ability in young children. *Journal of Personality, 29*, 396–413.
54. Manosevitz, M., Fling, S., & Prentice, N. M. (1977). Imaginary companions in young children: Relationships with intelligence, creativity and waiting ability. *Journal of Child Psychology and Psychiatry, 18*, 73–78.
55. This difference failed to reach significance because children were extremely variable in their waiting times.

56. Carlson, S. M., & Davis, A. C. (2005). *Executive function and pretense in preschool children* [Poster presentation]. Annual meeting of the Jean Piaget Society, Vancouver, BC.
57. Healy, D. (2005). *Attention deficit hyperactivity disorder and creativity: An investigation into their relationship* [Dissertation]. University of Canterbury, New Zealand.
58. Carson, S. H., Peterson, J. B., & Higgins, D. M. (2003). Decreased latent inhibition is associated with increased creative achievement in high-functioning individuals. *Journal of Personality and Social Psychology, 85*, 499–506.
59. Gopnik, A. (2009). *The philosophical baby*. Farrar, Straus, & Giroux.
60. Ibid., p. 73.
61. Ames, L. B., & Learned, J. (1946). Imaginary companions and related phenomena. *The Journal of Genetic Psychology, 69*, 147–167.
62. Jersild, A. T., Markey, F. V., & Jersild, C. L. (1933). *Children's fears, dreams, wishes, daydreams, likes, dislikes, pleasant and unpleasant memories* (Vol. 12). Teachers College, Columbia University.
63. Bairdain, E. F. (1959). Psychological characteristics of adolescents who have had imaginary companions. *Dissertation Abstracts International, 29*, 747.
64. Singer, D. G., & Singer, J. L. (1990). *The house of make-believe: Children's play and developing imagination*.
65. Chicoine, B. (2006). Self-talk, imaginary friends, and fantasy life. In D. McGuire & B. Chicoine (Eds.), *Mental wellness in adults with Down Syndrome: A guide to emotional and behavioral strengths and challenges* (pp.136–146). Woodbine House, Inc.

    Glenn, S. M., & Cunningham, C. C. (2000). Parents' reports of young people with Down syndrome talking out loud to themselves. *Mental Retardation, 38*(6), 498–505.
66. Mauro, J. (1991). *The friend that only I can see: A longitudinal investigation of children's imaginary companions*.
67. Taylor, M., & Carlson, S. M. (1997). The relation between individual differences in fantasy and theory of mind. *Child Development*.
68. Kalyan Masih, V. (1978). Imaginary companions of children. In R. B. R. Weizmann, P. J. Levinson, & P. A. Taylor (Eds.), *Piagetian theory and its implications for the helping professions*. University of Southern California.

    Manosevitz, M., Fling, S., & Prentice, N. M. (1977). Imaginary companions in young children: Relationships with intelligence, creativity and waiting ability. *Journal of Child Psychology and Psychiatry*.
69. Lillard, A. S., & Kavanaugh, R. D. (2014). The contribution of symbolic skills to the development of an explicit theory of mind. *Child Development, 85*(4), 1535–1551.
70. Bouldin, P., Bavin, E. L., & Pratt, C. (2002). An investigation of the verbal abilities of children with imaginary companions. *First Language, 22*(3), 249–264.
71. Baron-Cohen, S. (1987). Autism and symbolic play. *British Journal of Developmental Psychology, 5*, 139–148.
72. Davis, P. E., Simon, H., Meins, E., & Robins, D. L. (2018). Imaginary companions in children with autism spectrum disorder. *Journal of Autism and Developmental Disorders, 48*, 2790–2799.
73. Davis, P. E., Slater, J., Marshall, D., & Robins, D. L. (2023). Autistic children who create imaginary companions: Evidence of social benefits. *Autism, 27*(1), 244–252.
74. Ibid.

75. Roth, I. (2007). Autism and the imaginative mind. In I. Roth (Ed.), *Imaginative minds* (pp. 277–306). Oxford University Press.
76. Grandin, T. (1996). *Thinking in pictures*. Vintage.
77. Willey, L. H. (2014). *Pretending to be normal: Living with Asperger's syndrome (autism spectrum disorder)* (Expand. ed.). Jessica Kingsley Publishers.
78. Ibid., p.18.
79. Adamo, S. M. G. (2004). An adolescent and his imaginary companions: From quasi-delusional constructs to creative imagination. *Journal of Child Psychotherapy, 30*, 275–295.
    Williams, D. (1994). *Nobody nowhere: The extraordinary autobiography of an autistic*. Avon.
80. Tammet, D. (2006). *Born on a blue day: Inside the extraordinary mind of an autistic savant*. Free Press.
81. Note that the reduction of loneliness here is in relation poor peer relations, not a desire to continue positive relationships when none are available. These are different types of loneliness. In typically developing children, it's "I wish one of my friends could come over" and in children with autism, it's "I wish I had a friend."
82. Guilford, J. P. (1967). *The nature of human intelligence*. McGraw-Hill.
83. Hoff, E. (2005b). Imaginary companions, creativity, and self-image in middle childhood. *Creativity Research Journal, 17*, 167–180.
84. Schaefer, C. E. (1969). Imaginary companions and creative adolescents. *Developmental Psychology, 1*, 747–749.
85. Firth, L., Alderson-Day, B., Woods, N., & Fernyhough, C. (2015). Imaginary companions in childhood: Relations to imagination skills and autobiographical memory in adults. *Creativity Research Journal, 27*, 308–313. https://doi.org/10.1080/10400419.2015.1087240
86. Manosevitz, M., Fling, S., & Prentice, N. M. (1977). Imaginary companions in young children: Relationships with intelligence, creativity and waiting ability. *Journal of Child Psychology and Psychiatry*.
87. Mottweiler, C. M., & Taylor, M. (2014). Elaborated role play and creativity in preschool age children. *Journal of Aesthetics, Creativity and the Arts, 8*, 277–286.
88. Kalyan Masih, V. (1978). Imaginary companions of children. In R. B. R. Weizmann, P. J. Levinson, & P. A. Taylor (Eds.), *Piagetian theory and its implications for the helping professions*. University of Southern California.
    Mauro, J. (1991). *The friend that only I can see: A longitudinal investigation of children's imaginary companions* [Doctoral dissertation]. University of Oregon.
89. Ibid.
90. Trionfi, G., & Reese, E. (2009). A good story: Children with imaginary companions create richer narratives. *Child Development, 80*, 1301–1313.
91. Mottweiler, C. M., & Taylor, M. (2014). Elaborated role play and creativity in preschool age children. *Journal of Aesthetics, Creativity and the Arts, 8*, 277–286.
92. Imafuku, M., & Seto, A. (2022). Cognitive basis of drawing in young children: relationships with language and imaginary companions. *Early Child Development and Care, 192*(13), 2059–2065. https://doi.org/10.1080/03004430.2021.1977290

93. Karmiloff-Smith, A. (1990). Constraints on representational change: Evidence from children's drawing. *Cognition, 34,* 57–83. https://doi.org/10.1016/0010-0277(90)90031-E.
94. Mottweiler, C. M., & Taylor, M. (2014). Elaborated role play and creativity in preschool age children. *Journal of Aesthetics, Creativity and the Arts.*
95. Gleason, T. R. (2004). Imaginary companions and peer acceptance. *International Journal of Behavioral Development, 28,* 204–209.
96. Bouldin, P., & Pratt, C. (1999). Characteristics of preschool and school-age children with imaginary companions. *Journal of Genetic Psychology.*
97. Gleason, T. R., Jarudi, R. N., & Cheek, J. M. (2003). Imagination, personality, and imaginary companions. *Social Behavior and Personality: An International Journal, 31*(7), 721–737.
    Dierker, L. C., Davis, K. F., & Sanders, B. (1995). The imaginary companion phenomenon: An analysis of personality correlates and developmental antecedents. *Dissociation: Progress in the Dissociative Disorders, 8*(4), 220–228.
98. Mannering, A. M., & Taylor, M. (2009). Cross-modality correlations in the imagery of adults and 5-year-old children. *Imagination, Cognition, and Personality, 28,* 207–238.
99. Kozhevnikov M., Hegarty M., & Mayer R. E. (2002). Revising the visualizer-verbalizer dimension: Evidence for two types of visualizers, *Cognition and Instruction, 20*(1), 47–77.
    Lequerica A., Rapport L., Bradley N. A., Telmer K., & Whitman R. D. (2002). Subjective and objective assessment methods of mental imagery control: Construct validation of self-report measures, *Journal of Clinical and Experimental Neuropsychology, 24*(8), 1103–1116.
100. Aleman A., Nieuwenstein M. R., Böcker K. B. E., & de Hán, E. H. F. (2000). Music training and mental imagery ability, *Neuropsychologia, 38*(12), 1664–1668.
    Halpern A. R. (1988). Mental scanning in auditory imagery for songs. *Journal of Experimental Psychology: Learning, Memory, and Cognition, 14*(3), 434–443.
101. Mannering, A. M., & Taylor, M. (2009). Cross-modality correlations in the imagery of adults and 5-year-old children. *Imagination, Cognition, and Personality, 28,* 207–238. Mannering and Taylor also investigated auditory imagery tasks in which reaction time was used as the index of imagery use, but base rates for imagery were very low making the results inconclusive.
102. Kosslyn, S. M., Margolis, J. A., Barrett, A. M., Goldknopf, E. J., & Daly, P. F. (1990). Age differences in imagery abilities. *Child Development, 61*(4), 995–1010.
103. Mannering, A. M., & Taylor, M. (2009). Cross-modality correlations in the imagery of adults and 5-year-old children. *Imagination, Cognition, and Personality.*
104. Tahiroglu, D., Mannering, A. M., & Taylor, M. (2011). Visual and auditory imagery associated with children's imaginary companions. *Imagination, Cognition and Personality, 31,* 99–112.
105. Fernyhough, C., Bland, K., Meins, E., & Coltheart, M. (2007). Imaginary companions and young children's responses to ambiguous auditory stimuli: Implications for typical and atypical development. *Journal of Child Psychology and Psychiatry, 48*(11), 1094–1101.
106. Fernyhough, C. (2016). *The voices within: The history and science of how we talk to ourselves.* Basic Books.
107. Tahiroglu, D., Mannering, A. M., & Taylor, M. (2011). Visual and auditory imagery associated with children's imaginary companions. *Imagination, Cognition and Personality.*

108. Calvert, S. L., & Valkenburg, P. M. (2013). The influence of television, video games, and the Internet on children's creativity. In M. Taylor (Ed.), *The Oxford handbook of the development of imagination* (pp. 438–452). Oxford University Press.
109. The findings of this research suggests that fast-paced, violent content that is entertainment focused has deleterious effects on children's creativity, whereas slower, prosocial content that is educational in nature has more positive effects. Calvert and Valkenburg also suggest that participatory opportunities, such as interactive digital games like MINECRAFT, and content generation on social media apps such as Instagram and YouTube, provide opportunities for older children's digital creativity more so than more passive content (e.g., passively watching videos); however, they note their concerns about children's social media use, particularly for children who are underage users.
Cataldo, I., Lepri, B., Neoh, M. J. Y., & Esposito, G. (2021). Social media usage and development of psychiatric disorders in childhood and adolescence: A review. *Frontiers in Psychiatry, 11*, 508595.
110. Singer, D. G., & Singer, J. L. (2005). *Imagination and play in the electronic age.* Harvard University Press.
Taylor, M., & Carlson, S M. (1997). The relation between individual differences in fantasy and theory of mind. *Child Development, 68*, 436–455.
111. Rideout, V., & Robb, M. B. (2020). *The Common Sense census: Media use by kids age zero to eight, 2020.* Common Sense Media.
112. Legal & General. (2023). *A million imaginary friends.* Legal & General. https://www.legalandgeneral.com/insurance/life-insurance/imaginary-friends/
113. Singer, D. G., & Singer, J. L. (2005). *Imagination and play in the electronic age.*
114. Ibid.

Chapter 5
Children Who Create Imaginary Friends
The Influence of Family and Culture

> Eyabra was a mask with three faces (one large and two small ones), Akoam was a magic green staff, and Duke was a huge shield made of a turtle's case shell. Depending on the time of day, a face from the mask would tell me stories while I sat on the shell and the staff kept watch.
> **(Adult memory of his childhood imaginary friends in Gabon)**

Most research on imaginary friends has been conducted in the United States, much of it in Eugene, Oregon, a predominantly white, middle-class university town known for its counterculture hippie past (well, mostly the past). Could imaginary friends thrive in Eugene in a way that does not generalize to the rest of the world? The answer is no. Eugene is not special when it comes to imaginary friends. Imaginary friends seem to be pretty much everywhere (with maybe a few exceptions).[1] However, their prevalence and characteristics are influenced by the context of children's lives, both in their families and in their communities at large. Pretend play in general involves a complex interaction between the people and ideas in the child's environment and the individual preferences of the child. Cultural differences include the extent to which adults believe pretend play has value or significance, encourage pretend play (cultivation, tolerance, or curtailment), and participate as joint play partners.[2] Even within a particular culture and belief system, the circumstances of children's lives shape the probability of them having an imaginary friend and the form it will take. More specifically, birth order, parental attitudes, religion, and culture affect the characteristics and prevalence of children's imaginary friends.

Birth Order

Although children from large families (i.e., three or more children) do create imaginary friends,[3] only children and firstborn children are somewhat more likely to do so.[4] In particular, children with invisible friends are commonly only children or firstborn children (88%) as compared with children who have personified objects (67%) and children without any type of imaginary friend (45%).[5] Although a large study

Imaginary Friends and the People Who Create Them. Second Edition. Marjorie Taylor and Naomi R. Aguiar, Oxford University Press. © Oxford University Press (2024). DOI: 10.1093/9780190888916.003.0005

conducted in China did not find any effect of birth order,[6] a multicultural meta-analysis of 33 studies reported that firstborn children were almost three times more likely to have imaginary friends than other children.[7]

The prevalence of imaginary friends among firstborn children in most studies is consistent with the reports of parents that they first noticed the imaginary friend shortly after the birth of the second child, a time when children often receive less attention from parents. Nagera described how a child named Tony played and talked for hours with an imaginary friend named "Dackie" who appeared immediately after Tony's brother's birth: "Dackie was around most of the day, getting up in the morning with Tony and going to bed when Tony did."[8] The appearance of an imaginary friend is not necessarily a sign of psychological distress related to the general upheaval that accompanies a new birth. Firstborn, as well as only children, might simply have more of the kind of unstructured time by themselves that promotes this type of play. Any change that increases time alone might also result in more imaginary friends. For example, in a Japanese sample, Masanori Yamaguchi and Yusuke Moriguchi[9] found that the prevalence of personified objects increased in 2020 compared with the previous year, which they attributed to the decreased opportunities for playing with real friends due to the Covid-19 pandemic. The limited available evidence suggests that imaginary friends are not more prevalent in families where the biological parents are divorced, separated, remarried, or deceased[10]—but in one study, children in single-parent families had a greater number of imaginary friends.[11]

Attitudes of Parents and Other Adults

In the United States and many other countries, most developmental psychologists, clinicians, educators, and parents alike believe that pretend play is a valuable, even crucial, component of healthy development.[12] Angeline Lillard and her colleagues caution that the available research evidence has been overstated when such very strong claims about the importance of pretend play are made,[13] but pretend play, in general, is mostly held in high regard. Attitudes specifically about the creation of imaginary friends are more varied. As discussed in Chapter 4, in early research, imaginary friends were often seen as red flags, suggesting that children were having problems. However, in the 1990s, Dorothy and Jerome Singer ushered in a much more positive view of imaginary friends as a particularly healthy sign of children's development.[14]

Paul Harris also has a positive view of imaginary friends, but he is more focused on children's early-developing capacity to reproduce imaginatively what they have observed in the real world (e.g., pouring imaginary tea from a toy teapot). He is less interested in the kind of fantastical creative pretending that is often evident in imaginary friends, partly because he believes that adult input might be largely responsible for such content. While Harris finds the more exotic imaginary friends to be intriguing, it is the pretend play that is grounded in reality—closely copying what children have experienced in real life—that he believes is crucial in developing their understanding of their world.[15] We think he is underestimating children's ability to generate fantasy on their own, but we agree with his view that the pretend play of most children reflects their own everyday real-life observations and experiences (e.g., pretending to cook dinner, go to the beach, or play checkers with an imaginary friend).

Despite early negative attitudes about imaginary friends (as discussed in Chapter 4) and some debate among psychologists about the type of pretend play that is most important in development, the current attitudes of parents toward imaginary friends are mostly positive. An article in *The Atlantic* by Allie Volpe[16] illustrates the ways that parents in some families come to enjoy and appreciate their children's imaginary friends. First, the child's accounts of their exploits are entertaining. Volpe describes a 10-year-old girl's ongoing story of Tentacles (a giant invisible octopus with an extra tentacle) who is in love with another invisible octopus named Coral. These parents enjoyed the stories and encouraged their daughter to tell them. Second, the parents also recognized that Tentacle and his imaginary social network provided real-life benefits for their daughter (e.g., helped her manage migraine pain). According to the mother, Tentacle is a "good influence on the whole family. . . . You know when you meet a cool person who's doing interesting things, they've traveled to interesting places, and they know cool foods, and they're really nice to people. That's who Tentacle is."[17]

Parents and siblings often form fond attachments to children's imaginary friends. Tracy Gleason describes this love in her essay about her little sister's stuffed bunny, Murray (see Chapter 3 for more about Murray). The relationship between Shayna and Murray made the stuffed bunny special for the whole family. As her sister grew up and played less with Murray, Tracy felt protective of him.

> When I find him on the floor, I feel compelled to pick him up and sit him in a more comfortable position, perhaps placing a book nearby in case he gets bored. . . . I could no more walk past Murray as he lies in an uncomfortable position than I could ignore my sister's pleas to play with her or the cat's meows for food.[18]

A comedy sketch on *Saturday Night Live* some years ago depicted two parents fighting over whose child had the better (e.g., more unique, detailed, creative) imaginary friend, suggesting that they had become a status symbol rather than a red flag. This shift to a more positive view of imaginary friends is also evident in modern parenting advice. For example, *Sesame Street Magazine* provided parents with suggestions for introducing invisible guests into the child's pretend play (e.g., when the parent and child are pretending to drink tea, the parent might say, "Oh, Aunt Jane has come to see us! Could we pour her some tea?").[19]

Once when Marjorie visited a friend, the friend's 4-year-old daughter greeted her at the door by asking, "How do you make a pretend friend?" (The child's mother had told her daughter about the topic of Marjorie's research.) We have assumed that if the question has to be asked, it cannot be answered—but we might be wrong about that.

In a small study, Paige Davis and her colleagues guided nine children (eight girls and one boy aged 4–6 years) over a three-month period through activities designed to promote the development of an invisible friend (e.g., drawing the friend, introducing the friend to the other children in the group). Seven of the nine children created invisible friends who were described as "qualitatively equivalent" to the ones that are created spontaneously and were found to have been maintained when the children were interviewed six months later.[20] No information was collected from parents in this small exploratory study, so we don't know the extent to which the children interacted with the imaginary friends at home outside of the intervention context. In our lab, children sometimes make up imaginary friends on the spot when they are asked about them but do not carry on with this play at home or elsewhere. Still, given the extensive and lengthy intervention and the careful follow-up interviews, it is likely that Davis and her colleagues were indeed successful in demonstrating that children can be taught to create imaginary friends. We are less sure about the authors' belief that elicited imaginary friends might help children process emotions or develop social understanding. It remains to be seen if elicited imaginary friends become sufficiently incorporated into children's lives (without continuing guidance from adults) to provide the benefits associated with imaginary friends that are created spontaneously.

Many parents would not go so far as to plant the idea of an imaginary friend in their child's head, but once they discover their child has one, they support the fantasy in a variety of ways. One of the children in our research began to express her interest in dolphins as soon as she was old enough to talk and created Dipper, the first of several imaginary dolphin friends (more about Dipper in Chapter 3). When Marjorie visited this child's home, the large collection of dolphin toys and dolphin pictures on the walls of her bedroom were obvious evidence of her parent's supportive attitude. At the time of this visit, the mother was wearing a dolphin T-shirt that she wore to please her daughter. Parents often are drawn into the fantasy in other ways as well. One mother whose son had an imaginary dog described her involvement with the pretense:

> He has Candy, a dog. When I go for a walk with *my* dog, we take Candy; we have to take Candy to the edge of the pavement. I think he can really see this dog. In fact, I said to my husband. I think *I* can see this dog![21]

The parents in these families and many others like them go along with such games because they value imagination and hope to cultivate it in their children. And without question, parental support and encouragement promote children's engagement in fantasy. After decades of studying the development of imagination, Singer and Singer[22] placed the support of fantasy behavior by a key person in the child's life at the top of their list of common threads in early childhood that are linked to the development of imagination. According to Singer and Singer, adults can promote imagination in their children by treating children's inventions with delight and respect, and by providing children with unstructured time, a place, and simple props to stimulate their pretend play.

Studies in which parents are directly questioned about imaginary friends present a more mixed view of parental attitudes. Mauro,[23] for example, found that most mothers were positive about imaginary friends, indicating that they would encourage their child to play with the imaginary friend (70%), and that the friend would have a positive effect on their child (65%). In contrast, Brooks and Knowles[24] found that the parents, especially fathers, did not hold very positive attitudes about them. However, this negative result was not too surprising, given that parents were asked questions such as how they would feel about a child insisting that a separate place be set at a crowded table on Thanksgiving for the imaginary friend. Imaginary friends can be inconvenient at times, even if they are generally beloved. Some parents object to the nuisance factor of having an invisible entity in the household who must not be sat upon, requires its own space in the car, and can be slow or unwilling to get ready when the family is waiting to go out together. Even parents who enjoy following their children's lead and playing along with the fantasy are sometimes uncertain about the best way to react to stories about the imaginary friend or the child's requests. Should they leave the television on when the family goes out to keep the friend from getting bored? Should they wait for a large enough table at a restaurant to accommodate the entire family, both visible and invisible? Why is the imaginary friend often sick? Why does the imaginary friend's father smoke cigarettes?

The Influence of Socioeconomic Status on Parental Attitudes

Some variation in parental attitudes about pretend play is a function of socioeconomic status. Middle-class parents typically consider pretend play to be important for child development, whereas parents with a lower socioeconomic background tend to believe pretend play is not of consequence.[25] This relation between attitudes and socioeconomic status extends to imaginary friends as well. Jennifer Miner[26] asked middle-class parents and parents whose children qualified for Head Start (a federally funded program that provides comprehensive services to low-income children and families) about their reactions to a series of short vignettes involving a range of child behaviors, including interactions with imaginary friends. The children of the parents in the two groups had similar numbers of imaginary friends, but the Head Start parents expressed more negative attitudes about them. Miner speculated that the negativity expressed by the Head Start parents might have been due to the imaginary friends in their homes having characteristics that reflected more difficult home environments. For example, one child often insisted that everyone be quiet for the "Bad Guys," invisible adult men that appeared when the child's father was violent. The child's mother believed the Bad Guys helped her son cope, but she was relieved when they disappeared. Children often explore negative themes in their pretend play, such as death, violence, disease, or negative aspects of ongoing events in their lives.[27]

Although some degree of violence in the context of pretend play is normative for children, it can make parents uneasy.[28]

Parents who don't have any experience with imaginary friends (they did not have one themselves and their children don't have any) express more concerns about imaginary friends than parents with first- or secondhand experience.[29] However, positive feelings can quickly shift to concern if the imaginary friends are not well behaved (see Chapter 2). Parents also worry about whether talking about an imaginary friend is equivalent to lying, or to confusion about the fantasy/reality distinction, or is not age appropriate (for imaginary friends that appear after the preschool years). In what follows, we discuss each of these concerns. In addition, parents wonder if children with imaginary friends are at risk for psychological disorders or if the imaginary friend is a sign that the children are experiencing social or emotional difficulties. These latter concerns will be discussed in Chapter 7.

Is Pretending Equivalent to Lying?

Some of the negativity expressed about imaginary friends is related to the view that fantasy behavior is similar to deceit and could lead to habitual lying.[30] When lower-socioeconomic class mothers were asked to rate different kinds of child behaviors, their ratings for incidents involving imaginary friends were similar to their ratings for incidents involving children telling lies. The authors concluded that for these mothers, "fantasy and deceit were part of the same global category of children's behavior."[31] In this sample, the parents worried about the mental health of children with imaginary friends and wondered if talking about an imaginary friend would evolve into more global dishonesty.

Shirley Brice Heath[32] also found some evidence of a relation between a concern for truthfulness and negative attitudes about fantasy in her ethnographic work in a rural Southern white community. Her observations on this topic primarily concern parental attitudes about their children's storytelling. The children in this study were strongly discouraged from telling any sort of story that did not conform closely to actual events. Stories with made-up or fanciful characters and imagined happenings were not enjoyed as evidence of the child's growing imagination. Instead, they were considered to be "lies, without a piece of truth."[33] If children described an event in which they interacted with a fantasy character, they were severely admonished: "To do so would shock the adults and cause them to accuse her of 'telling a story' (i.e., changing a real incident to make it a lie). In this community 'Don't you tell me a story' means 'Don't you tell me a lie.'"[34]

Both lying and pretending involve statements or actions that are not literally true, but pretending does not involve the intention to deceive. This distinction can be subtle or even obscured (e.g., the wolf *pretends* to be Grandmother in order to *deceive* Little Red Riding Hood). Children lie ("I didn't do it") and pretend ("I am a tiger") from very early ages, but do they understand the difference? When Marjorie and her colleagues investigated the way the words "pretend" and "lie" are used, they found that both children and adults often describe scenarios designed to illustrate pretending as lying. However, when the pretend scenarios are based on familiar types of pretend play (e.g., taking on the role of another person), even 4-year-olds had no difficulty distinguishing pretend statements from lies.[35]

Confusion about What Is Real

Even very young children seem to be clear that invisible friends are pretend (see Chapter 8), but watching a child interact with an invisible companion can be disconcerting. Parents wonder if they should encourage this blurring of the fantasy/reality distinction, as described by a parent in research by Newson and Newson: "I'll tell you what it is—it worries me sometimes—he's got a vivid imagination; and it goes on and on until he *lives* it; and sometimes, these imaginary people, you have to *feed* them with him, do you see what I mean? It worries me."[36]

Korney Chukovsky,[37] a well-known author of books for children in the former Soviet Union, describes a period of time in Russia in which parents and educators were discouraged from telling fantasy stories and fairy tales to young children because of the potential for confusing children about the real world. But when the imaginative nature of the poetry he wrote for children was criticized as harmful, Chukovsky responded that fantasy content in stories and poetry

> not only does not interfere with the child's orientation to the world that surrounds him, but, on the contrary, strengthens in his mind a sense of the real: and that it is precisely to further the education of children in reality that such nonsense verse should be offered to them.[38]

According to Chukovsky, negative adult attitudes about fantasy do not substantially curb children's own pretend activities. He gives the example of the son of a noted Russian authority on children's education. The child's father espoused a negative view of fantasy because he believed that it had a detrimental impact on children's understanding of the real world. Despite his father's views, the boy created a host of imaginary animals, including a red elephant who lived in his room, a bear named Cora, and a tiny baby tiger that sat in his hand and ate from a small plate beside his own at the dinner table. Chukovsky used this type of example to support his view that children will create their own fantasy tales to supplement any deficit in the stories provided by adults.

How Old Is Too Old?

Parents who have some admiration for the creativity involved in a preschooler's invention of a pretend friend sometimes express concern when the child is still playing with the imaginary friend beyond the preschool years. For a 4-year-old, the imaginary friend is cute; for a 10-year-old, not so much. In a study by Sugarman, mothers who were very positive about their young children's imaginary friends nevertheless believed that having an imaginary friend into late childhood would have a negative effect on children's relationships with real peers and/or was a sign that a child was experiencing significant social difficulties.[39] Children become increasingly aware of the negative attitudes that imaginary friends sometimes elicit from onlookers. In the words of one mother, "she knows we're laughing at her, sort of thing—you have to laugh at her, because it seems peculiar for her to answer herself back, sort of thing—and she'll stop playing. She goes all red, you know, blushy."[40]

Dorothy and Jerome Singer describe fantasy play as going "underground" during middle childhood as a consequence of increasing disapproval from others.[41] Children who retain their imaginary friends beyond the preschool years are described as playing with them more privately and no longer making demands on other family members to play along (e.g., avoid sitting on the imaginary friend, carry it). The parents indicate that they no longer actively participated in the fantasy games of their children, and many express negative attitudes about such play. In some cases, social disapproval eventually results in the disappearance of imaginary friends.[42] As Newson and Newson point out, "ridicule is the enemy of fantasy."[43] (See Chapter 9.)

The Influence of Religious Beliefs

In an ethnographic study on culturally shared forms of fantasy, Cindy Dell Clark found that many parents who identified with fundamentalist Christianity were uncomfortable with fantasy behavior in their children. They worried that once children discovered the truth about Santa Claus and other cultural myths, they would start to question the existence of God.[44] After all, if parents lied about Santa, how was the child to know the parents were not also lying about Jesus? For example, one father recalled admitting, upon being questioned by his son, that he was the one carrying out the activities attributed to Santa Claus, the Tooth Fairy and the Easter Bunny. His son's response was to ask, "Are you God, too?"[45] Jehovah's Witnesses explicitly discourage parents from teaching children about Santa Claus for this reason. Clark provides the following quote from *The Watch Tower* (a religious magazine distributed by Jehovah's Witnesses): "One little fellow, sadly disillusioned about Santa Claus, said to a playmate: "Yes, and I'm going to look into this 'Jesus Christ' business too."[46]

According to Paul Harris, children are surprisingly sensitive to subtle distinctions in the way adults discuss God as compared with cultural myths, suggesting that the parents' concerns are unfounded.[47] In addition, Clark[48] found no evidence that when the children learned there was no Santa, they routinely lost their faith in God. And despite the influence of their churches and parents, all the children of fundamentalist Christian parents in Clark's study (with one exception) believed that Santa Claus was real. The exception involved a mother who believed it was better to tell children the truth about Santa and that it was wrong to give Santa credit for gifts and blessings that should be credited to God. Her son's behavior had raised concerns at school because he told many of the other children that Santa was fake, and he refused to join the other children in drawing Santa Claus on decorations for Christmas. When interviewed for this study, he pointed out to the interviewer that Santa was Satan with the letters changed.

The mention of Satan brings up the second type of concern that members of some fundamentalist groups have about fantasy, in general, and imaginary friends, in particular. This concern is espoused by a subset of fundamentalists who have a particular interest in or preoccupation with "spiritual warfare" and the need to protect their children from evil forces. Imaginary friends are sometimes explicitly discussed in this context. In their book on spiritual protection for children, Anderson, Vanderhook, and Vanderhook provide a prayer for parents to teach their children in which they confess to God that they have an imaginary friend and renounce this activity. These authors have the following advice for parents:

> Many children have imaginary "friends" they play with. It can be harmless unless the imaginary friend is talking back. Then it is no longer imaginary.... A child's dependence on spirit "friends" will eventually result in spiritual bondage. This must be identified as soon as possible. Satan disguises himself as an angel of light, so young children probably won't see the danger.[49]

How common is it for parents to worry that an imaginary friend could result in spiritual harm? No studies document the prevalence of this point of view, and any estimate might be an underestimate because fundamentalist parents with this belief system might be reluctant to participate in psychological research on imagination. They might question the goals of the research and worry about being misrepresented or misunderstood, concerns that one of Marjorie's research assistants encountered when she asked questions in Christian bookstores.

In Marjorie's research with 7-year-old children, two parents who identified themselves as fundamentalist Christians voiced this kind of concern. One mother told her that

> around our house we try to keep our kids from having imaginary companions. I think they are associated with the devil and it would be very bad if they had imaginary companions. I try to emphasize that imaginary companions are bad so he doesn't have an imaginary companion.

Another mother stated that imaginary friends were anti-Christ and that she was very concerned about her 6-year-old daughter's fantasies involving unicorns. Sometimes the little girl pretended to be a unicorn, shaking invisible wings and making fluttering sounds, and sometimes she seemed to be playing with an imaginary unicorn. The mother admitted that she sometimes played along with her daughter because she loved her, but she tried to hide her daughter's vivid imagination from other people, and she prayed every day for the Devil to leave her child.

This little girl was clearly very engaged with pretense, despite her mother's strong objections. This was also the case for the little boy whose mother was just quoted. While his mother was telling the interviewer that imaginary friends are associated with the Devil, the boy was telling a research assistant in the next room about his pretend moose friend. The mother was unaware of her son's private fantasy.

Not all fundamentalist Christians are preoccupied with issues related to spiritual warfare. Mennonites (and their Amish subgroups) are more concerned with leading a simple, truthful life of devotion to God. To accomplish this goal, they live separately from modern mainstream American culture without the conveniences of modern technology (e.g., phones, electricity, cars) and avoid the outside influences of television, movies, and public education.[50]

The Mennonite literature suggests that this community believes that pretend play is seen at best as a waste of time and at worst as a potential threat to the cohesion of the group because of its association with individual freedom of expression.[51] Mennonite children are discouraged from engaging in any pretend play that is not directly related to their future roles in the community as mothers, fathers, and farmers. Acceptable reading material is restricted to stories that represent an American rural way of life and teach a moral lesson (e.g., the value of hard work). Mennonite parents "do not want their children to read fairy tales or myths; many object to any stories that are not true such as those in which animals talk and act like people or stories that involve magic, such as 'The Pied Piper of Hamlin.'"[52]

Stephanie Carlson, Marjorie, and Gerard Levin wondered if the restrictions imposed on Mennonite children might actually stimulate private fantasy activity.[53] For example, Laura Weaver recalled that she and many of her Mennonite friends had imaginary friends who were "fancy" and thus allowed to wear clothes and play with toys that were off limits to the children themselves.[54] In order to learn more about Mennonite practices relating to children's imagination, Stephanie assisted the teachers in one school in rural Pennsylvania for six months. During her visits, she took great care in her dress, wearing clothing that was plain and traditional (i.e., long black skirt, high-collared blouse or sweater, black stockings, and flat shoes), keeping her hair in a bun, and not wearing any makeup, nail polish, perfume, or jewelry. Although the teachers and children were positive about her visits, the parents in this Old Order community did not approve, and the teacher was reprimanded by the elders of the community at a church meeting.

Despite this setback, Stephanie was able to interview 18 teachers from other Mennonite schools, as well as non-Mennonite private Christian elementary schools. Overall, the Mennonite teachers were not as positive about social pretense as the non-Mennonite teachers, but the reports concerning private fantasy activities painted a different picture. Specifically, the Mennonite teachers were more likely to say that they share their dreams and/or daydreams with their class, that they themselves had an active imagination, and they were more positive about imaginary friends. These teachers were the only ones who reported that their students, or even themselves, had imaginary friends. They tended to view having an imaginary friend as making up for a lack of social contact with real friends or siblings. Thus, some of these teachers agreed that they would talk to an imaginary friend for a child's benefit and believed that children would end this type of play on their own as they acquired real friends. The most detailed account was from a young Mennonite teacher's description of her own imaginary friend, described as her best friend until age 15. "Rachel" was the same age and size as the teacher. She had blond hair, dark brown eyes, and pretty clothes. They rode horses together and worked as clerks in a store that she imagined their families owned (in reality, her parents were farmers).

What about the Mennonite children? Stephanie observed that these children did not seem to have the conceptual understanding of pretense that would be expected in mainstream American 6-year-olds. For example, one day when the children gathered around to inspect a doll brought to school by one of the girls, a child said repeatedly, "It's not a right baby." When questioned, it became apparent that the child meant to communicate that the doll was not real but did not have the vocabulary for talking about fantasy. Another child asked, "What's pretend?," when he came across this word in a book. On the playground, Mennonite children's play themes adhered more closely to everyday family roles and activities than did children's play in the non-Mennonite Christian group, but some of the Old Order Mennonite teachers suspected that a few of the children had imaginary friends. One teacher reported that she saw a third-grade boy talking to an invisible friend and another boy talking to an imaginary dog.

The non-Mennonite fundamentalist Christian teachers who participated in this study were more suspicious of imaginary friends, voicing concerns about psychopathology or demonic possession. One teacher worried that imaginary friends could lead a child into "demon occultist activity." Another teacher stated, "I'd watch out for an imaginary friend. Children should have real friends," adding that a broken home life can lead to the "wrong kind" of imagination.[55]

Imaginary Friends around the Globe

In the past, much of the research on imaginary friends was conducted in the United States and England, with a few studies in Australia and Europe, notably Sweden. However, a growing number of studies are emerging in non-Western countries, with local assistants who speak the language and understand how tasks and questions about imaginary friends might need to be adapted to a particular region or culture. These studies sometimes clarify inconsistencies in past research, as well as provide insight concerning the ways that children are taught to understand and experience themselves and their perceptions in their culture. The prevalence of imaginary friends in these studies is often difficult to pinpoint for comparison with Western samples because of variation in definitions and methodologies, but in most cases a substantial minority of children report having imaginary friends. In what follows, we summarize some of the findings.

People's Republic of China

Qiyi Lin and his colleagues[56] have conducted several large-scale studies that highlight the importance of differences in types of imaginary relationships and provide information about imaginary friends in a Chinese context. In Lin et al.'s studies, birth order (firstborn vs. second- and third-born) was not related to the creation of imaginary friends, and there was mixed evidence about gender, with some (but not all) samples showing more girls than boys having imaginary friends. Of children between 4 and 6 years old, 34%–40% had imaginary friends, with a larger proportion of personified objects (about two-thirds) than invisible friends (about a third). Children with invisible friends (e.g., an invisible 3-year-old boy who lives in a cabin in the forest) and children with personified objects (e.g., a handmade donkey who enjoys sunshine) did not differ on teacher-assessed ratings of social competence or on 3 of the 4 measures of popularity.[57] Both invisible friends and personified objects were associated with greater emotional understanding and the tendency to anthropomorphize as compared with children who did not have imaginary friends.[58]

Some past research in the United States has linked the type of relationship children had with their imaginary friends—egalitarian, peerlike relationships or hierarchical relationships in which the child takes care of a less competent imaginary friend—with the type of imaginary friend (invisible or personified object),[59] but in Lin et al.'s research as well as in more recent US studies, egalitarian and hierarchical caretaking relationships occur equally often for both types of imaginary friends. Egalitarian relationships (with both invisible friends and personified objects) in the Chinese sample were related to better peer relationships reported by classmates and higher ratings of social competence reported by teachers.[60]

In Western samples, the evidence for a relation between imaginary friends and theory of mind has been somewhat mixed, but Chinese children with imaginary friends, particularly children with egalitarian relationships, scored higher on second-order theory of mind tasks (see Chapter 4).[61] Lin et al. suggest that some inconsistency in the theory-of-mind results in Western studies might be due to a floor effect; the across-the-board poor performance on theory of mind for young US children makes detecting a benefit for children with imaginary friends difficult. However, Chinese children are more advanced in theory-of-mind development over their US counterparts,[62] which makes detecting individual differences easier. Thus, the Chinese studies have helped to substantiate the relation between having an imaginary friend and theory-of-mind development.

Japan

In Japan, girls and boys are equally likely to have imaginary friends, and the overall prevalence is roughly similar to what is found in the United States, New Zealand / Australia, and Europe (39%–49%).[63] However, the majority of the Japanese imaginary friends (more than 80%) are personified objects.[64] According to Yusuke Moriguchi and colleagues, this difference in type might be related to parental attitudes. Although Japanese parents are generally positive about pretend play, including play with personified objects, they tend to voice concerns about interactions with invisible play partners.

Several Japanese studies have made important contributions to the literature linking theory of mind development with the creation of imaginary friends (see Chapter 4). In particular, the longitudinal studies of Motoshima, Moriguchi, and their colleagues have established a relation between parent/child theory-of-mind behaviors in infancy and the development of imaginary friends in later childhood. In one study, the frequency of mothers' use of mental state language (i.e., statements about desires, intentions, perceptions, emotions, thoughts and interests) during a 10-minute play session with their infants predicted the children's creation of imaginary friends when they were 3½ years old (e.g., an invisible kitten who lives in a nice house; a pink stuffed rabbit who is a playmate).[65] In addition, the children of mothers who were less controlling during the play session with them at 6 months were more likely to have imaginary friends at age 3½. Other Japanese studies have found links between anthropomorphism and having an imaginary friend. In a longitudinal investigation, infants who appeared to interpret the movements of an inanimate object as intentional were more likely to have imaginary friends at age 4.[66] In another study, preschool children with imaginary friends provided more anthropomorphic interpretations of the movements of geometric shapes than children who did not have imaginary friends (see Chapter 3).[67]

Türkiye

A study by Yazici Arici and colleagues reports descriptive information about the imaginary friends of 46 four- and five-year-old Turkish children.[68] The accounts were collected directly from the children themselves, who drew their imaginary friends and answered a series of questions about them. The children's responses showed many of the characteristics that we have found in studies with American children. For example, children gave details about their friend's clothing (e.g., rainbow dress), emotions (e.g., being happy and cheerful), and thoughts (e.g., thinking about friends and hobbies). Like American children, Turkish children had mostly positive things to say about their imaginary friends (e.g., likes to play, is beautiful, loves animals), but they also voiced a variety of complaints (e.g., uses bad words, doesn't do what the child says, doesn't share, needs to take a bath). The accounts of Turkish imaginary friends are particularly interesting because according to Deniz Tahiroglu, a developmental psychologist in Istanbul, Turkish parents tend to be quite negative about imaginary friends.[69] Thus, Turkish imaginary friends exist in a familial context that does support them. We don't know the prevalence of imaginary friends in Turkey, but a study conducted in another majority-Muslim country (Iran) found that

37% of adolescents reported having had imaginary friends, with the majority (64%) being invisible.[70]

India

Antonia Mills began her research in India by conducting an informal survey in which she asked psychologists as well as other adults if they knew of any children who had imaginary friends.[71] The answer was "no." At first, Mills attributed this result to Indian children rarely being alone, but later Mills realized there was an issue with the use of the word "imaginary." She discovered that when Indian children talk about entities that adults cannot perceive, the entity is referred to as invisible rather than imaginary. Some of these children are believed to be communicating with a being who exists on a spiritual realm, and some are believed to be remembering a past life.

Mills was particularly interested in the children who were believed to be speaking of past lives. There have been a few studies of such children in cultures where there is a widespread belief in reincarnation. For example, in a Sri Lankan study, these children were found to do better in school than a control group of children but to have more behavioral problems.[72] Memories for past lives are not as common (about .2% of children in Northern India) as US invisible imaginary friends, but Mills was able to interview 49 parents who claimed their children had such memories. She found that the time frame that is typical for imaginary friends was similar for past-life memories and that most of the children who talked about past lives were the youngest or next to youngest in the family. The adults around them encouraged the children's memories and guided the children's interpretation of them as from a past life. At about age 7, children were taught to let go of these memories because parents worried that the children would take on the past identity instead of pursuing their present one. Mills interpreted her work as showing "how children are socialized into paradigms of their culture, how they learn what is considered reality and what is called pretense or fantasy in cultures that use very different paradigms of what is real and what is fantasy."[73]

The example of memories for past lives raises the recurring issue of how to define "imaginary friend." In this book we have focused on interactions with entities that children and adults believe are imaginary. To the extent that the experiences Mills describes are understood as communications from invisible beings outside the self, the label "imaginary friend," reflecting our Euro-Western perspective, is questionable. Perhaps memories for past lives and the creation of imaginary friends are completely unrelated behaviors. However, Adams, Stanford, and Singh examined concepts of invisible entities across a wide range of fields (e.g., bereavement studies, parapsychology, psychiatry, anthropology, religion, and spirituality) and argued that these researchers might be investigating the same phenomena.[74] Similarly, Antonia Mills wondered if children who were thought to have imaginary friends in the United States would be thought to be remembering previous lives if they lived in India, and vice versa.

Kenya, Malawi, Nepal, and the Dominican Republic

J. Bradley Wigger, an ordained Presbyterian minister and educator who was intrigued by his daughter's relationship with an invisible friend, wondered if the capacity to be in relationships with invisible others underlies both children's imaginary friends and religious experience. He began his efforts to answer this question by interviewing parents and children in Louisville, Kentucky. His findings echoed many our own: the imaginary friends had imaginative names and descriptions, had similar functions, and were understood to be pretend ("They're *pretend!*," an emphatic put-down to Wigger when he asked a 4-year-old if her imaginary friends would like a sticker). The imaginary friends he collected varied in form, gender, personality, and pretty much everything else.

After this preliminary step, Wigger moved on to research in Kenya, Malawi, Nepal, and the Dominican Republic.[75] Taking a cue from Antonia Mills, Wigger avoided the words "imaginary" or "pretend" by asking children "Do you have a friend nobody else can see?" (However, he continued to refer to their descriptions as "imaginary.") In all four cultures, the adults tended to report that children did not have imaginary friends, but the children said otherwise. In Kenya (a Luo village near Lake Victoria), 23 of 100 children (21%; aged 3–8 years) described imaginary friends (e.g., an invisible girl named Emma that only God can see). In a rural area near Balaka Malawi, 57 of 220 children (aged 3–12 years) had imaginary friends (26%) (e.g., an invisible friend named "Secret"). In Pokhara Nepal, 5 out of 101 children (aged 5–8; younger children were too shy to be interviewed) had imaginary friends (e.g., a boy who played with an imaginary family). Finally, in the Dominican Republic, 29 out of 88 children (aged 3–8 years) (34%) had imaginary friends (e.g., two invisible friends named Alejandro, one little and one big).

Wigger was careful not to make too much of the exact percentages he found in each location due to the many factors that affect results (e.g., age of child, whether the imaginary friend is current or past, misunderstandings, and breakdowns in communication). His goal was more basic: Did children in these diverse cultures invent anything like imaginary friends? After years of interviewing hundreds of children across a range of cultural contexts, Wigger is convinced that they do. He also repeatedly emphasizes that children not only envision imaginary friends; they have "real" relationships with them, a phenomenon that he believes is related to the human capacity for religious experience.

Mexico

As part of her doctoral dissertation, Deborah Legoretta collected many cases of imaginary friends created by children in Mexico City, and in a subsequent study, she interviewed 46 Mexican parents (22 of Mayan descent) about children's pretend play.[76] The parents were told brief vignettes in which children engaged in behaviors involving different types of pretend play and then were asked to describe what children were doing and their reactions to the children's behaviors. The incidence of imaginary friends for these parents' children (54%) was similar to an American comparison group (50%), but the Mexican parents were less approving of imaginary friends and expressed a variety of concerns about them. Compared with 2.5% of the American parents, 20% of the Mexican parents described this behavior as being in touch with a spiritual world (e.g., "I was afraid it was something supernatural"). Differences also emerged in the extent to which parents equated pretending with lying; whereas 17% of the Mexican parents associated pretending with lying, none of the US parents did. JoAnn Farver and Carolee Howes also found differences in attitudes about pretend play between Mexican and US parents.[77] In their study, mothers in a community in Northern California believed pretend play to be important for the educational benefits it provided their children, whereas mothers in a small town in southern Mexico considered pretend play to be an activity that amused their children but was of no value in their development.

After decades of experience living and conducting research in a Mayan community in rural Mexico and reviewing ethnographic records across cultures, Suzanne Gaskins has a different view of pretend play.[78] She claims that the Mayan children she has observed not only do not have imaginary friends, they spend very little time engaged in any kind of pretending. Gaskins describes the cultural context of pretend play in this community as "curtailed" because adults do not see any intrinsic value, do not provide resources, do not participate, and restrict its expression. Instead, children work at jobs that are important to the community (e.g., child care) and are encouraged to carefully observe the activities of others rather than to spend time apart in play. To the extent that any pretend play occurs, Gaskins describes it as interpretive (i.e., imitative of adult behaviors in traditional roles) rather than inventive (i.e., fantastical transformations and/or characters that children do not encounter in everyday life). This view of pretend play shares Margaret Mead's emphasis on the input and attitudes of parents: "the great majority of children will not even imagine bears under the bed unless the adult provides the bear."[79] Gaskins views the absence of imaginary friends in the Mayan community in a positive light. According to Gaskins, the absence might be due to Mayan children being more protected than American children from adverse experiences in everyday life. In other words, Gaskins speculates that Mayan children do not need imaginary friends because they don't experience the types of stress that are common elsewhere. Note, however, that this theory assumes that imaginary friends are created primarily as a way to cope with difficulties.

Reviewing the large, complex ethnographic record on pretend play is beyond the scope of this book. Nevertheless, despite the numerous counterexamples in the studies by Wigger and others, Gaskins' research is a reminder that the widespread view of pretend play as a spontaneous, intrinsically motivated, and universal behavior is often based on research in cultures where pretend play is cultivated or at least accepted.

Summary

Imaginary friends are given interpretations by those around them in ways that reflect the values and beliefs of family members as well as the culture in which the children live. The prevalence of imaginary friends is at least somewhat influenced by these interpretations, as well as by variables that affect the amount of unstructured time the child has alone. The reactions of parents and other adults vary considerably as a function of age of the child, socioeconomic status, religion, and culture, but overall, supportive attitudes of parents do not seem to be *required* for children to create pretend friends, and parents' attempts at curbing their children's fantasy behavior are not always entirely successful. Imaginary friends have been identified in several different countries, sometimes in ways that blur the boundaries between categories of invisible beings and the distinction between "invisible" and "imaginary."

But *why* do children create them? One possibility suggested by the finding that children with imaginary friends tend to have fewer brothers and sisters is that children create pretend friends so they will have someone to play with when nobody else is around. In the next chapter, we discuss how imaginary friends provide companionship, as well as the many other functions that they serve.

Notes

1. Wigger, J. B. (2019). *Invisible companions: Encounters with imaginary friends, gods, ancestors, and angels.* Stanford University Press.
2. Gaskins, S., Haight, W., & Lancy, D. F. (2007). The cultural construction of play. In A. Göncü & S. Gaskins (Eds.), *Play and development* (pp. 184–207). Psychology Press.
   Gaskins, S. (2013). Pretend play as culturally constructed activity. In M. Taylor (Ed.), *The Oxford handbook of the development of imagination* (pp. 224–247). Oxford University Press.
3. Hoff, E. (2005a). A friend living inside me: The forms and functions of imaginary companions. *Imagination, Cognition and Personality, 24,* 151–189.
4. Gleason, T. R., Sebanc, A. M., & Hartup, W. W. (2000). Imaginary companions of preschool children. *Developmental Psychology, 36,* 419–428.
   Manosevitz, M., Prentice, N. M., & Wilson, F. (1973). Individual and family correlates of imaginary companions in preschool children. *Developmental Psychology, 8,* 72–79.
   Kalyan-Masih, V. (1986). Imaginary play companions: Characteristics and functions. *International Journal of Early Childhood, 18*(1), 30–40.
   Singer, D. G., & Singer, J. L. (1990). *The house of make-believe: Children's play and developing imagination.* Harvard University Press.
   Svendsen, M. (1934). Children's imaginary companions. *Archives of Neurology and Psychiatry, 2,* 985–999.
5. Gleason, T. R., Sebanc, A. M., & Hartup, W. W. (2000). Imaginary companions of preschool children. *Developmental Psychology.*

6. Lin, Q., Zhou, N., & Fu, H. (2020). Prevalence of imaginary companions among Chinese children aged 4 to 6 years. *Social Behavior and Personality: An International Journal, 48*(3), 1–11.
7. Moriguchi, Y., & Todo, N. (2018). Prevalence of imaginary companions in children: A meta-analysis. *Merrill-Palmer Quarterly, 64*(4), 459–482. https://doi.org/10.13110/merrpalmquar1982.64.4.0459
8. Nagera, H. (1969). The imaginary companion: Its significance for ego development and conflict resolution. *The Psychoanalytic Study of the Child, 24*, 165-196, see p. 183. https://doi.org/10.1080/00797308.1969.11822691
9. Yamaguchi, M., & Moriguchi, Y. (2022). Did children interact with their personified objects during the COVID-19 Pandemic? *Imagination, Cognition and Personality, 41*(3), 354–367.
10. Manosevitz, M., Prentice, N. M., & Wilson, F. (1973). Individual and family correlates of imaginary companions in preschool children. *Developmental Psychology*.
11. Yawkey, T. D., & Yawkey, M. L. (1983, June 29). Assessing young children for imaginativeness through oral reporting: Preliminary results [Paper presentation]. International Conference on Play and Play Environments: Research and Its Application to Play Settings, Austin, TX.
12. Hirsch-Pasek, K., Golinkoff, R., Berk, L., & Singer, D. (2009). *A mandate for playful learning in preschool: Presenting the evidence.* Oxford University Press.
    Vygotsky, L. S. (1978). *Mind in society.* Harvard University Press.
13. Lillard, A. S., Lerner, M. D., Hopkins, E. J., Dore, R. A., Smith, E. D., & Palmquist, C. M. (2013). The impact of pretend play on children's development: A review of the evidence. *Psychological Bulletin, 139*, 1.
    Note that Lillard is an important scholar of the teachings of Maria Montessori, the early childhood educator who famously eliminated imaginative play from her curriculum to focus on intellectual exercises and real-world activities that she believed children preferred.
    Lillard, A. S., & Taggart, J. (2018). Pretend play and fantasy: What if Montessori was right? *Child Development Perspectives, 6*, 1–6.
    Lillard, A. S. (2013). Playful learning and Montessori education. *Namta Journal, 38*(2), 137–174.
14. Singer, D. G., & Singer, J. L. (1990). *The house of make-believe: Children's play and developing imagination.* Harvard University Press.
15. Harris, P. L. (2021). Early constraints on the imagination: The realism of young children. *Child Development, 92*(2), 466–483.
16. Volpe, A. (2019, July 30). Why kids invent imaginary friends. *The Atlantic.* https://www.theatlantic.com/family/archive/2019/07/why-do-kids-have-imaginary-friends/594919/
17. Ibid.
18. Gleason, T. (2007). Murray: The stuffed bunny. In Turkle, S. (Ed.), *Evocative objects: Things we think with* (pp. 171–177). The MIT Press, see p. 175.
19. Couple. (1991, October). Fantastic voyages. *Sesame Street Magazine.*
20. Davis, P. E., King, N., Meins, E., & Fernyhough, C. (2023). "When my mummy and daddy aren't looking at me when I do my maths she helps me"; Children can be taught to create imaginary companions: A new method of studying imagination. *Infant and Child Development, 32*(2), e2390.

21. Newson, J., & Newson, E. (1968). *Four years old in an urban community.* George Allen & Unwin Ltd., p. 176.
22. Singer, D. G., & Singer, J. L. (1990). *The house of make-believe: Children's play and developing imagination.*
23. Mauro, J. (1991). *The friend that only I can see: A longitudinal investigation of children's imaginary companions.* [Doctoral dissertation.] University of Oregon.
24. Brooks, M., & Knowles, D. (1982). Parents' views of children's imaginary companions. *Child Welfare, 61,* 25–33.

    Unfortunately, a limitation in this study is that Brookes and Knowles did not determine how many of the parents in this research actually had children with imaginary friends, but the parents in this study were also somewhat negative when asked about their reactions to more neutral situations. For example, when asked about a situation in which a child's response to being asked to play quietly was to go outside and play with her imaginary friend, only 31% of the parents said they would encourage this behavior. There was a tendency for the parents of daughters to be more encouraging of imaginary companion behavior than the parents of sons.
25. Smilansky, S. (1968). *The effects of sociodramatic play on disadvantaged preschool children.* John Wiley & Sons.
26. Miner, J. L. (2004). *Parental attitudes toward pretend play and imaginary companions in preschool children.* [Unpublished honors thesis.] University of Oregon.
27. Dunn, J., & Hughes, C. (2001). "I got some swords and you're dead!": Violent fantasy, antisocial behavior, friendship, and moral sensibility in young children. *Child Development, 72*(2), 491–505.
28. Sutton-Smith, B. (2001). *The ambiguity of play.* Harvard University Press.
29. Sugarman, S. (2013). *An investigation into parents' attitudes to their children having imaginary companions.* [Doctoral dissertation.] University of London.
30. Newson, J., & Newson, E. (1976). *Seven years old in an urban environment.* George Allen & Unwin Ltd.
31. Ibid., p. 189.
32. Heath, S. B. (1983). *Ways with words: Language, life, and work in communities and classrooms.* Cambridge University Press.
33. Ibid., p. 158.
34. Ibid., p. 160.
35. Taylor, M, Lussier, G. L., & Maring, B. L. (2003). The distinction between lying and pretending. *Journal of Cognition and Development, 4,* 299–323.
36. Newson, J., & Newson, E. (1976). *Seven years old in an urban environment.* George Allen & Unwin Ltd. See p. 161.
37. Chukovsky, K. (1925/1968). *From two to five.* University of California Press.
38. Ibid., p. 90.
39. Sugarman, S. (2013). An investigation into parents' attitudes to their children having imaginary companions.
40. Newson, J., & Newson, E. (1976). *Seven years old in an urban environment,* p. 158.
41. Singer, D. G., & Singer, J. L. (1990). *The house of make-believe: Children's play and developing imagination.* Harvard University Press.
42. Hurlock, E. B., & Burnstein, M. (1932). The imaginary playmate: A questionnaire study. *Journal of Genetic Psychology, 41,* 380–391.

43. Newson, J., & Newson, E. (1976). *Seven years old in an urban environment*, p. 149.
44. Actually, many young children do seem to think Santa and God are connected in some way. Children in Clark's (1995) research suggested that God and Santa must live next door to each other and be friends, that God made Santa, that Santa knows whether children have been good or bad because God told him, and that God is the one who asks Santa to give presents to children.
45. Scheibe, C. (1987). Developmental differences in children's reasoning about Santa Claus and other fantasy characters. [Doctoral dissertation.] Cornell University. Cited in Clark, C. D. (1995). *Flights of fancy, leaps of faith: Children's myths in contemporary America*. University of Chicago Press.
46. Ibid., p. 56.
47. Harris, P. L. (2013). Fairy tales, history and religion. In M. Taylor (Ed.), *The Oxford handbook of the development of imagination* (pp. 31–41).
48. Clark, C. D. (1995). *Flights of fancy, leaps of faith: Children's myths in contemporary America*.
49. Anderson, N. T., Vanderhook, P., & Vanderhook, S. (1996). *Spiritual protection for your children*. Regal, pp. 195–196.
50. Hostetler, J. A., & Huntington, G. E. (1971). *Children in Amish Society: Socialization and Community Education*. Case Studies in Education and Culture Series. Holt, Rinehart and Winston, Inc., p. 9.
51. Redekop, C. (1989). *Mennonite society*. Johns Hopkins University Press.
52. Hostetler, J. A., & Huntington, G. E. (1971). Children in Amish Society: Socialization and Community Education, p. 46.
53. Carlson, S. M., Taylor, M., & Levin, G. R. (1998). The influence of culture on pretend play: The case of Mennonite children. *Merrill Palmer Quarterly, 44*(4), 538–556.
54. Weaver, L. H. (1982). Forbidden fancies: A child's vision of Mennonite plainness. *Journal of Ethnic Studies, 11*, 51–59.
55. Carlson, S. M., Taylor, M., Levin, G. R. (1998). The influence of culture on pretend play: The case of Mennonite children, p. 553.
56. Lin, Q., Zhou, N., & Fu, H. (2020). Prevalence of imaginary companions among Chinese children aged 4 to 6 years. *Social Behavior and Personality: An International Journal, 48*(3), 1–11.
57. Lin, Q., Fu, H., Wan, Y., Zhou, N., & Xu, H. (2018). Chinese children's imaginary companions: Relations with peer relationships and social competence. *International Journal of Psychology, 53*(5), 388–396.
    Children with invisible friends and children with personified objects did not differ on measures in which the children in their class were asked to identify the most popular classmates, the least popular classmates, and the classmates they least liked to play with. However, children with invisible friends were more likely to be named when classmates were asked whom they most liked to play with.
58. Lin, Q., Zhou, N., & Fu, H. (2020). Prevalence of imaginary companions among Chinese children aged 4 to 6 years.
    Lin, Q., Zhang, R., Zhang, Y., & Zhou, N. (2022). Did Chinese children with imaginary companions attribute more agencies to non-human items: Evidences from behavioral cues and appearance characteristics. *Frontiers in Psychology, 13*, 1–9.
59. Gleason, T. R., Sebanc, A. M., & Hartup, W. W. (2000). Imaginary companions of preschool children. *Developmental Psychology*.

60. Lin, Q., Fu, H., Wan, Y., Zhou, N., & Xu, H. (2018). Chinese children's imaginary companions: Relations with peer relationships and social competence. *International Journal of Psychology*.
61. Lin, Q., Zhou, N., Wan, Y., & Fu, H. (2020). Relationship between Chinese children's imaginary companions and their understanding of second-order false beliefs and emotions. *International Journal of Psychology, 55*(1), 98–105.
62. Liu, D., Wellman, H. M., Tardif, T., & Sabbagh, M. A. (2008). Theory of mind development in Chinese children: A meta-analysis of false-belief understanding across cultures and languages. *Developmental Psychology, 44*(2), 523.
63. Moriguchi, Y., & Todo, N. (2018). Prevalence of imaginary companions in Japanese children: A meta-analysis. *Merrill-Palmer Quarterly*.
    Motoshima, Y., Shinohara, I., Todo, N., & Moriguchi, Y. (2014). Parental behaviour and children's creation of imaginary companions: A longitudinal study. *European Journal of Developmental Psychology, 11*(6), 716–727.
    Yamaguchi, M., Okanda, M., Moriguchi, Y., & Itakura, S. (2023). Young adults with imaginary companions: The role of anthropomorphism, loneliness, and perceived stress. *Personality and Individual Differences, 207*, 112159.
64. Moriguchi, Y., & Todo, N. (2018). Prevalence of imaginary companions in Japanese children: A meta-analysis. *Merrill-Palmer Quarterly*.
65. Motoshima, Y., Shinohara, I., Todo, N., & Moriguchi, Y. (2014). Parental behaviour and children's creation of imaginary companions: A longitudinal study. *European Journal of Developmental Psychology*.
66. Moriguchi, Y., Kanakogi, Y., Todo, N., Okumura, Y., Shinohara, I., & Itakura, S. (2016). Goal attribution toward non-human objects during infancy predicts imaginary companion status during preschool years. *Frontiers in Psychology, 7*, 221.
67. Moriguchi, Y., Shinohara, I., & Ishibashi, M. (2016). Agent perception in children with and without imaginary companions. *Infant and Child Development, 25*(6), 550–564.
68. Yazıcı Arıcı, E., Keskin, H. K., Papadakis, S., & Kalogiannakis, M. (2022). Evaluation of children's discourses regarding imaginary companion: The case of Türkiye. *Sustainability, 14*, 16608. https://doi.org/10.3390/su142416608
69. Personal communication. March, 2023.
70. Zarei, T., Pourshahbaz, A., & Poshtmashhadi, M. (2021). Childhood imaginary companion and schizotypy in adolescents and adults. *Journal of Anomalous Experience and Cognition, 2*(1), 166–189.
71. Mills, A. (2003). Are children with imaginary playmates and children said to remember previous lives cross-culturally comparable categories? *Transcultural Psychiatry, 40*, 62–90.
72. Haraldsson, E., Fowler, P. C., & Periyannapillai, V. (2000). Psychological characteristics of children who speak of a previous life: A further field study on Sri Lanka. *Transcultural Psychiatry, 37*, 525–544.
73. Mills, A. (2003). Are children with imaginary playmates and children said to remember previous lives cross-culturally comparable categories? pp. 63–64.
74. Adams, K., Stanford, E., & Singh, H. (2022). Reconceptualizing imaginary friends: Interdisciplinary approaches for understanding invisible companions. *Journal of Childhood Studies, 47*, 32–49.
75. Wigger, J. B. (2019). *Invisible companions: Encounters with imaginary friends, gods, ancestors, and angels*.

76. Legorreta, M. D. (1999). *Relación entre amigos imaginarios, tipo psicológico y creatividad artística (on the relationship between imaginary companions, psychological type and artistic creativity)*, [Doctoral dissertation] Universidad Iberoamericana.
    Legorreta, M. D., & Taylor, M. (2002). Differences in Mexican and American parents; interpretations of chilkdren's imaginary companions. Unpublished data. University of Oregon, Eugene OR.
77. Farver, J. M., & Howes, C. (1993). Cultural differences in American and Mexican mother-child pretend play. *Merrill-Palmer Quarterly, 39*, 344–358.
78. Gaskins, S. (2013). Pretend play as culturally constructed activity. In M. Taylor (Ed.), *The Oxford handbook of the development of imagination* (pp. 224–250). Oxford University Press.
79. Mead, M. (1930). *Growing up in New Guinea*. William Morrow, p. 258.

Chapter 6
Why Do Children Create Imaginary Friends?

> I just pretend he is in our world when I want to see him, when I need to see him, when it's no fun outside, and not very much to do in the house. I make him up.
>
> (Five-year-old boy describing friendship with "Ian," his invisible friend)

This child's description reminds us of *The Cat in the Hat* by Dr. Seuss. That story begins with two bored children who can't go outside to play because it is too cold and wet. They are sitting around with nothing to do, when suddenly a tall black cat in a striped top hat walks through the door and saves the day by entertaining the children with his outrageous behavior. Everyone has a great time messing up the house until the grown-ups return. Scholars of popular culture differ in their interpretations of the title character of this story, but he sounds like an imaginary friend to us. For many children, someone like the Cat in the Hat would be an ideal solution to the problem of being stuck in the house on a rainy day, and it is likely that some imaginary friends have their beginnings in scenarios like the one described in Dr. Seuss's story.

But imaginary friends can be much more than partners in play. They are all-purpose, extraordinarily useful beings. Not only do they provide companionship when no one else is available, they also keep secrets, alleviate fears, help cope with life's difficulties, provide a reference point when bargaining with parents, and assist in storytelling and communications with other people.[1] Identifying the needs met by a particular imaginary friend is challenging because they are so diverse and their uses evolve over time and with changes in circumstance. Young children's answers to direct questions about why they created a pretend friend tend not to be particularly informative (e.g., "because I like him"). Older children sometimes are able to shed light, but many are reluctant to open up to researchers about the origins of imaginary friends.[2] Although parents can sometimes suggest possible reasons,[3] Jennifer Mauro found that mothers were mostly at a loss when asked why their children created an imaginary friend.[4]

Sometimes it is possible to construct a plausible story about the services an imaginary friend provides beyond the primary function of companionship by examining the match between child and companion on a case-by-case basis. The form that

Imaginary Friends and the People Who Create Them. Second edition. Marjorie Taylor and Naomi R. Aguiar, Oxford University Press. © Oxford University Press (2024). DOI: 10.1093/9780190888916.003.0006

they take, their activities—even their names—provide clues about what children are attending to in their environment and the functions that imaginary friends might be serving. "Phena" and "Barbara Tall" were created by a preschooler who heard references to the medication used by her father, "Fetiss" was created by two girls whose mother was pregnant, and "Pigsty" was created by a child whose untidy room was a source of annoyance for the mother.[5] Individual cases like these can provide insight, but in this chapter we go beyond anecdotes to shed light on common reasons for children's creation of their imaginary friends cited in research, including diary studies with parents, research on children's concepts of friendship, qualitative interviews with older children about their imaginary friends, and clinical case studies.

Friendship

Across many studies and a wide age range, close and trusted friendship is usually central to children's descriptions[6] (e.g., "We always know what the other one is going to say"; "I can trust them. . . . Like if I tell them a secret it's not like they can tell anyone.")[7] Who could potentially be a better partner in play than someone you make up for yourself? Some imaginary friends are closely modeled after children's real-life friends or are imaginary twins of the children themselves. Other imaginary beings who serve as play partners are zany characters like the Cat in the Hat or Bing Bong from the movie *Inside Out*, a cat/elephant/dolphin hybrid made mostly of cotton candy.[8] Bing Bong is a particularly good depiction of a beloved imaginary friend. The scenes from the child's early life show her playing happily with Bing Bong, but when as an 11-year-old, she is struggling with an unwelcome move to a new city, Bing Bong—who lives in long-term memory—helps out behind the scenes.[9] Like this fictional example, imaginary friends in real life are fun playmates but also provide comfort and support during stressful times. They reflect the child's idiosyncratic interests, have characteristics that are not necessarily logical or internally consistent, and shift to suit the whims and needs of their creators. Several of the 10-year-olds in a study conducted in Sweden reported that their imaginary friends were *better* than real-life friends ("It's different 'cause for example when you talk to her then she understands"; "With the pretend playmates you can do what you want to do").[10]

In Chapter 2 we highlighted some of the difficulties children have with unruly imaginary friends, but imaginary friends are typically easier to control than their real-life counterparts. They can mostly be depended upon to play the game of the child's choice and go along with all the child's ideas and preferences. They do not make unwelcome suggestions for changing the game or insist on taking their turn at the most interesting point. The child doesn't have to worry about imaginary friends getting cranky and threatening to take their toys and go home. On the other hand, the child can walk out on the imaginary friend at any point without repercussions, and, in most cases, the imaginary friend will be cheerfully ready to start up again at a moment's notice. The exceptions to this good-natured compliance and empathy are fascinating, but it is important not to lose sight of the fact that it is the child who endows the imaginary friend with personality flaws—which are usually combined with characteristics that make the companion a good friend most of the time.

According to mothers, invisible friends are more likely than personified objects to function like real-life friends; thus, children's exploration of friendship seems to be particularly evident in play with invisible friends.[11] Consistent with this idea, children with invisible friends have an understanding of friendship that is more developmentally advanced than children with personified objects or children who do not have any type of imaginary friend.[12] In addition, a study with preschoolers found that 4-year-old children who had an egalitarian, peerlike relationship with their imaginary friend (as compared with a caregiving relationship or no imaginary friend) used more constructive and positive coping strategies in real-life interactions with other children involving aggression, teasing, and social exclusion.[13] Thus, imaginary friends might provide opportunities to practice friendships with freedom from consequences that can have a positive impact on real-world relationships.

Children's descriptions of their imaginary friends include many of the characteristics of close friendships with real-life peers,[14] but do children really think their imaginary relationships are like real-life ones? According to Gleason and Hohmann, the answer is yes.[15] They explored this idea in a series of studies in which preschool children were asked to name three children with whom they "most liked to play." Then the children were asked to report on the benefits and social opportunities (e.g., companionship, reliable alliance, affection, enhancement of self-worth) that they experienced with (1) reciprocal friends (someone the child named as a preferred playmate who also named the child), (2) unilateral friends (someone the child named who did not name the child), (3) nonfriends (neither child named the other one) and imaginary friends (for children who had one). In general, children made clear distinctions between reciprocal friends, unilateral friends, and nonfriends on the types of social opportunities these relationships can or cannot provide. However, the responses for imaginary friends did not differ from the responses for reciprocal friends. In other words, children conceptualized their imaginary friends as similar to real-life best friendships.

A particularly interesting finding in this research involves the reciprocity of the relationships. In real life, close friendships are mutual; both individuals consider the other to be their friend and both contribute to the relationship. The "contributions" of an imaginary friend are unobservable to other people (unless the child speaks aloud for an imaginary friend), but children imagine those contributions and they are important to the relationship. For example, the child loves the imaginary friend and feels loved in return. The child and imaginary friend argue with each other, laugh at each other's jokes, take turns in games, and share secrets. Despite their being imaginary, reciprocity is a defining feature of relationships with pretend friends.

Loneliness

Perhaps the claim that children create imaginary friends because they are lonely is only another way of saying that pretend friends provide companionship, but it has a hollower sound. The "deficit" hypothesis—that imaginary friends are created to compensate for a lack of real-life friends—is sometimes voiced by children who are asked to explain why they have imaginary friends[16] (e.g., "They ... come when I am very lonely.... .They are a great comfort to me when I am all alone").[17] Although we suspect that most of these children are talking about situations in which their friends are temporarily unavailable, there are cases in which children create imaginary friends to alleviate a deeper aloneness than having no one to play with one day.[18] More generally, fantasy activities can help children through extended periods of loneliness. For example, Francis Ford Coppola, the director of *The Godfather* and many other films, passed the time during a year spent alone in his room as an 8-year-old recovering from polio by acting out stories with his puppets, an unusually intensive fantasy experience that may have contributed to his later choice of career.[19] While the deficit hypothesis might account for some imaginary friends, most imaginary friends are not created to address deficiencies in a person's social functioning or opportunities.[20]

Perhaps the strongest evidence against the deficit hypothesis comes from Tracy Gleason's research in which preschool children were asked to name the classmates with whom they most liked to play.[21] Children with imaginary friends did not differ from other children in the number of reciprocal friendships.[22] In other words, they have just as many real-world friendships as children who do not have imaginary friends. In addition, Mathur and Smith found no difference between children with and without imaginary friends in their interactions with real peers and concluded that children with imaginary friends, are "socially well-adjusted, being neither overly 'needy' or self-chosen social isolates."[23]

According to Inge Seiffge-Krenke, "undoubtedly, at times imaginary relationships alleviate feelings of loneliness, but to ascribe their existence solely to this purpose seems to underestimate the range and variety of roles that they may play."[24] This conclusion was based on her study of 241 adolescents aged 12–17, including 94 adolescents who kept diaries with the entries addressed to an imaginary friend.[25] Adolescents with imaginary friends were just as likely as adolescents without imaginary friends to report close relationships and to be socially competent; they had imaginary friends in addition to—not instead of—real friends.

In her review of the literature, Gleason concluded,

> Children with imaginary friends thus are not creating them because they have few or no real friends. They appear to be as well-liked as children without imaginary companions. Concerns, therefore, that children might be creating imaginary companions because they cannot create satisfactory relationships with real peers seem unfounded.[26]

While imaginary friends can help in coping with occasional situational loneliness, they should not be interpreted as a sign of a chronically lonely child with no real friends. The bottom line is that children's imaginary friends do not typically serve as replacements for friendships with peers.

Storytelling

Parents who collected regular observations of their children for two weeks reported that storytelling was a particularly common activity for children who have invisible friends.[27] There are stories about the friend's first appearance ("It was when I was building a snow sculpture. Then I made a small house and then it struck me that someone could live there and then I pretended that a mouse fell down from the sky")[28] and stories about ongoing and past activities ("He loved to talk about situations and experiences that he hadn't had but Mick Nick had").[29] In the lab, we have also heard children's stories about the imaginary social worlds of their invisible friends, imaginary places where they live, and the ongoing events that happen there. Thus, having an invisible friend is not just about needing or wanting an extra companion, and direct personal interaction is not the only way that imaginary friends are experienced by young children. Children also use their invisible friends as the main characters in stories that they tell to parents and other family members, as well as to themselves.

This finding dovetails with research described in Chapter 4 about the enhanced narrative skills and greater creativity in the stories of children with invisible friends.[30] Storytelling can turn into a shared activity when parents scaffold their children's narratives by asking questions and listening as the child works out the details, an activity that can be exciting for budding storytellers and their parents alike. To illustrate, Table 6.1 provides a transcript of a father and his 3-year-old daughter discussing the activities of Hermione, an invisible white cat who likes to live in places that are white.[31]

In this example, the father is listening carefully and mostly following the child's lead. Sometimes she answers his questions directly, and sometimes she ignores a particular direction suggested by his comments. But his attention clearly acknowledges that she is the knowledgeable one when it comes to the activities of her invisible cat, a heady (and unusual!) experience for a 3-year-old child.

A Vehicle for Communicating with Others

Sometimes asking questions about a "friend's" situation or describing the reactions of a "friend" is easier than talking about yourself. Hence, communications to doctors, psychologists, and other professionals are sometimes prefaced by "I have a friend who wants to know. . ." or "I have a friend who has this problem. . . ." It is clear to

Table 6.1 A father and daughter's collaborative storytelling

(Child prints the words "pink cheshie" on a piece of paper.)
FATHER: Tell me about "pink cheshie"? What language is that?
CHILD: You know "pink" is English. And then "cheshie" is Antarctican.
FATHER: Antarctican? And how does Hermione know Antarctican?
CHILD: She was in the Antarctic for a bit before she moved to the Moon.
FATHER: What was she doing in the Antarctic?
CHILD: Do you know what she used to keep warm? Do you know what? She got leopard seal's fur, she got leopard seal's skin and fur to make a coat. And then put buttons on it.
FATHER: And what prompted her to move from Antarctica to the Moon?
CHILD: Because she wanted a place higher. But now she is thinking she wants to move back to Antarctica because it's too high up and she thinks it is not as easy as on Earth to jump from planet to planet.
FATHER: I see. . . . What does she eat on the Moon?
CHILD: We need to send her some food. All she can have . . . all she has up there is one onion and house mice. One onion and house mice.
FATHER: House mice?
CHILD: Yes.

---

everyone involved that the person is actually talking about themselves. Imaginary friends can provide a veil in this way, making communication easier for a young child. For example, Singer and Singer[32] describe a child who cautioned his parents to make sure Poh, the imaginary friend, did not go down the drain when they were taking a bath together. The parents believed the child was using Poh to express his own fear of the drain, an interpretation that is consistent with their observation that he was much relieved after hearing Mister Rogers sing the "You can't go down the drain" song.

One of the children studied by Newson and Newson used her companion for expressing negative emotions in a way that cushioned their possible impact. When she was upset with her mother, this child would say, "I don't love you, but Noddy (the imaginary friend) does!"[33] The continued love of Noddy might have seemed to the child to weaken the blow by indicating that in some part of herself she still loved her mother. Similarly, Jean Piaget's daughter Jacqueline disparaged the father of her imaginary friend (e.g., "Marecage has a horrid father"; "Her mother chose badly") as a way to communicate displeasure with her own father.[34] The child might also use the imaginary friend to bargain with parents. For example, one 3-year-old boy who claimed to have a pretend friend living in his throat had a habit of saying things like "My Throat says I don't like peas," or "Throat says I'm not sleepy." This boy's mom sometimes asked her son to open his mouth so she could have it out with Throat directly.[35]

Parents can exploit the imaginary friend for their own communicative purposes. If you want to know more about how your child is feeling about a potentially sensitive topic, you might try asking about the imaginary friend (e.g., what does the imaginary friend think about the large dog who has moved in next door?). It also can sometimes be easier for children to express difficult things by whispering to an imaginary friend in the presence of a parent than by telling the parent directly.

Coping with Fears

Children's capacity to experience emotional reactions to imagined events is consistent with the view that an important function of pretend play is the management of emotion.[36] More specifically, fantasy play of various types can play a powerful role in children's ability to overcome fear (e.g., "There was always a little circle of security about Aida Paida and we moved in it with her. Things that might have got us never could. Aida Paida never did anything to them, but they could never get at us. She made them keep their distance").[37] The imaginary friend might be protective like Aida Paida or might help simply by providing company (e.g., "... it's someone to be with you in the dark.")[38]

In some cases, the fear is overcome when children comfort or protect an imaginary friend. This point was brought home to Marjorie by her daughter's reaction at the age of 3 to the gift of a small box described as containing a "baby ghost." Amber had developed a fear of ghosts that disrupted her sleep and made her anxious when left alone at bedtime. However, when asked if she would like to take care of the baby ghost, she was eager to do so. For over a week she carried the box with its invisible contents wherever she went and was very much absorbed in this fantasy.[39] The baby ghost and its box were abandoned after a week or so for other toys, but Amber was never again bothered by a fear of ghosts. Conceptualizing the ghost in the box as something weak, tiny, and in need of care seemed to remove the scariness from her thoughts about ghosts in general.

In the baby ghost example, an adult scaffolded the child's use of fantasy to deal with the fear, but children often discover fantasy solutions for dealing with fears by themselves. Gottman describes two children who frequently pretended to comfort dolls who were afraid of the dark.[40] The game was abruptly dropped when the children were no longer bothered by fear of the dark in their own lives. Singer and Singer describe a child who replaced her regular imaginary friend named Louisa after an incident in which the child was outside during a heavy rain. When asked if a place should be set at the table for Louisa, the child announced that "Louisa was drownded in the big puddle" and then requested that a place be set for her new imaginary friend, Frogman, who was "not afraid of puddles."[41] Claire Golomb and Regina Kuersten[42] observed that children often ramp down the scariness of a pretend game by changing something within the play to make it less frightening. For example, when pretend play involving monsters gets too intense, children can adjust the type of monster (e.g., "Look, all the monster's teeth fell out"; "It's just a baby monster").

The role that fantasy can play in the overcoming of fears is well known to play therapists. One clinical technique, known as emotive imagery, was specifically designed for helping children cope with their fears and anxieties by working hero images into stories involving the child's fears. For example, a child who is afraid of the dark and loves Superman might be told to imagine situations in which he is waiting in a dark place for instructions for helping Superman. Lazarus found that the positive aspects of such imagery helped children overcome their fears and that there were no negative side effects. For example, children who were treated with emotive imagery procedures did not subsequently have difficulties differentiating fantasy from reality.[43]

Anna Freud[44] described a case of a boy (age 7) who had an imaginary tame tiger who loved and obeyed the boy but scared everyone else. In another case study, a child created an imaginary friend named Laughing Tiger at a time when she was afraid of animals, especially some dogs who lived nearby. The important thing about Laughing Tiger was that he laughed instead of growled and that he was extremely gentle and compliant. He was quite afraid of children, especially his creator, who tended to boss him around. There was immediate improvement in the child's fear of animals when Laughing Tiger first appeared, and by the time he disappeared, the fear was essentially gone. Fraiberg noted that the child might have coped with her fears in some other much less productive way such as avoiding animals, not leaving the home, or staying close to her parents. "If we watch closely, we shall see how the imaginary companions and enemies fade away at about the same time that the fear dissolves, which means that the child who has overcome his tigers in his play has learned to master his fear."[45]

Issues of Competence

A child might fashion an imaginary friend to help achieve feelings of competence or mastery in several ways.[46] First of all, children sometimes endow imaginary friends with negative characteristics that the children want to distance from themselves. The 10-year-olds in a study by Eva Hoff often described their imaginary friends as stupid, lazy, and/or not brave ("they're so chicken"; they're always worrying about new things").[47] According to Hoff, a child's self-esteem might be enhanced by feeling superior to this type of imaginary friend. Another way for the child to feel competent is to take on a caretaking or teaching role for an incompetent imaginary friend ("Well I could count a little so I taught him that").[48] In contrast, some children create highly competent imaginary friends with characteristics that the children desire for themselves ("he has taught me to become more inventive").[49] Imaginary friends can be powerful allies or knowledgeable teachers who bolster the child's confidence. Wigger[50] describes two invisible friends (Katie Fendus and Nellie Brosus) who "taught" the child how to spell (although they sometimes made mistakes such as spelling "meat" as "meqfeq").

Boys might be more likely than girls to opt for an imaginary friend who is more competent than the children themselves ("He can run faster than all the other children"; "He is bigger than me, and he can draw better and skip better"; "On the jungle gym, he gets to the top fastest"). Here is a particularly good example of a very competent imaginary friend:

> His name is Christian the Monster Magician, and he can do lots of things, a lot! He's tall, he's big, he's bigger than me. He can jump so high, he can jump from the barbershop, where he cuts his hair, all the way home. He can jump pretty far, can't he? He can jump on both feet and make one foot go up and he can make magic, he can make a stilt come out of his foot! That's hard to walk on, high stilts, but that's what Christian can do, the highest stilts in the world! That's scary, but he's not scared. Not Christian the Monster Magician, no sir![51]

In the same study, many of the girls created imaginary friends who were described as less competent than themselves ("She doesn't know any colors, so I have to tell her"; "I can run faster than they can, so when they get tired they watch me run"; "I have to teach him his letters every day because he can't remember so good"). Here is more detailed example of an incompetent imaginary friend:

> His name is Kitty Cat. When I'm doing puzzles, he gets them undone. He doesn't know how. He doesn't have friends, just me. He's usually bad. He usually falls off [the jungle gym] and I catch him; he's kinda scared so I get him down. He can't tie his shoes so I tie them for him, I tie his paws. He can't count, he just meows. He doesn't know how to swing, so I push him, but he falls off. I have to help him hop. He's scared at night, so I get him waked up and put him in my bed.[52]

We don't want to make too much of this gender difference because it is not found in every study.[53] For example, in a study with children aged 3–7 years, many of the boys as well as the girls described their imaginary friends as less competent than themselves. There are also examples throughout this book of girls with highly competent imaginary friends (e.g., "Alice," who bravely faced a giant crocodile and "that time when the monstrous rat at my grandmother's was about to bite me and she came out of who knows where to save me at the right moment"). For us, the interesting point is that competence—either positive or negative—is frequently part of children's descriptions. However, figuring out exactly why a particular child invokes competence in describing an imaginary friend tends to be a post hoc exercise of working backward from the child's lived experience on a case-by-case basis. This approach is not very satisfying, but general claims averaging across large numbers of children are apt to be misleading by underestimating the diversity in how or why a particular characteristic of imaginary friends, such as competence, is important or useful to children.

Coping with Restrictions, Limitations, and Physical Challenges

Imaginary friends can fill in to help the child satisfy a wish that is subject to restrictions in real life. For example, a girl in research by Karen Majors who was not allowed to have a pet created imaginary horses ("But if you, like, don't have an animal... and you want an animal. Like I'm desperate to have an animal.").[54] Majors also provides examples of children with imaginary friends who had skills that the children were trying to acquire (e.g., a 6-year-old boy who was learning to swim created "Ducky," an imaginary friend who was an excellent swimmer).[55] Imaginary friends do not have to eat foods the child doesn't like and do not have to go to bed if they feel like staying up. Sometimes, the events and circumstances in the imaginary friend's life are bigger and better versions of what is happening with the child (e.g., on the day a child was given a small bowl of fish, the imaginary friend acquired a giant tank of sharks). Another example is provided by Jean Piaget, who described how his daughter consoled herself after failing to "tame" a grasshopper by commenting on the ability of her imaginary friend Marecage to do so. "Marecage tamed a grasshopper. She had one that followed her everywhere; it went for walks with her and came home with her."[56]

Sometimes, the most central traits of the companion correspond to more pervasive types of restrictions or limitations in the child's life. For example, although the play of blind children generally tends to be more reality oriented than the play of sighted children, many blind 8-to-12-year-old children had an imaginary friend who was sighted who could "read others' mail, find hidden things, or wander freely about the school."[57] According to Singer and Lenahan, deaf children, like blind children, tend to have more concrete and less creative pretend play, but about a third of the deaf children (12–13 years old) in their study had imaginary friends.[58] Singer and Lenahan did not provide descriptive details about these imaginary friends, but an autobiographical account by Frances Warfield suggests that the imaginary friend she created when she was 6 years old played an important role in the expression of her feelings about being hard of hearing. In fact, Warfield dedicated her autobiography to him. Here is an excerpt:

> Wrinkel was invisible and inaudible, which left him free to do and say whatever he wanted. The first time he entered a room he found the exact center of the ceiling and drove in a large invisible staple. He tossed an invisible rope ladder through the staple, festooning it over the tops of pictures, curtain poles, and chandeliers, and climbed over people's heads, listening to their talk and making nonsense of it. Wrinkel... didn't care whether he heard perfectly or not. He chose to hear, and to act on what he heard, strictly as he had a mind to.... When people talked and talked and Wrinkel didn't make sense of what they said, that wasn't because he didn't hear it. It was because he liked to make nonsense by weaving his own name in and out of their sentences.... He killed people off for me all the time. He killed off all the ones I didn't like—the ones who cleared their throats pointedly or raised their voices at me, as if they thought I might not hear them. He killed off the deadpans, when they mumbled some question at me.[59]

In a study by Smith[60] with 12 blind, 13 deaf, and 26 hearing and seeing, ethnically diverse 8-to-12-year-old children, 76.9% of the deaf children reported having an imaginary friend, compared with 33.3% of the blind children and 53.8% of the hearing and seeing children. Although the children in this study did not differ in their reports of loneliness, other research suggests that blind and deaf children have fewer friends, possibly because they are less likely to engage in some of the social activities that promote the development of social networks.[61] Smith attributed the lower numbers of imaginary friends in the blind versus deaf children as due to particular problems in blind children in developing pretend play and in theory of mind development, but her findings suggest that both deaf and blind children might be motivated to create imaginary friends to supplement or compensate for a smaller social network.

There are several case histories of imaginary friends created by children with other sorts of challenges (see Chapter 7). A 10-year-old child who struggled with clumsiness, tics, and grimaces had an imaginary monkey friend named Fatto who was graceful, agile, and strong ("Fatto can swim and jump over the Empire State Building").[62] Sally, a little girl whose family had suffered substantial financial difficulties, created Sally the Second, a little girl who dressed in a blue velvet coat trimmed with fur and whose father gave her everything she wanted because he was so very rich.[63] Sometimes, the imaginary friend might substitute for a relationship that the child does not have in real life. For example, one young boy whose father was absent created an imaginary one who was better than everyone else ("his feet were bigger than anyone else's"; "he owned a big car with lots of wheels on it"; "he had golden hair and lovely pink eyes").[64] The fantasy father, as well as being a strategy for coping with the absence of a real father, provided the child with a strong and powerful ally.

The psychologists reporting these cases believe that imaginary friends play a positive, constructive role because they help children respond to unsatisfactory experiences owing to unfavorable social, physical, or economic conditions. According to Bender and Vogel,

> far from representing a willful and malicious "flight from reality," this phantasy represents the child's normal effort to compensate for a weak and inadequate reality to round out his incomplete life experiences and to help create a more integrated personality to deal with the conflicts of his individual life.[65]

As children encounter problems in their everyday lives or become frustrated in their efforts to accomplish a goal, they often make up stories about an imaginary friend overcoming the difficulty of the moment. These types of narratives are yet another example of how imaginary friends can support children's understanding of their world and their place in it.

Avoiding Blame

Imaginary friends can be convenient scapegoats. Princess Margaret of the House of Windsor is said to have used her imaginary friend in this way. Whenever she was confronted by her nanny about having done something wrong, she would say, "It wasn't me—it was Cousin Halifax."[66] Similarly, one of the parents interviewed by Newson and Newson reported that her son blamed an invisible girl named Choany whenever there was a mishap ("I think she must be his naughty self, because every time anything goes wrong, Choany has done it.").[67] Although interviews with children[68] and parents[69] suggest that children's attempts to blame their imaginary friends for mishaps or bad behaviors do not happen often, they are often amusing and memorable. Sometimes the child seems quite indignant about what the imaginary friend has done: "'Gerald [the imaginary companion], did you break daddy's pipes?' the boy demands to know."[70] Hoff described a child who cut her own bangs and then blamed her imaginary friend for making a mess of it.[71] In our research, we met a little girl whose brother habitually blamed things on her, stuttering (She-she did it). The little girl's imaginary friend was a naughty invisible girl named She-She who was held responsible for anything that went wrong.

The scapegoat function has multiple interpretations. One view is that using the imaginary friend to avoid blame is part of the process in which these children develop self-control. The process of blaming and sometimes punishing the friend might also help children to identify and internalize the expectations of parents or help children resolve issues about the own behaviors and characteristics that others deem unacceptable.[72] When the child blames the imaginary friend for something that they know is wrong or undesirable, the behavior or characteristic is distanced from the self. By doing so, children are trying to avoid criticism from the parents and maintain their self-esteem.

A Tool for Processing and Understanding Lived Experience

> I thought it was amazing that she could develop so many distinct personalities . . . with strengths and weaknesses for each. Seemed like she was teaching herself about people and diversity, as well as having a huge stable of characters to play out any emotions and situations she experienced or wanted to experiment with.
> **(Parent reflecting on her daughters play with stuffed animals)**

According to Jerome Bruner, fictional narratives extend our experience beyond our own personal circumstances.[73] Research with adults supports this idea, showing that engaging with fictional stories involves the simulation of emotional experiences in a way that sheds light on behavior that might be difficult to understand in real life.[74] We believe that the development of pretend play narratives can provide similar benefits for children. Many of the topics listed in this chapter—issues of mastery or competence, coping with fears—are examples of how interactions with imaginary friends include elements from children's lives and provide a forum for thinking about real-life themes and challenges. More generally, Paul Harris has argued that by imagining different possibilities in their pretend play, children are developing their understanding of reality.[75]

In their interactions with imaginary friends, children experience emotional reactions and imagine the possible responses to those feelings ("If I want to say something to my friends I can say it to her, and then maybe she would understand how I am feeling and that's what good about her."[76]) Three of the eight children interviewed by Karen Majors described how having an imaginary friend helped them manage their emotions. For example, one 8-year-old child who had difficulty controlling his temper had an 18-year-old imaginary friend named Tom who was described as similar to the child—both liked coffee, did not like brussels sprouts, and had bad tempers. Sometimes the boy imagined hitting the imaginary friend ("It takes my anger out without actually hurting someone"), but he explained that "Tom's not an imaginary human punch bag. He's friends."[77]

An imaginary friend can also provide a vehicle for thinking about things that a child has heard about, but not experienced firsthand—cultural backgrounds, lifestyles, or world events that capture the child's attention. Mary Jalongo describes a case in which a 4-year-old white child invented an imaginary friend who was Indigenous American. Imagining her companion allowed this child to have a connection with a culture that was not accessible to her in real life.[78] Hoff described a child whose response to learning about the suffering of people in war zones was to create Bambina, an imaginary friend who traveled with the child in her imagination to tend to the injured ("She has such different medicines that, well, she maybe pours them onto the wounds and then suddenly everything is alright again.").[79]

In their pretend play, children can enact over and over again any situation or event, an activity that often helps reduce any anxiety associated with the event and gain understanding of it.[80] For example, when someone in the family is sick, the child might pretend that the imaginary friend is sick and act out a variety of hospital and home scenarios associated with the illness. The characters, scenes, and plot lines in children's interactions with imaginary friends thus provide a window on children's interests, fears, conflicts, and concerns.

Summary

Why do children create imaginary friends? Because they can. It is a fun way for them to stretch their growing imaginations, and once pretend friends have shown up, they can help out in all sorts of ways. Their primary function is typically friendship, but they also provide a vehicle for storytelling, communication, dealing with fears, restrictions, and issues related to competence, and generally mulling over lived experience. Many have characteristics that appear customized to meet the ever-shifting idiosyncratic whims and needs of the child creators. The capacity of young children to use their imaginary friends for all these purposes is impressive—or even magical.

All of this makes pinning down the exact reason why a particular child created a particular type of imaginary friend difficult. In fact, when we ask, "Why do children create imaginary friends?," the question itself presumes a singular answer, which could not be further from the truth. In most studies, children are interviewed once, giving the researcher a snapshot—a still life—of what the imaginary friend is like on that particular day. But imaginary friends are multifunctional moving targets. They shapeshift, multiply, grow and shrink ("he is any size you want!"), and evolve with the child's needs. They are not easily categorized in terms of functions, and researchers must take care to avoid being misleading, out of date, or simplistic. Still, comparing what is going on in children's lives with the characteristics of their imaginary friends is fascinating. And sometimes such observations can be useful information for parents, therapists, and others who want to help children cope with psychological needs that are more substantive than a desire to escape blame or tell a story. In the next chapter, we focus more specifically on the extent to which imaginary friends serve as vehicles for coping with serious trauma, mental health problems, and adversity.

Notes

1. Armah, A., & Landers-Potts, M. (2021). A review of imaginary companions and their implications for development. *Imagination, Cognition and Personality, 41*(1), 31–53.
Hoff, E. (2005a). A friend living inside me: The forms and functions of imaginary companions. *Imagination, Cognition and Personality, 24*, 151–189.
2. Majors, K. (2013). Children's perceptions of their imaginary companions and the purposes they serve: An exploratory study in the United Kingdom. *Childhood, 20*, 550–565. https://doi.org/10.1177/0907568213476899
3. Gleason, T. R., Sebanc, A. M., & Hartup, W. W. (2000). Imaginary companions of preschool children. *Developmental Psychology, 36*, 419–428.
4. Mauro, J. (1991). *The friend that only I can see: A longitudinal investigation of children's imaginary companions* [Doctoral dissertation]. University of Oregon.
5. Singer, D. G. (1993). *Playing for their lives: Helping troubled children through play therapy.* The Free Press, pp. 135–136.
6. Ibid.
Kalyan Masih, V. (1978). Imaginary companions of children. In R. B. R. Weizmann, P. J. Levinson, & P. A. Taylor (Eds.), *Piagetian theory and its implications for the helping professions.* University of Southern California.
Majors, K. (2013). Children's perceptions of their imaginary companions and the purposes they serve: An exploratory study in the United Kingdom. *Childhood.*
Manosevitz, M., Prentice, N. M., & Wilson, F. (1973). Individual and family correlates of imaginary companions in preschool children. *Developmental Psychology, 8*, 72–79.
7. Hoff, E. (2005a). A friend living inside me: The forms and functions of imaginary companions. *Imagination, Cognition and Personality, 24*, 151–189, see p. 158.
8. Docter, P. *Inside out* [Film] (2015). Walt Disney Studios.
9. And then fades away to nothing and is gone forever—a sad moment for us.

10. Hoff, E. (2005a). A friend living inside me: The forms and functions of imaginary companions. *Imagination, Cognition and Personality*, p. 168.
11. Gleason, T. R., Sebanc, A. M., & Hartup, W. W. (2000). Imaginary companions of preschool children. *Developmental Psychology, 36*, 419–428.
12. Gleason, T. R. (2002). Social provisions of real and imaginary relationships in early childhood, *Developmental Psychology, 38*, 979–992.
13. Gleason, T. R., & Kalpidou, M. (2014). Imaginary companions and young children's coping and competence. *Social Development, 23*(4), 820–839.
14. Parker, J. G., & Asher, S. R. (1993). Friendship and friendship quality in middle childhood: Links with peer group acceptance and feelings of loneliness and social dissatisfaction. *Developmental Psychology, 29*(4), 611–621.
15. Gleason, T. R., & Hohmann, L. M. (2006). Concepts of real and imaginary friendships in early childhood. *Social Development, 15*(1), 128–144.
16. Majors, K. (2013). Children's perceptions of their imaginary companions and the purposes they serve: An exploratory study in the United Kingdom. *Childhood*.
17. Bender, L., & Vogel, B. F. (1941). Imaginary companions of children. *American Journal of Orthopsychiatry, 11*, 56–65, see p. 59.
18. Nagera, H. (1969). The imaginary companion: Its significance for ego development and conflict resolution. *The Psychoanalytic Study of the Child, 24*, 89–99.
19. Lindsey, R. (1988, July 24). Promises to keep. *New York Times Magazine*, 23–24.
20. Gleason, T. R., Sebanc, A. M., & Hartup, W. W. (2000). Imaginary companions of preschool children. *Developmental Psychology*.
    Bouldin, P., & Pratt, C. (1999). Characteristics of preschool and school-age children with imaginary companions. *The Journal of Genetic Psychology, 160*(4), 397–410.
21. Gleason, T. (2004). Imaginary companions and peer acceptance. *International Journal of Behavioral Development, 28*(3), 204–209.
    Singer, D. G., & Singer, J. L. (1990). *The house of make-believe: Children's play and developing imagination*. Harvard University Press.
22. Gleason, T. (2004). Imaginary companions and peer acceptance. *International Journal of Behavioral Development*.
    Bouldin, P., & Pratt, C. (1999). Characteristics of preschool and school-age children with imaginary companions. *The Journal of Genetic Psychology, 160*(4), 397–410.
23. Mathur, R., & Smith, M. C. (2008). An investigation of imaginary companions in an ethnic and grade diverse sample. *Imagination, Cognition and Personality, 27*(4), 313–336, see p. 332.
24. Seiffge-Krenke, I. (1993). Close friendship and imaginary companions in adolescence. In B. Laursen (Ed.), *Close friendships in adolescence*. (pp. 73–87). Jossey-Bass, see p. 261.
25. Adolescents frequently write diary entries as if they were letters to an imaginary friend. The most famous example is the diary of Anne Frank, which was addressed to her imaginary friend "Kitty."
    Frank, A. (2003). *The diary of Anne Frank: The revised critical edition*. Doubleday Books.
26. Gleason, T. (2004). Imaginary companions and peer acceptance. *International Journal of Behavioral Development*, p. 208.
27. Gleason, T., & White, R. (2005, April). Talking to a tiger: Children's day-to-day interactions with their imaginary companions [Paper presentation]. Biennial meeting of the Society for Research in Child Development, Atlanta.

28. Sugarman, S. (2013). *An investigation into parents' attitudes to their children having imaginary companions* [Doctoral dissertation], University of London.
29. Hoff, E. (2005a). A friend living inside me: The forms and functions of imaginary companions. *Imagination, Cognition and Personality*, p. 157.
30. Trionfi, G., & Reese, E. (2009). A good story: Children with imaginary companions create richer narratives. *Child Development*, 80, 1301–1313.
31. This transcript is from a video made by Marjorie's cousin.
32. Singer, D. G., & Singer, J. L. (1990). *The house of make-believe: Children's play and developing imagination.* Harvard University Press.
33. Newson, J., & Newson, E. (1968). *Four years old in an urban community.* George Allen & Unwin Ltd., p. 183.
34. Piaget, J. (1962). *Play, dreams, and imitation in childhood.* Norton.
35. Imperiale, N. (1992, September 30). Imaginary pals say lots about kids, *Orlando Sentinel Tribune*, p. E1.
36. Bretherton, I. (1989). Pretense: The form and function of make-believe play. *Developmental Review*, 9, 383–401.
    Sutton-Smith, B. (2001). *The ambiguity of play.* Harvard University Press.
    Vygotsky, L. S. (1978). *Mind in society.* Harvard University Press.
37. Wickes, F. G. (1927). *The inner world of childhood.* D. Appleton & Company, pp. 162–163.
38. Majors, K. (2013). Children's perceptions of their imaginary companions and the purposes they serve: An exploratory study in the United Kingdom. *Childhood*, p. 560.
39. The children at her daycare took turns taking the box into the bathroom, turning out the light, and letting the ghost out of the box. In the pitch dark of the windowless bathroom, all the children were able to enjoy playing with the baby ghost.
40. Gottman, J. M., & Parker, J. G. (1986). *Conversations of friends: Speculations on affective development.* Cambridge University Press.
41. Singer, D. G., & Singer, J. L. (1990). *The house of make-believe: Children's play and developing imagination.* Harvard University Press.
42. Golomb, C., & Kuersten, R. (1996). On the transition from pretence play to reality: What are the rules of the game? *British Journal of Developmental Psychology*, 14(2), 203–217.
43. Lazurus, A. (1984). *In the mind's eye: The power of imagery for personal enrichment.* Guilford Press, p. 103.
44. Freud, A. (1966). A short history of child analysis. *The Psychoanalytic Study of the Child*, 21(1), 7–14.
45. Fraiberg, S. H. (1959). *The magic years.* Charles Scribner's Sons, p. 19.
46. Harter, S., & Chao, C. (1992). The role of competence in children's creation of imaginary friends. *Merrill-Palmer Quarterly*, 38, 350–363.
    Hoff, E. (2005a). A friend living inside me: The forms and functions of imaginary companions. *Imagination, Cognition and Personality*.
47. Ibid., p. 166.
48. Ibid., p. 167.
49. Ibid., p. 167.
50. Wigger, J. B. (2019). *Invisible companions: Encounters with imaginary friends, gods, ancestors, and angels.* Stanford University Press.
51. Harter, S., & Chao, C. (1992). The role of competence in children's creation of imaginary friends. *Merrill-Palmer Quarterly*, p. 359.

52. Ibid., p. 358.
53. Coetzee, H., & Shute, R. (2003). "I run faster than him because I have faster shoes": Perceptions of competence and gender role stereotyping in children's imaginary friends. *Child Study Journal, 33*(4), 257–272.

    Hoff, E. (2005a). A friend living inside me: The forms and functions of imaginary companions. *Imagination, Cognition and Personality*.
54. Majors, K. (2013). Children's perceptions of their imaginary companions and the purposes they serve: An exploratory study in the United Kingdom. *Childhood*, p. 560.
55. Ibid.
56. Piaget, J. (1962). *Play, dreams, and imitation in childhood*. Norton, p. 132.
57. Singer, J. L., & Streiner, B. F. (1966). Imaginative content in the dreams and fantasy play of blind and sighted children. *Perceptual and Motor Skills, 22*, 475–482, see p. 480.
58. Singer, D. G., & Lenahan, M. L. (1976). Imagination content in dreams of deaf children. *American Annals of the Deaf, 121*(1), 44–48.
59. Warfield, F. (1948). *Cotton in my ears*. The Viking Press, pp. 7–9.
60. Smith, M. C. (2019). Imaginary companions of blind, deaf, and typically developing school children. *Imagination, Cognition and Personality, 38*, 290–314.
61. Huurre, T., & Aro, H. (2000). The psychological well-being of Finnish adolescents with visual impairments versus those with chronic conditions and no disabilities. *Journal of Visual Impairment & Blindness, 94*, 625–637.
62. Bender, L., & Vogel, B. F. (1941). Imaginary companions of children. *American Journal of Orthopsychiatry*, p. 62.
63. Wickes, F. G. (1927). *The inner world of childhood*. D. Appleton & Company.
64. Machtlinger, V. J. (1976). Psychoanalytic theory: Pre-oedipal and oedipal phases with special reference to the father. In M. E. Lamb (Ed.), *The role of the father in child development* (pp. 277–305). Wiley, p. 298.

    Burlingham, D., & Freud, A. (1944). *Infants without families*. George Allen & Unwin.
65. Bender, L., & Vogel, B. F. (1941). Imaginary companions of children. *American Journal of Orthopsychiatry*, p. 64.
66. Sakol, J. & Latham, C. (1988). *The Royals*. Congdon & Weed.
67. Newson, J., & Newson, E. (1968). *Four years old in an urban community*.
68. Hoff, E. (2005a). A friend living inside me: The forms and functions of imaginary companions. *Imagination, Cognition and Personality*.
69. Gleason, T. R., Sebanc, A. M., & Hartup, W. W. (2000). Imaginary companions of preschool children. *Developmental Psychology*.

    Sugarman, S. (2013). *An investigation into parents' attitudes to their children having imaginary companions*.
70. Fraiberg, S. H. (1959). *The magic years*. Charles Scribner's Sons, p. 141.
71. Hoff, E. (2005a). A friend living inside me: The forms and functions of imaginary companions. *Imagination, Cognition and Personality*.
72. Singer, D. G., & Singer, J. L. (1990). *The house of make-believe: Children's play and developing imagination*. Harvard University Press.
73. Bruner, J. (1986). *Actual minds, possible worlds*. Harvard University Press.
74. Mar, R. A., & Oatley, K. (2008). The function of fiction is the abstraction and simulation of social experience. *Perspectives on Psychological Science, 3*(3), 173–192.

Zunshine, L. (2006). *Why we read fiction: Theory of mind and the novel.* Ohio State University Press.
75. Harris, P. L. (2000). *The work of the imagination.* Basil Blackwell.
76. Majors, K. (2013). Children's perceptions of their imaginary companions and the purposes they serve: An exploratory study in the United Kingdom. *Childhood,* p. 559.
77. Ibid., p. 558.
78. Jalongo, M. R. (1984). Imaginary companions in children's lives and literature. *Childhood Education, 60,* 166–171, see p. 167.
79. Hoff, E. (2005a). A friend living inside me: The forms and functions of imaginary companions. *Imagination, Cognition and* Personality, see p. 169.
80. Ibid.
    Majors, K. (2013). Children's perceptions of their imaginary companions and the purposes they serve: An exploratory study in the United Kingdom. *Childhood.*
    Newson, J., & Newson, E. (1968). *Four years old in an urban community.*

Chapter 7
Do Imaginary Friends Help Children Cope with Adversity?

One of the most powerful resources available to young children for coping with stressful situations is their imagination. With their imaginations, children can work through and make sense of the difficult events happening to them and gain a sense of mastery and understanding of their own experiences.[1] In their pretend play, children cope with terrible life events and chronic stressors—the loss of a home to an environmental disaster, the death of a parent, toxic home environments, ongoing neglect and/or abuse, intractable poverty, serious medical conditions, and protracted regional violence.

Clinical accounts documenting such cases sometimes includes descriptions of imaginary friends by therapists trying to piece together an understanding of the inner experiences of troubled children. The insights of skilled clinicians are instructive, but these are exactly the kinds of writings that have contributed to the association of imaginary friends with emotional disturbance, especially in the past when engaging with imaginary friends was often interpreted as a maladaptive coping strategy or as indicative of emotional, social, or psychological problems.[2] Although some clinicians are careful to point out that the children were not referred to them because of their imaginary friends, the negative impression created of imaginary friends is hard to avoid.

The fact is that many children with emotional problems and children living in stressful situations have imaginary friends. Why? Because imaginary friends love you when you feel rejected by others, listen when you need to talk to someone, and can be trusted not to repeat what you say. A famous example is the imaginary friend named Kitty who was the recipient of Anne Frank's diary entries about the trauma of being hidden in an attic for two years during World War II.[3] In another example, an adult who grew up in a dysfunctional home recalled having an imaginary friend with

> the most beautiful chocolate skin, great big happy eyes, a million-dollar smile and long black curly hair . . . she gave me her undivided attention as I poured out all my hurts, all my betrayals, all my goodness and my badness. She never told. She never scolded me.[4]

No wonder this woman recalled deep feelings of love for the little invisible girl.

Therapists vary in their interpretation of how imaginary friends reflect or are otherwise related to children's difficulties, but Dorothy Singer argued that the presence of

Imaginary Friends and the People Who Create Them. Second edition. Marjorie Taylor and Naomi R. Aguiar, Oxford University Press. © Oxford University Press (2024). DOI: 10.1093/9780190888916.003.0007

imaginary friends in therapy should be taken as a positive sign that children are using their own resources to cope with distress.[5] She gives the example of a little boy whose attention deficit disorder and hyperactivity had affected his language development, making it difficult for him to understand what was being said and to express himself. With his imaginary friend, Petey, there were none of the frustrations involved in trying communicate with real people:

> I watched as Marty "talked" to Petey . . . his speech, racing along, was unintelligible to me, filled with nonsense words, his own private vocabulary, but obviously affording him pleasure. He was peaceful as he played—for the longest time he had remained with one game . . . Petey was Marty's "friend." Petey made no demands on Marty.[6]

The tricky point here is that although children with problems often have imaginary friends, having an imaginary friend does not mean that the child has problems. Most imaginary friends come along on their own without a concomitant crisis. With this point firmly in mind, we next explore how—when the need arises—imaginary friends can help children cope with a host of external and internal stressors.

Children Living in Difficult Home Environments

The creation of a steadfast companion to scaffold the complexities of adverse events and support emotion regulation could be invaluable for children—not only in their ability to cope with living in a chaotic, stressful, or abusive home environment, but also in their ability to recover from these experiences and become resilient adults. Humberto Nagera provided several clinical case studies of children who seemed to benefit from having an imaginary friend.[7] For example, a 5-year-old child named Miriam created an imaginary friend, "Susan," at the time that her parents divorced and her mother was hospitalized for mental illness. Miriam talked for hours to "Susan," often asking her questions such as "What happened to Mummy?" and consulting her for advice.[8] Two older children in the family reacted with school difficulties, sleeping disturbances, and regression (e.g., bed wetting). Nagera attributed Miriam's lack of these symptoms to the benefit she received from her imaginary friend.

Therapists sometimes provide stuffed animals in therapy to help children express themselves and communicate their worries. Nagera described a 4-year-old boy who used stuffed animals (a crocodile and tiger) during sessions in which he felt anxious after he had been aggressive toward the therapist. The child would kick the therapist and then warn him that the stuffed animals would defend the child if the therapist retaliated. Nagera writes that

> . . . later in treatment when his fear of being smacked by the father increased—a fear that had a reality basis—he began to protect himself further by taking the two

powerful allies home. If this was not allowed, he took them in his "imagination" by pretending that he had put them into his pocket. In the following sessions he would comment spontaneously or in response to my questions how these animals had frightened his father, who then did not dare smack him.[9]

In another case study, a 6-year-old boy whose disabled mother actively rejected him and whose father had a cognitive disability developed a fantasy about being the leader of a pretend gang. By describing the gang to the therapist, he was able to express his fears:

They run away so I got running away (the child had run away from home). The biggest one is 14 years. I'm the littlest. I am the leader. They want me to be. They just sit there. They don't do anything else. The big boy got the idea first. His mother isn't good to him. That is why he runs away. His mother killed his father with a knife. I don't like my mother because the other boys don't like their mothers. I'm afraid my mother will kill my father. She doesn't like my father, nor me, or the baby—not anybody.[10]

Many examples from therapists are associated with physical and/or sexual abuse, and experts agree that children who have experienced abuse often create imaginary friends.[11] In one study with adults who had experienced abuse as children, 14 of the 22 participants (63%) recalled having imaginary friends.[12] In another study with 23 ten-year-olds who had experienced maltreatment, 52% reported having imaginary friends.[13] Some of these imaginary friends were described as performing functions specific to maltreatment, such as taking pain and abuse for the child or keeping the child's secrets.[14]

One child in Marjorie's research told her about an invisible sister who was the same size and age as the little girl herself. The pretend sister was a very good girl who cleaned the kitchen, swept the floor, and dusted the house. Her parents reported that their daughter started to talk about the imaginary friend shortly after she had been sexually abused by a neighbor. One of the noteworthy aspects of this example is that the child talked about her pretend sister openly and with affection. This point is important because some psychologists have suggested that a child will talk freely about an imaginary friend only if it serves the normal purposes of fun and companionship.[15] However, our research suggests that at least some children will talk openly about their imaginary friends, even when the timing of their appearance coincides with abuse.

According to Sawa and colleagues, the imaginary friends of traumatized patients are often useful to a therapist. They might provide clues about the patient's beliefs and desires and at times can even act as intermediaries with patients who have difficulty expressing themselves to the therapist. Sawa and colleagues have found that "by incorporating them into the therapeutic strategy as a presence supporting the patient's growth, it is possible that the psychotherapy may proceed more smoothly."[16]

Therefore, these imaginary friends should be considered a response, not the primary driver, of the children's mental health challenges.[17]

The Imaginary Friends of Children Who Have Been in Foster Care

Children who have lived in foster care are a particularly vulnerable population due to the situations that resulted in their entering the foster care system (e.g., severe neglect, physical and/or sexual abuse) and the stress associated with foster care (e.g., disruption of family relationships, changes in schools, ineffective foster parenting, frequent transitions in and out of multiple foster care homes).[18] Along with all the other difficulties associated with these traumatizing experiences, they can have deleterious effects on children's friendships.[19]

This population is at high risk for a range of negative outcomes, but not all foster children inevitably grow up to be troubled adolescents and adults. Some are able to overcome the adversity in their early lives to become healthy and highly functioning members of society.[20] Does a history of maltreatment and the stress related to foster care motivate some children to create imaginary friends who can provide companionship that is not prone to disruption by all these upheavals? To find out, Naomi and her colleagues interviewed 21 children (9- to 14-year-olds) who had been removed from their families of origin when they were 3–6 years old and placed in foster care but were currently in permanent placements.[21] As a comparison group, 39 children were interviewed who were similar in age and were also from a low socioeconomic community but had no history of maltreatment and had never been in foster care.[22]

The prevalence rates of imaginary friends did not differ by group, and the overall rate (43%) was comparable to the general rates reported for 9- to 12-year-olds by Pearson and colleagues.[23] Although one might expect that the imaginary friends of these children would be likely to have negative characteristics, the children in both groups described them in positive ways—supportive friends who were fun to be around (see Table 7.1). A few had a mix of positive and negative characteristics (e.g., an invisible bear named Louie who was funny and often cheered the child up but also enjoyed sneaking up on the child and scaring her), but not a single child described an imaginary friend in a primarily negative way.

We were also interested in the type of relationship that these children created with their imaginary friends. None of the children described a relationship in which the child was the caregiver who looked after a vulnerable imaginary friend. When imaginary friends were described as needing care (e.g., an invisible panda who needed the child to play music to cheer him up when he was sad), children also mentioned ways in which these companions helped the children themselves in return. In most cases, the imaginary friend was described as a highly competent individual, often with super powers (e.g., the ability to fly, shapeshift) who helped the child rather

Table 7.1 Examples of imaginary friends created by children who had lived in foster care and children from a low-SES community sample

Male 9 yrs 7 mos Foster care	An invisible Siberian tiger described as a "good best friend." Helps the child feel better when he is angry or lonely. Described as having power swipes, but also needs the child to help him feel better when he is sad, and seeks comfort during rainy nights.
Male 13 yrs 5 mos Foster care	A stuffed gorilla described as "funny" because of the clothes he wore. Helped the child feel better when his grandfather passed away. He was "pretty good" at things, but child did not like that they would sometimes disagree about activities (e.g., whether to go to the park).
Female 9 yrs 11 mos Foster care	An invisible milk carton described as "very kind and kind of like a conscience." Helped the child feel better when her sister did things she was not allowed to do. Child helped Milk learn to run, jump rope, and hula-hoop. She liked that the milk carton was "not like a human being." "I learned a lot about Milk and Milk learned a lot about me."
Female 9 yrs 1 mo Community sample	A tiny invisible boy who is "always there for... giving me ideas" and "very rarely needs me to cheer him up." A mind reader who "finds out your secrets" and who is good at being "in very, very tight places." Lives in a little house in a wall in her bedroom. Helps child feel better when her sister is being mean. Likes that "he's kind and generous" and dislikes that he "sometimes pulls my hair."
Female 10 yrs 2 mos Community sample	A stuffed lion described as "nice and almost always happy" and "likes to talk." Sometimes feels "left out" and "gets mad at me when I... talk to people about him." Helps the child feel better by talking to him when she is lonely. Really good at "swinging on the swings and... playing board games." Likes that "we always play together."
Female 13 yrs 5 mos Community sample	An invisible girl who could fly. Described as "really nice," "funny," and "like a superhero" that "succeeded... followed through and helped me." Helped the child by hanging out with her when she was sad. Was "a part of my family and was there all the time." Liked that "she was there when I needed her."

than the reverse. (Note that in this study competency was not related to having been in foster care or to sex.)

Both the children who had lived in foster care and the children in the comparison group described how their imaginary friends supported them by simply being there ("she was there when I needed her"; "was there for giving me ideas"; "followed through and helped me"). They also described how their imaginary friends helped them cope with particularly difficult experiences. One 13-year-old boy who had lived in foster care described his stuffed gorilla as helping him when his grandfather passed away: "when I would get upset about something that happened that I didn't want to happen—like when our grandpa died—he helped me with that." A 13-year-old girl who had lived in foster care described how her stuffed pony had helped her cope with negative emotions: "whenever I got sad or mad or I wanted to throw something and break it . . . it was . . . like what a mom would do, try to calm someone down." Another 9-year-old boy from the community sample described how an invisible boy would talk with him about what was bothering him: "when I'm upset he makes me talk sometimes. He makes me feel a little bit better." Children also described their imaginary friends as helping them in other ways, such as working with them on homework and teaching them new things (e.g., the colors of the rainbow). In many ways their descriptions were similar to those provided by the 10-year-olds in Hoff's study who were from a middle-class population that was not identified as having experienced significant trauma. The imaginary friends in both studies were positive, competent play partners who provided the children with companionship and support. The children in the foster care study clearly believed that their imaginary friends had helped them cope with the challenges in their lives.

The Imaginary Friends of Low-SES, High-Risk Middle-School Children

In a 2010 study, Marjorie and her colleagues departed from their usual practice of interviewing preschool children and their parents from a normative community sample. They wanted to determine if having an imaginary friend might be a red flag for older children, as some have claimed.[24] Their idea was to identify a group of middle-school children who were already having problems and were at risk for future difficulties and then to determine if the children in this group who had imaginary friends had different trajectories than the children who did not have imaginary friends. The research team started by identifying 152 twelve-year-olds who were considered by their teachers as showing the highest levels of poor school adjustment, and by extension, the most likely to continue and escalate problem behavior in later adolescence. They were failing in school, getting into fights, and living in families that were dealing with poverty, missing parents, and addiction. Basically, these kids were chosen by the teachers as the least likely to succeed.

Thirteen of these children had imaginary friends (e.g., a brainiac who was cool, knew everything, and tried to keep the child out of trouble; a boy with dirty blond hair and long lashes who always knew what the child was going to say). This group of children scored higher than the other children on a measure of positive strategies for making themselves feel better when they were upset (e.g., go for a walk instead of hitting someone). But they were rated by their parents as having more behavioral problems, and they were not well liked by their peers. The question was whether having an imaginary friend at age 12 in this high-risk sample was predictive of particularly negative outcomes down the road or, alternatively, if such friendships might be a source of resilience. Would the children with imaginary friends at age 12 overcome their early difficulties and be doing better six years later when they were 18 years old?

At the follow-up assessment at age 18, the research team considered adolescents to be doing well if they (1) had graduated from high school, (2) did not have a diagnosis of mental illness, (3) did not have a history of police arrest, and (4) were not using illegal drugs. The adolescents who had described imaginary friends at age 12 when they were in middle school were much more likely to meet these criteria for a positive outcome (72.7%) than the other adolescents in this high-risk sample. Only 27.5% of the adolescents who did not have imaginary friends at age 12 showed this positive pattern of outcomes at the end of high school.

From this study, it is temping to conclude that imaginary friends contribute directly to resilience by helping children work through difficulties. But perhaps children who have the capacity and inclination to supplement their social world with their imagination are less vulnerable to the attractions of involvement with deviant peers (a significant risk factor for poor outcomes). Moreover, given the small number of children with imaginary friends, these findings should be interpreted with caution. What we can say with some confidence is that the results of this study provide no evidence that having an imaginary friend in early adolescence is a sign of impending behavioral or mental health problems for high-risk children. In fact, having an imaginary friend in middle school was associated with a positive pattern of adjustment at the end of high school.

Imaginary Friends of Children Coping with Mental Illness

Not only mentally healthy children have imaginary friends; children who are mentally ill have them too. *Born Schizophrenic: January's Story*, a documentary about a young girl struggling with childhood schizophrenia, presents a particularly vivid portrayal of the way a host of invisible friends named after numbers (e.g., "Three," "Seven") were intermixed with her symptoms.[25] Individual cases like January's sometimes include accounts of imaginary friends with characteristics that are thematically linked to pathology or appear designed to address the difficulties that mentally ill children experience.

In some clinical examples, the psychological process known as "splitting"—when a person's desirable and undesirable characteristics are separated into polar extremes—might have a superficial resemblance to the creation of pretend friends. However, there is an order of magnitude between the splitting observed in clinical disorders and the inclination of some children to associate primarily good or primarily bad behaviors with one or more imaginary friends (e.g., a good invisible person named Folkers and a bad invisible person named Favors). Lenore Terr, a child psychiatrist who is an expert on childhood trauma, provides a clinical example of an imaginary friend created by a boy who had been kidnapped and held for ransom at the age of 3:

> I called my fake person "Olive." I named him for a jar of stuffed olives I saw on the table. I made him up a couple of years ago when I was five, and I still have him in my mind. Olive never speaks . . . I pretend Olive is dead. I look up at the sky now and I

see his face. Olive was just my age. He had black hair, a light blue face and yellow eyes . . . I made him up because I picked up a rotten olive. . . . On my birthday, Olive died. He was going outside and he had a heart attack. I called the hospital. And they said they were all filled up. Then I didn't know what to do. Then Olive died.[26]

According to Terr, the child had split off the weaker, less positive aspects of himself to create Olive. She suggested that the boy's good adjustment after the kidnapping—his ability to do well in school, have many friends, and be well behaved—was in part due to the Olive fantasy. In therapy, she was able to help him be more accepting of his own imperfections and accept the characteristics of Olive as part of himself.

In psychopathology, splitting tends to be associated with serious disorders such as borderline personality disorder and dissociative identity disorder, in which two or more distinct personalities exist within the same person. In borderline personality disorder, individuals show serious disturbances in basic identity or sense of self and tend to have unstable relationships, distorted self-image, and impulsivity. Patients with borderline personality disorder are actually less likely to recall playing with imaginary friends than patients with other types of disorders. Dissociative identity disorder (previously known as multiple personality disorder) is diagnosed when a person seems to have more than one distinct personality that at times take control of the person's body outside of their awareness. A person with dissociative identity disorder might suddenly realize that they cannot remember what has happened over the past few days or even months, a time when the alter personality was active. Experts consider this disorder to be closely tied to child abuse.[27]

Imaginary Friends Associated with Dissociative Identity Disorder

Only a subset of people with dissociative identity disorder report having had imaginary friends in childhood, but these cases teach us something about the characteristics of imaginary friends invented as a response to abuse. According to Barbara Sanders, the experience of having an imaginary friend is quite different for abused children who go on to develop dissociative identity disorder as adults than for other children. Sanders interviewed 22 adults with dissociatve identity disorder and found that 14 remembered having had imaginary friends as children (e.g., an impish brat who answered back and was defiant; a tall male bodyguard). Although the primary function served by most of the imaginary friends was companionship, Sanders' patients also mentioned a variety of functions that were related to the experience of abuse. Their imaginary friends kept secrets; held memories; endured sex, pain, and abuse; and felt sad for these children.

Although the imaginary friends do not take over in the same way as an alter, Sanders speculated that imaginary friends of children who go on to develop dissociative identity disorder as adults might be more likely than the imaginary friends of nonabused children to engage in actions that run counter to the child's wishes or for which the child is amnesic. In a study with children (7–12 years) receiving psychiatric care at a clinic in Finland, many of the children reported that their imaginary friends did not want the children to tell others about their existence, and a few children discussed wanting their imaginary friends to go away or finding them annoying or controlling.[28]

The usefulness of information about imaginary friends in the diagnosis of dissociative disorders depends upon the ability to accurately distinguish the characteristics of normative imaginary friends from those of dissociative children. On the basis of her clinical work with young children, Joyanna Silberg proposed three main differences between pathological and normative experiences of imaginary friends: (1) whether the child or the imaginary friend has control, (2) whether the child feels bothered by the presence of the imaginary friend, and (3) whether the imaginary friend gives the child competing messages about how to behave. Silberg, as well as other clinicians, have also suggested that the vividness of the companions created by maltreated children makes them qualitatively different from the imaginary companions in normative samples.[29]

This list is problematic, however, because most of the characteristics of imaginary friends that are suggested as associated with pathological dissociation (e.g., vividness and uncontrollability) are common in the imaginary friends created by children who have not experienced abuse (see Chapters 2 and 3).[30] Mentally healthy, nonabused children create imaginary friends that are vivid, difficult to control, argumentative, bothersome, or unruly. Even in cases in which no abuse has occurred, children who are intensely involved with their imaginary friends can sometimes feel unable to control their actions (see Chapter 2).

Research that associates imaginary friends with dissociation also has methodological challenges. Stephanie Carlson, Deniz Tahiroglu, and Marjorie[31] found that children with imaginary friends scored higher than children without such friends on the most widely used assessment tool for dissociative disorders in young children (the Child Dissociative Checklist);[32] however, this difference was due to the items on this checklist that specifically asked about imaginary friends. When we omitted these items, the difference between the two groups of children was no longer significant. Moreover, having an imaginary friend in this study was not associated with any of our measures of difficulties in children's lives (behavior problems, fears, and nightmares).

What is the relationship between imaginary friends and the split personalities of dissociative identity disorder? Unlike alter personalities, imaginary friends do not completely take over the child's personality and do not operate outside the child's awareness. In some cases, however, an alter personality can be traced back to the imaginary friend the child had at the time the abuse was happening, or an imaginary friend that was created to help cope with the abusive situation.[33] This link, however, does not in any way suggest that children with imaginary friends are at risk for developing dissociative identity disorder. First of all, the vast majority of imaginary friends are created for reasons that have nothing to do with abuse. Second, although individuals with dissociative identity disorder typically have a history of abuse, the victims of child abuse do not typically develop alter personalities. Dissociative identity disorder is now being diagnosed more frequently than in the past, but it is still rare, certainly much rarer than child abuse.

A final point regarding links between imaginary friends and dissociation is that highly imaginative play is not of concern to therapists who treat troubled children. In fact, the play of many abused and neglected children is strikingly *less* creative than that of their peers.[34] In addition, abused children tend to show none of the joy and delight that routinely accompanies the everyday play of other children—including play with imaginary friends. Lenore Terr characterized the play that follows trauma as "grim and monotonous." Left to their own devices in a play therapy room, abused children engage in activities that lack coherence, spontaneity, and positive affect. Their pretense appears unimaginative and literal, such as "the child who sweeps the floor, washes the play dishes and play clothes, carefully arranges stray toys and then quietly waits for his or her parent to arrive."[35] Thus, although some children create imaginary friends as a response to trauma, in and of themselves these friends are not a bad sign. The children who lack the capacity to play freely, creatively, and happily are more likely to elicit the concern of clinicians.

Imaginary Friends of Children Coping with Physical Illness and Injury

In Chapter 6, we discussed how children might create imaginary friends to cope with physical differences such as being blind or deaf. Pretend play can also a source of coping and resilience for children dealing with illness, either because they are sick themselves or because they are worried about the illness of others. Cindy Dell Clark interviewed children and their parents and collected observations at summer camps specialized for children with asthma and with diabetes.[36] Her rich descriptions document the important role of pretend play in children's coping responses: a little boy with severe asthma who imagined the mask he wore during a nebulizer treatment to be a pilot's mask and the toy airplane he held to carry him away through the mist; the laughter of children at a summer camp at a skit in which the wolf in *The Three Pigs* could not blow down the pigs' houses because he had asthma; and a 6-year-old boy's attachment to a Power Ranger toy who also had diabetes. Clark's research is about pretend play in general, rather than focusing specifically on imaginary friends, but many of her examples suggest that imaginary friends might be important for chronically ill children.

Imaginary friends might also have a role in supporting young children are who injured in some way and have to spend time in the hospital or have repeated visits to the doctor. These experiences can result in considerable trauma associated with the pain of the injury, fear about medical procedures, and anxiety about being separated from home and family. In her book, *The Widening World of Childhood*, Lois Murphy gives a detailed description of how one 3-year-old coped with the traumatic events associated with an accidental amputation of his finger, which included surgery to reattach the finger, being given injections of penicillin over the course of treatment, and repeated visits to the doctor's office to have the dressing changed.

The office visits were particularly difficult for the child, in part because of the doctor's decision not to allow the mother in the treatment room. At the beginning of the appointment when the child was taken to the treatment room, he typically had to be pried off his mother while screaming, "I want my Mommy!" About a week after these visits began, the boy told his mother that an elf named Woody had appeared in the treatment room to keep him company. After this first appearance, Woody turned up on a regular basis, both at home and at the doctor's office.

> Playing doctor, Sam said to me, "You take your medicine and you won't have to have penicillin. You have to stay in the hospital all day and all night." When I asked him how I could manage to do that he told me there was a little elf, "Woody," who would stay with me, just like it was at Dr. H's office—Woody was there with him because I couldn't be with him.
>
> At Dr. H's office he cried hard when leaving me and while soaking his finger . . . I asked him why he had made such a fuss at the doctor's office and he said, "Because Woody wasn't there—he was on vacation." Later, when we were making brownies he said, "Woody used to make brownies when he was a little boy—he told me that at Dr. H's office."[37]

Woody clearly played an important role in Sam's ability to cope with his injury. Once Woody started showing up in the treatment room, Sam's crying and fussing abated, and he became focused on asking the doctor detailed questions about the stitches, the shaping of the new fingernail, and so on. Later on, when Sam started school he experienced some difficulty with the separation from his mother, and once again Woody helped out by showing up at school when Sam needed him.

Imaginary Friends of Children Coping with War-Related Experiences

In her book on play therapy, *Playing for Their Lives*, Dorothy Singer describes how pretend play can serve as a way for children to make sense of what is happening in their lives and to process emotions associated with current circumstances. In the case of maltreatment, the trauma experienced by children is private, personal, and often secretive.[38] In the context of war, the experience of trauma is a collective one. The security, consistency, and rhythms of day-to-day life are violently disrupted for children and adults alike. One of Singer's examples, a particularly grim one, is that children living in the concentration camp at Auschwitz during World War II were observed playing a game called "going to the gas chamber."[39] In another case study from World War II, a child in England created a brood of imaginary animals that were dependent on her for care. This child was temporarily displaced from home during the war, and lived for 18 months in a nursery set up for children before being reunited with her mother and stepfather. The return home was difficult, as she missed her caretaker and the other children in the nursery. According to her mother, she had

> ... [a] brood of imaginary animals, cats and chickens which live with her and share all her activities. It is quite uncanny the way she looks at them, just as though she could really see them. Often, she tells me off for clumsily kicking one of them or I have to lift them up over the pavement and am told that "they are too small," or they can't manage.[40]

The interpretation given to these fantasies was that in assuming a caretaking role for these imaginary animals—helping them and looking after their needs—the little girl was somehow coping with her traumatic history and adjusting to her changed circumstances.

These speculations are based on examples from a war that occurred a long time ago, but studies conducted during the Israeli/Lebanon conflict in 2006[41] provide similar accounts. Israeli children (2–7 years old) who had lived in temporary refugee camps experienced high levels of trauma-induced stress, including trouble sleeping, separation anxiety, disinterest in play, and increased startle responses. Instead of collecting descriptions of spontaneously created imaginary friends, Avi Sadeh and his colleagues investigated the possibility that an intervention in which children were guided in the use of a stuffed animal as a personified object might help them transition to their lives back at home. The children were randomly assigned to either a Standard Educational Intervention or a "Huggy Puppy Intervention." In the Standard Educational Intervention, the children's parents were provided with information about how to address their children's fears and anxieties as they returned to normal life after the war. In the Huggy Puppy Intervention, each child was given a stuffed dog that was described as being far from home, emotionally vulnerable, and in need of care. Children in this group were asked to care for the dog by playing with it, hugging it, and sleeping with it at night.

After three weeks, children in the Huggy Puppy Intervention experienced a larger drop in the number and severity of their stress-related symptoms compared with the children in the Standard Education Intervention. The more attached that children were to the stuffed dog, the more successful the intervention was in reducing children's symptoms. These results were later replicated by Sadeh and his colleagues with another larger group of elementary school children who had also been adversely affected by the war. According to Dr. Shai Hen-Gal, a clinical psychologist who worked on the Huggy Puppy Intervention, taking on a caretaking role with an imaginary friend allowed children to shift their attention from their own thoughts and feelings toward the needs of the imaginary other:[42]

> It's important to remember that every person, and especially every child, has a strong natural inner compass that directs them towards growth, that allows them to successfully overcome difficult life events. Therefore, often a brief intervention is enough to get them back on track for development and flourishing.

One question is the extent to which the details of this particular description of the stuffed dog are essential for the success of this intervention. Does the Huggy Puppy *need* to be described as vulnerable and in need of care in order to activate children's internal coping resources? Our work with foster care children showed that spontaneously created imaginary friends did not include any that were primarily in need of care. Instead, the imaginary friends were powerful allies, or the children and imaginary friends took care of each other. In a study investigating peer relations by Tracy Gleason and Maria Kalpidou, parents reported that preschool-aged children in caretaking relationships with their imaginary friends used less competent coping strategies (e.g., aggression) compared with children who had more equal friendships with their imaginary friends.[43] Although vulnerable imaginary friends were effective in the study by Sadeh and colleagues, maybe competent imaginary friends might be even more successful in helping children cope with stressors beyond their control.

Kushnir and Sadeh tested this idea with an intervention study focused on alleviating young children's nighttime fears, one of the symptoms associated with war-related trauma.[44] Over one hundred 4-to-6-year-old Israeli children were randomly assigned to one of two intervention conditions: (1) the original Huggy Puppy Intervention or (2) a modified version in which the Huggy Puppy was described as a competent friend who could help the children cope with their fears. These two groups of children were compared with children who had not yet participated in the intervention (they were on the waitlist). The results showed that both types of cover stories were effective. Children in both interventions showed a significant reduction in their nighttime fears from the very start (one week following the intervention) that was still evident six months later.[45]

Although not all children spontaneously create imaginary friends to cope with life's challenges, these interventions suggest that guiding children to use personified objects to cope with trauma is possible. The success of these interventions is promising in that they did not require substantial fiscal or human resources; they can be implemented fairly quickly, so long as there is access to the stuffed animals and adults to talk to the children about them.[46] Given the relatively low costs of these interventions, it might be possible to positively impact children coping with a range of adverse experiences. And in fact, Dr. Hen Gal has now conducted Huggy

Puppy interventions with children in Gaza border communities, in Japan following the tsunami in 2011, and with children fleeing the war in Ukraine. An intervention that is built on a natural strength of young children—their imaginations—was beneficial in helping them cope with the negative effects of being exposed to war and related trauma.

Summary

Imaginary friends provide companionship and comfort during stressful life events and might serve as a protective factor for children in high-risk social environments and a vehicle for coping with both acute and chronic stressors. Given that having an imaginary friend can function as a way to cope with trauma, and the well-established links between trauma and dissociation, the creation of imaginary friends has sometimes been seen as a potential early marker of pathological dissociation. But having an imaginary friend is better characterized as an early marker of creativity and social understanding (Chapter 5) than as the first sign of mental illness. And intervention work by Sadeh and his colleagues provides compelling evidence that children's imaginary friends can have a real and potentially lasting impact in helping children deal with adversity.[47]

In many of the clinical examples, the strength of children's attachment might raise questions about the extent to which the imaginary friends had become real for the children who created them. Even when there are no mental health issues, parents and other adults sometimes wonder if imaginative children have a firm grasp of the distinction between fantasy and reality. More specifically, do children understand that their imaginary friends are pretend? This question is the topic of the next chapter.

Notes

1. Bretherton, I. (1989). Pretense: The form and function of make-believe play. *Developmental Review, 9*, 383–401.
Partington, J. T., & Grant, C. (1984). Imaginary playmates and other useful fantasies. *Play in Animals and Humans*, 217–240.
2. Benson, R. M., & Pryor, D. B. (1973). When friends fall out: Developmental interference with the function of some imaginary companions. *Journal of the American Psychoanalytic Association, 21*, 457–468.
3. Frank, A. (2003). *The diary of Anne Frank: The revised critical edition*. Doubleday Books.
4. Imperiale, N. (1992, September 30). Imaginary pals say lots about kids, *Orlando Sentinel Tribune*, p. e1.
5. Singer, D. G. (1993). *Playing for their lives: Helping troubled children through play therapy*. The Free Press.
6. Ibid., pp. 135–136.

7. Nagera, H. (1969). The imaginary companion: Its significance for ego development and conflict resolution. *The Psychoanalytic Study of the Child, 24*, 165-196. https://doi.org/10.1080/00797308.1969.11822691
8. Susan eventually faded away when Miriam developed a very close friendship with a child at her school.
9. Nagera, H. (1969). The imaginary companion: Its significance for ego development and conflict resolution. *The Psychoanalytic Study of the Child*, p. 170.
10. Bender, L., & Vogel, B. F. (1941). Imaginary companions of children. *American Journal of Orthopsychiatry, 11*, 56–65, p. 60.
11. Putnam, F. W. (1989). *Diagnosis and treatment of Multiple Personality Disorder.* Guilford Press.
12. Sanders, B. (1992). The imaginary companion experience in multiple personality disorder. *Dissociation, 5*, 159–162.
    It is not clear if the prevalence in this population is due to better accuracy in remembering imaginary friends from childhood (since rates in retrospective reports are typically lower) or an actual higher prevalence in these populations. It is possible that traumatized children keep their imaginary friends longer than nontraumatized children and thus would be remembered better.
13. Trujillo, K., Lewis, D. O., Yeager, C. A., & Gidlow, B. (1996). Imaginary companions of school boys and boys with Dissociative Identity Disorder/Multiple Personality Disorder: A normal to pathological continuum. *Child and Adolescent Psychiatric Clinics of North America, 5*, 375–391.
14. McLewin, L. A., & Muller, R. T. (2006). Childhood trauma, imaginary companions, and the development of pathological dissociation. *Aggression and Violent Behavior, 11*, 531–545. https://doi.org/10.1016/j.avb.2006.02.001
    Trujillo, K., Lewis, D. O., Yeager, C. A., & Gidlow, B. (1996). Imaginary companions of school boys and boys with Dissociative Identity Disorder/Multiple Personality Disorder: A normal to pathological continuum. *Child and Adolescent Psychiatric Clinics of North America.*
15. Nagera, H. (1969). The imaginary companion: Its significance for ego development and conflict resolution. *The Psychoanalytic Study of the Child.*
16. Sawa, T., Oae, H., Abiru, T., Ogawa, T., & Takahashi, T. (2004). Role of imaginary companion in promoting the psychotherapeutic process. *Psychiatry and Clinical Neurosciences, 58*(2), 145–151, p. 145.
17. McLewin, L. A., & Muller, R. T. (2006). Childhood trauma, imaginary companions, and the development of pathological dissociation. *Aggression and Violent Behavior, 11*, 531–545. https://doi.org/10.1016/j.avb.2006.02.001
18. Fisher, P. A., Burraston, B., & Pears, K. (2005). The early intervention foster care program: Permanent placement outcomes from a randomized trial. *Child Maltreatment, 10*(1), 61–71. https://doi.org/10.1177/1077559504271561
19. Shook, J. J., Vaughn, M. G., Litschge, C., Kolivoski, K., & Schelbe, L. (2009). The importance of friends among foster youth aging out of care: Cluster profiles of deviant peer associations. *Children and Youth Services Review, 31*, 284–291. https://doi.org/10.1016/j.childyouth.2008.07.024
20. Fisher, P. A., Gunnar, M. R., Dozier, M., Bruce, J., & Pears, K. C. (2006). Effects of therapeutic interventions for foster children on behavioral problems, caregiver attachment,

and stress regulatory neural systems. *Annals of the New York Academy of Sciences, 1094*(1), 215–225.

21. Aguiar, N. R., Mottweiler, C. M., Taylor, M., & Fisher, P. (2017). The imaginary companions created by children who have lived in foster care. *Imagination, Cognition and Personality, 36*(4), 340–355.
22. Families were included in the low-SES comparison group if the child lived consistently with at least one biological parent, the annual household income was no more than $30,000, parental education was less than a 4-year college degree, and the family did not have any previous involvement with child welfare services as verified by child welfare services records. Children in the low-SES group did not significantly differ in age from children who had lived in foster care.
23. Pearson, D., Rouse, H., Doswell, S., Ainsworth, C., Dawson, O., Simms, K., Edwards, L., & Faulconbridge, J. (2001). Prevalence of imaginary companions in normal child population. *Child: Care, Health and Development, 27*, 12–22. https://doi.org/10.1046/j.1365-2214.2001.00167.x
24. Taylor, M., Hulette, A. C., & Dishion, T. J. (2010). Longitudinal outcomes of young high-risk adolescents with imaginary companions. *Developmental Psychology, 46*, 1632–1636.
Gupta, A., & Desai, N. G. (2006). Pathological fantasy friend phenomenon. *International Journal of Psychiatry in Clinical Practice, 10*(2), 149–151. https://doi.org/10.1080/13651500600578961
25. Gribbon, B. (Director). (2010). *Born schizophrenic: January's story*. Homerun Entertainment.
26. Terr, L. (1990). *Too scared to cry: Psychic trauma in childhood*. Basic Books, pp. 202–203.
27. Kluft, R. P. (1984). Treatment of multiple personality disorder: A study of 33 cases. *Psychiatric Clinics of North America, 7*, 9–29.
28. Huolman, M., & Peltonen, K. (2022). Dissociative features related to imaginary companions in the assessment of childhood adversity and dissociation: A pilot study. *European Journal of Trauma & Dissociation, 6*(4), 100295.
29. Silberg, J. L. (2021). *The child survivor: Healing developmental trauma and dissociation*. Routledge.
McLewin, L. A., & Muller, R. T. (2006). Childhood trauma, imaginary companions, and the development of pathological dissociation. *Aggression and Violent Behavior, 11*, 531–545. https://doi.org/10.1016/j.avb.2006.02.00
Trujillo, K., Lewis, D. O., Yeager, C. A., & Gidlow, B. (1996). Imaginary companions of school boys and boys with Dissociative Identity Disorder/Multiple Personality Disorder: A normal to pathological continuum. *Child and Adolescent Psychiatric Clinics of North America, 5*, 375–391.
Sanders, B. (1992). The imaginary companion experience in multiple personality disorder. *Dissociation, 5*, 159–162.
30. Taylor, M., Carlson, S. M., & Shawber, A. B. (2007). Autonomy and control in children's interactions with imaginary companions. In I. Roth (Ed.), *Imaginative minds* (pp. 81–100). British Academy and Oxford University Press.
31. Carlson, S. M., Tahiroglu, D., & Taylor. M. (2008). Links between dissociation and role play in a non-clinical sample of preschool children. *Journal of Trauma and Dissociation, 9*, 149–171.

32. Putnam, F. W. (1989). *Diagnosis and treatment of Multiple Personality Disorder*. Guilford Press.
33. Lovinger, S. L. (1983). Multiple personality: A theoretical view. *Psychotherapy: Theory, Research & Practice, 20*(4), 425–434. https://doi.org/10.1037/h0088503
    Sanders, B. (1992). The imaginary companion experience in multiple personality disorder.
34. White, J., & Allers, C. T. (1994). Play therapy with abused children: A review of the literature. *Journal of Counseling & Development, 72*(4), 390–394.
35. Terr, L. (1990). *Too scared to cry: Psychic trauma in childhood*. Basic Books, p. 238.
36. Clark, C. D. (1998). Childhood imagination in the face of chronic illness. In J. de Rivers & T. R. Sarbin (Eds.), *Believed-in imaginings: The narrative construction of reality* (pp. 87–100). American Psychological Association.
    Clark, C. D. (2003). *In sickness and in play: Children coping with chronic illness*. Rutgers University Press.
37. Murphy, L. B. (1965). *The widening world of childhood: Paths toward mastery*. Basic Books, p. 125.
38. Singer, D. G. (1993). *Playing for their lives: Helping troubled children through play therapy*. Free Press.
39. Opie, I., & Opie, P. (1959). *The lore and language of school children*. Oxford University Press.
40. Nagera, H. (1969). The imaginary companion: Its significance for ego development and conflict resolution. *The Psychoanalytic Study of the Child*. See pp. 187–188.
41. Sadeh, A., Hen-Gal, S., & Tikotzky, L. (2008). Young children's reactions to war-related stress: A survey and assessment of an innovative intervention. *Pediatrics, 121*, 46–53.
42. Shtarkman, R. (2022, April 24). This puppet from Israel helps Ukrainian kids cope with unspeakable trauma. *Haaretz*. https://www.haaretz.com/israel-news/2022-04-24/ty-article-magazine/a-doll-from-israel-helps-ukrainian-children-cope-with-unspeakable-trauma/00000180-5bee-de8c-a1aa-dbee4c070000
43. Gleason, T. R., & Kalpidou, M. (2014). Imaginary companions and young children's coping and competence. *Social Development, 23*(4), 820–839.
44. Kushnir, J., & Sadeh, A. (2012). Assessment of brief interventions for nighttime fears in preschool children. *European Journal of Pediatrics, 171*, 67–75.
45. The Huggy Puppy Intervention builds on a type of play that is familiar for most children—interacting with a stuffed animal. Paige Davis and her colleagues wondered if it would be possible to help children create an imaginary friend that was invisible. Over a three-month period, nine children were guided through activities designed to promote the development of an invisible friend (e.g., drawing them). Eight of the nine children created invisible friends that were sustained for several months and that Davis and colleagues described as "qualitatively equivalent" to invisible friends that are create spontaneously. There was no information collected from parents in this small exploratory study, so we don't know the extent to which children interacted with the imaginary friends at home outside of the intervention context. Children can sometimes make up imaginary friends on the spot when asked to do so but do not carry on with this play at home or elsewhere. Wigger (2019) reported that children resisted this type of suggestion (e.g., "it just didn't work . . . it was boring; he never built anything!"). However, we don't know of any other study in which there was such an extensive 3-month long attempt to encourage this type of

play. We should note that Davis was primarily interested in whether children would create invisible friends when instructed to do so. The study did not investigate if the children derived any benefit from the activity.

Davis, P. E., King, N., Meins, E., & Fernyhough, C. (2023). 'When my mummy and daddy aren't looking at me when I do my maths she helps me"; Children can be taught to create imaginary companions: An exploratory study. *Infant and Child Development, 32*(2), e2390.

Wigger, J. B. (2019). *Invisible companions: Encounters with imaginary friends, gods, ancestors, and angels.* Stanford University Press.

46. Dr. Hen Gal indicates in the following article that these specific Huggy Puppies are the most effective in helping children cope because they look sad: Shtarkman, R. (2022, April 24). This puppet from Israel helps Ukrainian kids cope with unspeakable trauma. *Haaretz.*

47. Kushnir, J., & Sadeh, A. (2012). Assessment of brief interventions for nighttime fears in preschool children. *European Journal of Pediatrics.*

Sadeh, A., Hen-Gal, S., & Tikotzky, L. (2008). Young children's reactions to war-related stress: A survey and assessment of an innovative intervention. *Pediatrics, 121,* 46–53.

Chapter 8
Do Children Think Their Imaginary Friends Are Real?

> Alice laughed: "There's no use trying," she said; "one can't believe impossible things." "I daresay you haven't had much practice," said the Queen. "When I was younger, I always did it for half an hour a day. Why, sometimes I've believed as many as six impossible things before breakfast."
> (*Through the Looking Glass* by Lewis Carroll)[1]

On the first leg of a family trip, a 6-year-old boy inadvertently left behind his small stuffed dog at a picnic site. The family had traveled many miles before the absence was noted, so the parents vetoed the child's request to go back immediately to retrieve the toy. The little boy initially handled this decision pretty well, but over the course of the weekend, he was preoccupied with thoughts about what the dog might be doing to pass the time while waiting for the family's return. The fate of his pretend friend weighed on his mind. Two days later, the family embarked on the return journey home. As they neared the location of the picnic, the boy's excitement and the parents' uneasiness mounted. They warned their son that the toy might be gone, but nothing they could say affected their son's anticipation. When they reached the site, the little dog was seated at the picnic table, looking none the worse for wear. The child was overjoyed and hugged him tightly the rest of the way home. Although the parents were relieved, their son's reaction was worrisome to them. What did it mean that he was so sure the dog would be "waiting" for them at the picnic site? Wasn't his joy at the reunion a little overblown for a child his age?

Episodes like this fuel parents' concern that their children's relationships with pretend friends are not completely healthy. In many homes, hours are spent each week searching for a misplaced stuffed animal whose presence seems to be a prerequisite for the child's happiness and the parents' peace of mind. Some children expect the whole family to wait at restaurants until a table large enough to accommodate their invisible friends, as well as the rest of the family, is available, or they insist that the TV be turned on whenever the family goes out so that the pretend friend won't be lonely when nobody is home. For many parents, flickers of worry are associated with such demands, as well as with other evidence of the intense relationship between their child and an imaginary friend. Is the child fully aware that the imaginary friend is "just" pretend?

Interacting with an imaginary friend is only one example of the many types of experiences in children's lives that involve the distinction between fantasy and reality. Even very young children are inundated with fantasy information, often mixed seamlessly with real-world content. Children in American homes watch videos portraying mermaids and superheroes and are read story books that are filled with talking animals who are dressed and act like people. They participate in family rituals where such characters as the Tooth Fairy, Santa Claus, and the Easter Bunny figure prominently and are taken to magic shows where rabbits emerge from hats and coins disappear. Adults tell them about entities that used to exist (e.g., dinosaurs), might exist (e.g., extraterrestrial life), and never existed (unicorns).[2] They need to learn the difference between events that are improbable (e.g., a person drinking onion juice) and events that are impossible (e.g., a person drinking lightning).[3] There is so much to sort out!

Given all these different kinds of fantasy contexts, keeping track of what is real and what is not is a substantial undertaking. Nevertheless, young children are surprisingly adept at it. For example, 3- and 4-year-old children are impressive in their early understanding of the words "real" and "pretend" their ability to answer questions about the differences between real and pretend entities, and their understanding that imagining is a private mental process occurring in a person's mind.[4] When asked to sort a variety of objects into real and not-real boxes, they put the ghosts, monsters, and witches in the "make-believe" box and the dogs, houses, and bears in the "real-life" box.[5] At 3 years of age, children realize that knowledge reflects reality more accurately than imagination, and objects they have been asked to imagine have not materialized in real life.[6] They do not use fantastical explanations for everyday events when they are aware of more naturalistic ones, and they can accurately distinguish between magical outcomes (e.g., a marble is moved from one box to another by a person thinking hard) and ordinary outcomes (e.g., the marble is moved by the person's hands).[7] And even toddlers are not confused when adults talk to stuffed animals as if the toys could understand, act as if mud pie is something desirable to eat, and react to a child's gentle push by falling violently to the ground. When a mother speaks into a banana as if it were a telephone, the child does not become confused about either bananas or phones.[8]

But these same preschoolers who are so comfortable with the dual worlds of fantasy and reality in their pretend play might believe there really is a Santa Claus or wake up wondering if a dream was real. They might have difficulty distinguishing animals that once existed (e.g., dinosaurs) and creatures that belong to the realm of fantasy (e.g., monsters). They might mistake the real events portrayed in a television program as fictional or misconstrue the fantastical stories read to them at bedtime as involving real-life characters and events. And if an adult plays the role of a roaring lion too well in a pretend game, the child might become truly frightened and start to cry. Many authors have been struck by these difficulties and conclude that children cannot distinguish fantasy from reality. This claim crops up in myriad contexts, baldly stated as truth in newspaper columns, magazines for parents, as well books on child development. Benjamin Spock, the respected advisor of American parents, wrote,

> This is an appropriate time, while we are discussing imaginary companions, to think about how rudimentary small children's grasp of reality is. It is difficult for inexperienced parents to realize that children sense very little difference between something that they have imagined and something that has actually happened.... One of the most important everyday jobs that parents have to take on as a matter of course is to teach their children—gradually over the months and years—to distinguish between fantasy and fact."[9]

Dr. Spock was not the only child expert to support this position. Developmental psychologists also belonged to the ranks of those who believed children were incompetent when it came to negotiating the boundary between fantasy and reality. Jean Piaget, the famous Swiss psychologist, described young children as living "in a dream world of imagination" and argued that children did not master the distinction between fantasy and reality until about age 12.[10] Similarly, according to psychologists Newson and Newson,

> On the whole, the four-year-old is protected from real dangers in a way which will necessarily have to change once he starts school; but from the perils which are conjured up by his imagination there is little protection, and it is to these that he is most vulnerable. He is probably now at the peak of his imaginative powers, without the firm grasp on reality which can allow an older child to subdue its fears; and because of this, the adult's reasoned assurances are often quite ineffective in calming a panicky four-year-old.[11]

So where do imaginary friends belong in this assortment of contradictory findings and claims? To answer this question, we first briefly discuss children's ability to negotiate the fantasy/reality distinction in cultural myths, storybooks, television programs, and joint pretend play with other people. This discussion provides the context for considering children's understanding of this distinction more specifically as it relates to their imaginary friends.

Cultural Myths and Rituals

An interesting blend of fantasy and reality occurs with cultural myths, such as those involving Santa Claus, the Easter Bunny and the Tooth Fairy. These myths have clear cues to fantasy in their content, but the characters are presented to children as real and involve rituals that provide both direct and indirect evidence of the characters' "real" existence.[12] For example, in the Western/European canon, Santa Claus is described to children as if he were a real person who lives at the North Pole and who makes a yearly distribution of presents depending upon the child's behavior. The entire community pitches in to provide direct evidence that Santa is real and encourage children to believe in him. Children are taken to meet Santa in person at malls, see him interviewed on TV, and even might have the chance to talk to him on the phone.[13] Parents and other family members also provide indirect evidence with rituals such as mailing children's letters to Santa, tracking Santa's location online, and leaving cookies out for him on Christmas Eve.

Parents' commitment to the Santa Claus myth was demonstrated in the reactions elicited by a gym teacher at an elementary school in Washington state who told his students there was no Santa.[14] The entire community was outraged. One angry parent was quoted as saying "I think the majority of this community wants their kids to believe in Santa. Nobody has the right to rape our kids of that belief." In an attempt to undo some of the "damage," teachers read *The Polar Express* by Chris van Allsburg[15] to the children. In this story, a child who has been told by a friend that there is no Santa takes a trip on a train to the North Pole where he sees Santa and his elves for himself and brings home a bell from Santa's sleigh. Movies are also sometimes used to instill belief. Nonbelievers learn there really is a Santa Claus in *Miracle on 34th Street* (the classic example) or *The Santa Clause*. There can also be a negative message about nonbelievers, either explicitly or implicitly: if the child fails to believe, maybe Santa will fail to visit. The consequences of not believing in Santa might be ones that children do not want to risk.

But do young children actually believe that a character like Santa Claus is real? Yes, they do. In some surveys, results are based on the parents' perceptions of their children's beliefs, while others rely on interviews with the children themselves. Regardless of method, the results show that the majority of preschoolers whose cultural background includes the celebration of Christmas[16] believe that Santa Claus is real. In a study with children, 85% of the 4-year-olds strongly believed in Santa, 10% were nonbelievers, and 5% were categorized as transitional (i.e., the child was not sure and told the interviewer the evidence for both sides of the debate).[17] In a study in which parents were asked about their children's (aged 4–6 years) beliefs, 81% reported that their children believed in Santa. In the same survey, 25% of the 8-year-olds were believers, 55% were nonbelievers, and 20% were transitional.[18]

Many young children also believe in the reality of other fantasy characters (e.g., Easter Bunny, Tooth Fairy). In her book on cultural myths, Cindy Dell Clark[19] presents examples of children commenting on the existence of these characters. One child speculated that the Tooth Fairy probably lived in a dentist's office ("If she's an inch small like I think she is, she'd be in a drawer somewhere").[20] Clark also documented the practices of parents who want their children to believe in the Tooth Fairy and other cultural favorites. One parent reported that she wrote notes to her children in very tiny script signed by the Tooth Fairy. Another mother fabricated the following story when her child became upset about losing a tooth down a drain:

> He couldn't leave his tooth for the Tooth Fairy if he didn't have the tooth....And I said, "It's OK, Jimmy, I'll call Uncle Joe ... and maybe he could take the sink apart and get the tooth." I wasn't really going to ask him to take the sink apart, but he had to get to school. And then I told him that night "they couldn't get it apart. But it happened to a friend of ours, when they did take it apart, they couldn't find the tooth anyway. But maybe if you left a letter for the Tooth Fairy." So he did and taped it to the front door.[21]

As Clark points out, parents perpetuate these cultural myths as much for themselves as for their children. Parents enjoy vicariously experiencing the excitement of a visit from Santa or the Tooth Fairy along with their children. Some parents associate belief in fantasy characters with the innocence of childhood and do not look forward to the time when their children would no longer believe.

> I think I might, the day I have to explain about Santa and the Tooth Fairy, I think I'll be a little crushed. Because it's almost like a magic spell I've broken a part of, another sign of growing up, when this [ends,] the fairy tale, the imagination.[22]

Still, the logical impossibilities in cultural myths do not escape the notice of even quite young children. How does Santa get into homes without chimneys or manage to transport all the toys needed for his task on one sleigh in a single night to children all around the world? How does the Tooth Fairy know when a child has lost a tooth? The authors of some children's books have developed stories that present ways to deal with these difficulties. For example, *The Real Tooth Fairy* by Marilyn Kaye[23] explains why a child who is pretending to be asleep might see her parent, instead of a fairy, exchange money for the tooth under the pillow. The child in the story is told that the Tooth Fairy changes her appearance to that of someone the child loves when she makes her visits because once a child woke up during her visit and was frightened to see a stranger in the room.

Overall, the majority of children under 8 years of age believe that characters in cultural myths are real; however, some children believe more than others. One might suspect that children who engage in fantasy in other parts of their lives might be particularly likely to believe in cultural myths, but the evidence suggests this is not the case. Children who spend a lot of time pretending, who have imaginary friends, or report having many dreams are no more likely to believe in fantasy characters than other children.[24] In one study, high-fantasy children actually were better able to identify the characters in cultural myths as make-believe than other children.[25] This finding suggests that "children with a high fantasy orientation might be viewed as experts within that domain; although they are intrigued by the fantasy world, they may be sophisticated in their ability to navigate it."[26] The extent to which parents promote these beliefs is a better predictor of how fully the child believes than the child's overall interest in fantasy. The children of parents who support and encourage their children to think fantasy characters are real (e.g., take them to the mall to see

Santa) are more likely to express belief than the children of parents who discourage or are ambivalent about their children's acceptance of cultural myths.

Jacqueline Woolley and her colleagues[27] avoided some of the methodological problems in studies of belief in cultural myths (e.g., differences in familiarity with the myth and parental practices) by inventing a new myth and controlling children's exposure to it. Preschool children were told a story about the Candy Witch—a nice witch who only ate candy and was able to replenish her supplies by visiting children's homes on Halloween night and trading toys for the children's candy. The children learned about the Candy Witch at school, saw a drawing of her, and participated in a school art project with a Candy Witch theme. At home, their parents supported the Candy Witch story by calling her on the phone to arrange for a Halloween visit, and making the toys-for-candy exchange after their children were in bed. The older preschoolers were more likely than the younger ones to believe the Candy Witch was real and more likely to be convinced about her reality by an actual visit of the Candy Witch to their home on Halloween. Woolley and colleagues interpreted this finding as supporting the view that it takes a degree of cognitive maturity to believe a story about something that is outside everyday experience but that has cultural support. Children who believed other cultural myths were also more likely to believe this one, suggesting that these children might have recognized similarities between the Candy Witch and other characters who they believed were real (e.g., the Candy Witch and Santa Claus both come at night and leave toys) and be receptive to the possibility of another unusual character.

Should we interpret belief in characters such as Santa Claus as evidence that a child has a poor grasp of fantasy and reality? We don't think so. Children are not the originators of cultural myths; they are told about them in the same way they are told about characters and events that are meant to be understood as real or to really have happened (e.g., the way they are told about dinosaurs or stories from the Bible). In addition, parents take concrete steps to blur the fantasy–reality boundary by leaving traces of the characters' actions.[28] Actually, it is quite impressive that by 8 years of age, the majority of children have figured out that Santa Claus and other fantasy characters are not real.[29]

Storybooks and Television

In addition to cultural myths centering on special occasions or holidays, young children listen to or watch many types of narratives that unfold in picture books and on screens with content that blurs fantasy and reality.[30] Children's books and films are populated with talking animals, mermaids, dragons, witches, ghosts, monsters, fairies, and other fantasy characters (e.g., Batman, Mickey Mouse). In some cases, belief in the characters featured in these narratives is explicitly encouraged. Consider the power attributed to children's belief in fairies in the story of Peter Pan. When children affirm their belief by clapping their hands, Tinkerbell is brought back from the brink of death. In *The Velveteen Rabbit*,[31] the love of a child for his stuffed bunny transforms the toy into a living creature; similarly, love by his maker transformed Pinocchio from wood to human flesh and blood.

Across a variety of different kinds of storytelling media, 3-year-olds exhibit considerable confusion about fantasy and reality. A child commenting on the distinction between fantasy and reality on *Sesame Street* explains, "I know that Big Bird isn't real. That's just a costume. There's just a plain bird inside."[32] In some studies, children have been shown pictures from realistic and fantasy storybooks and asked to categorize the depicted events.[33] The 3-year-olds in one study reported that a moose cooking in a kitchen and a girl riding a horse were equally likely to happen in real life.[34] By 5 years of age, children are much better at identifying events as realistic or fantasy but sometimes report that real-life events (e.g., being questioned by the police) could not actually happen. In addition, children often claimed that scary events, whether they were realistic or fantastical, could not happen in real life.[35] In studies in which children were read the whole story (instead of being asked to categorize individual pictures), the most common error was also to claim that real-life events and characters were fantasy.[36]

Children's ability to distinguish fantasy and reality in material presented in film or on television shows a similar pattern. In one study, children named their favorite TV show and then were asked a series of questions about whether what happened on the show was in real life or just on TV.[37] The 5-year-olds mostly assumed that all televised events or stories were fiction. Similarly, according to the *New York Times* (June 12, 2005), many children assumed that the documentary *The March of the Penguins* was a story created with animation and special effects. On the other hand, when asked questions about the characters, the same 5-year-olds tended to underestimate how much the actors were following scripts and seemed confused about there being a difference between the characters that actors play on television and their off-screen life.

Confusion between characters and actors isn't unique to children (see Chapter 10). An occupational hazard of playing a nasty character on television is that sometimes these actors are treated badly when encountered by viewers of the program. This phenomenon is not new and not restricted to television roles. In 1841 when Little Nell in Dickens' serialization of *The Old Curiosity Shop* died, a sense of loss swept England. Dickens received so many letters from mourners he felt like he had committed a real murder.[38]

In addition to stories that are primarily for entertainment, other narratives are designed to teach real-world information that children would be unlikely to acquire firsthand (e.g., a story about exploration in the Arctic).[39] And sometimes fantasy material is used as a vehicle for teaching this information. The fantasy context is used to capture children's attention, but the message is meant to pertain to real life (e.g., morals, values, understanding of divorce, death). Thus, children are expected to extract the elements of a fantasy story that are meant to be relevant to the real world (e.g., a story about a young rabbit who learned to love her baby brother instead of resent him). Children do not always successfully make this transfer.[40] A striking example comes from research on children's understanding of instructional videos.[41] Children aged 4–6 years were shown an animated video about animal characters who initially were afraid of a three-legged dog but discovered that his disability was not contagious, he could do many tasks without help, he wanted to be treated normally, and he was good company. The goal of the video was to teach children to be accepting of people with disabilities, but only about 9% of the children got the intended message. Instead, many children reported that they had learned to be kind to three-legged dogs or that three-legged dogs are scary.

Paul Harris and his colleagues[42] have extended past work on the fantasy/reality distinction by investigating children's ability to assess what people tell them, including simple statements and descriptions, as well as more fully formed narratives. The development of general knowledge about many topics (e.g., scientific entities such as germs, microscopic animals, and black holes) relies on such "testimony" when there is no possibility for firsthand experience. Children's success in learning via testimony depends upon their ability to distinguish real-world information from fiction. Although young children have sometimes been characterized as believing everything that they are told,[43] children actually are cautious (sometimes overly so) in accepting the claims of others as veridical information about the world.[44] They tend to rely on the extent to which the new information connects in some way to their own experience or observations. The research on testimony suggests that children can be quite sensitive to the subtle cues about fantasy versus reality in the way a topic is discussed.[45] For example, when children learn about germs, there is no discussion of whether or not they exist. However, the existence of God is commented on in statements like "I believe in God." Koenig and Harris claim that such comments actually shed doubt on God's existence by calling it into question.

Social Games of Pretense

When you consider how much children need to learn about real-life people and social interactions, it starts to seem downright bizarre that they spend so much time thinking about and interacting with people that do not exist. Some years ago, Alan Leslie raised the more general point about the early emerging capacity to pretend:

> Pretending ought to strike the cognitive psychologist as a very odd sort of ability. After all, from an evolutionary point of view, there ought to be a high premium on the veridicality of cognitive processes. The perceiving, thinking organism ought, as far as possible, to get things right. Yet pretense flies in the face of this fundamental principle. In pretense we deliberately distort reality. How odd then that this ability is not the sober culmination of intellectual development but instead makes its appearance playfully and precociously at the very beginning of childhood.[46]

This is a deceptively simple observation. Leslie made the everyday behavior of young children seem exotic. He was a fish who noticed the water.

Young children's ability to understand pretend actions and statements and to act accordingly has been carefully documented in a series of experiments by Paul Harris and Robert Kavanaugh.[47] For example, children watched a pretend sequence in which a puppet tipped an empty milk carton over an empty bowl, picked up the bowl, and dumped its imaginary contents over the head of an unsuspecting stuffed monkey. Two-year-olds described the monkey as all soggy with milk, although in reality nothing came out of the milk carton and the monkey remained dry. This research shows that even very young children can comprehend a sequence of pretend actions performed by another person.

Once the game of pretense begins, children are pretty much expected to figure out for themselves which of the things their partner says and does are meant to be understood as pretense and which have to do with the real world. Sometimes the invitation to pretend is implicit in the partner's actions—a parent picks up a toy and makes it talk to the child. Other times the context of pretense is made explicit—"Let's pretend that the rock is a bear." DiLalla and Watson[48] wondered how children manage to keep track of an ongoing game of pretense while simultaneously coping with real-world demands. To study this issue, they observed the reactions of children aged 2½–6½ years of age as they played a game of pretense involving superheroes and a monster with a researcher who interrupted the game by: (1) suggesting that a table in the room being used as a tower might be changed to a cave; (2) being called out of the room briefly, leaving the child alone; and (3) suddenly pretending to be the monster instead of the child's partner in the search for the monster. The older children could handle these changes and interruptions smoothly, often incorporating them into the storyline of the game. In contrast, the 3-year-olds were confused and had difficulty coping with interruptions to their game and tended to reject the proposed changes ("No, you're not the monster"). Their response to the interruptions was often to stop playing and resist the researcher's attempt to pick up where things left off.

In social games of pretense with other children, 5-year-olds are highly skilled in assigning or taking roles, designating props, setting the scene, and building collaborative pretend play scripts.[49] They easily step in and out of their fantasy roles in ongoing games to give stage directions to other children (e.g., "No, you are supposed to be the baby").[50] They also are not confused when engaged in fantasy play with an adult who acts as if she has lost track of reality (e.g., taking a real bite out of a play dough cookie during a pretend picnic). Even 3- and 4-year-olds react strongly to this type of transgression ("Oh, you took a real bite. Now your teeth are all pink. How does it taste? Yuck, do you always eat that play dough?").[51] Their surprise was evidence that, although they were engrossed in the game of pretense, they continued to view play dough as an inedible substance and expected that their play partner would not violate the rules of the game.

Although these results indicate that young children can distinguish fantasy and reality while engaged in a game of pretense, preschool children sometimes become genuinely afraid when engaged in scary pretend play. Paul Harris and his colleagues [52] investigated this issue in a study in which children were asked to pretend there was a big scary monster inside a box, a monster that liked to bite children's fingers. Although they had previously seen that the box was empty, some children did not want to be left alone with it, and most of the children chose to poke a stick into a hole in the box rather than to use their finger. Many of the children who agreed to be left alone in the room with the box looked inside it and later told the researcher that they had wondered if there really was a monster in the box.

Note that in this procedure, the context of joint pretense was explicit. There was talk of pretending that a monster was in the box, and the researcher never acted as if, in reality, he believed there was anything in the empty box. Yet once children joined the researcher in pretending there was a monster in a box, they subsequently were apprehensive. According to Carl Johnson and Paul Harris,[53] once children create an imaginary being in their mind, the vividness of the image and the ease in recreating it makes the possibility of the entity really existing seem more plausible, and the children check inside the box just to be sure. Children act similarly even when the pretense involves nonscary pretend entities (e.g., a fairy).[54] In fact, 5- and 6-year-old children frequently examine the contents of *transparent* boxes that have previously been the location of pretend objects, although there could be no ambiguity of the actual contents.[55]

In some cases, children's apparent confusion might actually reflect a breakdown in communication between the adult asking the questions and the child who is answering. Children might interpret "Is it a real monster?" as "Is it a real pretend monster?" or "Are you pretending it is a real monster?" Maybe the child is still pretending when the researcher starts to ask "serious" test questions. A child in one study responded to a question about whether or not a monster was pretend by opening the empty box in which the child and adult had been pretending there was a monster, looking inside and replying "a real monster."[56] This child was clearly continuing to pretend although the question was meant to pertain to the real state of affairs. When the context of pretending is clearly ended[57] or someone who has not been part of the pretending asked questions,[58] children show no signs of confusion about what is real and what is pretend. For example, in one study children were asked to pretend there was a pencil in a box, and then a second adult entered the room and asked for a pencil. In response to this unambiguous request for a real pencil, children did not refer the adult to the box containing the pretend one.[59]

Overall, young children are quite competent in keeping track of the status of pretend and real entities, but without a doubt, children can become genuinely afraid when engaged in scary pretend play.[60] Perhaps maintaining the boundary between what is real and what is pretend might be especially difficult when fantasy or pretend play arouses strong emotion.[61] But emotion can be elicited by fantasy with no loss in the individual's grasp of the fantasy–reality distinction. Children, as well as adults, seek emotional experiences involving imaginary inputs that would never be enjoyed or desired if the input were real. Children become afraid in monster games but nevertheless want to play them, and some adults particularly like movies that make them feel afraid, sad, or horrified. The child who retreats from a scary game of monster may be akin to the adult who understands that the movie is fiction but walks out because it has crossed the line of what the adult experiences as the pleasurable arousal of fear.[62] In many ways, our emotions seem strangely disconnected from our knowledge. The physiological reactions of people watching a scary movie (e.g., pounding of the heart, adrenaline flowing, and muscles tensing) are those of real fear, but in no way do moviegoers act as if they feel personally endangered or feel the need to intercede in the events taking place on the screen.[63] We know the outcome of a detective movie we have seen before, yet we still have a feeling of suspense as the events unfold.[64]

According to Thalia Goldstein,[65] sad movies are pleasurable for adults because, unlike real-life sad events, which elicit a combination of sadness and anxiety, sad movies allow for an experience of sadness that is "unadulterated" by anxiety; there is no expectation or obligation for the adult viewer to intervene or respond to the sad events. Goldstein suggests that "experiencing sadness in fiction allows us to explore and understand it and this may make us more prepared to deal with it in our real lives."[66] Similarly, in role play, children might work through and make sense of events happening to them, gaining a sense of mastery and understanding of their own experiences (see Chapter 5).[67] An appreciation of the pretend status of the simulation allows for the safe exploration of emotional space. Although the emotional reactions to imagined and real input can be similar, the benefits of role play and simulation likely depend partly on maintaining a clear distinction between what is real and what is pretend.

If children's grasp of reality is not faulty, then trying to calm a frightened child by assuring her that a scary pretend entity is not real is likely to be ineffective. Children might be well aware that ghosts and monsters don't exist, but when they think about them, they are scared anyway. On the other hand, children and adults might differ in how they interpret the experience of fear elicited by fantasy material. The experience of a strong emotional response to the fantasy might confuse children and result in their being less sure about what is real. Sometimes it might help if parents are able to work within the pretense context and change the nature of how the entity is conceptualized—help children imagine the entity as having characteristics that make it less scary. For example, Golomb and Kuersten[68] found that some children were able to manage fear elicited by a scary game of pretense involving a monster by changing the nature of the game. Children, who appeared genuinely afraid, changed the emotional tone of the play by describing the monster as "a little beast" (that was subsequently destroyed in a play oven), or as being friendly.[69]

Imaginary Friends

"Real isn't how you are made," said the Skin Horse. "It's a thing that happens to you. When a child loves you for a long, long time, not just to play with, but REALLY loves you, then you become Real."

The Velveteen Rabbit[70]

Our discussion of cultural myths, storybooks, television, and social games of pretense is just a sampling of the many fantasy/reality distinctions that confront children. Overall, children are reasonably successful in negotiating the many variations. But what about imaginary friends? Are children aware that their imaginary friends are make-believe? There are several reasons why adults might sometimes wonder about the child's understanding of the imaginary friend as fictional. One reason has to do with the strong emotions elicited by these friends. Children express great love for their imaginary friends. In addition, when they are asked explicit questions about their experience of an invisible friend (e.g., Can you see her the way you see me? Do you think I can see her right now?), the majority of the children claim that both they and the researcher can see and touch their imaginary friends.[71] However, many of the children in this study also explicitly told the researcher that the imaginary friend was not real (e.g., "she's not here for real"; "we're just pretending"). So, on the one hand, these children reported they could see their friend the same way they could see the researcher, but the same children cautioned the researcher in an aside that the friend was not real.

Other signs suggest that even quite young children never completely lose touch with the fantasy status of their imaginary friends. Even the fact that they readily answer the question, "Do you have a pretend friend?" by describing imaginary friends indicates that they think of the friends as pretend. We have the distinct impression that after children spend a period of time being interviewed about an imaginary friend by a researcher who listens carefully and takes notes, they begin to wonder if the researcher might be confused. At some point during the interview, children are apt to clarify by saying "it's just pretend you know" or "she isn't real." Even when children do not use the term "pretend friend" to refer to their companion, the pretend status is frequently acknowledged up front, as illustrated in the following exchange with a 5-year-old girl:

> RESEARCHER: Do you have a pretend friend?
> CHILD: No. . . . Well, I only have my house ghost.
> RESEARCHER: Your house ghost. Is your house ghost pretend or real?
> CHILD: Pretend.
> RESEARCHER: Does your house ghost have a name?
> CHILD: George.
> RESEARCHER: And is George a stuffed animal or a doll or is George completely pretend?
> CHILD: He's just pretend.
> RESEARCHER: He's invisible?
> CHILD: Yeah.
> RESEARCHER: Okay. And is George a person, an animal, or something else?
> CHILD: He's just a house ghost.

How often do children explicitly comment on the fictional nature of their imaginary friends? To find out, Marjorie and her colleagues[72] reviewed the interviews of 86 children (4–6 years old) who were categorized as having invisible friends in three

Table 8.1 Four- and five-year-old children's spontaneous references to the fantasy status of their imaginary friends

---

"I can pretend he's whatever I want him to be."
"I just imagination."
"She does not talk because she's not a real baby."
"She is really not real, just a funny play bear."
"I made it up."
"I just made him up in my head."
"She's just my imaginary friend."
"It's just pretend."
"Her is a fake animal."
"It's really just because it's pretend."
"He's not in real life."
"She pretends that she's real."
"I pretend they're real but they're not."

---

studies and found that 39.5% of the children spontaneously and explicitly pointed out the pretend status of their invisible friends (see Table 8.1).

Next, the transcripts of the interviews were carefully examined for any indications that the children were confused about the pretend status of their invisible friends. Instead of confusion, it was rare for children to say anything that suggested they thought their pretend friends were real. Of the 86 children in this study, it happened four times. One child described a vivid invisible friend named Yosa, a little boy who was always there at his side and, in fact, was present at the time of the interview. This child referred to Yosa as a pretend friend and said that he had "made him up," but he also said, "Sometimes he turns real and he talks real so everybody can hear him." Similarly, a second child described her friend Emma as "pretend" but commented, "She's actually real to me, but she's invisible to my mom and sister."

The remaining two children showed more significant signs of confusion about their invisible friends. In one case, the child said "no" when asked if she had a pretend friend, but her mother reported that the child had many pretend friends called "Sailor Scouts" (characters in a Japanese animation movie). When asked why the child did not mention the Sailor Scouts during the original interview, the parent said that the child "sometimes won't admit that they are pretend." In the follow-up interview with the child, she described Phoenix (a made-up Sailor Scout, not actually one of the characters in the movie), who was "really beautiful and good at defending." The child said that she met Phoenix when "we were walking and we bonked heads and became friends." Overall, this child did not seem completely sure about the fantasy status of the invisible friend.

Only one child clearly and unambiguously believed that her invisible friend was real. When initially asked if she had a pretend friend, this child paused and replied, "there's a real friend that I have, but she's invisible," and she went on to describe a little girl named Carly who she met one day when she saw Carly walking on the sidewalk ("I only can see her; nobody else"). Carly did not like where she was living, so she moved into the child's house. The child described Carly's physical appearance (e.g., "Her body is orange and her tummy is kind of skinny, her hands are black, she looks kind of weird. . . "), habits (e.g., "she always sleeps in late"), personality (e.g., "She always be's funny sometimes . . . she always makes up stories that are really funny and I like it because they make me laugh a lot"). Repeatedly, the child stressed that her friend was invisible, but real ("She is really really invisible and I can really hear her when she talks"). At one point during the interview, the child looked to her left, laughed, and said "Carly just told a joke to you." The experimenter asked if Carly was in the room, and the child said, "No, she told me on our invisible cell phones." The child's mother also provided extensive information about Carly and reported that her daughter played with or talked to Carly almost every day. She said that she was uncomfortable about Carly because "I like to deal with things I can see, and I can't see Carly. [The child] really thinks that she's real."

If children tended to experience their pretend friends as real, we would expect more children to provide the type of description and commentary that we observed in this case. But she was only one of 86 children who participated in this study. This child's account of a colorful invisible girl with a cell phone stands out in marked contrast to what usually happens when we ask children about their pretend friends; the exception that proves the rule. Despite children's detailed descriptions and emotional attachments to their invisible friends, the vast majority of them understand that imaginary friends are pretend. They might wish the imaginary friend were real and like to pretend that the imaginary friend is real, but deep down they know that they made it up.

Summary

There are many different kinds of fantasy/reality distinctions, each requiring different sorts of insights and having different developmental trajectories. Overall, children are impressive in their ability to negotiate the boundary between fantasy and reality.[73] Of the numerous dimensions on which fantasy experiences vary, the one that we suspect is particularly relevant to children's ability to differentiate fantasy and reality is the extent to which children have some creative control over the experience.[74] Fantasy content is often presented ready-made to children. In cultural myths, parents and other adults present a convincing case for the existence of the characters, and children's belief in characters like Santa Claus is well documented. In storybooks, movies, and verbal testimony, adults and others present information to children in various ways, but in most cases, children's roles in these experiences are passive; they sit and listen. In social games of pretense, all participants have at least the possibility of contributing to the unfolding fantasy narrative, although sometimes a bossy play partner might actually be calling most of the shots. Children mostly are excellent at keeping track of the fantasy/reality distinction in such play. They might become scared when the fantasy is emotionally charged, but an emotional response to fantasy is not an unambiguous sign of confusion.

In the case of imaginary friends, children tend to make up most everything for themselves. The children are the ones in control of these fantasies, and they typically understand exactly what is going on. Thus, the answer to the question raised in the title of this chapter is no—young children do not think their imaginary friends are real. Perhaps that is why children do not mourn them when they are gone. In the next chapter, we discuss the fate of imaginary friends when their child creators grow up.

Notes

1. Carroll, L. (1871). *Through the looking glass*. Macmillan, p. 47.
2. Harris, P. L., Pasquini, E. S., Duke, S., Asscher, J. J., & Pons, F. (2006). Germs and angels: The role of testimony in young children's ontology. *Developmental Science, 9*(1), 76–96.
3. Shtulman, A., & Carey, S. (2007). Improbable or impossible? How children reason about extraordinary events. *Child Development, 78*, 1015–1032.
4. Bretherton, I., & Beeghley, M. (1982). Talking about internal states: The acquisition of an explicit theory of mind. *Developmental Psychology, 18*, 906–921.
    Flavell, J. H., Flavell, E. R., & Green, F. L. (1987). Young children's knowledge about the apparent-real and pretend-real distinctions. *Developmental Psychology, 23*, 816–822.
    Wellman, H. M., & Estes, D. (1986). Early understanding of mental entities: A reexamination of childhood realism. *Child Development, 57*, 910–923.
    When shown a boy described as pretending to have a cookie and a boy described as really having a cookie, children as young as 3 years are very accurate in their judgments about which boy could eat the cookie, touch the cookie, save the cookie for tomorrow, and share the cookie with friends.
    Woolley, J. D., & Wellman, H. M. (1993). Origin and truth: Young children's understanding of imaginary mental representations. *Child Development, 64*, 1–17.
5. Harris, P. L., Brown, E., Marriott, C., Whittall, S., & Harmer, S. (1991). Monsters, ghosts and witches: Testing the limits of the fantasy-reality distinction in young children. *British Journal of Developmental Psychology, 9*, 105–123.
6. Woolley, J. D., & Wellman, H. M. (1993). Origin and truth: Young children's understanding of imaginary mental representations. *Child Development, 64*, 1–17.
7. Subbotsky, E. V. (1993). *Foundations of the mind*. Harvard University Press.
8. Leslie, A. M. (1987). Pretense and representation: The origins of "theory of mind." *Psychological Review, 94*, 412–426.
9. Spock, B. (1974). *Bringing up children in a difficult time*. The Bodley Head, p. 50.
10. Piaget, J. (1923/1973). *Language and thought of the child. Concept of the mind*. Routledge Classics, p. 63.
11. Newson, J., & Newson, E. (1968). *Four years old in an urban community*. George Allen & Unwin Ltd., p. 193.

12. Kapitány, R., Nelson, N., Burdett, E. R., & Goldstein, T. R. (2020). The child's pantheon: Children's hierarchical belief structure in real and non-real figures. *PLOS ONE, 15*(6), e0234142.
    Goldstein, T. R., & Woolley, J. (2016). Ho! Ho! Who? Parent promotion of belief in and live encounters with Santa Claus. *Cognitive Development, 39,* 113-127.
13. Clark, C. D. (1995). *Flights of fancy; leaps of faith: Children's myths in contemporary America.* University of Chicago Press.
14. Teacher says there's no Santa; parents outraged. *Oregon Daily Emerald,* 1994, January 7, p. 14.
15. van Allsburg, C. (1985). *The polar express.* Houghton Mifflin.
16. Some Jewish children also believe that Santa Claus is a real person.
    Prentice, N. M., Gordon, D. (1986). Santa Claus and the Tooth Fairy for the Jewish child and parent. *Journal of Genetic Psychology, 148,* 139-151.
17. Prentice, N. M., Manosevitz, M., & Hubbs, L. (1978). Imaginary figures of early childhood: Santa Claus, Easter Bunny and the Tooth Fairy. *American Journal of Orthopsychiatry, 48,* 618-628.
18. Rosengren, K. S., Kalish, C. W., Hickling, A. K., & Gelman, S. A (1994). Exploring the relation between preschool children's magical beliefs and causal thinking. *British Journal of Developmental Psychology, 12,* 69-82.
19. Clark, C. D. (1995). *Flights of fancy; leaps of faith: Children's myths in contemporary America.* University of Chicago Press.
20. Clark, C. D. (1995). *Flights of fancy; leaps of faith: Children's myths in contemporary America,* p. 6.
21. Ibid.
22. Ibid., pp. 17-18.
23. Kaye, M. (1990). *The real tooth fairy.* Harcourt, Brace, & Co.
24. Prentice, N. M., Manosevitz, M., & Hubbs, L. (1978). Imaginary figures of early childhood: Santa Claus, Easter Bunny and the Tooth Fairy. *American Journal of Orthopsychiatry, 48,* 618-628.
    Taylor, M., Cartwright, B. S., & Carlson, S. M. (1993). A developmental investigation of children's imaginary companions. *Developmental Psychology, 29,* 276-285.
25. Sharon, T., & Woolley, J. D. (2004). Do monsters dream? Young children's understanding of the fantasy/reality distinction. *British Journal of Developmental Psychology, 22*(2), 293-310.
26. Woolley, J. D., Boerger, E. A., & Markman, A. B. (2004). A visit from the Candy Witch: Factors in influencing young children's belief in a novel fantastical being. *Developmental Science, 7,* 456-468.
27. Ibid., p. 457.
    Also see Rosengren, K. S., Johnson, C., & Harris, P. L. (Eds.). (2000). *Imagining the impossible: The development of magical, scientific, and religious thinking in contemporary society.* Cambridge University Press.
28. We do not mean to say that children make no contributions. In many families, children create their own variations to rituals associated with cultural myths and parents accept them. Yet, even in these cases, children are following the leads of others in their participation.

29. Some children might intellectually understand that an imaginary entity is not real, but they decide to believe that it is real all the same. Thus, for some children and to some extent, belief can be a choice.
30. A full discussion of the many levels of fantasy/reality distinctions on television (e.g., cartoons vs. live action, documentaries vs. fictionalized events, commercials, actors, and the roles they portray) is beyond the scope of this book. For more complete coverage of children's understanding of fantasy on television see Singer & Singer (1981, 2011):
    Singer, J. L., & Singer, D. G. (1981).*Television, imagination and aggression.* Lawrence Erlbaum.
    Singer, D. G., & Singer, J. L. (Eds.). (2012). *Handbook of children and the media.* Sage Publications Inc.
31. Williams, M. (1975). *The velveteen rabbit.* Avon Books, p. 13.
32. Morison, P., & Gardner, H. (1978). Dragons and dinosaurs: On distinguishing the realms of reality and fantasy. *Child Development, 49,* 642–648.
33. Taylor, B., & Howell, R. J. (1973). The ability of three-, four-, and five-year-old children to distinguish fantasy from reality. *Journal of Genetic Psychology, 122,* 315–318.
    Samuels, A., & Taylor, M. (1994). Children's ability to distinguish fantasy events from real-life events. *British Journal of Developmental Psychology, 12,* 417–427.
    Morison, P., & Gardner, H. (1978). Dragons and dinosaurs: On distinguishing the realms of reality and fantasy. *Child Development.*
    Scarlett, W. G., & Wolf, D. (1979). When it's only make-believe: The construction of a boundary between fantasy and reality in storytelling. In E. W. H. Gardner (Ed.), *New directions for child development: Fact, fiction and fantasy in childhood.* Jossey-Bass, pp. 29–40.
34. Samuels, A., & Taylor, M. (1994). Children's ability to distinguish fantasy events from real-life events. *British Journal of Developmental Psychology.*
35. Perhaps when children feel afraid of an entity, they are motivated to think of the entity as fantasy as a defense against the negative emotion.
36. Woolley, J. D., & Cox, V. (2007). Development of beliefs about storybook reality. *Developmental Science, 10,* 681–693.
37. Some of children's difficulty reflects misunderstandings about the technology used to communicate a story (Wright et al., 1994). For example, preschool children sometimes question how characters get inside a television, speculating that somehow the characters might become smaller and enter through the plug in the wall (Quarforth, 1979). Another group of researchers showed children a televised image of a bowl of popcorn and found that some 3-year-olds reported that the popcorn would spill out if the top of the TV were taken off and the TV were turned upside down (Flavell et al., 1990). In addition, young children fail to recognize the economic motives underlying the messages in commercials (i.e., products are portrayed in an overly positive way) and sometimes mistakenly believe that a person beaten or killed in a show has actually been hurt.
    Flavell, J. H., Flavell, E. R., Green, F. L., & Korfmacher, J. E. (1990). Do young children think of television images as pictures or real objects? *Journal of Broadcasting and Electronic Media, 34,* 399–419.
    Quarforth, J. M. (1979). Children's understanding of the nature of television characters. *Journal of Communication, 29,* 210–218.

Dorr, A. (1983). No shortcuts to judging reality. In J. Bryant & D. R. Anderson (Eds.), *Children's understanding of television* (pp. 199–220). Academic Press.

Wright, J. C., Huston, A. C., Reitz, A. L., & Piemyat, S. (1994). Young children's perceptions of television reality: Determinants and developmental differences. *Developmental Psychology, 30*, 229–239.

38. Wullschlager, J. (1996). *Inventing Wonderland*. The Free Press.

    Perhaps the most famous incident in which adults confused a fictional program for reality was the 1939 radio show *War of the Worlds* by Orson Wells, which used a news format to tell the fictional story of an invasion of Earth from outer space. Hundreds of adult listeners thought the report was real news and mass hysteria ensued.

39. Harris, P. L. (2012). *Trusting what you have been told: How children learn from others*. Belknap Press/Harvard University Press.

40. Ganea, P. A., Pickard, M. B., & DeLoache, J. S. (2008). Transfer between picture books and the real world by very young children. *Journal of Cognition and Development, 9*(1), 46–66.

    Richert, R. A., Shawber, A. B., Hoffman, R. I., & Taylor, M. (2009). Learning from real and fantasy characters in preschool and kindergarten. *Cognition and Development, 10*, 41–66.

    Richert, R. A., & Smith, E. I. (2011). Preschoolers' quarantining of fantasy stories. *Child Development, 82*(4), 1106–1119.

41. Mares, M. L., & Acosta, E. (2008). Be kind to three-legged dogs: Children's literal interpretations of television's metaphorical messages about tolerance. *Media Psychology, 11*, 377–399.

42. Koenig, M. A., & Harris, P. L. (2005). Preschoolers mistrust ignorant and inaccurate speakers. *Child Development, 76*(6), 1261–1277.

    Koenig, M. A., & Harris, P. L. (2007). The basis of epistemic trust: Reliable testimony or reliable sources? *Episteme, 4*(3), 264–284.

    Harris, P. L. (2012). *Trusting what you're told: How children learn from others*. Harvard University Press.

43. Dawkins. R. (January/February, 1995). Putting away childish things. *Skeptical Inquirer, 19*, 31–36.

    Piaget, J. (1929). *The child's conception of the world*. Routledge and Kegan Paul, p. 94.

44. Li, H., Boguszewski, K., & Lillard, A. S. (2015). Can that really happen? Children's knowledge about the reality status of fantastical events in television. *Journal of Experimental Child Psychology, 139*, 99–114.

    Woolley, J. D., & Ghossainy, M. E. (2013). Revisiting the fantasy–reality distinction: Children as naïve skeptics. *Child Development, 84*(5), 1496–1510.

45. Koenig, M. A., & Harris, P. L. (2005). Preschoolers mistrust ignorant and inaccurate speakers. *Child Development, 76*(6), 1261–1277.

46. Leslie, A. M. (1987). Pretense and representation: The origins of "theory of mind." *Psychological Review, 94*, 412–426, see p. 412.

47. Harris, P. L., Kavanaugh, R. D., & Meredith, M. C. (1994). Young children's comprehension of pretend episodes: The integration of successive actions. *Child Development, 65*, 16–30.

    Harris, P. L., & Kavanaugh, R. D. (1993). Young children's understanding of pretense. *Monographs of the Society for Research in Child Development, 58*(1), i–107.

48. DiLalla, L. F., & Watson, M. W. (1988). Differentiation of fantasy and reality: Preschoolers' reactions to interruptions in their play. *Developmental Psychology, 24,* 286-291.
49. Golomb, C., & Galasso, L. (1995). Make believe and reality: Explorations of the imaginary realm. *Developmental Psychology, 31,* 800-810.
    Golomb, C., & Kuersten, R. (1996). On the transition from pretence play to reality: What are the rules of the game? *British Journal of Developmental Psychology, 14,* 203-217.
    Lloyd, B., & Goodwin, R. (1995). Let's pretend: Casting the characters and setting the scene. *British Journal of Developmental Psychology, 13*(3), 261-270.
50. Ibid., p. 208.
51. Ibid., p. 208.
52. Harris, P. L., Brown, E., Marriot, C., Whittall, S., & Harmer, S. (1991). Monsters, ghosts and witches: Testing the limits of the fantasy-reality distinction in young children. *British Journal of Developmental Psychology, 9,* 105-123.
53. Johnson, C., & Harris, P. L. (1994). Magic: Special but not excluded. *British Journal of Developmental Psychology, 12,* 35-51.
54. Bourchier, A., & Davis, A. (2000). Individual and developmental differences in children's understanding of the fantasy-reality distinction. *British Journal of Developmental Psychology, 18*(3), 353-368.
55. Golomb, C., & Galasso, L. (1995). Make believe and reality: Explorations of the imaginary realm. *Developmental Psychology, 31,* 800-810.
56. Ibid., p. 802.
57. Ibid.
58. Woolley, J. D., & Phelps, K. E. (1994). Young children's practical reasoning about imagination. *British Journal of Developmental Psychology, 12,* 53-67.
59. Ibid.
60. Bourchier, A., & Davis, A. (2000). Individual and developmental differences in children's understanding of the fantasy-reality distinction. *British Journal of Developmental Psychology, 18*(3), 353-368.
    DiLalla, L. F., & Watson, M. W. (1988). Differentiation of fantasy and reality: Preschoolers' reactions to interruptions in their play. *Developmental Psychology, 24,* 286-291.
61. Harris, P. L. (2000). *The work of the imagination.* Basil Blackwell.
    Lillard, A. (1994). Making sense of pretence. In C. Lewis & P. Mitchell (Eds.), *Children's early understanding of mind* (pp. 211-234). Lawrence Erlbaum.
62. Gerrig, R. J. (1993). *Experiencing narrative worlds: On the psychological activities of reading.* Yale University Press.
    Goldstein, T. R. (2009). The pleasure of unadulterated sadness: Experiencing sorrow in fiction, nonfiction and "in person." *Psychology of Aesthetics, Creativity, and the Arts, 3,* 232-237.
63. Walton, K. L. (1990). *Mimesis as make-believe.* Harvard University Press
64. Gerrig, R. J. (1993). *Experiencing narrative worlds: On the psychological activities of reading.* Yale University Press.
65. Goldstein, T. R. (2009). The pleasure of unadulterated sadness: Experiencing sorrow in fiction, nonfiction and "in person." *Psychology of Aesthetics, Creativity, and the Arts, 3,* 232-237.
66. Ibid., p. 237.

67. Bretherton, I. (1989). Pretense: The form and function of make-believe play. *Developmental Review, 9*, 383–401.
    Partington, J. T., & Grant, C. (1984). Imaginary playmates and other useful fantasies. In P. K.Smith (Ed.), *Play in Animals and Humans* (pp. 217–240). Basil Blackwell.
68. Golomb, C., & Kuersten, R. (1996). On the transition from pretence play to reality: What are the rules of the game? *British Journal of Developmental Psychology, 14*, 203–217.
69. Sayfan, L., & Lagattuta, K. H. (2009). Scaring the monster away: What children know about managing fears of real and imaginary creatures. *Child Development, 80*(6), 1756–1774.
70. Williams, M. (1975). *The velveteen rabbit.* Avon Books.
71. Taylor, M., Cartwright, B. S., & Carlson, S. M. (1993). A developmental investigation of children's imaginary companions. *Developmental Psychology, 29*(2), 276–285.
72. Taylor, M., Shawber, A. B., & Mannering, A. M. (2009). Children's imaginary companions: What is it like to have an invisible friend? In K. Markman, W. Klein, & J. Suhr (Eds.), *The handbook of imagination and mental simulation* (pp. 211–224). Psychology Press.
73. Woolley, J. (1997). Thinking about fantasy: Are children fundamentally different thinkers and believers from adults? *Child Development, 68*, 991–1011.
74. Taylor, M. (1997). The role of creative control and culture in children's fantasy/reality judgments. *Child Development, 68*, 1015–1017.
    We do not mean to suggest that fantasy activities fall neatly into categories with children either as passive recipients of fantasy created entirely by others or as isolated fantasy masterminds untouched by the influences of environment and culture. Actually, the child's role is probably rarely all or nothing. Still, fantasy experiences vary considerably in how much control is exercised by children.

Chapter 9
What Happens to the Imaginary Friends Created in Early Childhood?

Children's friendships with imaginary friends are often intense, emotional, and absorbing, but they (mostly) don't last forever. One day, parents realize that the pretend friend they had been hearing about for months, or even years, is no longer mentioned. A once-cherished stuffed animal ends up in the back of the closet; invisible beings disappear without a trace. These endings are typically difficult to pinpoint and can be as perplexing as the initial appearances. When children are asked what happened to their imaginary friends, they usually say that they don't remember. Curiously, they also express very little sadness or regret.[1] Note that in Peter, Paul, and Mary's well-known song, it is Puff the Magic Dragon, not Jackie Paper, who cries and sadly retreats into his cave when their relationship is over.[2] In real life most children, like the fictional Jackie, give up imaginary friends without fuss or fanfare. When they are finished with their pretend friends, they move on to other activities and often forget about them completely. McAnally and her colleagues[3] found that the majority of 16-year-old adolescents (78%) who had described imaginary friends when they were 4 years old did not remember them, even when provided with cues (e.g., the imaginary friend's name and description).

Parents and other family members who have become accustomed to the imaginary addition to the family are less cavalier and sometimes become invested in keeping the memory alive. Marjorie interviewed a woman who reported that her parents insisted on telling anyone she brought to their home about the invisible green gunkies she played with as a child. In an article published in the *LA Times*, Nancy Rivera Brooks described the feelings of loss that her family and friends experienced when her son stopped playing with Norey Porto, an imaginary boy with dark hair and green eyes who lived nearby with his family in a black house with blue trim:

> Norey was Cord's imaginary playmate, and after spending a significant amount of time with us during the past three years, Norey has gone the way of baby bottles and potty chairs. But since this perfectly normal, age-appropriate milestone occurred, the strangest thing has happened: I've started to miss old Norey. My husband and 7-year-old daughter, when quizzed, have made similar reluctant confessions.

Imaginary Friends and the People Who Create Them. Second Edition. Marjorie Taylor and Naomi R. Aguiar, Oxford University Press. © Oxford University Press (2024). DOI: 10.1093/9780190888916.003.0009

Are we in mourning for Cord's lost toddler-hood? Is this one of those bittersweet passage of time things? Naw. I think we are pining for Norey himself and his odd family and their lavish lifestyle, all courtesy of the imaginings of our budding wordsmith.[4]

Given the description that Brooks provides of Norey, it is not surprising that the family misses him. Norey was pretty special. He had more birthday parties than any other kid, owned every imaginable toy (except Barbie), and had lots of pets, including buffalos, a hippo, a lion, and a hyena, as well as the more conventional ones. His family was also noteworthy. On Valentine's Day, Norey's mom (who was so tall she could touch the ceiling) found a dead snake and cooked it for Norey's dad. One sister died when someone stepped on her, and the other was a baby who drank out of Power Ranger bottles. Brooks compared the demise of Norey with the ending of a good movie or book. She missed hearing about all the strange events that occurred in Norey's life. In the end, though, she decided that his disappearance was for the best because, "you know you are in trouble when your kid's imaginary creations have a more interesting life than you do."

Christopher Milne, who inspired his father's (A. A. Milne's) stories about Winnie-the-Pooh, experienced this nostalgic response of others to his childhood imaginary friends on a larger scale. He found that people were disappointed that he no longer possessed his collection of stuffed animals. Fans of the *Winnie-the-Pooh* books somehow wanted and expected the real-life Christopher Robin to retain an attachment to Winnie-the-Pooh, Eeyore, Piglet, Kanga, Roo, and Tigger—the famous companions of his childhood. Thus, as an elderly man, Milne found it necessary to carefully explain that he liked to surround himself with the things he currently enjoyed, rather than the things he had played with as a little boy.[5]

In any case, most children do not seem to mourn the passing of imaginary friends. This point underlines their utilitarian nature. They tend to be abandoned when they have outlived their usefulness. Their disappearance in no way indicates that the children's emotional attachment to their pretend friends was not real or important. As many of the descriptions in this book clearly show, children love their imaginary friends very much. And if the relationship ends prematurely, children are not so nonchalant. For example, sometimes a toy that has functioned as a personified object is accidentally destroyed or lost. This sort of event can elicit strong emotional responses from young children. When Naomi's child lost Ellie the Elephant, the tears didn't stop flowing until Ellie was recovered a day later.

Another example illustrates this scenario. From early childhood, Lynn had a brown teddy bear named DeeZee who was her constant companion. The whole family was aware of Lynn's special relationship with her bear, and he is still mentioned in family stories. One day Lynn was playing with DeeZee in a huge sand pile that had been created in her parents' yard in preparation for a landscaping project. The game involved lots of tunneling in the sand. Things got a little out of control—"DeeZee dug too far"—and the bear disappeared in the sand pile and could not be found.

Lynn was upset but hoped to find DeeZee as the project progressed. Unfortunately, insects located him before the landscapers did. When DeeZee finally surfaced, he was infested with bugs and Lynn's parents threw him out. Lynn remembers picking him out of the garbage and hugging him, bugs and all, but her mother insisted that he had to go (see Chapter 3 for other examples of reactions to lost personified objects).

What about the circumstances associated with the final exits of imaginary friends that are not lost, but are given up voluntarily? We have pieced together a few empirical findings and case histories in an attempt to come up with something more substantive to say than simply recounting the speculations and assumptions of parents and psychologists. If we knew more about when and how imaginary friends disappear, we might understand more fully the roles they play in the children's lives—why they were created in the first place.

Why Do Children Give Up Their Imaginary Friends?

What makes children ready to give up an imaginary friend that was once so important to them? When asked about the circumstances of the disappearance, most parents reported that they did not know why the imaginary friend was gone and that their children did not seem to be bothered by the loss—the imaginary friend simply disappeared.[6] The children who reported that they no longer played with an imaginary friend also had little explanation for its disappearance, although a few children gave reasons such as there being a fight between the imaginary friend and the child or the imaginary friend moving away.[7] For many children, the memory of the imaginary friend fades in the same way as memories for favorite childhood toys or playmates.

Loss of Interest

The disappearances of many imaginary friends are not that mysterious. Children simply lose interest in this type of play. In these cases, giving up an imaginary friend would not be much different from giving up play with blocks or finger paints. The activity becomes less absorbing or interesting over time, and the child moves on to other things. For example, one adult informant described the end of her relationship with an imaginary girl named Alice. For quite some time the child had enjoyed the imagined adventures of Alice, a brave girl who was nevertheless afraid of her stepmother, a witchlike woman who beat her with a Gucci belt (she "was very evil, but also very elegant"). Alice hid under the table one day to escape her stepmother's notice and realized that she liked living under the table. She still visited the little girl from time to time, but she no longer had much to say—after all, there are limited opportunities for adventure when you live under a table. The little girl found she didn't enjoy Alice's visits as much as before. One day, Alice, along with a pink rabbit, escaped from the stepmother's house altogether, stopping by the little girl's home to say goodbye before they hopped away to a place where they would be safe. The girl never saw them again.

The minority of adults who recall having had imaginary friends in childhood can sometimes provide insight about the end of the relationships. In a study by Robert Kastenbaum and Lynn Fox,[8] 22 of 37 adults who remembered childhood imaginary friends reported that the friend had simply faded away; one adult reported that the imaginary friend was still with her; and 14 adults had specific memories about the end of the imaginary friend. In six cases, it was a matter of the child growing up and moving on:

> I was getting cleverer and smarter and learning new things all the time and she was still the same. I hate to say it, but Loppy was getting boring and I had more exciting friends and things to do.[9]

Creation of a New Imaginary Friend

Sometimes the child loses interest in a particular imaginary friend, but not in the activity itself. As children's needs and interests change, their current imaginary friend might be outgrown. Thus, the imaginary friends that are created early in childhood drop out as the children dream up new ones. The revolving-door aspect of play with imaginary friends was described in a story by J. D. Salinger,[10] "Uncle Wiggily in Connecticut," about a little girl who had an imaginary friend named Jimmy Jimmereeno. The mother was exasperated by Jimmy and his constant presence. "I get it all day long. Jimmy eats with her. Takes a bath with her. Sleeps with her. She sleeps way over to one side of the bed, so's not to roll over and hurt him."[11] One day the girl abruptly announced that Jimmy had been run over and killed. However, the mother later observed that the child was still sleeping so far to the edge of her bed that she was in danger of falling on the floor. She shook the child awake and demanded to know why she wasn't sleeping in the middle of the bed now that Jimmy was dead. The child replied that she didn't want to hurt Mickey Mickeranno. This was the last straw for the frazzled mother who had enough trouble dealing with her real-life child, let alone the comings and goings of imaginary ones.

Like the girl in Salinger's story, many children routinely replace old imaginary friends with new ones. Marjorie and her colleagues[12] first realized that imaginary friends have a high rate of turnover when we interviewed a group of 12 four-year-old children seven months after they had originally told us about their pretend friends. Seven of the 12 children still played with these friends and were happy to provide updated descriptions, but the other 5 children had new imaginary friends and were not particularly interested in discussing the previous ones. The following is part of an interview with one of these children, a boy who originally told us about two invisible pretend friends, a girl named Tippy and a boy named Tompy. They were described as being 5 years old, having blond hair and blue eyes, and being great playmates. At the time of the first interview, the child's mother confirmed the existence of Tippy and Tompy and reported that her son played with them regularly. Seven months later, it was difficult to engage the child in conversation about the pretend friends he had once discussed with great enthusiasm.

>ADULT: Do you have a pretend friend named Tompy?
>CHILD: Oh. Tompy, Tompy. They were dead. They got dead today. Oh ... the day before the day. They just got dead, 'cause ... (stops and points to ceiling). What's up there?
>ADULT: I don't know. Can you tell me about Tompy before he died? Is that a boy or a girl?
>CHILD: Oh, she was a girl.
>ADULT: So how old is Tompy?
>CHILD: Well, he's 7200 years old.
>ADULT: Is it a boy or a girl?
>CHILD: Well ... the other one's a girl. But Tompy's real defective. He has a sore knee. Sore leg though but.... There's lots of times that Tompy ... we're really good friends...
>ADULT: They're good friends?
>CHILD: Yeah, they were.
>ADULT: They were? So, are they still alive?
>CHILD: Oh, they are still alive but ... (makes sound effect and falls back as though hit).
>Have I told you to do that to my speeders! (speaking to someone other than the adult conducting the interview).
>ADULT: Who did that?
>CHILD: Oh, Gadget.
>ADULT: Gadget?
>CHILD: Gadget's a girl. Now go back to sleep! (says to pocket)
>ADULT: Can you tell me about Gadget?
>(Adult asks child several questions about Gadget, who is described as a small invisible and very frisky mouse. Then the adult tries to return to the topic of Tompy.)
>ADULT: Do you play with Tompy sometimes?
>CHILD: (in critical tone of voice) Did you forget about what I told you? Ouch! (reacting to some action of Gadget's)

This transcript gives some idea of how tricky it can be to extract information from preschoolers. The child seemed to be censoring some material, was inconsistent in some of his comments, and was distracted by the antics of a new imaginary friend (verified by the parent) who had come along to the interview uninvited. His comments about "the other one" being a girl make sense to someone who knew the history of Tippy and Tompy but were bewildering to the researcher conducting the interview.

She had only been told that the child used to have a pretend friend named Tompy and was instructed to try to elicit information about Tompy. (We did not want the second interviews in this study to be influenced by the interviewer's knowledge of what the children had said seven months earlier.) The interviewer was unsuccessful in learning much about Tompy, other than that he had been a good friend but was "defective." The child's words and his tone of voice suggested that Tompy was remembered with some fondness, but no profound sense of loss. Gadget had clearly taken over.

Adults Take Control of the Imaginary Friend

One of the endearing things about many imaginary friends is that children can boss them around and direct their activities. Even when an imaginary friend is mean and annoying instead of obedient and faithful (see Chapter 2) or experienced as having its own thoughts and feelings (see Chapter 13), the child is the one who communicates the imaginary friend's narrative to others. A few case studies suggest that if the child's sense of control over the imaginary friend is diminished because of outside influences, the pretend friend sometimes disappears. For example, Ronald Benson and David Pryor[13] described the disappearance of an imaginary friend that was clearly associated with an adult taking over the narrative of the imaginary friend's behavior. The imaginary friend in question was created by a 4-year-old girl who was the eldest of three children in the family (her mother was pregnant with the third child at the time Nosey joined the family). Nosey was a black and white dog, about five feet tall, who walked on his hind legs, always wore a skirt, and usually was holding a mop or broom in his hands. The mother reported that Nosey was accepted by the other members of the family and was a regular participant in family events.

Nosey was abandoned suddenly after an incident that took place at the home of the child's grandparents. Unbeknown to the child, the grandfather had installed a remote control for opening and closing his garage door. After coming home from a drive, the grandfather asked if Nosey could help by opening the garage door. The child relayed this request to Nosey, and then the grandfather surreptitiously opened the door with the remote control. The child appeared to be stunned by the opening of the door on cue. A few weeks later the child's mother realized that Nosey had not been mentioned for some time and asked her daughter about him. The child reported that Nosey had stayed with her grandparents to help them with their garage door. She recalled that she had left him on the garage steps sweeping with his broom. An imaginary cat who also walked on her hind legs was beside him. Although this ending was abrupt, it did not seem to be associated with any upset feelings. At age 16, the girl recalled the incident as a pleasant memory about Nosey staying where he was needed.

Benson and Pryor interpreted this case study as suggesting that interventions by others that take the imaginary friend out of the realm of the imaginary and give it a different meaning might lead to the abandonment of the fantasy. As additional evidence for this interpretation, Benson and Pryor reported a second case of an imaginary friend who was given up as a consequence of outside intervention, but this case involved a child who was being treated in a psychiatric hospital for emotional problems. The friend was described as an extraterrestrial creature named Ronzar. According to the boy who invented her, Ronzar gave him advice and helped him with his homework. Sometimes he felt that Ronzar transported him mentally to other planets. The psychotherapist convinced him that Ronzar was a substitute for interactions with everyday people. The boy acknowledged that there might be some truth to this interpretation because he was aware that Ronzar helped him control angry feelings toward other people. He was disturbed by the thought of not having Ronzar ("I don't know what I'd do without Ronzar. I don't know how I would handle my hate"), but shortly after the psychotherapist proposed this view of Ronzar, the boy announced that Ronzar had been killed in a meteorite shower. The psychotherapist's interpretation of Ronzar's functions made the boy rethink the relationship and abandon it.[14]

These last examples are a little surprising because many children enjoy the participation of others in their fantasy about an imaginary friend. Parents in our research have uniformly reported that when they pretend to see or hear the imaginary friend, their children react with delight. The children may even insist upon the parent taking part in the fantasy by drying the imaginary friend after a bath or buckling the imaginary friend into the car with a seat belt. One parent described how a restaurant server played along when his young daughter asked for a high chair for her imaginary friend. The server not only added a highchair to the family's table; she brought a small plate of raw onions (the imaginary friend's favorite food) from the kitchen and set it on the high chair's tray. Perhaps the key to the child's enjoyment is that the child retains the role of director and thus is in control of exactly how other people participate.

Marjorie and her colleagues[15] found that children resist an adult's attempts to dictate the actions of imaginary friends when they tried unsuccessfully to do this in the lab. We were interested in the possibility that children might experience their imaginary friends as more real when the play was emotionally charged. To create this type of play, we set up a situation in which the child and the imaginary friend were both present. Then the researcher gave an attractive toy to the imaginary friend and told the child that the imaginary friend refused to share the toy. This procedure simply did not work. The children became annoyed with the researcher, not their companion. It was clear that these children were not about to relinquish their authority over the activities of the imaginary friend to someone else.

Parental Disapproval

When their children are preschoolers, some parents delight in their children's inventions, but parental enjoyment of a child's fantasy gives way to concern if the child continues in such play after the age that the parent believes it to be appropriate (see Chapter 5). Parental disapproval does not eliminate fantasy play, but children's increasing awareness of negative parental attitudes is bound to make them more secretive. Children also report being teased at school about an imaginary friend, which led to them being more private about having one. Pearson and his colleagues[16] reported that some of the children over 10 years of age were clearly hesitant about telling the researchers that they had an imaginary friend. In fact after the study was completed, some of them confessed informally that they did have an imaginary friend although they had denied that in the interview. In at least some cases, it is likely that social disapproval instigates the disappearance of imaginary friends. Thus, one reason why at least some children might give up an imaginary friend is because as they get older this kind of play is no longer tolerated by the people around them.

Child Acquires More Real Friends

As discussed in Chapter 4, imaginary friends fulfill a variety of needs for young children. If the imaginary friend was created to serve a particular need, then it makes sense that the pretend friend would disappear when the need was satisfied. This is true for any of the needs listed in Chapter 4, but here we have singled out companionship because it is one of the primary functions served by imaginary friends.

In children's books, a common theme is that imaginary friends disappear when the child character acquires some real friends and the imaginary friend is no longer needed. Guy-guy, Bickerina, and Mr. Dobie are never heard from again when the little girl in "The Three Funny Friends" by Charlotte Zolotow[17] makes friends with a child who lives next door. The substitution of real friends for imaginary ones seems to be viewed by the authors of children's books as the most suitable or satisfying way to wrap things up.

This sort of ending also characterizes the reports of parents. When pressed for an explanation, parents sometimes link the fading of the imaginary friend with the beginning of school when there is a marked increase in opportunities to socialize with real children.[18] And certainly there is a pronounced drop in imaginary friends when we compare parental reports for preschool children and children older than 6 years, the age when most children start school. In Newson and Newson's sample, only 3% of 700 seven-year-olds were identified by their parents as having imaginary friends (as compared with 22% of these children at age 4).[19]

However, there is reason to question the tendency of parents to equate the disappearance of imaginary friends with the increase in real-life friends that comes with the beginning of school. There could be other reasons why children might stop playing with imaginary friends as they reach school age (e.g., parental disapproval). Plus, parental reports, even for younger children, are not that accurate and become worse as children get older (see Chapter 1). When researchers interview school children, they often discover that, unbeknown to the parents, the pretend friends are still active in the children's fantasy lives.[20] The discrepancy between what children and parents report was particularly striking in Jennifer Mauro's research. By the time the children were 7 years old, all 38 parents reported that their children no longer played with the imaginary friends, but most of these same children claimed that either the imaginary friend was still around or that they had created a new one. Thus, many children continue to play with their imaginary friends into the school years, but parents do not know about it. The tendency of older children to show less overt acting out of fantasy could account for the fact that parents underestimate the ages at which imaginary friends are abandoned.

Although some children might stop playing with imaginary friends when real ones become more available, imaginary friends are not typically created because a child does not have friends. Children with imaginary friends have as many real-life friends as other children (see Chapter 6). In many cases, pretend companions have their own charms; they are not simply substitutes for real children. Interactions with pretend friends can involve unique imaginative scenarios (e.g., a tiny friend who lives in the family's mailbox), and imaginary friends often have special qualities as play partners (e.g., they can engage in bad behavior with no consequences) that are not found in real children. Thus, an imaginary friend is not always a pale substitute for the "real" thing. Children who enjoy using their imagination in this way are not necessarily going to give up fantasy friends when real life ones come along.

Imaginary Friends Who Die

When children are finished with the invisible type of pretend friend, these companions mostly just fade gradually away, but sometimes the children invent stories about their demise. One example of an abrupt ending was described by a colleague who played with three tiny invisible bears when she was a little girl. The bears lived on her hand. In some ways this was a convenient location because they were always nearby, but it also required keeping track of which hand they were in and switching the bears frequently from one hand to another with the demands of everyday life. Although she was usually very careful to keep the bears out of harm's way, one day she forgot to transfer the bears when her mother took her hand to cross the street. The bears were crushed and died.

In recalling the bear story, this woman wondered what it meant that she had been so calm and accepting of this violent death. But her attitude is just another example of children's indifference about the old friends who are no longer part of their lives.[21] And it is not unusual for imaginary friends to meet violent ends. There are many examples of children responding to questions about a missing companion by announcing that it is dead, was killed, or has drowned. One child told a story about her imaginary dinosaur Gawkin being hit by a truck. She was holding his hand, but he lagged behind and the truck killed him. There were no tears or bad feelings—Gawkin was dead and that was the end of the story. The end can sometimes be a little mysterious: a 3-year-old reports that Coda died when "he took too big a bite," with no further explanation.[22] Daniel Tammet describes the sad day when his very old invisible friend Anne told him she was dying and it was time to say goodbye. Although most children do not react strongly to the end of the relationship, Tammet recalled crying until he no longer had any tears.[23]

Kastenbaum and Fox[24] were particularly interested in the eight cases in their study in which imaginary friends were reported to have died. They speculated that "the comings and goings of imaginary companions could offer a fresh perspective on the ways that change, loss and death are conceived within the minds of children."[25] Two of the imaginary friends in their study died of benign neglect. In these cases, the children were not initially aware of the death but realized it had occurred after a period of the imaginary friend's absence. One child noticed that "Emmy," an imaginary friend with perfect teeth and a bright smile (the child's father was a dentist), wasn't around anymore. "She just stopped breathing, dead. I had stopped thinking about her, so that's what happened."[26] The other child did not notice the absence of "Fred the Kangeroo" until a Ouija board told her that he was dead. Her imaginary friend had died because she forgot about him.

For another child, death was a series of endings rather than a final one. "Fred" did not die in a specific way; he just died. But then he returned for special occasions. "I let him come back to have a good time on Halloween. He wore the cool sunglasses and Hawaii shirt, the stuff he always wears." Fred died after Halloween, but his death was not final: ". . . he could come back again. Yeah, he could probably die again . . . I think he will be with me the rest of my life."[27]

A couple of deaths happened in response to the actions of other people. When one child wanted a serving of homemade ice cream for his invisible friend, his mother replied that there wasn't enough for everyone and that he needed to share his serving with "Bobby." This did not go over very well: "I didn't like that, and Bobby didn't like that. He said he was going away and not coming back. He died. Bobby was very upset that he could not be part of the family any more, and he died. That was the end of Bobby."[28] In another case, when a neighbor girl was pushy about wanting to play with "Barneybus," the child responded that "he had gone to the hospital because he was dead."[29] Although this was something that "just popped into her head," once she said it, it was true. In three other cases, there were violent deaths. "Todd" was run over and killed by a fire truck ("He just ran out in the street to see what was happening and the fire engine got him . . . I didn't feel too sad about it. . . . Just something that happened").[30] "Sarah" died in a real-life house fire. "Mawblez," a tiny transparent friend who liked to hide in the child's pocket and sing, died when some furniture fell over and crushed him ("I told everyone he died").

Imagining the death of a pretend friend is another example of how children might use an imaginary friend to explore their ideas and develop their understanding of real-life challenges and circumstances (see Chapter 6). Maybe imagining the death of an imaginary friends is a way to think about what it means to die, to be alive, or even to be real? But note that most imaginary friends do not explicitly die; they just fade away. And neither type of ending—even when the death is violent—seems to elicit much sadness or regret.

Are They Really Gone?
They Have a Life of Their Own

In the fall of 1995, Bill Watterson announced that he had decided to stop producing his comic strip about a small boy and his stuffed tiger. His many fans were going to have to adjust to life without a daily fix of "Calvin and Hobbes." As the date for the final strip approached, Marjorie wondered how Watterson would choose to close this chapter of the Calvin and Hobbes saga. She was not the only one engaged in such speculation—one parody of the final panel depicted Hobbes dumped unceremoniously into a garbage can. However, on December 31, 1995, Watterson drew Calvin and Hobbes as excited to discover that everything outside was covered with a fresh layer of snow. The final panel shows them tobogganing away together down a hill, full of anticipation for the day ahead and their continued adventures.

The theme of the imaginary friend somehow carrying on is common in fictional depictions. One version is that the imaginary friend is recycled; when one child doesn't need the pretend friend anymore, he/she/it moves on to another child, sometimes with a transitional stay in a temporary group home (e.g., the cartoon *Foster's Home for Imaginary Friends* about a place "where good ideas are not forgotten"). In *Confessions of an Imaginary Friend*, the pretend friend who has been forgotten by his child calls for help from the "Imaginary Office of Reassignment," selecting from long menu of options (e.g., "Press 1 if you have been imagined as a houseplant; Press 2 if you have been imagined as a trademarked character and are worried about legal issues; . . . Press 99 if you have been imagined as the thing you hate most. . .").[31]

Children also sometimes report that the imaginary friends they used to play with are still alive and well but living somewhere else. For example, children sometimes describe pretend friends as moving away to another city or state, retiring, or going on sabbatical.[32] Marjorie encountered one example of an imaginary friend that moved on to a second child. It started with a 3-year-old boy who was apprehensive about attending a play group. His mother was worried about how her son would adjust to this change but was relieved to find him relaxed and happy when she picked him up after his first day. He explained that he had met a little girl named Margarine who was really nice to him. After hearing several references to Margarine over the next few weeks, the mother decided to contact her parents to convey how much she appreciated their daughter's thoughtfulness and caring behavior. Clearly, Margarine had been a big factor in her son's easy transition to the group play experience. But it turned out to be a challenge to locate Margarine or her parents. The play group leader and the boy's mother searched the list of children in the play group for a

What Happens to the Imaginary Friends Created in Early Childhood?

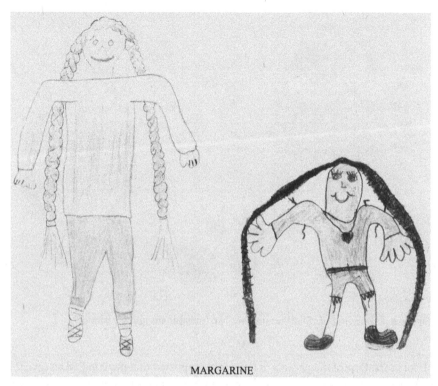

Figure 9.1 Drawings of "Margarine" by 8-year-old boy (left) and his 5-year-old sister (right).

"Marjorie" or "Margaret," or any name with a passing resemblance to "Margarine." Nothing. The mother then asked her son for more information and learned that Margarine had long yellow braids that dragged behind her on the floor. Margarine was an imaginary girl. A few years later, when the boy's little sister started preschool, the change in schedule was easy for her too. You guessed it—Margarine was on hand at the preschool to make her feel welcome and ease her transition (see Figure 9.1).

Long-Lasting Imaginary Friends

Some imaginary friends last well beyond the preschool years.[33] About half of the adults who remember having imaginary friends indicate that they stopped playing with them after they were 10 years of age.[34] Many schoolchildren report they still play with their imaginary friends, at home and sometimes at school. One 10-year-old boy described playing with his imaginary friend at recess break; a 7-year-old told us about Skate Board Guy (see Figure 9.2), who waits in his shirt pocket during school but then entertains the child as he walks home with his skateboarding tricks. Newson and Newson[35] also include descriptions of imaginary friends that lasted into the

Figure 9.2 Drawing of "Skateboard Guy," an invisible imaginary friend.

school years. One of the parents in their study reported that her son had an invisible friend named Lion who would reassure him when his mother was late coming home from work.

Ronald Siegel[36] gives one detailed report of a 14-year-old girl who was still playing with Chopsticks, the imaginary dragon who had been her friend since early childhood. Chopsticks was a striking example of an imaginary friend. He was a royal blue color with pointed ears, green eyes, a poodle-like face, reptile feet, a little white beer belly, and the ability to shrink from his normal height of eight feet to fit any space. The mother described Chopsticks as being ferocious—"Watch out for Chopsticks, He'll rip your head off"—but otherwise didn't know much about him. When asked why, she replied, "That's because Nancy rarely talks about him and I'm always afraid to ask."[37] The girl had stopped playing publicly with Chopsticks since the age of 10 but carried on long conversations with him when she was alone in her room. Chopsticks helped the girl plan her 16th birthday party, but he did not show up for the event and was never heard from again.

In some cases, traces of a childhood imaginary friend can be found in the lives of adults. We know a young woman who had an image of her childhood invisible friend tattooed on her arm. When Dorothy Juba became one of the top models of the 1950s, she used "Dovima" (the name of the imaginary friend she invented as a child when she was bedridden with rheumatic fever) as her professional name.[38] When Frances Warfield published her autobiography, she dedicated the book to her imaginary friend (see Chapter 6). More examples of the lasting influence of childhood imaginary friends, as well as some pretend friends that continue to provide companionship into adulthood, are provided in Chapter 12.

Summary

The majority of imaginary friends simply fade away without much fanfare, although in some cases, children and adults recall specific events that triggered the disappearance. Typically, children do not express much emotion about these events even when they are violent. Sometimes old imaginary friends get replaced with new ones, but mostly children simply lose interest in this type of play and move on. In some cases, imaginary friends die or disappear because of unwelcome attention from parents or others who try to insert themselves into the activity or express disapproval. But part of the story regarding the ultimate fate of imaginary friends created by preschool children is that, contrary to popular belief, they might continue on in some form beyond early childhood. In fact, some older children develop entire worlds for their imaginary friends to live in. These "paracosms" are the subject of the next chapter.

Notes

1. Kastenbaum, R., & Fox, L. (2008). Do imaginary companions die?: An exploratory study. *OMEGA, 56*, 123–152.
   Mauro, J. (1991). *The friend that only I can see: A longitudinal investigation of children's imaginary companions* [Doctoral dissertation]. University of Oregon.
2. Yarrow, P., & Lipton, L. (1963). Puff (the magic dragon) [Song recorded by Peter, Paul and Mary on *Moving*]. Warner Bros.
3. McAnally, H. M., Forsyth, B. J., Taylor, M., & Reese, E. (2020). Imaginary companions in childhood: What can prospective longitudinal research tell us about their fate by adolescence? *The Journal of Creative Behavior, 55*, 276–283. https://www.do./org/10.1002/jocb.468
4. Brooks, N. R. (1997). Goodbye to an imaginary friend. *LA Times*. https://www.latimes.com/archives/la-xpm-1997-01-19-ls-20055-story.html.
5. Milne, C. (1974). *The enchanted places*. Eyre Methuen Ltd.
6. Mauro, J. (1991). *The friend that only I can see: A longitudinal investigation of children's imaginary companions.*
7. Taylor, M., Carlson, S. M., Maring, B. L., Gerow, L., & Charley, C. (2004). The characteristics and correlates of high fantasy in school-aged children: Imaginary companions, impersonation and social understanding. *Developmental Psychology, 40*, 1173–1187.
8. Kastenbaum, R., & Fox, L. (2008). Do imaginary companions die?
9. Ibid., p. 138.
10. Salinger, J. D. (1953). *Nine stories*. Little.
11. Ibid., p. 27
12. Taylor, M., Cartwright, B. S., & Carlson, S. M. (1993). A developmental investigation of children's imaginary companions. *Developmental Psychology, 29*(2), 276–285.
13. Benson, R. M., & Pryor, D. B. (1973). When friends fall out: Developmental interference with the function of some imaginary companions. *Journal of the American Psychoanalytic Association, 21*, p. 457–468.
14. Ibid., pp. 470–471.

15. Taylor, M., Cartwright, B. S., & Carlson, S. M. (1993). A developmental investigation of children's imaginary companions.
16. Pearson, D., Rouse, H., Doswell, S., Ainsworth, C., Dawson, O., Simms, K., & Faulconbridge, J. (2001). Prevalence of imaginary companions in a normal child population. *Child: Care, Health and Development, 27*(1), 13–22.
17. Zolotow, C. (1961). *The three funny friends*. New York: Harper & Brothers.
18. Manosevitz, M., Prentice, N. M., & Wilson, F. (1973). Individual and family correlates of imaginary companions in preschool children. *Developmental Psychology, 8*, 72–79.
19. Newson, J., & Newson, E. (1976). *Seven years old in an urban environment*. George Allen & Unwin Ltd., p. 158.
20. Taylor, M., Carlson, S. M., Maring, B. L., Gerow, L., & Charley, C. (2004). The characteristics and correlates of high fantasy in school-aged children: Imaginary companions, impersonation and social understanding.
21. Newson, J., & Newson, E. (1968). *Four years old in an urban community*. George Allen & Unwin Ltd.
22. Wigger, J. B. (2019). *Invisible companions: Encounters with imaginary friends, gods, ancestors, and angels*. Stanford University Press, p. 43.
23. Tammet, D. (2006). *Born on a blue day: Inside the extraordinary mind of an autistic savant*. Free Press.
24. Kastenbaum, R., & Fox, L. (2007). Do imaginary companions die?
25. Ibid., p. 124.
26. Ibid., p. 142.
27. Ibid., p. 140.
28. Ibid., p. 141.
29. Ibid.
30. Ibid., p. 141.
31. Buevas, M. (2015). *Confessions of an imaginary friend: You are only as invisible as you feel*. Puffin Books.
    The concept of having an imaginary friend has been explored in many works of fiction. This novel is one of our favorites.
32. Taylor, M., Carlson, S. M., Maring, B. L., Gerow, L., & Charley, C. (2004). The characteristics and correlates of high fantasy in school-aged children: Imaginary companions, impersonation and social understanding.
33. Pearson, D., Rouse, H., Doswell, S., Ainsworth, C., Dawson, O., Simms, K., & Faulconbridge, J. (2001). Prevalence of imaginary companions in a normal child population.
34. Kavanaugh, R., & Taylor, M. (April, 1997). *Adult correlates of childhood fantasy*. Poster presented at the Biennial Meeting of the Society for Research in Child Development, Washington, DC.
35. Newson, J., & Newson, E. (1976). *Seven years old in an urban environment*. George Allen & Unwin Ltd.
36. Siegel, R.K. (1992). *Fire in the brain: Clinical tales of hallucination*. Penguin Books USA Inc.
37. Ibid., p. 141.
38. Morris, B. (1990, May 5). Dovima, a regal model of the 50s is dead at 63. *The New York Times*, p. 31.

Chapter 10
Paracosms

The Imaginary Worlds of Middle Childhood

> It makes me feel free. I mean, I can design it however I want to. It's my very own world. I can play it by myself, I can play it with friends...
> **(from interview with an 8-year-old)**

"Abixia," the mother said, "is his imaginary world inhabited by soldier cats." She went on to explain that Abixia had a king, its own flag, national anthem, currency, and language. Her son had drawn maps of Abixian geography, written about its history, and worked out many details of everyday life. For example, Swiss Army knives were revered because in Abixian's creation story, a horse God named Aht carved the world using a Swiss Army knife with a special attachment. Accordingly, Swiss Army knifeology was the largest field of study at Abixian University and Abixians sometimes made pilgrimages to Switzerland. But Abixia is located in a different solar system from Earth and is set in 1943 with primitive technology. The interplanetary travel that such pilgrimages required had to be coordinated with Rontuia, a neighboring world (also inhabited by soldier cats) created by the boy's best friend. Technology was highly developed in Rontuia: healing was accomplished by taking pills that had remotely controlled robots inside, shipping was done with magnetic levitation trains that travel 300 miles per hour, and the military was entirely composed of mass-produced robotic insects (making it easier to tailor the size of the military depending on whether there was a current conflict). Rontuian airliners were hypersonic vessels equipped for space travel, so they potentially could be booked by Abixians for trips to Earth. The complication was that Abixians and Rontuians did not get along. When the boys got together—sometimes with other children who also had imaginary worlds (e.g., Lethiopian, Berakeyaran, and Dragonian)—there were treaties to be worked out, alliances to be formed, and battles to be fought. Emotions ran high; tears were shed.

"So," the mother asked, "is this normal?"

Bewildered/astonished/intrigued/concerned parents often ask if other children have imaginary friends that are too busy to play (yes), live in the child's hair (yes), or swear a lot (yes). But coordinated imaginary worlds inhabited by soldier cats? This variation got our attention. We were aware of "paracosms"—entire imaginary societies or worlds—because of well-known historical examples, the work of Robert Silvey, and passing references to them when we interviewed children about imaginary friends. But the account of Abixia and Rontuia made us want to take a closer look.

The Childhood Paracosms of Famous Adults

For adults, the creation of imaginary worlds can be all in a day's work. *The Dictionary of Imaginary Places*[1] lists over 1,000 imaginary worlds from literary works of fiction, with entries including realms such as Wonderland (Carroll, 1865) and Middle Earth (Tolkien, 1937). Many more examples could be added today (Hogwarts, Wakanda, and Panem). At least some of this world-making begins in childhood. Accounts of childhood paracosms are sometimes present in the biographies and autobiographies of individuals who later became famous for their creative work. The most well-known examples come from the Brontë children—Emily, Charlotte, Anne, and Branwell—who in the 1820s imagined a set of kingdoms as the settings for the exploits of their toy soldiers.[2] When this play began, the children were under 10 years of age, but Angria, Glass Town, and Gondal lasted well into the Brontë siblings' 20s. Along the way, the children created tiny hand-sewn books, some of which have been preserved in library archives (see Figure 10.1), as well as maps, histories, poems, stories—even editorials in a tiny magazine. There are also carefully drawn and painted portraits of the leading citizens of Angria, Glass Town, and Gondal. These paracosms were important to the Brontë children and a major focus of their attention and time during their early lives.

More accounts of paracosms created by children who went on to become accomplished authors, artists, musicians, and scientists are comprehensively documented by Michele Root-Bernstein.[3] The inspiration for her book was likely her own daughter's creation of Karland, an island nation accessible through a portal inside a washing machine. Karland was inhabited with many types of animals and plants and a primitive hunter/gatherer tribe with its own language, arithmetic, and art. Michele also describes the childhood paracosms of Robert Louis Stevenson (the rival kingdoms of *Nosingtonia* and *Encyclopedia*), Friedrich Nietzsche (an imaginary world ruled by King Squirrel with its own plays, poems, and art gallery) and C. S. Lewis (*Boxen*, a combination of India and an earlier *Animal-land* that was inhabited by animals dressed like people and medieval knights). *Boxen* was ruled by a frog named Lord Big and documented with maps, stories, and histories that Lewis later brought together in the *Encyclopedia Boxoniana*. Another well-documented literary case is described in a biography of Barbara Follett, a writer who achieved early fame as a novelist. According to her biographers, she was engrossed for several years as a young girl and teenager in the creation of an imaginary world called *Farksolia*, complete with plants, animals, people, a detailed history, and its own language, Farksoo (e.g., "Ar peen maiburs barge craik coo" means "As the mayflowers begin to come").[4]

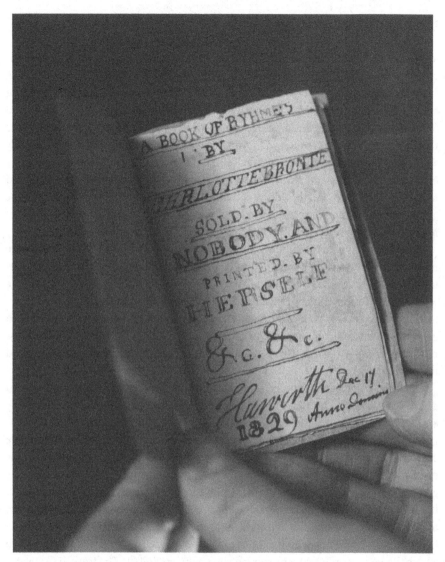

Figure 10.1 Tiny book created by Charlotte Brontë for her paracosm.
© Clark Hodgin.

A more recent example comes from Alma Deutscher, a celebrated composer, virtuoso pianist and concert violinist who began her music career as a child prodigy and is frequently compared to Mozart. (She was born in 2005 and starting composing when she was 4 years old.) In an interview with the *Washingtion Post*,[5] she admitted that she stole a beautiful aria for her first opera from Antonin Yellowsink. But he didn't mind. Yellowsink is one of the several imaginary composer friends she created to live in her paracosm, *Transylvanian*. Alma consults them when she needs inspiration or ideas for a new piece.

Past Investigations of Paracosms

The first large-scale collection of imaginary worlds was the brainchild of Robert Silvey, who coined the word "paracosm" (parallel world). As a child, Silvey had created "The New Hentian States"—complete with a constitution, government, budget, and cabinet ministers. As a retired adult, Silvey looked back on this activity and wondered if it was shared by other children. He ran an ad in a British newspaper asking, "was there ever a time, gentle reader, when you invented an imaginary world?"[6] Ultimately Silvey and his colleague Stephen MacKeith collected 64 descriptions of paracosms created by 57 adults and three children with about equal numbers of males and females. After Silvey's death, Cohen and MacKeith[7] published a book describing the governments, religions, royalty, languages, special animals, customs, artifacts (e.g., maps, flags, and written histories), and many other features of these paracosms.

The paracosms described in this report were extremely varied; 17 of the 64 were magical kinds of places, 45 were naturalistic, and 2 combined both magical and naturalistic features. Some of the worlds were based on toy or object props, and some were entirely in the minds of the creators. They also varied in the amount of structure and artifacts associated with them. Some of the paracosms were equipped with government systems, documents, maps, cultures, religions, histories, public transportation systems, currency, national anthems, magazines, and languages specified by the child.

One child had created a special script for his imaginary world, which was based on a Tamil primer brought back from India by his father. Another parasosm (shared by an 8-year-old girl and a 10-year-old boy) was populated by children called Friskies, good-natured hedgehog-like animals called Big Dears and Little Dears, and horrible creatures called Naughts. "Friskyland" was described as "a pleasant land, somehow not far away, but out of sight until you were there, and then you were amongst its green and pleasant fields and undulating hills . . . there were no houses in Friskyland, but very many Friskies."[8] Other paracosms included an imaginary village with a list of 282 residents. The child used the village as the setting for a series of stories she told herself about the people who lived there. Another paracosm, Coneland, was a place with hollowed-out giant cones in which you could live and fly. The trees in Coneland were the tallest in the world, and their soft insides were tinned as "good Conish food." One 8-year-old girl and her brother created a world inhabited by a tiny race of people called the Minaturians.

Although these descriptions were collected in a relatively unsystematic way—primarily by advertising in journals and newspapers for individuals who remembered having a paracosm when they were younger—they are valuable for the rich detail and insight they provide about the fantasy lives of school-aged children. Some of the paracosms invented by these individuals were freely shared with family and friends at the time of their creation, while others were kept private until the participants decided to respond to Silvey's ad. Some of the creators received support from their parents, some kept their paracosms private, and others had parents who knew about the paracosms and actively discouraged the children's involvement. One participant recalled that his father found a list of the radio and television programs available in the paracosm and wrote "rubbish" across it. But for the most part, the participants in Silvey and MacKeith's research seemed to have enjoyed happy family lives. Their paracosms were not a way to escape from a hostile environment. The inventors of imaginary worlds also did not appear to suffer from isolation or an inability to get along with others. In fact, many of the worlds were shared among several children. Interest in paracosms peaked at about age 9 and were less common after age 12. They were described as eventually fading away, as the child lost interest and began to spend more time participating in other activities. In most cases they were abandoned by 18 years of age, although some of the informants reported having some participation in fantasy worlds even as adults.

Michele and Robert Root-Bernstein[9] wondered if the creation of a paracosm in childhood might be an early sign of exceptional creativity or might set the stage for later developing creative endeavors. They investigated this possibility by recruiting 90 adults who had been recognized for their creativity with MacArthur Awards and comparing their responses to questions about paracosms with those of a control group of 262 college students. They found that the prevalence of paracosms was higher for the MacArthur Fellows (26%) than for the college students (12%), suggesting that highly creative people were more likely to have had them. In addition, many of the MacArthur Fellows assigned importance to having a childhood paracosm and saw it being connected to their work as adults (e.g., developing the capacity to consider alternative possibilities).

The results of this study indicated that although the creation of an imaginary world is not widespread, it is not as rare as Silvey and MacKeith had suspected. We have also found that once you start looking for accounts of paracosms, they are surprisingly easy to come by. Our informal inquiries resulted in several examples, including a preschooler who regularly told his mother about "the planet Geranium," a 10-year-old who created an imaginary institute complete with an invisible train to take him there and back, and a child who began to talk about Martians at an early age and over the years developed an increasingly elaborated fantasy about Mars. This child's parents initially interpreted his fantasy as reflecting a special interest in learning about Mars; however, when they supplied him with factual information about the planet, he would inform them that things operated differently on *his* Mars.

More examples of paracosms are reported in Eva Hoff's study of 26 Swedish 10-year-olds who had or used to have imaginary friends.[10] Thirteen of these children described elaborated fantasies about places that Hoff categorized as paracosms, including a secret country that could be reached in five seconds from the child's bedroom using the magic power of an imaginary panther; a jungle where the child visited with lions, moose, and birds; idyllic worlds where no one died and there were no wars; and an impoverished place with a beat-up shed that had rotting walls.

Our Research on Paracosms

The historical accounts of paracosms and descriptions provided by adults reflecting on their childhoods are fascinating, but they do not provide reliable information about how common it is for children to develop their own imaginary worlds. The reports collected directly from children also do not address prevalence because they have tended to be individual case studies or the children were selected because they had imaginary friends.

Assessing the prevalence of paracosms requires interviews with a large, random sample of children in the age range when paracosms are believed to be most common. We wanted to interview children themselves instead of relying on what a sample of adults could recall about their childhoods. However, collecting information about paracosms is challenging because they tend to be multifaceted and idiosyncratic, differing dramatically in their content, structure, and associated artifacts. Most paracosms have been developed over a period of years, and there is a lot of ground to be covered. An interview that included questions about all the possible topics that are explored in paracosms might take hours. When asked about paracosms, some children explicitly state that knowing where to start is difficult because so much could be included ("if you haven't been in on it from the beginning, it's going to take a long time to explain"), or because they are reluctant to describe complicated aspects of a paracosm (e.g., "[animal inhabitants] are really complicated . . . the simplest one, there are three versions of it and in the seasons, the versions vary").

Our first step with this research was to pilot a streamlined interview that was designed for the efficient collection of information about the level of detail, scope, and variation of paracosms.[11] Our strategy was to begin the interview by showing children a list of 43 topics (e.g., geography, languages) that have been identified in past research as featured in some children's paracosms. Then children selected the topics that were important for their own paracosms, and the interview focused on the children's selections.

We tried out this approach with the boys who had created Abixia and Rontuia and two 10-year-old girls who also had coordinated paracosms (see Table 10.1 for overviews of Chapaki and Cektrikx). All four children were excellent informants, as their paracosms had been an important part of their everyday lives for several years and they had created many types of artifacts, including maps, flags, architecture, newspapers, stories, comic strips, and drawings of characters and landscapes.

Abixia, in particular, was well documented with minted Abixian coins, printed Abixian money (see Figure 10.2), a dictionary of the Abixian language, a gospel for the Abixian religion, and a tourist guide to Abixia. The comments of the children suggested that they were still discovering things about their paracosms, as if the paracosms existed independently and they were learning about them rather than creating them. For example, when one of the boys described the language of his paracosm he mentioned that he was not "fluent . . . only knows a bit" and that he did not understand all of the spelling rules (e.g., "I don't know why there's a

Table 10.1 Brief descriptions of coordinated paracosms (Chapaki and Cektrikz) created by two 10-year-old girls

Cektrikx is a ruby planet in a parallel universe with a population of about 100 animals, mostly walking cats and dogs, although there are also bats, mice, and other animals. The inhabitants of Cektrikx are vegetarians except that they like to eat deep-fried blue-green ladybugs. Many are excellent cooks who prepare specialty dishes, including star leaves (leaves and lettuce with sweet and spicy sauce), and candied spider webs. Ruby bites are drinks made from four types of berries that are grown, along with other plants, by the Berry Cats. Another important plant is monark leaf, which is used for healing anything from cuts and bruises to serious medical problems. All the animals rely on power stones kept in special jars to give them the abilities or powers that determine their jobs. Power stones can make them smart, fast, invisible, or really good at cooking. The enemy of the animals is Bow Girl and the other 5-year-old girls who live in Bow Town and "want to put bows on everything and make everyone wear dresses and stuff. They have this machine where they can hypnotize the animals with this machine so that they all have to love bows and dresses." There used to be a pet shop in Bow Town where animals were mistreated, but the citizens of Cektrikx went to war and liberated the animals from the pet shop. The date of liberation is celebrated as a holiday like the 4th of July with food, lights, music and presents.

Chapaki is located in a distant solar system with a star that is much larger than our Sun. The 201 inhabitants include a few humans, but mostly intelligent animals (primarily winged cats) who live and work in a very tall tower (15 million stories) equipped with an elevator that travels at 3/4s the speed of light. Power stones that are connected to the life forces of the inhabitants are stored in the hollow core of Chapaki Star. Travel on Chapaki is accomplished by starships, which range from the size of bicycles to giant 10-mile-wide mansion-like ships equipped with swimming pools, hot tubs, jungle gyms, and many other amenities. There are also little glowing orbs that are used to transport objects. Instead of mailboxes, inhabitants have orbs hovering outside their doors. The leader of Chapaki is Charger, an 8' dog with a sonic bark ("if you happened to be in the range, you would feel like you were getting hit by a brick wall"). Bow Girl is the enemy ("she basically wants to take over the world by putting everyone in dresses and bows and girly stuff"). On Chapaki, tornados are made out of northern lights and are harmless. When a warning is broadcasted, the inhabitants like to go outside and get tossed by the tornado, as if they are on an amusement park ride. Chapaki has a hidden connection to Earth via Diamond City where dog- and cat-like creatures have individual designations as keepers (e.g., Keeper of Colors, Keeper of Stars, Keeper of Fashion, Keeper of Ecosystems, Keeper of Awesomeness). The entrance to Diamond City is through a well on Earth that is filled with water.

---

silent f"). The parents confirmed that the paracosms were very much a presence in their household and that the children regularly discussed the affairs of their paracosms, often sounding as if they were talking about real-world events.

Our strategy of focusing on the topics the child selected from a comprehensive list worked equally well for the dramatically different structures and concerns of Abixian and Rontuia compared with Chapaki and Cektrikx. We subsequently used this approach with 169 children aged 8 to 12 years, who were asked if they liked to think about an imaginary place.[12] Sometimes children said "yes," but the rest of the interview indicated little or no evidence of repeated engagement with the place or not much elaborated detail. Sometimes children described a fictional place from a book, movie, or video game or a real place the child had visited or would like to visit in the future (e.g., Venice). None of these were counted as paracosms. However, 29 children

Figure 10.2 Front and back of Abixian currency.

(17%) provided detailed accounts of imaginary worlds (see Table 10.2) that included information about environments (e.g., forests, lakes, caves), inhabitants (e.g., bandits, goblins, zebras, hamsters), and idiosyncratic details (e.g., fountains that spray honey). We next examined the 33 descriptions (29 from the large studies and 4 from our case study) for information about the inhabitants, relation to children's real-life interests, and the social context of paracosms.

The Inhabitants of Imaginary Worlds

The majority of the children (83%) who created paracosms also described having had imaginary friends. For many of these children (54%), creating a paracosm for the imaginary friend to live in seemed like the next step in the elaboration of their pretending. But for other children (46%), imaginary friends and paracosms were

Table 10.2 Examples of paracosms

Vera-sigh (8-year-old girl). Vera-sigh is located on a distant planet and ruled by Vera, who was abandoned after birth on a lonely island because although she was a "misfit of evil," she was good inside. There are many types of creatures on Vera-Sigh, including purple snakes, spiders, "sonny woos," blue butterfly armies, etc. Vera leads the fight against the Goblin King and his goblin followers. Life is hard because of the constant fight against the goblins, but Vera and some of the others have magical warrior powers and that helps.

An unnamed miniature world (12-year-old girl). A world in which everything is tiny—people, cars, TVs, food, money, etc. The inhabitants work in gardens, run shops and like to ride skateboards. Everyone is equal, however, there is a giant rabbit that the child described as similar to Godzilla causing significant damage when jumping through the world.

Somalockta (11-year-old girl): A planet with two rings. There are two races that inhabit the planet in different areas: Somas and Locklas. Somas love nature and plants and are responsible for plants and animals. Locklas are responsible for maintaining the lava and rocks and they are not affected by heat or fire. The inhabitants look like humans, but do not breathe, so they can go underwater and fly into space. The two lands sometimes go to war. There are important characters, particularly Nature and her evil sister Firestorm, who the child creates stories about.

Spirit Realm (12-year-old boy): An imaginary place with no physical constraints and a geographical layout that is always shifting, such as changing mountain ranges. The architecture of the buildings is a cross between religious temples and old university-looking buildings. There are no cars, but people do travel on the train, which is the only place where the child imagines other people. The child imagines visiting to reflect when confused about something, and imagines it as a peaceful place, free of "the problems of the real world."

The White Square (8-year-old boy): The White Square looks like a wall; it is invisible from 20 feet away, but when you walked closer "it would turn." Child's imaginary friends (Alexander, Furry Face, Sinister, and Mystery) live there and the child has a house located there. Everyone eats corn-dogs, and speaks a language called "Plifcy" (e.g., "ver" means "that"). No one wears clothes. The rules are no running, no flipping, no hurting anyone, and no cars (everyone walks). Newspapers and books cover everything child did in the past week.

Imaginary forest (13-year-old girl): The child imagines that she is the ruler of a magical forest filled with friendly, cute animals and imagines that she has a home inside a tree there. The child is concerned about the welfare of the inhabitants, who all have special powers. There is no conflict or evil and everyone gets along. The child described the imaginary forest as making her feel happy, calm, and safe.

Candyland (12-year-old girl): An imaginary place based on the game Candyland and the film *Wreck-It Ralph*. Everything is made of candy: candy cars, candy buildings, candy racetracks, a chocolate milk river. There is art made of Skittles, M&Ms, and chocolate chips. Everything is edible and after being eaten will grow back. Christmas is celebrated with an ice-cream cone tree, Halloween pumpkins are made of candy, and the city is decorated with Peeps to celebrate other holidays. The child is the Queen. The only rule in Candyland is that you cannot murder; the punishment for murder is jail time and healthy food.

Wonderland (12-year-old boy): An imaginary place adapted from *Alice in Wonderland*. The child generated new characters based on members of his family and homes for the inhabitants of Wonderland to live in. The child imaged having tea parties with the Mad Hatter and that there were lots of hats everywhere. He also enjoyed creating maps and designing details for his version of Wonderland.

unrelated. For example, one child described Vera, the leader of Vera-Sigh, in great detail, but Vera was a character in the narrative of the paracosm, not the child's imaginary friend. The child had several stuffed animals that served that function. Perhaps the relation between these activities is based more generally on a proclivity for fantasy or storytelling. Preschool children often use imaginary friends as the vehicles for stories (see Chapter 6), and the construction of a fantasy narrative is one of the central features in the development of paracosms.[13]

Regardless of imaginary friend status, paracosms are inhabited, and in some cases the development of characters is of primary importance. The kingdoms of Chapaki and Cektrikx had 100 and 201 inhabitants, respectively, and the girls appeared to have developed individual characteristics for the majority of them (see Figure 10.3). For example, Charger, the President of Chapaki, is a giant white dog with black ears and tail who lives with his mate Wycoboa (a platypus/cat hybrid) in a room made of ice near the top of Chapaki tower. Charger sends the inhabitants on missions and makes laws with the help of the ruling class, which includes Storm Gear, a gray tomcat who works as a sky mechanic; Gear, a black cat with a mechanical tail and spiky hair who works as a mechanic and in the food industry; and Cutsie, a red cat who also

Figure 10.3 Drawings of characters who live in Chapaki.

serves as the leader of Cektrikx. There used to be a Goddess of Chapaki (an abnormally tall human), but she disappeared and no one knows where she is. Delgado, a German shepherd/Collie mix, is in charge of sending messages, such as tornado warnings.

In contrast, the characters of other paracosms are not the primary focus. The anonymous quality of characters was particularly striking in Abixia and Rontuia, which were both inhabited by soldier-cats. According to one of the parents, "there seem to be more institutions than individuals," an observation that was consistent with the boys' focus on various aspects of the government, transportation, geography, history, and military operations of their paracosms. And while all four children in the case study discussed conflicts, Abixia and Rontuia were at war with each other, whereas Chapaki and Cektrikx worked together to fight a common enemy (Bow Girl, the leader of 5-year-old girls). The gender differences suggested by the case study were interesting but did not show up in our larger sample of 29 paracosms. Variation in the development and use of characters in the larger sample was distributed equally across boys and girls.

In some ways, the creation of a paracosm might appear similar to pretend play involving imaginary friends. But we agree with Silvey and MacKeith and Root-Bernstein that these two types of play are distinct. Imaginary friends are much more common, are associated with an earlier period of development, and typically do not involve the same amount of documentation. In addition, imaginary friends typically provide love, support, and companionship.[14] In contrast, the child's role in a paracosm is more like that of a creator or an observer than a participant in social interactions. In our research, the roles that children described for themselves included discoverer, creator, master, protector, inhabitant, God, president, and politician.

Real-Life Interests

Cohen and MacKeith speculated that paracosms served as a way to explore real-life events and interests ("many of the worlds suggest that, having created them, the children perpetuate them as a vehicle for their latest hobby").[15] For example, two adults in their study recalled the invention of "Possumbulese" as the language spoken in *Possumbol* when they started studying languages at school. One of the other participants, who had been fascinated by languages as a boy, invented a language of his own called "Ktu" and then created The Republic of Ktu so that Ktu could be spoken. Many of the adult participants in that study recalled shifts in the focus of their childhood paracosms as their real-life interests changed. In addition, fictional events in their paracosms were often triggered by real-world events (e.g., a general election in Britain was followed by one in Bearland).

Sometimes the study of real-life topics (e.g., peerages, medals, and heraldic emblems) were undertaken in order to incorporate them accurately into the paracosms. For example, the creator of Karland described the process of designing clothes for the inhabitants as follows:

> I would get out as many books as I could find in the house or the library or both, and go through and look at pictures of what other ancient people from all types of cultures wore as clothes. And I would pick bits out of those and put them together and try to find some synthesis of all those.[16]

This type of imaginative blending of ideas—combining and modifying existing concepts to create something new—is common in descriptions of paracosms and has been described more generally as key to the creative process.[17]

Similar to the accounts of Cohen and MacKeith, in our research we also found that many paracosms were explicitly described as vehicles for the exploration of the child's real-world interests. For example, in real life the boy who created Abixia collected Swiss Army knives, rode horses, was fascinated by foreign currency, and studied French and Arabic. All of these interests featured prominently in the content of his paracosm. According to his mother, new experiences in her son's life often showed up in some form in Abixia. For example, when he discovered a new favorite food, he added it to the rations for Abixian soldiers; when his mother was given a necklace that her son admired, he designated it as part of the Abixian crown jewels. The creator of Rontuia noted that if a real-world celebration (e.g., the Olympics) was happening, "then my friends and I will decide where to host the games, and a war might break out from it." In many of the paracosms in our research, we found that children similarly drew upon and extended their actual experience in the context of their imaginary worlds.

Paracosms might also reflect children's concerns and worries as well as their interests and hobbies. Naomi, Marjorie, and their colleagues found some evidence of this possibility in a smaller interview study with 60 children from low-socioeconomic status families (21 of the children had spent time in foster care).[18] Eleven of these children (18.3%) described paracosms, including several that had themes of abundance and material possessions (e.g., a place where there was lots of candy, no rules, and the child could get anything he wanted). This result suggests that paracosms, like imaginary friends, could serve as vehicles for children to reflect on and cope with challenges they face in their everyday lives.

Social Context

For some children, creating their own world is a private or even secret activity, but the development of paracosms is not always a solitary activity. In fact, the best-known historical examples of paracosms have a social context. C. S. Lewis (1955) wrote that when he was alone, his childhood imaginary world "Animal-Land" involved mice and rabbits dressed in medieval armor, but that it shifted to a preoccupation with trains, steamships, and the geography of India when he was joined by his brother. Silvey and MacKeith were surprised by how many of the paracosms in their study were shared with siblings and/or friends.

For some children, social interactions are central to paracosm-related activity. Of the 33 children in our research, 12 (41.4%) reported that developing their paracosms was a social activity shared with family members or friends. In one case, the paracosm was widely shared among a large number of children who developed its structure and narrative both individually and in various group settings. Parents indicated that when their children worked together on the narratives for their paracosms, the interactions were intense, emotional, and deeply absorbing. Two parents reported that the paracosm activities helped their children learn to resolve interpersonal conflict, and many parents reported having positive feelings about the social effects of this activity on their children. Perhaps as children develop the shared narratives of their paracosms, they are developing their ability to cooperate, collaborate, and negotiate with others.

Characteristics of Children Who Create Paracosms

> She's excited about life and loves to share her interests and ideas. She can talk with anyone; one of her "best friends" is 60+. She loves to "teach" him things. She is kind and caring to her friend's younger siblings and she loves to "babysit." She talks/sings almost nonstop. She has a great sense of humor. She's very out-going and can make a friend anywhere.
> **(Parent describing her 8-year-old daughter who has a paracosm)**

What does the invention of a paracosm say about its creator? In the movie *Heavenly Creatures*,[19] two adolescent girls in New Zealand developed a close friendship based, in part, on their shared imaginary world. The girls spent countless hours together discussing the interpersonal intrigues of an imaginary royal family and making clay figurines of their favorite characters. Their preoccupation with this invented world made an upcoming separation so unthinkable that the girls committed an actual murder to prevent it. Once again, moviegoers are exposed to the uncomfortable idea that elaborate fantasy can spiral out of control.

Heavenly Creatures is actually based on a real-life case, but fortunately it is not representative of children who create paracosms! With a couple of exceptions, children with paracosms are similar to their peers in most respects. In our research they did not differ from other children in verbal comprehension, working memory, or the most widely used creativity task (i.e., the Unusual Uses task, in which children are asked to generate possible uses for a common object). One of the exceptions was that children with paracosms had more difficulty with inhibitory control tasks in which they had to ignore distractors or inhibit the usual response (e.g., say "night" instead of "day" when shown a drawing of a sun). Inhibitory control (i.e., the ability to suppress thought processes that interfere with goal-directed behavior) has a complex relationship with creativity. Sometimes it is negatively correlated with creative behavior,[20] but there is also evidence of a positive relation between the development of inhibitory control and imagination tasks involving pretend play in preschool children.[21] In their literature review, Carlson and White[22] acknowledge the complexity of this relation and report the existence of a subset of highly imaginative children who have difficulty with inhibitory control (see Chapter 4).

The most striking difference between children with and without paracosms was for creativity tasks involving social content. Although these children did not differ from other children when asked to generate uses for a familiar object, they were more creative than other children when asked to generate different ways that someone at a new school could make friends (e.g., "at lunch sit next to someone else who is new"; "give the other children candy"). In addition, children with paracosms were more creative in their solutions to a task in which we asked children to draw "a real person" and "an imaginary person, someone you make up."

Most of all, children with paracosms stood out in the creativity of their storytelling. We measured this by telling the beginning of a story with the use of dolls and props and then asking children to finish the story ("Now it is your turn. What happens next?"). (See Chapter 4 for details of this task.) The children with paracosms produced endings to the story that were rated by adult judges as more creative than the ones produced by the other children.

As they mature, perhaps narrative and storytelling will continue to be a favorite fantasy pastime for children who have paracosms, or maybe the experience of creating a paracosm will contribute to the development of their skills as storytellers. This view was clearly held by C. S. Lewis:

> It will be clear that at this time—at the age of six, seven and eight—I was living almost entirely in my imagination; or at least that the imaginative experience of those years seems to me more important than anything else . . . in mapping and chronicling Animal-Land I was training myself to be a novelist.[23]

Summary

Paracosms are so elaborate and inventive that they seem like they must be rare. But although paracosms are not as common as imaginary friends, a substantial minority of children (about 17%) create them—places where, for example, people only read the books they have written themselves, cats fly, or snowball fighting is the national sport. The currently available evidence suggests that the children who create paracosms are similar to their peers in verbal comprehension, working memory, and the most commonly used creativity tasks. Where they do stand out is in storytelling. Not only were the narratives of their paracosms impressive; they invented more creative endings to a story than the endings proposed by other children.

Although inventing a paracosm tends to happen later in life than creating an imaginary friend, these activities have substantial overlap, including a general proclivity for storytelling. Older children and adolescents also engage in other types of fantasy activities, including imaginary interactions with celebrities and other individuals who they will never know in real life. This type of imaginary activity is referred to as having a parasocial relationship, and it is the subject of the next chapter.

Notes

1. Manguel, A., & Guadalupi, G. (1980). *The dictionary of imaginary places*. Macmillan.
2. Rachford, F. E. (1949). *The Brontës' web of childhood*. Columbia University Press.
3. Root-Bernstein, M. (2014). *Inventing imaginary worlds: From childhood play to adult creativity across the arts and sciences*. Rowman & Littlefield Publishers.
4. McCurdy, H. G., & Follett, H. (1966). *Barbara: The unconscious autobiography of a child genius*. The University of North Carolina Press.
5. Meet the next Mozart, an 11-year-old who just wrote her first opera. *Washington Post*. (2016, November 18). https://www.washingtonpost.com/lifestyle/kidspost/meet-the-next-mozart-an-11-year-old-girl-who-just-wrote-her-first-opera/2016/11/18/93876bf0-ada7-11e6-8b45-f8e493f06fcd_story.html
6. The wording of Silvey's ad is provided in Root-Bernstein, M. (2014). *Inventing imaginary worlds: From childhood play to adult creativity across the arts and sciences*. p. 23.
7. Cohen, D., & MacKeith, S. A. (1991). *The development of imagination: The private worlds of childhood*. Routledge.
8. Ibid., p. 31.
9. Root-Bernstein, M., & Root-Bernstein, R. (2006). Imaginary worldplay in childhood and maturity and its impact on adult creativity. *Creativity Research Journal, 18*(4), 405–425.
10. Hoff, E. (2005a). A friend living inside me: The forms and functions of imaginary companions. *Imagination, Cognition and Personality, 24*, 151–189.
11. Taylor, M., Mottweiler, C. M. Naylor, E., & Levernier, J. (2015). Imaginary worlds in middle childhood: A qualitative study of two pairs of coordinated paracosms. *Creativity Research Journal, 27*, 167–174.
12. Taylor, M., Mottweiler, C. M., Aguiar, N. R., Naylor, E. R., & Levernier, J. G. (2018). Paracosms: The imaginary worlds of middle childhood. *Child Development, 91*, 164–178. doi: 10.1111/cdev.13162
13. Root-Bernstein, M. (2014). *Inventing imaginary worlds*.
14. Gleason, T. R. (2002). Social provisions of real and imaginary relationships in early childhood. *Developmental Psychology, 38*, 979–992.
15. Cohen, D., & MacKeith, S. A. (1991). *The development of imagination: The private worlds of childhood*, p. 103.
16. Root-Bernstein, M. (2021). Creating imaginary worlds across the lifespan. In S. W. Russ, J. D. Hoffmann, & J. C. Kaufman (Eds.), *The Cambridge handbook of lifespan development of creativity* (pp. 327–350). Cambridge University Press, p. 337.

17. Turner, M. (1996). *The literary mind.* Oxford University Press.
18. Aguiar, N. R., Mottweiler, C. M., Taylor, M., & Fisher, P. (2017). The imaginary companions created by children who have lived in foster care. *Imagination, Cognition and Personality, 36*(4), 340–355.
19. Jackon, P. (Director). (1994). *Heavenly creatures.* Miramax.
20. Martindale, C. (1999). Biological basis of creativity. In R. Sternberg (Ed.), *Handbook of creativity* (pp. 137–152). Cambridge University Press.
    White, H. A., & Shah, P. (2006). Uninhibited imaginations: Creativity in adults with attention-deficit/hyperactivity disorder. *Personality and Individual Differences, 40*(6), 1121–1131.
21. Carlson, S. M., & White, R. E., Davis-Unger, A. C. (2014). Evidence for a relation between executive function and pretense representation in preschool children. *Cognitive Development, 29*, 1–16.
22. Carlson, S. M., & White, R. E. (2013). Executive function, pretend play, and imagination. In M. Taylor (Ed.), *The Oxford handbook of the development of imagination* (161–174). Oxford University Press.
23. Lewis, C. S. (1955). *Surprised by joy: The shape of my early life.* Harcourt Brace & Co., p. 15.

Chapter 11
Parasocial Relationships with Celebrities and Media Characters

> ... does an imaginary friend count on like a video game where they talk to me and like to hang out?
>
> **(from an interview with an 8-year-old child)**

This is an excellent question. In theory, the answer is relatively straightforward. When the partners or "targets" in imagined relationships are invented by us, they are called imaginary friends. When the targets are either real people (e.g., celebrities) or fictional characters invented by others (e.g., Harry Potter), they are called parasocial relationships. The targets of imaginary friendships and parasocial relationships differ in how and to what extent they participate in the relationship. Children envision their imaginary friends as interacting directly with them in a reciprocal or back-and-forth way, whereas parasocial relationships are described as one-sided because it is not usually possible to interact directly with a target. In most cases, the target of a parasocial relationship does not know the other person exists.[1] However, the products of our imagination do not fit so neatly into distinct categories. In practice, the line between imaginary friendships and parasocial relationships is fuzzy and getting more so all the time.

In the original 1956 definition, "parasocial interactions" was a term used in communications research to refer to one-sided interactions that some adults had with actors, newscasters, and other celebrities as they watched them on television.[2] In later research, these parasocial interactions were described as the building blocks upon which a parasocial *relationship* is formed. Parasocial relationships occur outside of the media context, involve an emotional connection, and are more ongoing than parasocial interactions.[3] The targets in early research—celebrities encountered on television—had very little or no direct contact with their audiences, but today there are many more potential targets and things are generally more complicated. For example, social media and technological advances in artificial intelligence (AI) provide opportunities for developing bonds and even receiving communications from people we will never meet in the physical world, such as social media influencers, fictional media characters (e.g., Big Bird), virtual online characters (e.g., MINECRAFT Steve), and voice-activated systems (e.g., "Alexa").

Imaginary Friends and the People Who Create Them. Second Edition. Marjorie Taylor and Naomi R. Aguiar, Oxford University Press. © Oxford University Press (2024). DOI: 10.1093/9780190888916.003.0011

Parasocial relationships are clearly different from relationships with invisible, one-of-a-kind imaginary friends who are envisioned as knowing their creators personally and as having imagined intimate interactions with them, but the distinction between imaginary friendships and parasocial relationships can sometimes be a close call. For example, many parasocial relationships are based on fictional media characters invented by adults for children in educational media (e.g., Elmo from Sesame Street) and/or entertainment media (e.g., Lego Ninjago characters), but fictional media characters also sometimes inspire the creation of imaginary friends (see Chapter 2). In such cases, the child takes over the narrative of the character, moving beyond the storyline presented in the media to include imagined personal conversations and shared activities. However, it is often not so easy to decide when a relationship with a media character has enough interactive, original content to be considered an imaginary friend as opposed to a parasocial relationship.

There are other definitional issues as well. Parasocial relationships are more than a strong interest in a famous individual or character. Liking and admiring a celebrity is not the same as feeling personally connected to them and having an imagined *relationship* with them. But in practice, it can be difficult to determine when a fan's interest is deep and emotional enough to be called a parasocial relationship. Unfortunately, some studies in this area do not clearly make this distinction and in popular parlance, "parasocial relationship" often seems to be used as a synonym for "fan." Another possible confusion involves the imagined conversations that people sometimes have with real-life partners. These imagined interactions are not evidence of a parasocial relationship.[4] As Tracy Gleason[5] points out, imagining a conversation with someone we know in real life should be considered part of a *real* relationship rather than constituting a parasocial one. We also exclude cases in which the individual—either adult or child—pretends to *be* a celebrity or a fictional character (see Chapter 2). When we pretend to be a character, we take on the identity as if it were our own, rather than imagining a relationship with a separate individual. When as a little girl, Naomi pretended to be Ariel from *The Little Mermaid*, Naomi was nowhere to be found! However, when we have imaginary relationships with other characters, our individual identities are preserved, and our focus is on the imagined interactions we have with these characters.

Variations in what is included as a parasocial relationship is one of the many challenges in interpreting the results of research in this area. For example, estimates of their overall prevalence depend upon the extent to which the research focuses on one or more types of targets (e.g., famous celebrities, social media influencer). Amanda Tolbert and Kristin Drogos[6] reported the prevalence for parasocial relationships with social media influencers on YouTube was 53% for 9-to-12-year-old children; however, Gleason and colleagues[7] reported the prevalence of parasocial relationships with famous celebrities was higher, at 61% for adolescents. Studies also vary in the age of the participants and how the information is collected.

Despite some uncertainty about exactly what they are and how best to study them, we believe the number of parasocial relationships is likely growing and their nature is evolving as our technological landscape evolves. In our view, parasocial relationships have some overlap with imaginary friendships, but thinking about the ways that they differ helps to better understand how imaginary friends are unique.

Children's Parasocial Relationships

For preschoolers and young school-aged children, most parasocial relationships are with fictional media characters from popular TV programs, books, movies, and video games.[8] It is not always possible to determine exactly where children first learned about the character or which platform inspired the parasocial relationship. For example, Dora the Explorer was a popular character that first appeared in a children's TV show produced by Nick Jr. in 2001, but soon after Dora could be found in books, video games, stuffed toys, dolls, and other branded merchandise (e.g., clothing, bedding, backpacks). It's possible that some children befriended Dora first through means other than the television program. Sometimes companies create the toys first and then follow up with TV shows as another vehicle for marketing products directly to children (e.g., Mattel's "He-Man" and "She-Ra").[9] Parents also play an important role by providing opportunities for their children to interact with the characters on various platforms and by purchasing toy versions. Children learn about media characters in other ways as well.[10] Naomi's child first became infatuated with the *PJ Masks* animated series after a friend at preschool showed up daily with a PJ Mask backpack and action figures. The friend and the toys are what drove Isabelle's desire to watch the series—a total marketing win!

Because of issues in defining parasocial relationships with young children, estimating how many children develop these bonds is tricky. In some of the research with preschoolers, if children say "yes" and provide a name when asked if they have a favorite media character, then they are counted as having a parasocial relationship.[11] However, many children like media characters but do not necessarily feel a strong personal connection to them. Moreover, in research studies, parents and children often disagree on who a child's favorite media character even is,[12] possibly because children's choices change frequently.

The rapid turnover in favorite media characters might reflect—in part—the extent to which children are now awash with an endless array of characters to interact with via touch devices and online streaming services. One quick view of Netflix Kids is enough to overwhelm—and that's just one of many streaming services now available to American families. Most of these characters do not change much in age or activities, so it is also possible that favorites change as children develop new interests.[13] Children might shift their affections from characters they have outgrown and go on to form new relationships with media characters that are older and have more desirable, age-appropriate (and sometimes gendered) characteristics. We suspect that the relatively fixed nature of fictional characters and their rapid turnover as favorites is one way that parasocial relationships might differ from imaginary friendships.

Although some children create a series of imaginary friends, our best guess is that imaginary friendships are more likely to be long-lasting than children's parasocial relationships, possibly because imaginary friends can evolve to reflect age-related transitions in interests. For example, Elfie Welfie (see Chapter 2) was described as a baby when the child was 4, but as an adult veterinarian when the child was 7. But this is only one of the differences between parasocial relationships and imaginary friendships. In what follows, we discuss possible differences in function, the extent to which the interactions are one-sided, and—most important of all—creative control.

Children's Parasocial Relationships versus Imaginary Friendships

Function

When young children interact with their favorite characters in educational media, they can learn new factual information and skills. For example, beloved Sesame Street characters have helped to teach numbers and letters to generations of young children. In much of the work in this area, researchers have investigated whether having a parasocial relationship with a character promotes this type of learning. The answer is yes. Young children are more likely to learn from digital media when they know, like, and trust the characters teaching the educational content.[14] For example, in a study by Alexis Lauricella and colleagues[15] American toddlers watched a video of either a familiar media character (i.e., Elmo, the well-known Sesame Street character) or an unfamiliar media character (i.e., DoDo, a character popular in Taiwan but unfamiliar in the United States) perform a seriation task in which the character stacked nested cups. Toddlers who watched Elmo were better able to perform the task than toddlers who watched Dodo. Similar results have emerged in studies with preschool-aged children. Molly Schlesinger and colleagues[16] tested 3-to-6-year-old children's ability to explain and complete a simple engineering task after watching a popular media character complete the task in a 90-second video clip. After viewing the clip, preschoolers who reported higher levels of trust in the media character were better able to explain the task to researchers and more likely to correctly complete the same task with similar objects.

Parasocial relationships with media characters also provide opportunities for learning when these characters are programmed to respond to children in socially contingent ways. One example comes from a series of studies conducted by Sandra Calvert and her colleagues.[17] The popular media character, Dora the Explorer, was put into a screen-based math game that taught preschool-aged children the "add-one rule" (i.e., the idea that when you add a single item to a group of items, it increases the total number of items by one). In some conditions, Dora responded to children contingently in real time, based on children's responses to math prompts. Dora also "knew" when children had made a mistake and helped them arrive at the correct answer.[18] In another condition, Dora simply moved through the game regardless of how children responded (as a TV program would). Preschoolers who experienced the contingent version of Dora responded more quickly and accurately to math prompts than children who did not and were better able to transfer what they learned to a similar task with physical objects. Children who had stronger parasocial relationships with Dora (as measured by a verbal survey) were even more likely to answer quickly and accurately to math prompts.

The results of these experiments suggest that methods for creating or enhancing a media character's contingent interaction with a child facilitate learning—especially when the child already has an established parasocial relationship with the media character. Rather than passive television/video viewing, which has dominated young children's digital lives,[19] interactive media characters that are artificially intelligent could be an effective new tool for helping children learn. Research on educational interventions using these technologies is underway at institutions like Carnegie Mellon, where Justine Cassell and her colleagues are programming AI virtual characters to build rapport with school-aged children with the goal of using these characters to improve academic performance.[20]

The educational opportunities that parasocial relationships afford could be one way in which these relationships are distinct from imaginary friendships. While children often incorporate real-world interests into their stories about imaginary friends, they are not learning new factual information directly from them. Instead, imaginary friends function more often as a source of entertainment, companionship, and emotional support (see Chapter 6). However, like imaginary friends, parasocial relationships also provide entertainment for children. In fact, the characters preferred by older children are more likely to be embedded in media designed for entertainment than for education.[21] But do parasocial relationships also function as supportive companions in the same way as imaginary friends?

To address this question, Naomi and Marjorie consulted the intuitions of preschool children about the possible functions of a virtual dog viewed on a screen as compared with an ordinary stuffed dog that was matched on physical appearance (e.g., same color and breed).[22] Our idea was that the virtual dog was the sort of entity that could inspire a parasocial relationship. It was programmed to simulate contingent responses (e.g., the virtual dog came when called, responded to being petted on a touch screen, and reacted in other ways to the child's voice) and was generally appealing and entertaining. The stuffed dog was the sort of toy that a children might use as a personified object.

After becoming familiar with both dogs, the children played a game in which they watched a real child in a video make a series of statements about a dog without specifying whether the statements referred to the virtual dog or the stuffed dog. The children's task was to guess which dog the child in the video was talking about. Although the virtual dog clearly moved around on its own and interacted with the child and the stuffed dog just sat there, the children viewed both dogs as being able to do things independently. Overall, children did not often differentiate between the two dogs, but when they did, the stuffed dog tended to be associated with statements relevant to friendship (e.g., "He/She keeps me company when I am lonely"), whereas the virtual dog was associated with statements relevant to entertainment (e.g., "S/he makes me laugh").

Naomi followed up this research by examining how school-aged children's concepts of an artificially intelligent child on a computer screen compared with a range of other potential relationship partners, including an inanimate doll. Graphic designers used photographs of real children to create realistic but slightly cartoonish depictions of children portrayed on a computer screen (the AI child), and dolls that closely resembled them (see Figure 11.1).[23] Five-to-eight-year-old children were shown the images and given brief descriptions (i.e., "Beth/Ben is a girl/boy character that you play with on a video game"; "Patty/Noah is a girl/boy doll that you play with"). Then the children were asked if each of a set of functions was true for the AI child and/or the doll (e.g., "S/he can keep you company,"; "S/he can help you feel better when you are sad"). The main finding was that children (both boys and girls) indicated that they were more likely to experience reciprocal love, companionship, and trust from the inanimate doll than they were from the virtual child.

Overall, the research findings suggest that there is overlap in the functions of parasocial relationships and imaginary friends (e.g., sources of entertainment), but they have different roles in children's lives. Parasocial relationships are distinctive in providing opportunities for acquiring new factual information and skills that children might seek out for themselves or that adults might use as educational tools. The available evidence suggests that parasocial relationships can provide emotional support, but love and companionship are more clearly the functions of imaginary friends.

Contingent Responding

Parasocial relationships do not typically have the personal two-sided imagined exchanges that characterize interactions with imaginary friends (e.g., conversations about pets, playing checkers, and arguing about what TV show to watch). The one-sided nature of parasocial relationships is widely listed as a defining characteristic. However, the types of exchanges that are possible within a parasocial relationship are changing as writers, directors, toy designers, and programmers develop techniques and technology to make interactions with media characters and personalities feel less one-sided. For example, one tried-and-true technique used in children's educational TV programs such as *Mr. Rogers' Neighborhood* and the modern take on this series, *Daniel Tiger's Neighborhood*, is to simulate a sense of characters interacting with young viewers by having them look directly into the camera as if they were making eye contact, ask questions of child viewers, and pause after asking a question, as if waiting for a response.

Parasocial Relationships with Celebrities and Media Characters 185

Figure 11.1 Naomi used photographs of four real boys and four real girls as the base images in her (2021) research. A team of graphic designers used each of these photographs to create corresponding images of (1) a child on a video chat program, (2) an AI child, and (3) a doll (for a total of 32 images—eight sets of four). Using multiple images helped to ensure that children's responses were not based on idiosyncratic features of a particular character (e.g., gender, hair color). This figure shows one of the sets of girl character images.

Image of real child printed by permission from Shutterstock. Images of children on a video chat program, AI children, and dolls printed by permission from Oslund Design Inc.

More striking are the communications that are made possible by AI. Parasocial relationships with fictional media characters can involve simulated social interactions in which the characters are perceived as responding directly and contingently to children in real time. The virtual pet game used in our study is one such example, and the AI version of Dora the Explorer in the study by Sandra Calvert and her colleagues is another. In these examples, the virtual characters responded to children in real time. Thus, the one-sidedness of parasocial relationships is disappearing as technology develops new ways for screen characters and smart toys to interact with children.

The digitized embodiment of such virtual characters combined with their programming for contingent responding presents children with a dilemma: What are these things? Are they alive or not alive? Can they think and do they feel? When viewed on a screen, they move independently, their voices are audible, and their emotions are detectable.[24] Many such characters have a presence in the real world, showing up on clothing, as toys or collectible action figures, and even in live action scenarios (e.g., children can meet characters "in real life" at Disneyland or Disney World). Perhaps it is not surprising that children tend to perceive fictional media characters as inhabiting the physical world beyond the page or the screen.[25] In other words, children (especially those under 6 years of age)[26] tend to believe fictional media characters are real rather than imaginary. In contrast, children are well aware that their imaginary friends are just pretend, at least in part because they were the ones who made them up (see Chapter 8).

Conversational agents or bots like "Siri" or "Alexa" are a different type of relationship partner because they don't have bodies or faces, but they excel in responding contingently (e.g., a child can ask "Alexa," questions and "Alexa" will respond based on what the child asked). In a study by Sandra Calvert and her colleagues, parents reported that their preschool-aged children had parasocial interactions with such conversational agents (asking questions such as "What happens when you die?" and "Are you a princess?") and developed emotional ties to them.[27] These findings suggest that the contingency that occurs through voice-activated systems might be enough to support the creation of a parasocial relationship. However, there are some cautions about drawing this conclusion. These findings were based on a one-time online parent survey, and the children were not questioned about the conversational agents directly or observed interacting with them. In addition, although the parents reported having the conversational agent in the household for about two years, it is unclear if the children's relationships with the agent endured over time.[28] Also, conversational agents differ from other media characters in the extent to which they are shared by whole households. Parents model how to interact with them—which might affect both the opportunities that children have to interact with these conversational agents and the relationships that they will develop with them.[29] Nevertheless, the Alexa example highlights the ways in which AI systems could become a type of relationship partner for children.

Currently there are too few studies examining how children interact with and respond to interactive AI characters on screens. We don't know the extent to which children actually *need* AI to help promote their learning from digital media or the extent that AI fosters parasocial relationships. Children's interactions with AI also have a downside. Smart toys marketed to children outside of carefully controlled educational settings can have unanticipated consequences. For example, when Hello Barbie entered the retail market in 2015, it was met with a lot of enthusiasm and media hype. Thanks to an embedded conversational agent, Barbie could now actually "talk to" and "get to know" her child playmates. But then it was discovered that Hello Barbie could be controlled by hackers and turned into a surveillance system, accessing children's personal information and conversations with the toy.[30] Hello Barbie was quickly discontinued.

The Hello Barbie fiasco raises bigger issues: we don't currently know what will happen to the data that children feed into AI systems, or what impact interactive

AI will have on children's long-term social, emotional, and academic development. The positive impacts of these technologies will likely be dependent on how they are designed (e.g., child-centered vs. profit-centered), what they will be designed for (e.g., education, therapeutic interventions, entertainment), what safeguards are put in place (e.g., firewalls, data encryption, opt-outs, user control), and who will benefit from their existence (e.g., children, families, product developers, companies).

In our view, interactive characters powered by AI are more suited for education than for lasting friendship. Children don't mention smart toys when they talk about their imaginary friends (see Chapter 3) or even when they are asked about their parasocial relationships.[31] Despite advances in AI designed to make the targets of parasocial relationships more interactive, the contingent responding that occurs in parasocial relationships is still qualitatively different from the reciprocity that is routine in imaginary friendships.

Creative Control

The most important difference between parasocial relationships and imaginary friendships involves creative control. With the fictional media characters that are the targets of children's parasocial relationships, the child is not the author of the character's appearance, personality characteristics, the places they live, or the other people or characters in their fictional lives. Everything has already been created for them. Children have much more creative control over their imaginary friends than the targets of parasocial relationships. This difference is most obvious with idiosyncratic invisible friends but is still true for personified objects and imaginary friends based on fictional media characters. A toy that becomes a personified object comes with a set appearance, but the child has creative control over its personality and the kind of relationship they have with it. A stuffed bear could be a fun-loving and shy friend who likes snuggling and being read to, or a loud and unruly prankster who is funny and fun but always getting into trouble. In the case of imaginary friends based on fictional media characters, children can pick and choose among the existing characteristics of the character and then elaborate to make up their own version. The influence of the media is usually limited to superficial characteristics, such as name and appearance.[32]

Children also have more creative control over their interactions with imaginary friends. Unlike AI generated responses, an imaginary friend's contributions to an interaction are part of what the child imagines. The creative control that children exercise over what the imaginary friend says, does, and feels is crucial to the experience of the relationship. Even in the instances in which imaginary friends are unruly, disobedient, or otherwise experienced as having minds of their own, their autonomy is imagined rather than the actual autonomy of the partners in parasocial relationships.

We suspect that adult efforts to increase the realism and contingent responsiveness of smart toys might not increase the scope of children's interactions with them or make these toys preferred companions. Moreover, programming could interfere with children's ability to explore friendships beyond the scripts that drive the characters in these games. For instance, in the study with the AI dog, most children played with the dog in the ways supported by the programming, which was designed to help children learn how to take care of real pets (e.g., feeding, grooming), rather than to provide a lasting relationship. Maybe no AI system can truly compare to a child's imagination.

Adults' Parasocial Relationships

One of the interesting things about parasocial relationships is that they are associated with a much wider age range than imaginary friends, which peak in childhood. Lots of adults have parasocial relationships, and the adult versions get a lot of attention on podcasts (e.g., episodes of *Doxxed*[33]) and the press (e.g., the *New York Times*).[34] Is an adult parasocial relationship like an adult version of having an imaginary friend? This possibility seems to be the view of both *The Atlantic* ("Parasocial Relationships Are Just Imaginary Friends for Adults")[35] and the *New York Times* ("When Grown-Ups Have Imaginary Friends: 'Parasocial relationships' Explain Why You Think Influencers Are Your Pals").[36]

We would not go that far, but parasocial relationships are interesting in their own right and are worth some discussion. They might be one of few socially acceptable types of imaginary relationships adults can have that are not automatically assumed to be markers of social, mental, or emotional problems. And yet, when we think of adults having parasocial relationships, pathological examples of obsessed fans come to mind, such as John Hinkley Jr.'s attempt to impress Jodie Foster by shooting President Reagan or Mark Chapman's murder of John Lennon. There are other examples of unhinged fans killing celebrities (e.g., Selena, Rebecca Shaeffer) and many more of them sending death threats. For example, Brenock O'Connor, who played the character "Olly" on *Game of Thrones*, received real death threats after killing the beloved fictional character Jon Snow in Season 6 of the TV series.[37]

According to cultural anthropologist John Caughey,[38] these extreme and violent examples make us overlook how common and normal imagined relationships are in the general population. In a fascinating book, *Imaginary Social Worlds*, Caughey claimed that the social worlds of *most* people include a large number of individuals whom they know only through television, books, and movies. Caughey exhaustively described these adult parasocial relationships and the roles they play in people's lives, including historical examples in which parasocial relationships can be a source of advice or an avenue for intellectual debate (e.g., Machiavelli having imaginary dinner conversations with ancient poets and with powerful individuals such as Moses, Romulus, and Theseus). But mostly Caughey focuses on his ethnographic research with adults who provided rich descriptions of their feelings of personal connection to the targets of their parasocial relationships. For example, a 21-year-old fan of Roger Daltrey of The Who recalled her experience of attending a concert: "I felt as though The Who were playing their songs just for me. I was surrounded by their music. When I left the concert, I felt exhilarated, as though I had actually met The Who in person."[39]

Caughey's book was written long before the rise of social media, so his informants mostly described relationships with musicians, actors, and athletes. Today there are many more possible targets, including social media influencers, Peloton coaches, reality TV stars, podcasters, gaming live streamers, and others. Research with adults tends to focus on parasocial relationships with real people who have never been encountered in life,[40] but adults as well as adolescents form similar bonds with fictional media characters (e.g., anime characters, Yoda from *Star Wars*). Just take a look at all the Discord servers devoted to anime characters alone to get a sense of just how prevalent and deep these relationships can be among adults.[41]

Emotional bonds with media characters develop in ways similar to real friendships. Initial attraction to and identification with the on-screen character lead to repeated parasocial interactions in which the person sees and has the opportunity to engage with the character through the media platform.[42] In turn, these repeated parasocial interactions become the basis upon which an enduring bond is formed.[43] With real people (e.g., celebrities), research tends to address specific aspects of parasocial relationships, such as "wishful identification" with the person.[44] Often the focus of these relationships is love and/or sexual attraction, such as imagined romantic attachments to famous actors and musicians, such as Harry Styles and Beyoncé.[45] In these instances, parasocial relationships are thought to serve as safe spaces for adolescents and young adults to experiment with their identities through identification with media personas, as well as explore their sexuality and the emotional intimacies of romantic relationships without the risk of rejection.[46]

Numerous studies indicate that parasocial relationships can affect emotional states, sense of well-being, and identity.[47] Much of the impact occurs via social media. For instance, an analysis of reactions on X (formerly Twitter) over the first 10 days following the death of the beloved character Jon Snow in *Game of Thrones* indicated that fans experienced the stages of grief associated with the loss of real people (i.e., denial, bargaining, acceptance).[48] Parasocial relationships also can function as a source of information, affecting the way people think about an issue or the products they buy. Even the targets that are based on fictional media characters often have their own social media accounts with "posts" that are attributed to the character but nevertheless might be taken seriously. For example, in 2021 a US senator (a real person in a position of authority) responded seriously to ideas attributed to a fictional character (a post on X, formerly Twitter, by Big Bird).[49]

The emotional and educational function of parasocial relationships can influence adolescents and adults in both positive and negative ways.[50] Celebrities and social media influencers can promote important health and safely information[51] but also model risky health behaviors, such as vaping and experimenting with extreme diets.[52]

Influencers can create safe spaces to build community and to cope with stressors,[53] while also promoting materialism, fame, and negative social comparisons.[54] According to Cynthia Hoffner and Bradley Bond,[55] the net effect of parasocial relationships that occur on social media is still unknown, although in their review of the research, they identified more positive than negative effects of these relationships. Any negative effects of parasocial relationships with influencers and celebrities might be due—at least in part—to the ways in which social media algorithms promote user profiles and content and the characteristics of the adults who have them. In some studies, adults who have insecure attachments to the real people in their lives tend to form more intense parasocial relationships and be more strongly affected by the statements and actions of the targets than those who are securely attached to real others.[56]

The targets of most adult parasocial relationships do not have to be imagined—they are mostly real people or fictional media characters that have well-known personalities and storylines. And especially in the past, these relationships were one-sided because the targets were inaccessible and did not have ways to interact directly. But as discussed with the parasocial relationships of children, things are changing. With advances in AI, fictional media characters are increasingly able to provide autonomous responses, and of course, relationships with conversational agents like Alexa are all about the immediate and contingent responses of the agent. In addition, many celebrities try to increase their fans' sense of personal connection by interacting with them on platforms such as YouTube, SnapChat, TikTok, Meta, and Instagram. On sites like Patreon and Cameo, fans can pay a fee to receive detailed information and/or have personal interactions with their favorite stars and influencers. On X (formerly Twitter), fans of famous musicians can—through solo or collective action—communicate with artists about their music and sometimes influence their choices. For example, the popular '90s band, Weezer, chose to cover the song "Africa"[57] after a fan insisted on social media that they cover it.[58] With the increase in real or AI-generated communications from the targets of parasocial relationships, one-sidedness does not seem to be such a defining feature anymore. But note that the adults creating these parasocial relationships are not the authors of these types of direct communications. Adults are listening to and watching their targets' contingent responses rather than imagining them.

Summary

The 8-year-old quoted at the beginning of this chapter asked if hanging out with a character on a video game counts as an imaginary friend. We think his description sounds more like a parasocial relationship. While both types of relationships involve imagination and can have real-world impact on thoughts, feeling, attitudes, and behaviors, there are qualitative differences. For children, parasocial relationships provide entertainment and educational opportunities, but they might not offer as much in the way of companionship compared with what children can create for themselves. Limitations in creative control over the targets themselves and interactions with them are what best distinguish parasocial relationships from imaginary friends. Children invent their imaginary friends without help from their parents or other people to bring these relationships about and to benefit from them. Parasocial relationships will never be solely the product of one person's imagination.

The personal communications of the celebrities, media characters, conversational agents, and other targets of parasocial relationships are increasing with social media platforms and advances in AI, but the interactive possibilities of parasocial relationships are a long way from what routinely happens with imaginary friends. Should we be surprised? Generations of parents have watched their children push aside a fancy toy to play with the box it arrived in, but we still often underestimate children's ability to entertain themselves by exploring the open-ended possibilities of their imaginations. Still, our ability to develop a sense of personal connection in a parasocial relationship has an interesting history and, given the rise of social media influencers and advanced technology, a fascinating future.

We have made the case that the parasocial relationships of adults should not be considered adult versions of what children experience with their imaginary friends. But do adults ever have imaginary friends that are similar to the child phenomenon in both relationship reciprocity and creative control? Yes, they do. In Chapter 12, we discuss the imaginary friends that linger well beyond childhood or appear for the first time later in life.

Notes

1. Hoffner, C. (2008). Parasocial and online social relationships. In S. L. Calvert & B. J. Wilson (Eds.), *The handbook of children, media, and development* (pp. 309–333). Wiley-Blackwell.
2. Horton, D., & Richard Wohl, R. (1956). Mass communication and para-social interaction: Observations on intimacy at a distance. *Psychiatry, 19*(3), 215–229.
3. Dibble, J. L., & Rosaen, S. F. (2011). Parasocial interaction as more than friendship: Evidence for parasocial interactions with disliked media figures. *Journal of Media Psychology: Theories, Methods, and Applications, 23*(3), 122. https://doi.org/10.1027/1864-1105/a000044
4. Honeycutt, J. M. (2020). Imagined interactions and inner speech. *Imagination, Cognition and Personality, 39*(4), 386–396.
5. Gleason, T. R. (2013). Imaginary relationships. In M. Taylor (Ed.), *The Oxford handbook of the development of imagination* (pp. 251–271). Oxford University Press. https://doi.org/10.1093/oxfordhb/9,780,195,395,761.013.0017
6. Tolbert, A. N., & Drogos, K. L. (2019). Tweens' wishful identification and parasocial relationships with YouTubers. *Frontiers in Psychology, 10*, 1–15.
7. Gleason, T. R., Theran, S. A., & Newberg, E. M. (2017). Parasocial interactions and relationships in early adolescence. *Frontiers in Psychology, 8*, 1–11. https://doi.org/10.3389/fpsyg.2017.00255

8. Aguiar, N. R., Richards, M. N., Bond, B. J., Brunick, K. L., & Calvert, S. L. (2019). Parents' perceptions of their children's parasocial relationships: The recontact study. *Imagination, Cognition and Personality, 38*(3), 221–249. https://doi.org/10.1177/0276236618771537
9. Frost, B. J. (Writer) & Stern, T. (Director). (2017). *He-man* (Season 1, episode 3) [TV series episode]. In B. Volk-Weiss, T. Stern, A. Carkeet, & E. Zane (Executive Producers), *The Toys that Made Us*. The Nacelle Company, Netflix.
10. Bond, B. J., & Calvert, S. L. (2014). A model and measure of US parents' perceptions of young children's parasocial relationships. *Journal of Children and Media, 8*, 286–304. https://doi.org/10.1080/17,482,798.2014.890948
11. Richards, M. N., & Calvert, S. L. (2016). Parent versus child report of young children's parasocial relationships in the United States. *Journal of Children and Media, 10*, 462–480. https://doi.org/10.1080/17,482,798.2016.1157502
12. Ibid.
13. There are some notable exceptions such as like Harry Potter, who grows up over the course of the book series.
14. Gola, A. A., Richards, M. N., Lauricella, A. R., & Calvert, S. L. (2013). Building meaningful parasocial relationships between toddlers and media characters to teach early mathematical skills. *Media Psychology, 16*(4), 390–411. https://doi.org/10.1080/15,213,269.2013.783774
    Calvert, S. L., Putnam, M. M., Aguiar, N. R., Ryan, R. M., Wright, C. A., Liu, Y. H. A., & Barba, E. (2020). Young children's mathematical learning from intelligent characters. *Child Development, 91*(5), 1491–1508. https://doi.org/10.1111/cdev.13341
    Schlesinger, M. A., Flynn, R. M., & Richert, R. A. (2016). US preschoolers' trust of and learning from media characters. *Journal of Children and Media, 10*(3), 321–340. https://doi.org/10.1080/17,482,798.2016.1162184
15. Lauricella, A. R., Gola, A. A. H., & Calvert, S. L. (2011). Toddlers' learning from socially meaningful video characters. *Media Psychology, 14*, 216–232. https://doi.org/10.1080/15,213,269.2011.573465
16. Schlesinger, M. A., Flynn, R. M., & Richert, R. A. (2016). US preschoolers' trust of and learning from media characters. *Journal of Children and Media*.
17. Calvert, S. L., Putnam, M. M., Aguiar, N. R., Ryan, R. M., Wright, C. A., Liu, Y. H. A., & Barba, E. (2020). Young children's mathematical learning from intelligent characters. *Child Development*.
18. To make Dora appear artificially intelligent, experimenters used a "Wizard of Oz" approach, where an experimenter hid behind a screen with a computer and selected a set of programed responses based on how the children responded to each question.
19. Rideout, V., & Robb, M. B. (2020). *The Common Sense census: Media use by kids age zero to eight, 2020*. Common Sense Media. https://www.commonsensemedia.org/sites/default/files/research/report/2020_zero_to_eight_census_final_web.pdf
20. Zhao, R., Papangelis, A., & Cassell, J. (2014). Towards a dyadic computational model of rapport management for human-virtual agent interaction. In G. Goos (Ed.), *International Conference on Intelligent Virtual Agents* (pp. 514–527). Springer International Publishing.
    Finkelstein, S., Yarzebinski, E., Vaughn, C., & Cassell, J. (2013). Modeling ethnicity into technology: Using virtual agents to understand sociolinguistic variation. *In Proceedings of NWA, 42*, 17–20.

21. Aguiar, N. R., Richards, M. N., Bond, B. J., Putnam, M. M., & Calvert, S. L. (2019). Children's parasocial breakups with media characters from the perspective of the parent. *Imagination, Cognition and Personality, 38*(3), 193–220. https://doi.org/10.1177/0276236618809902
22. Aguiar, N. A., & Taylor, M. (2015). Children's concepts of the social affordances of a virtual dog and a stuffed dog. *Cognitive Development, 34,* 16–27.
23. Aguiar, N. R. (2021). A paradigm for assessing adults' and children's concepts of artificially intelligent virtual characters. *Human Behavior and Emerging Technologies, 3*(4), 618–634.
24. This incongruence in children's concepts has been captured in the "new ontological category" hypothesis (see Kahn, Gary, & Shen, 2013), which attempts to account for children's complex and multifaceted judgments about the reality status of social robots (Jipson & Gelman, 2007; Severson & Carlson, 2010). According to this view, children and adults treat new technologies that simulate both social exchanges and social relationships as a new and unique category of human artifacts—nonbiological agents that are neither "alive" nor "not alive" (see Kahn et al., 2013; Severson & Carlson, 2010).

    Jipson, J. L., & Gelman, S. A. (2007). Robots and rodents: Children's inferences about living and nonliving kinds. *Child Development, 78*(6), 1675–1688.

    Kahn, P. H., Jr., Gary, H. E., & Shen, S. (2013). Children's social relationships with current and near-future robots. *Child Development Perspectives, 7,* 32–37.

    Severson, R. L., & Carlson, S. M. (2010). Behaving as or behaving as if? Children's conceptions of personified robots and the emergence of a new ontological category. *Neural Networks, 23,* 1099–1103.
25. Aguiar, N. R., Richards, M. N., Bond, B. J., Brunick, K. L., & Calvert, S. L. (2019). Parents' perceptions of their children's parasocial relationships: The recontact study. *Imagination, Cognition and Personality, 38*(3), 221–249. https://doi.org/10.1177/0276236618771537
26. Hoffman, A., Owen, D., & Calvert, S. L. (2021). Parent reports of children's parasocial relationships with conversational agents: Trusted voices in children's lives. *Human Behavior and Emerging Technologies, 3*(4), 606–617.
27. Ibid.
28. Aguiar, N. R., Richards, M. N., Bond, B. J., Putnam, M. M., & Calvert, S. L. (2019). Children's parasocial breakups with media characters from the perspective of the parent. *Imagination, Cognition and Personality, 38*(3), 193–220. https://doi.org/10.1177/0276236618809902
29. Naomi has often found her daughter and her daughter's friends' interactions with conversational agents jarring at best and annoying at worst. "Alexa" is asked to play music at inopportune times or to answer questions that can sometimes be silly or inappropriate (e.g., potty humor).
30. Gibbs, S. (2016, November 26). Hackers can hijack Wi-Fi Hello Barbie to spy on your children. *The Guardian.* https://www.theguardian.com/technology/2015/nov/26/hackers-can-hijack-wi-fi-hello-barbie-to-spy-on-your-children
31. Richards, M. N., & Calvert, S. L. (2017). Measuring young U.S. children's parasocial relationships: Toward the creation of a child self-report survey. *Journal of Children and Media, 11,* 229–240. https://doi.org/10.1080/17,482,798.2017.1304969
32. Ruben, E., French, J. A., Lee, H. J., Aguiar, N. R., & Richert, R. (2023, March). *Let it go: Media influences on imaginary companions in early childhood* [poster presentation]. Biennial Meeting of the Society for Research in Child Development, Salt Lake City, UT.

33. Renee, R., & Bonis, J. (Hosts). (2023, April 26). Parasocial relationship pitfalls (No. 5) [Audio podcast episode]. In *Doxxed The Podcast.*(RSS.com). https://rss.com/podcasts/doxxedthepodcast/910459/
34. Grose, J. (2021, May 5). When grown-ups have imaginary friends: "Parasocial relationships" explain why you think influencers are your pals. *The New York Times.* https://www.nytimes.com/2021/05/05/parenting/influencers-social-media-relationships.html?searchResultPosition=1

    Ng, B. (2021, December 17). *Did you see what Big Bird tweeted? Social media is fueling our "parasocial relationships" with TV characters. The New York Times.* https://www.nytimes.com/2021/12/17/style/sesame-street-social-media-parasocial-relationships.html?searchResultPosition=3

    Botsman, R. (2017, October). Co-parenting with Alexa. *The New York Times.* https://www.nytimes.com/2017/10/07/opinion/sunday/children-alexa-echo-robots.html?searchResultPosition=5

    Newman, J. (2014, October 17). To Siri, with love. *The New York Times.* https://www.nytimes.com/2014/10/19/fashion/how-apples-siri-became-one-autistic-boys-bff.html
35. Brooks, A. C. (2023, April). Parasocial relationships are just imaginary friends for adults: if you get too invested in a fake friendship, your real ones might suffer. *The Atlantic.* https://www.theatlantic.com/family/archive/2023/04/parasocial-relationships-imaginary-connections-fans-celebrities/673645/
36. Grose, J. (2021, May). When grown-ups have imaginary friends: "Parasocial relationships" explain why you think influencers are your pals. *The New York Times.*
37. Robinson, M. (2016, May). A teen actor from "Game of Thrones" has been getting death threats from viewers. *Business Insider.* https://www.businessinsider.com/olly-actor-game-of-thrones-death-threats-2016-5
38. Caughey, J. L. (1984). *Imaginary social worlds: A cultural approach.* University of Nebraska Press.
39. Ibid., p. 42.
40. Gleason, T. R., Theran, S. A., & Newberg, E. M. (2017). Parasocial interactions and relationships in early adolescence. *Frontiers in Psychology, 8,* 1–11. https://doi.org/10.3389/fpsyg.2017.00255
41. Note that fan fiction is another way that fans can engage with their favorite characters and storylines.
42. Auter, P. J., & Palmgreen, P. (2000). Development and validation of a parasocial interaction measure: The audience-persona interaction scale. *Communication Research Reports, 17*(1), 79–89.

    Rubin, A. M., Perse, E. M., & Powell, R. A. (1985). Loneliness, parasocial interaction, and local television news viewing. *Human Communication Research, 12,* 155–180. https://doi.org/10.1111/j.1468-2958.1985.tb00071.x
43. Dibble, J. L., Hartmann, T., & Rosaen, S. F. (2016). Parasocial interaction and parasocial relationship: Conceptual clarification and a critical assessment of measures. *Human Communication Research, 42*(1), 21–44. https://doi.org/10.1111/hcre.12063

    Giles, D. C. (2002). Parasocial interaction: A review of the literature and a model for future research. *Media Psychology, 4*(3), 279–305. https://doi.org/10.1207/S1532785XMEP0403_04

Schramm, H., & Hartmann, T. (2008). The PSI-process scales. A new measure to assess the intensity and breadth of parasocial processes. *Communications: The European Journal of Communication Research, 33*, 385–401. https://doi.org/10.1515/COMM.2008.025

44. Hoffner, C. (2008). Parasocial and online social relationships. In S. L. Calvert & B. J. Wilson (Eds.), *The handbook of children, media, and development* (pp. 309–333). Wiley-Blackwell.

    Gleason, T. R., Theran, S. A., & Newberg, E. M. (2017). Parasocial interactions and relationships in early adolescence. *Frontiers in Psychology, 8*, 1–11. https://doi.org/10.3389/fpsyg.2017.00255

    Lim, J. S., Choe, M. J., Zhang, J., & Noh, G. Y. (2020). The role of wishful identification, emotional engagement, and parasocial relationships in repeated viewing of live-streaming games: A social cognitive theory perspective. *Computers in Human Behavior, 108*, 106327.

45. Adam, A., & Sizemore, B. (2013). Parasocial romance: A social exchange perspective. *Interpersona: An International Journal on Personal Relationships, 7*(1), 12–25.

    Erickson, S. E., Harrison, K., & Dal Cin, S. (2018). Toward a multi-dimensional model of adolescent romantic parasocial attachment. *Communication Theory, 28*(3), 376–399.

46. Hoffner, C. A., & Bond, B. J. (2022). Parasocial relationships, social media, & well-being. *Current Opinion in Psychology, 45*, 101306.

47. Ibid.

48. Daniel, E. S., Jr., & Westerman, D. K. (2017). Valar Morghulis (all parasocial men must die): Having nonfictional responses to a fictional character. *Communication Research Reports, 34*(2), 143–152.

49. Ng, B. (2021, December 17). *Did you see what Big Bird tweeted? Social media is fueling our "parasocial relationships" with TV characters*. New York Times.

50. Hoffner, C. A., & Bond, B. J. (2022). Parasocial relationships, social media, & well-being.

51. Kang, S., Dove, S., Ebright, H., Morales, S., & Kim, H. (2021). Does virtual reality affect behavioral intention? Testing engagement processes in a K-Pop video on YouTube. *Computers in Human Behavior, 123*, 106875.

    Kresovich, A., & Noar, S. M. (2020). The power of celebrity health events: Meta-analysis of the relationship between audience involvement and behavioral intentions. *Journal of Health Communication, 25*(6), 501–513.

52. Daniel, E. S., Jr., Crawford Jackson, E. C., & Westerman, D. K. (2018). The influence of social media influencers: Understanding online vaping communities and parasocial interaction through the lens of Taylor's six-segment strategy wheel. *Journal of Interactive Advertising, 18*(2), 96–109.

    Myrick, J. G., & Erlichman, S. (2020). How audience involvement and social norms foster vulnerability to celebrity-based dietary misinformation. *Psychology of Popular Media, 9*(3), 367.

53. Niu, S., Bartolome, A., Mai, C., & Ha, N. B. (2021, May). # StayHome# WithMe: How do YouTubers help with COVID-19 loneliness? In Y. Yoshifumi & A. Quigley (Eds.), *Proceedings of the 2021 CHI conference on human factors in computing systems* (pp. 1–15). Association for Computing Machinery.

54. Hoffner, C. A., & Bond, B. J. (2022). Parasocial relationships, social media, & well-being.

55. Ibid.

56. Cole, T., & Leets, L. (1999). Attachment styles and intimate television viewing: Insecurely forming relationships in a parasocial way. *Journal of Social and Personal Relationships, 16,* 495–511.
57. See both the original song and Weezer's cover here: https://www.youtube.com/watch?v=FTQbiNvZqaY; https://www.youtube.com/watch?v=mk5Dwg5zm2U
58. Greene, D. (Host). (2018, May 30). Weezer gives in to fans and covers Toto's "Africa." [Audio radio episode]. On *Morning edition.* NPR. https://www.npr.org/2018/05/30/615388548/weezer-gives-in-to-fans-and-covers-totos-africa

Chapter 12
The Imaginary Friends of Adults

"How old do you have to be before having an imaginary friend is a bad thing?" We have been asked variations of this question many times, and often the look on the asker's face suggests that they have a personal stake in the answer. Why do we get nervous about adults having imaginary friends? After all, adults engage in a wide range of fantasy activities such as role playing in games in real life or online, (e.g., *Dungeons and Dragons*, *Final Fantasy*), historical re-enactments like those of the Society for Creative Anachronism, and acting in theatrical or film productions. According to Paul Bloom,

> our main leisure activity is, by a long shot, participating in activities that we know are not real. When we are free to do whatever we want, we retreat to the imagination—to worlds created by others, as in books, movies, video games, and television (over four hours a day for the average American) and to worlds we ourselves create, as when daydreaming and fantasizing.[1]

The actors, producers, and writers who supply us with an unending flow of movies, television shows, and novels are paid some of the highest salaries in our nation. The avid consumption of fantasy material by adults includes fantastical worlds that originally were created for children. As Jennifer Barnes points out,

> A single person could have sat around from the dawn of man until now doing nothing but reading *Harry Potter* and watching the *Harry Potter* movies, and that still would not encompass the amount of time people have invested in the franchise since the first book was published in 1997.[2]

The importance of fictional characters to adults was underscored when two imaginary people (Anne of Green Gables, the protagonist in L. M. Montgomery's novels and Evangeline, the heroine of Henry Wadsworth Longfellow's famous poem) were included in *Maclean's Magazine* list compiled by a prestigious panel of judges of the 100 most important Canadians in history, side by side with real people like Alexander Graham Bell, Wayne Gretsky, and Pierre Trudeau. But even more so than with children, adults who create and interact with invisible friends are often assumed to be disturbed.[3]

This view is reflected in fictional portrayals such as Elwood Dowd in Mary Chase's play *Harvey*[4] (Jimmy Stewart's character in the movie adaptation). Elwood's sister attempts to commit Elwood to a sanatorium because Elwood's best friend is a

Imaginary Friends and the People Who Create Them. Second Edition. Marjorie Taylor and Naomi R. Aguiar,
Oxford University Press. © Oxford University Press (2024). DOI: 10.1093/9780190888916.003.0012

6' 3½" invisible white rabbit named Harvey. But Elwood's practice of introducing Harvey to everyone he met was just part of what made Elwood odd. Despite his age, his naive personality and sheltered existence (unmarried, unemployed, living with his sisters) made him more like a child than a grown-up. In another fictional account (*Who's Afraid of Virginia Woolf*), Edward Albee[5] (1962) introduces us to George and Martha, an unhappily married couple who have collaborated for years on an elaborate fantasy about an imaginary son. In Act Three ("The Exorcism"), the son is revealed as fantasy to the other characters in the play when Martha reacts violently to George's decision to imagine that the son, now a 21-year-old college student, has been killed in a car accident. Their fantasy about an imaginary son is the basis for George and Martha being described in literary commentary as mentally ill.[6] There is also the unnamed Narrator from the movie *Fight Club*[7] (played by Edward Norton), whose character brawls with an imaginary friend (enemy?), Tyler Durden (played by Brad Pitt). In fact, when you start to look for fictional examples of such relationships, they abound. What they have in common is that none of the adults are portrayed as having good mental health.

Is this assessment necessarily true? The erroneous assumption here is that having an imaginary friend is like having a delusion or hallucination—the creator, whether a child or an adult, believes the friend to be real. This sort of behavior might be tolerated to some extent in children because of the widespread belief that childhood is a stage of life in which it is normal to lack a firm grasp on reality (a view we do not support). But in adults, the expression of unusual beliefs or hallucinations is often central to the identification of mental illness. However, we have argued that even very young children understand that their imaginary friends are pretend (see Chapter 8). Thus, if we want to identify an adult version of the phenomenon, we need to identify imaginary friends that the adults know are not real. We should look for something closer to the imaginary friends of typically developing children, rather than rely on examples based on those suffering from psychosis.

The restrictions that (1) the friend is imaginary and (2) the adult *knows* the friend is imaginary rule out lots of entities that bear a passing resemblance to imaginary friends. For example, people sometimes ask about guardian angels, Jesus, fairies, ghosts, and creatures from outer space. Should any of these be considered imaginary friends? We think not. In these cases, the perceived realities of these entities depend on the person. This point is most clear in the domain of religion. Many adults strongly believe that God, angels, and spirits of various sorts are real. Faith, the capacity to believe without doubt, is prayed for and highly valued. An atheist observing the practices of someone who believes in God might refer to the person as having an imaginary friend. But for people of faith, applying the word "imaginary" to their relationship with God would be considered insulting because it undermines or calls into question this faith.

As for ghosts, creatures from outer space, and other similar beings, the case is less clear. For one thing, people disagree about whether these beings are imaginary or have some basis in reality. Although no accepted scientific evidence for the paranormal currently exists, a 2001 Gallup Poll showed an increase from 1990 in adults' beliefs in a range of paranormal experiences involving these entities.[8] More recently, a poll by Ipsos (Institut Public de Sondage d'Opinion Secteur) revealed that about 46% of adults in the United States believe in ghosts.[9] If we broaden our view to take a cross-cultural perspective, the problem of how to decide what is real and what is fantasy becomes even more challenging. Reality can be viewed as culturally constructed—in other words, there is not one universally accepted and "objective" truth (see Chapter 6). A belief can be judged as a delusion or not depending on the culture of the believer.[10] In any case, the point is that to qualify as an imaginary friend, the entity in question has to be considered imaginary by both the person and their culture.

Fortunately, it is not necessary for us to decide whether a particular invisible entity is real or not. All that matters is the belief of the person who communes with it. In order to be similar to the childhood phenomenon of imaginary friends, adults who claim to interact with ghosts, for example, would have to conceptualize the ghosts as figments of their imagination. In many cases, however, adults who claim to interact with entities like ghosts believe they are real.

Do Adults Have Imaginary Friends?

One of the examples used in a newspaper article on the "crazy" behaviors of airline passengers featured an adult with an imaginary friend. According to a flight attendant,

> a passenger told her, "I'll have a scotch and soda and he (gesturing to the empty seat beside her) will have a scotch and soda." The attendant placed two drinks in front of the woman who complained, "Well, aren't you going to let his tray down and give him a napkin?" The attendant let down the tray and placed one of the drinks in front of the empty seat and then said, "That will be $5 please." The woman gestured to her invisible companion, and said, "He'll pay for it."[11]

This anecdote was reported in the *Chicago Tribune*, but is it for real? If so, we are not sure about this woman's mental health.

Some reports of imaginary friends created by adults are found in clinical cases studies,[12] but do adults who are psychologically healthy and have adult lifestyles with adult responsibilities ever have imaginary friends? Yes, they do. These kinds of experiences include intellectual exercises such as Hillary Clinton's imagined conversations with Eleanor Roosevelt and more fully developed fantasies about imaginary friends that are a source of support, advice, and entertainment. For example, Karl-Anthony Towns, a star basketball player for the Minnesota Timberwolves of the National Basketball Association, is well known for his on-court communications with an imaginary friend named Karlito who sits on his shoulder. According to Towns, Karlito provides a critique of his ongoing performance in a game, helps him figure out what he needs to work on, and serves as a distraction that prevents him from talking back to a coach.[13]

Some adults create imaginary relationships with close loved ones who have recently died, such as spouses, siblings, or children.[14] These imaginary relationships are referred to as continuing bonds, and are thought by many scholars to be a normative part of the grieving process.[15] What is striking about continuing bonds is that they can evolve over time, growing and changing along with the living adult.[16] For instance, some adults turn to their deceased spouse for advice with new important or difficult life decisions. Much like other imaginary relationships, adults report that continuing bonds make them feel loved, valued, and supported.[17,18]

How often do adults have imaginary friends that are similar to the childhood phenomenon? In the past, interview questions about imaginary friends have reflected the assumption that they are long gone and the adults are describing memories from childhood (e.g., "How old were you when you stopped playing with the imaginary companion?"). Early on, Marjorie was guilty of asking this type of leading question. However, a few adults reported that they still interacted with their imaginary friends. For example, one woman described how her imaginary friend served as the voice of reason when she was thinking through an issue in her life.[19] A couple of respondents reported that they still cherished stuffed animals who had been with them since childhood ("I still tell my bunny my problems"). One professional adult described how she used a stuffed animal as a go-between when discussing difficult issues with her husband. Another couple discussed their collection of stuffed animals in a way that was reminiscent of parents talking about their children. The husband, an award-winning writer of fiction, also shared the characters of his novels with his wife. Together, they recounted some of the past exploits of these characters, in and out of their respective novels.[20] Research by Stephen Jay Lynn and his colleagues on fantasy-prone adults provides a few additional examples of adults with imaginary friends. One woman described Alexis, an invisible girl who had been her friend as a small child. "As I grew older, she seemed to grow with me, age with me. When I am afraid, I sometimes talk to her, and she is a source of comfort. When I have writer's block, she is my muse. We are separate yet together. It is the separateness that is still enriching..."[21]

In a large online study, Charles Fernyhough and his colleagues[22] asked, "Do you have an imaginary friend now?," and 110 adults (7.5% of the 1,472 adults in the sample) answered "yes." Eighty-four of these adults were referring to childhood friends that persisted, and 26 were talking about imaginary friends that emerged in adulthood. The authors cautioned that this sample was not representative of the general population. The adults were a highly educated group (80% had a graduate degree), 76% were female, and the questions were part of a study of mental imagery, which could have selected for individuals who had particularly vivid imagery and thus were interested in participating in the study. Nevertheless, the finding that so many adults claimed to have imaginary friends might surprise some readers. For Marjorie, not so much. When she started looking more carefully, it became clear that some adults derive a great deal of pleasure and comfort from imaginary friends.

Biographies, Diaries, and Documentaries as Sources of Information

Over the past two decades, Marjorie and her colleagues have collected more than 1,000 descriptions of imaginary friends from studies in which we have interviewed children, parents, and adults. However, Marjorie also collects descriptions wherever she finds them—in magazine and newspaper articles, from people who write to her via the Internet, and from casual encounters. If the person sitting next to her on an airplane starts to tell her about their memories of an imaginary friend, she is apt to whip out a questionnaire and ask for permission to use the description in her writing or talks.

When Marjorie first started examining biographies, autobiographies, and diaries, she was looking for retrospective accounts of childhood imaginary friends. She was curious about the possibility that having an imaginary friend as a child might be associated with creative achievement as an adult. If so, one might expect the biographies of people who became famous in adulthood for their creative work to be particularly likely to include descriptions of childhood imaginary friends. And some of them do. Here is an example from a diary entry (Sunday, March 26, 1905) by Lucy Maud Montgomery (1874–1942):

> As far back as consciousness runs, *Katie Maurice* and *Lucy Gray* lived in the fairy room behind the bookcase. *Katie* was a little girl like myself and I loved her dearly. I would stand before that door and prattle to her for hours, giving and receiving confidences... *Lucy Gray* was grown-up—and a *widow*! I did not like her as well as Katie. She was always sad and always had dismal stories of her troubles to relate to me; nevertheless, I always visited her scrupulously in turn, lest her feelings should be hurt, because she was jealous of *Katie*, who also disliked her.[23]

Montgomery was 31 years old when she wrote this entry—a month or so before she began her most famous novel, *Anne of Green Gables*. Those who have read *Anne of Green Gables* will recognize Katie because she appears in the book as Anne's imaginary friend, a point that Montgomery mentions in a diary entry several years later (1911): "The *Katie Maurice* of Anne was *my* Katie Maurice—that imaginary playmate of the glass bookcase door in our sitting room."[24]

Montgomery does not write about relationships with imaginary friends as an adult, except for occasionally referring to "flights of fancy" or brief references to having conversations with imaginary friends when she went for walks in the woods. However, some other people's diaries, biographies, or documentaries provide accounts of lifelong attachments to imaginary friends. Sometimes, the information is scant, is secondhand, and requires inferential leaps. For example, why did Kurt Cobain (1967–1994) address his suicide note to "Boddha," the name of the childhood imaginary friend documented in *Kurt and Courtney* by his Aunt Mary?[25] Did Cobain have a lingering attachment to his childhood imaginary friend, or was this a one-time turning to an old memory? Or perhaps he had some other entirely different private meaning for "Boddha."

Another hint about an imaginary friend who might have lasted in some form beyond childhood comes from the diary of Frida Kahlo, the renowned Mexican artist. The entry titled "Origin of The Two Fridas" in which Kahlo writes about an imaginary friend from her childhood (an invisible girl the same age as Frida) has been described as one of the "most revealing and intimate" of the entire diary.[26] Like some of the children we have interviewed, Kahlo had a ritual for meeting her friend. She blew on her bedroom window to create mist and then drew a door which opened to an imaginary meadow. "I would cross all the field I could see until I reached a dairy store named PINZÓN. . . . Through the 'O' of PINZÓN I entered and descended impetuously to the entrails of the earth, where 'my imaginary friend' always waited for me."[27] Kahlo remembered the joy of those meetings and how her friend laughed, danced, and listened to Kahlo's secrets. "It has been 34 years since I lived that magical friendship and every time I remember it, it comes alive and grows more and more inside my world."[28] Beside this diary entry there is a sketch of a child drawing the window that served as the porthole to Kahlo's imaginary world. The sketch is titled "Las Dos Fridas," which is also the title of one of Kahlo's most famous paintings depicting two adult Fridas seated side by side holding hands. (see Figure 12.1).

Many imaginary friends vanish without a trace, but Kahlo's words speak for the adults who still cherish and are inspired by the memory of an imaginary friend. Thus far, the amount of information in these examples is minimal, but other sources provide more extensive firsthand accounts of imaginary friends who are still important to their adult creators. The most detailed descriptions we have found are in the autobiographies of two exceptionally productive and long-lived creative artists: Agatha Christie, the prolific writer of mystery novels, and Paul Taylor, the acclaimed dancer/choreographer. Perhaps their fame and the widespread admiration for their talent made it possible for them to be more forthcoming than others in disclosing their relationships with imaginary friends. They did not have to worry about being accused of mental illness. In both cases, their imaginary friends were created in childhood but persisted and evolved throughout Christie's and Taylor's lives. Given their thoughtful and extensive accounts of how their imaginary friends functioned in their adult lives, these descriptions deserve special attention.

The Imaginary Friends of Adults   203

Figure 12.1 *The Two Fridas* by Frida Kahlo.

© 2024 Banco de México Diego Rivera Museums Trust, Mexico, D.F. /Artists Rights Society (ARS), New York. Photo Credit: Schalkwijk/Art Resource, New York. Artist: Frida Kahlo (1907–1954), © ARS, New York 2024. Description: *The Two Fridas* (Las Dos Fridas). 1939. Oil on canvas, 173 × 173 cm (5' 8 1/2" × 5' 8 1/2"). Location: Museo Nacional de Arte Moderno/Mexico City.

Agatha Christie and "The Girls"

Agatha Christie (1890–1976) wrote 66 mystery novels and dozens of stories, plays, essays, and other writings. More than a billion of her books have been sold in the English language and another billion in other languages. Christie started her autobiography in 1950 and finished it in 1965. She did not feel compelled to make it comprehensive; large parts of her life are omitted or skimmed. However, she describes in detail and with great fondness a series of imaginary friends who kept her company over the years. She started to invent them from an early age ("From as early as I can remember, I had various companions of my own choosing"),[29] and she continued to have thoughts and fantasies about imaginary friends up until the time that she finished writing her autobiography at age 75.

Agatha grew up in a home with few playmates. Her "Nursie," although much beloved, was an elderly woman who did not participate in the playing of games. Her older brother and sister were mostly away at school. No matter—Agatha derived great pleasure from inventing scores of her own playmates, starting with a group of imaginary kittens and followed by a large family of an indeterminate species—part human and part dog. When Christie's family moved to France, for a year, she created "The Girls," imaginary friends that became her lifelong companions.

> The first girls to arrive were Ethel Smith who was 11 and Annie who was 9. Ethel was dark, with a great mane of hair. She was clever, good at games, had a deep voice and must have been rather masculine in appearance. Annie Gray, her great friend, was a complete contrast. She had pale flaxen hair, blue eyes. And was shy and nervous and easily reduced to tears. She clung to Ethel who protected her on every occasion...
>
> After Ethel and Annie, I added two more: Isabella Sullivan, who was rich, golden-haired, brown-eyed, and beautiful. She was 11 years of age. Isabella, I did not like—in fact I disliked her a good deal...Elsie Green was her cousin. Elsie was rather Irish; she had dark hair, blue eyes, curls, and was gay and laughed a good deal . . . Elsie was poor; she wore Isabel's castoff clothes.[30]

The autobiography contains descriptions of the girls traveling together, riding horses, gardening, and playing croquet. Agatha actively disliked Isabella and rooted against her. She describes how she was intentionally reckless when playing for Isabella in croquet, but in spite of her careless shots (or perhaps because of them) Isabella tended to win. Agatha frequently added new members to The Girls:

> Ella was conscientious, industrious and dull. She had bushy hair, and was good at lessons . . . played a fair game of croquet. Sue de Verte was curiously colorless in appearance and in personality . . . the seventh girl was Sue's step sister Vera de Verte—13 years old . . . She was not at the moment beautiful but she was going to be a raving beauty. There was a mystery about her parentage.[31]

Some of the later additions were Adelaide, Beatrice, and Rose and Iris Reed (two sisters). Ethel never married; she lived in a cottage with Annie.

The imaginary girls never faded away. Christie was bemused by this and pokes fun at herself as a grown woman who talks to and thinks about imaginary girls. "It makes me laugh when I do it, but there the girls are *still*, though unlike me they have not grown old. Twenty-three is the oldest I have ever imagined them."[32] The attention and affection that Christie devotes to her imaginary girls in this autobiography contrasts with her treatment of Hercule Poirot and Miss Jane Marple. Her private imaginary friends clearly win out over the renowned characters from her books. The Girls were personal favorites of Christie's; her relationships with Poirot and Marple were more professional. Poirot was initially created in 1916 for Christie's first detective novel (*The Mysterious Affair at Styles*). She was delighted when the novel was accepted for publication (after a number of rejections), but her reminisce is tinged with irony. She writes that when she went out with her husband to celebrate that night, "there was a third party with us, though I did not know it. Hercule Poirot, my Belgian invention, was hanging around my neck, firmly attached there like the old man of the sea."[33] He was to appear in 33 novels and over 50 short stories. If the public had not embraced Poirot so enthusiastically, Christie might not have continued with his exploits.

Miss Jane Marple had an even more inauspicious beginning in *The Murder at the Vicarage* (1930). "I cannot remember when or how I wrote it, why I came to write it, or even what suggested to me that I should have a new character—Miss Marple—to act as the sleuth in the story. Certainly, at the time I had no intention of continuing her for the rest of my life."[34] Both Poirot and Marple would likely have been designed differently if Christie had had a vision of the future. Neither one would have been old. "What a mistake I made there. The result is that my fictional detective must really be well over a hundred by now... I ought to have abandoned after the first three or four books and begun again with someone much younger."[35]

Apart from describing their beginnings, Christie scarcely mentions Poirot or Marple in the rest of her autobiography. They did not seem to be part of her private emotional life in the same way as The Girls. However, Christie does draw some parallels between the way she interacted with characters as she developed storylines and the way she liked to talk to her imaginary friends. In the end, she reflects upon the writing of novels by saying, "Oh well, I suppose it is just the same as when I was four years old and talking to the Kittens. Am I still talking to the Kittens, in fact?"[36] For Christie, interacting with imaginary others started early and became the basis for her professional success. Storytelling was second nature to her in both her professional and private life. Early on, The Girls might have been used for companionship when she was living abroad, but their primary function for Christie as an adult seemed to have been as a source of amusement in her private life.

Paul Taylor and George Tacet, Ph.D.

Paul Taylor (1930–2018) was the director of the Paul Taylor Dance Company (and Paul Taylor 2) and widely recognized as one of the leading choreographers of his generation. He received many awards for his accomplishments in dance, including the MacArthur "Genius" award. Taylor's autobiography, *Private Domain*,[37] starts with a matter-of-fact account of a difficult childhood. His mother had three children with her first husband, who died after five years of marriage. She then had a brief and unhappy marriage to Paul Taylor Sr., with Paul Jr. being their only child. After the divorce, Paul's mother worked hard to support the family and Paul was often alone. He was much younger than his half-siblings (the eldest was 16 years his senior), and his mother worked long hours as a single parent to support the family. However, Paul recalls that he was never lonely because there were always imaginary friends around to entertain him.

The most enduring of Paul's childhood friends, George H. Tacet, Ph.D., was discovered one day at the end of one of the halls in the Brighton Hotel in Washington where Paul's mother operated a dining room. Tacet was a doctor of phrenology (an early interest of Taylor's) with a misshapen head, bony knees, and raspy voice, who talked a great deal and had a grandiose manner.[38] Originally and for some time, Tacet seemed to function as sort of a kindly substitute father. Whenever Taylor formed an important relationship with an adult male, he compared him with Tacet. The headmaster at Taylor's prep school: "An avid scholar of Latin and Greek, he's a dead ringer for Tacet, only his skull has no lumps and I doubt he'll be talking me up on his knee."[39] And when Taylor went to Syracuse University and joined the swimming team, he commented that his coach reminded him of Tacet, in part because both were fond of women.

Over the years, Tacet evolved into a lifelong friend and advisor. His function seems to have been more fundamental to Taylor's emotional well-being than The Girls were for Agatha Christie. Tacet assumed the second side in internal debates over various problems and worries. Note that Tacet was also a source of amusement. There is a lot of humor in both the description of Tacet and his pedantic (sometimes incomprehensible) ways of expressing himself. When Taylor was upset at the end of an affair, Tacet referred to Taylor's heartbreak as "the extraordinarily injurious extrapolation which rent my interpersonal connection bondings."[40] Taylor refers to him variously as "the old geezer," "Doc T," "my alias," "troublemaker Tacet," and "that venerable old fraud." He described Tacet as loving women, high living, and refined manners. According to Taylor, Tacet's lecherous side could be observed when he said goodbye to the dancers before they went on tour—"with his farewell hugs, pressing his frame against people he's barely met, finding other excuses to touch his delectable dancers or trying to blow on their ears, wheezing, waving, and displaying his tawny teeth."[41]

But in addition to Taylor's enjoyment of imagining Tacet, there was something more serious in his function that might account for his continuing usefulness to Taylor into adulthood. In fact, the most common role for Tacet was as the giver of advice. In Latin, Tacet means "he is silent," but he rarely seemed to be. Taylor quoted Tacet's wisdom throughout his autobiography:

> ON ART AND FOOTBALL: "My general impression is that art of all kinds has a taint to it. Nice people worked for a living, and good boys played football. Everyone has been very definite about that. Even so, old Tacet and I agree that football is ridiculous and work something to avoid."[42]
>
> ON TRYING TO FIND A REAL SUBSTITUTE FATHER: "The more thou diggest, my boy, the emptier thine hole."[43]
>
> ON THE DRAFT FOR KOREA: "Dodge, my boy, dodge the indignities of soldier life, cling to your inalienable rights as a Creative Artist."[44]
>
> ON TAYLOR'S QUESTIONABLE FUTURE: "Have you the heart of a lion, the soul of a saint? Or even, dear boy, the fecundity of a hare?"[45]

Tacet was important when Taylor needed to think through an issue in his life and needed a sounding board. "Things need to be sorted out, and it's times like this that old Tacet comes in handy."[46] For example, at a major turning point in Taylor's life, he describes the discussion with Tacet about the pros and cons of breaking with Martha Graham, after six years as a member of her company. Taylor wrote two pages of dialogue between himself and Tacet. Here is an excerpt:

> TACET: How darst she dump you! She is merely using Bathsabee's parsimony as an excuse. The indignity of it! What inadequate appreciation of your adoration, what...
> I let him go on for a while, then say,
> "Maybe you're right, Pops, maybe not. Gee, and I thought Martha was getting to like me. It looks like I went and shaved off my beard for nothing. (Taylor had shaved his beard when Martha requested.)
> TACET: Mark my words, Sonny, that woman is a Delilah and wants to clip our career short, not to mention other unkind acts...[47]

Tacet came down clearly on the side of leaving the company, and that is what Taylor did. Throughout the book, Taylor refers to requesting advice from Tacet, sometimes on matters of importance (what direction he should take in his choreography) and other times on matters of inconsequence (how to react when Martha jabbed him with a pin while fitting a costume): "As usual, Tacet is waiting someplace in the gloom, wanting to express opinions. I'm needing career advice, so maybe it won't hurt to let him play devil's advocate. 'Hey, Doc, what are you thinking?'";[48] "Although he is only imaginary, sometimes his advice has been worth listening to."[49]

Tacet also seemed to do his fair share of listening to Taylor's complaints, worries, and fears. As director of his company, Taylor often had no one to gripe to except Tacet. There is one long dialogue in his autobiography that takes place near the end of Taylor's dancing career at age 44, when he has serious health problems. "The fears that I am confiding to him are ones that I have never told anyone."[50] At bad times like these, Tacet served as the voice of encouragement.

In addition to his role in Taylor's private life, Tacet was involved in the life of Taylor's company. When dancers came home from being on tour, they often brought home gifts for Tacet. In addition, Tacet sometimes appeared on the dance programs as in charge of the costumes, props, or lighting (see Figure 12.2). He was listed as the coproducer for some performances, and on one tour he signed on as official "Aesthetical Executor." Taylor reported that Tacet's work was well received, and the company was sent many letters asking if Tacet was available to work on other productions. Also, the dancers are described as referring to Tacet's costume design and his promises to make sure they get the prettiest ones. These examples suggest that another function of Tacet might have been communication from Taylor to his company or perhaps also the reverse, not unlike the function of some childhood imaginary friends for communicating about concerns or fears.

> **CITY CENTER**
>
> Wednesday Evening, April 16, Friday, Evening, April 18,
> Saturday Evening, April 26, Thursday Evening, May 1, 1980
>
> **AUREOLE**
> Music by George Frederic Handel
> *Excerpts from Concerti Grossi in C, F and Jeptha*
> *Choreography by* Paul Taylor
> *Costumes by* George Tacet
> *Lighting by* Thomas Skelton
>
> *First performed in 1962*
>
> 1st Movement .... Carolyn Adams, Monica Morris,
> Lila York & Christopher Gillis
> 2nd Movement .... Elie Chaib
> 3rd Movement .... Carolyn Adams, Monica Morris,
> Lila York & Christopher Gillis
> 4th Movement .... Monica Morris & Elie Chaib
> 5th Movement .... full cast
>
> *3 MINUTE PAUSE*
>
> **3 EPITAPHS**
> American Folk Music
>
> *Choreography by* Paul Taylor
> *Costumes by* Robert Rauschenberg
> *Lighting by* Jennifer Tipton
>
> *First performed in 1956*
>
> Linda Kent   Thomas Evert
> Ruth Andrien   Susan McGuire   Cathy McCann

Figure 12.2 Page from *Playbill* for The Paul Taylor Dance Company 1980. Taylor's imaginary friend, George Tacet, is credited for costumes.
Used by permission. All rights reserved Playbill Inc.

Mostly Tacet seems not to have gone on tour with the company. But that does not mean he was forgotten. Taylor reports missing him and thinking about both what Tacet would have said and done if he were there and what he might be doing on his own while Taylor was away. Taylor provided examples of three letters that he wrote while on tour—to his mother, his best friend George Wilson, and to Tacet. The longest, most personal, and most detailed by far was to Tacet. But Tacet was plenty busy while Taylor was away; he had his own autobiography to write.

Summary

We might assume that imaginary friends fade away along with favorite blankets, picture books, nursery rhymes, and other paraphernalia from childhood, but at least some adults create imaginary friends that resemble the childhood phenomenon. In some cases, the childhood imaginary friend continues into adulthood in a diminished role or as a cherished memory, and in other cases, the imaginary friend appears for the first time in adulthood. The most detailed information that we found were descriptions in published diaries and biographies of imaginary friends that started in childhood but continue into adulthood to provide a lasting source of comfort, entertainment, and companionship. Although the available descriptions are limited, these long-lasting pretend friends might be just as varied as the preschool variety and mirror some of the same themes. We described the examples of Agatha Christie's "Girls" and Paul Taylor's "George Tacet" at some length because they show how an adult might make use of an imaginary friend as a private source of amusement or more seriously as a voice in internal debates about important concerns and decisions.

While hunting for descriptions of imaginary friends in biographies, we learned about another type of interaction with imaginary others—the invention of an imaginary person for the purpose of creating a work of fiction. Like children who regularly imagine the exploits of pretend friends, writers imagine fictional characters and the invented worlds they inhabit. In the next chapter, we discuss the extent to which the relationships of authors with their characters might sometimes resemble interactions with imaginary friends.

Notes

1. Bloom, P. (2010). *How pleasure works: The new science of why we like what we like.* W. W. Norton & Co., p. 155.
2. Barnes, J. (2012). Fiction, imagination and social cognition: Insights from autism. *Poetics, 40*, 299–316.
3. Svendsen, M. (1934). Children's imaginary companions. *Archives of Neurology and Psychiatry, 2*, 985–999.
4. Chase, M. (1944). *Harvey.* Dramatists Play Service.
5. Albee, E. (1962). *Who's afraid of Virginia Woolf?* Atheneum.
6. Roudane, M. C. (1990). *Who's afraid of Virginia Woolf?: Necessary fictions, terrifying realities.* Twayne Publishers.

7. Fincher, D. (1999). *Fight Club*. 20th Century Studios.
8. Newport, F., & Strausberg, M. (2001, June 8). *Americans' belief in psychic and paranormal phenomena is up over the last decade*. https://news.gallup.com/poll/4483/americans-belief-psychic-paranormal-phenomena-over-last-decade.aspx

   Belief in the paranormal is not limited to a particular social class or educational level. For example, Sir Arthur Conan Doyle, who is famous for his stories about Sherlock Holmes (ironically, a detective who found natural explanations for events that struck others as supernatural), had an intense interest in the occult in his private life. In his book *The Coming of Fairies*, he documented his efforts to determine the authenticity of a series of photographs taken by cousins Frances and Elsie Cottingley (aged 10 and 16) showing small, winged people. He concluded that fairies, gnomes, and other small humanlike beings exist and speculated that some of them might have evolved from insects. At one time the Cottingley photographs were considered the strongest evidence for the existence of fairies and were the basis for a movie titled *Fairies: A True Story*, but the cousins later confessed that they had been faked. Nevertheless, there continues to be debate over the status of many such creatures, with skeptics dismissing believers as mentally deranged or, at best, unintelligent, and believers criticizing skeptics as narrow-minded.

   Kottmeyer, M. (1996). Fairies. In G. Stein (Ed.), *The encyclopedia of the paranormal*. Promethesus Books.

9. Kambhampaty, A. P. (2021, October 28). *Many Americans say that they believe in ghosts. Do you? Beliefs in paranormal phenomena may be a way of grappling with the unknown*. https://www.nytimes.com/2021/10/28/style/do-you-believe-in-ghosts.html 2

   Jackson, C., & Yi, J. (2019, October 24). *Less than half of Americans believe ghosts are real. Vast majority of parents eat their child's Halloween candy*. https://www.ipsos.com/en-us/news-polls/halloween-2019

10. Heise, D. R. (1988). Delusions and the construction of reality. In T. F. Oltmanns & B. A. Maher (Eds.), *Delusional beliefs* (pp. 259–272). Wiley.
11. Arnold, J. (1986, March 11). High jinks: O'Hare may handle more flights but none as crazy as the New York-to-Miami run. *Chicago Tribune*, p. 1.
12. Bass, H. (1983). The development of an adult's imaginary companion. *Psychoanalytic Review, 70*(4), 519–533.
13. Auerbach (2015, March 25). Kentucky's Karl-Anthony Towns fueled by criticism, "Karl-ito." *USA Today*. https://www.usatoday.com/
14. Gleason, T. R. (2013). Imaginary relationships. In M. Taylor (Ed.), *The Oxford Handbook of the Development of Imagination* (pp. 251-271). Oxford University Press. https://doi.org/10.1093/oxfordhb/9,780,195,395,761.013.0017
15. Klass, D. (2006). Continuing conversation about continuing bonds. *Death Studies, 30*(9), 843-858.

    Klass, D., Silverman, P. R., & Nickman, S. L. (Eds.). (2014). *Continuing bonds: New understanding of grief*. Taylor & Francis.
16. Gleason, T. R. (2013). Imaginary relationships. In M. Taylor (Ed.), *The Oxford handbook of the development of imagination.*
17. Dannenbaum, S., & Kinnier, R. (2009). Imaginal relationships with the dead: Applications for psychotherapy. *Journal of Humanistic Psychology, 49*, 100–113.
18. Artificially intelligent systems (such as generative AI chatbots) have the potential to reshape the nature of continuing bonds. For instance, it is now possible to carry on

conversations with imaginary versions of deceased loved ones by training AI models on recordings of the deceased person's voice, tone, and manner. So far this type of chatbot has had mixed success, and the extent to which this is healthy for processing loss is not currently known. This technology also opens the door to imaginary relationships with celebrities (living or dead) via AI chatbots that mimic their characteristics. Paul Bloom speculates about such possibilities on Substack: (2024, March 25). *Small potatoes, be right back.* https://smallpotatoes.paulbloom.net/p/be-right-back.

Also see Carballo, R. (2023, December 11). Using A.I. to talk to the dead. *The New York Times.* https://www.nytimes.com/2023/12/11/technology/ai-chatbots-dead-relatives.html

19. Honeycutt, J. M. (2003). *Imagined interactions: Daydreaming about communication.* Hampton.

20. Some adults have such active imaginations that psychologists refer to them as fantasy prone (Wilson & Barber, 1981). This relatively small segment of the population (about 3%–4%) spend half or more of their waking hours absorbed in fantasies involving elaborate scenarios, much like real-life Walter Mittys. Fantasy proneness has been associated with extreme life circumstances and is often viewed negatively, but other researchers (e.g., Sanders, 1992) believe that the ability to fantasize contributes to psychological well-being and helps these individuals cope with stressful life events. According to Klinger, Henning, and Janssen (2009), the component of fantasy proneness that involves enjoyment of make-believe is unrelated to any disorders.

Klinger, E., Henning, V. R., & Janssen, J. M. (2009). Fantasy-proneness dimensionalized: Dissociative component is related to psychopathology, daydreaming is not. *Journal of Research in Personality, 43,* 506–510.

Sanders, B. (1992). The imaginary companion experience in multiple personality disorder. *Dissociation, 5,* 159–162.

Wilson, S. C., & Barber, T. X. (1981). Vivid fantasy and hallucinatory abilities in the life histories of excellent hypnotic subjects ("somnambules"): Preliminary report with female subjects. In E. Klinger (Ed.), *Imagery, Vol 2: Concepts, results, and applications* (pp. 341–387). Plenum Press.

21. Lynn, S. J., Pintar, J., & Rhue, J. W. (2013). Fantasy proneness, dissociation, and narrative construction. In S. Krippner & S. M. Powers (Eds.), *Broken Images, Broken Selves* (274–302). Brunner/Mazel, pp. 274–275.

22. Fernyhough, C., Watson, A., Bernini, M., Moseley, P., & Alderson-Day, B. (2019). Imaginary companions, inner speech, and auditory hallucinations: What are the relations? *Frontiers in Psychology, 10,* 1665.

23. Rubio, M., & Waterson, E. (Eds.). (1985). *The selected journals of L. M. Montgomery, Vol 1:1889–1910.* Oxford University Press, Toronto, p. 306.

24. Ibid., p. 41.

25. Broomfield, N. (Director). (1998). *Kurt & Courtney* [Film]. Capital Films.

26. Ibid., p. 245.

27. Kahlo, F. (1995). *The diary of Frida Kahlo: An intimate self-portrait.* (Introduction by Carlos Fuentes, essay by Sarah Lowe). Harry N. Abrams, Inc.

28. Ibid.

29. Christie, A. (1977). *Agatha Christie: An autobiography.* Dodd, Mead & Co., p.11

30. Ibid, p. 106.

31. Ibid., pp. 106–107.
32. Ibid., pp. 107–108.
33. Ibid., p. 328.
34. Ibid., p. 333.
35. Ibid.
36. Ibid., p. 531.
37. Taylor, P. (1987). *Private domain: An autobiography.* Alfred A. Knopf.
38. Ibid., p. 10.
39. Ibid., p. 19.
40. Ibid., p. 275.
41. Ibid., p. 200.
42. Ibid., p. 17.
43. Ibid., p. 26.
44. Ibid., p. 38.
45. Ibid., p. 58.
46. Ibid., p. 72.
47. Ibid., pp. 72–73.
48. Ibid., p. 143.
49. Ibid., p. 175.
50. Ibid., p. 339.

Chapter 13
Adult Fiction Writers and Their Characters

> Might we not say that every child at play behaves like a creative writer, in that he creates a world of his own . . ."
>
> **(Sigmund Freud)**[1]

Freud considered creative writers to be "strange beings" and wondered how best to study their "mysterious" process. One of his suggestions was to start with something simpler—the pretend play of children.[2] Was Freud right about there being a link between early pretending and fiction writing? Are children who imagine the exploits of pretend friends similar to adults who create characters for their novels, plays, and movies? Perhaps the creation of an imaginary friend is an early manifestation of the capacity of adults to imagine entire fictional worlds and the people who live in them.

Freud seemed to think that studying children would be simpler than accessing the "mysterious" process of fiction writing, but in our experience collecting information about imaginary friends from young children and even adolescents has significant challenges. Young children are limited in their ability to reflect on their experiences and sometimes misconstrue interview questions (e.g., when asked if they have a pretend friend, they answer "no" because they call her a "ghost sister"). Adolescents understand what is being asked but often have forgotten about past imaginary friends and can be secretive about current ones to avoid ridicule. In contrast, adult fiction writers are articulate informants; the existence of their characters is public knowledge; and fiction writing is a highly valued activity with results that are typically shared rather than kept private. Are adult fiction writers a potentially useful source of information about the experience of interacting with imaginary friends?

The goals and activities of an adult novelist have obvious differences from those of children playing, but like children with pretend friends, writers imagine fictional characters and the invented worlds they inhabit on a daily basis. One of the possible differences is that children confide in their imaginary friends and listen to what they have to say about life in the real world. The job of writing fiction does not require authors to develop such personal reciprocal interactions, but actually some authors do describe having friendlike relationships with characters and imagined conversations with them.[3] In addition, one of the more peculiar characteristics of imaginary friends—that they can be difficult to control—has at least a superficial similarity to

Imaginary Friends and the People Who Create Them. Second Edition. Marjorie Taylor and Naomi R. Aguiar,
Oxford University Press. © Oxford University Press (2024). DOI: 10.1093/9780190888916.003.0013

some adult authors' accounts of their creative process. Characters created by adults for works of fiction are sometimes experienced as if they were narrating the story or even having their own agenda for it. Is there a relation between independent-minded fictional characters in novels and unruly imaginary friends?[4] Although we believe that children, despite their limitations, are usually the best informants about imaginary friends, in this chapter we explore the possibility that fiction writers might be able to shed light on some of children's experiences with them.

Fictional Characters with Minds of Their Own

We were particularly interested in the possibility that fiction writers might help us better understand a part of children's experience that we had puzzled over for years: their complaints about imaginary friends who talk too loudly, do not share, and generally do not do as they are told (see Chapter 2). In one study in which children were specifically asked, "Does your friend always do what you want them to do?," only one child out of 36 said yes. The other 35 children were happy to have the opportunity to unload about their imaginary friends. Perhaps these children were simply exploring the role of the disciplinarian or the aggrieved/rejected in a safe way—mirroring some of the less desirable behaviors they confronted with real-life companions (e.g., bossiness, not helping, not wanting to play the child's favorite game). However, at least some of these children seemed like they were truly experiencing their imaginary friends as sometimes acting as independent agents.

Marjorie's informal survey of fiction writers talking about their characters as having minds of their own is what first inspired her to take a closer look at adult authors. She hoped to gain insight about the behaviors of imaginary friends by investigating how often and under what circumstances adult authors similarly experience their characters as autonomous. Judging from the autobiographies and biographies of fiction writers, the phenomenon of characters acquiring autonomy—taking over the story and expressing their own ideas—might be quite common. In her book *Invisible Guests*, Mary Watkins[5] provides many striking examples documenting the experience of having characters narrate the story to the author, as described by Enid Blyton:

> I don't know what anyone is going to say or do. I don't know what is going to happen. I am in the happy position of being able to write a story and read it for the first time, at one and the same moment.... Sometimes a character makes a joke, a really funny one, that makes me laugh as I type it on the paper—and I think, "Well, I couldn't have thought of that myself in a hundred years!" And then I think, "Well, who *did* think of it, then?"[6]

This sort of description can be found in interviews and writings of authors as varied as Henry James, Jean Paul Sartre, Fyodor Dostoevsky, Marcel Proust, Kurt Vonnegut, and J. K. Rowling. The events of the story are generated by the characters' actions, and the writer's job becomes merely to observe and record. According to Ursula Le Guin, "I don't feel so much as if I were 'making it up'; I know I am, but that's not what it feels like. It feels like being there and looking around, and listening."[7]

Siegel (1992) discusses this phenomenon as a kind of channeling, using the example of ventriloquist Edgar Bergen and his wooden dummy, Charlie McCarthy:

> One day, a visitor came into Bergen's room and found him talking—not rehearsing—with Charlie. Bergen was asking Charlie a number of philosophical questions about the nature of life, virtue, and love. Charlie was responding with brilliant Socratic answers. When Bergen noticed that he had a visitor, he turned red and said that he was talking with Charlie, the wisest person he knew. The visitor pointed out that it was Bergen's own mind and voice coming through the wooden dummy. Bergen replied, "Well, I guess ultimately it is, but I ask Charlie these questions and he answers, and I haven't the faintest idea of what he's going to say and I'm astonished by his brilliance—so much more than I know."[8]

In some ways, these examples sound like Csikszentmihalyi's concept of "flow"—the pleasurable experience of being totally absorbed in an activity that becomes effortless and unselfconscious.[9] The person loses track of time and ideas seem to arrive on their own outside of conscious control. Authors do sometimes report being in flow while writing,[10] but flow does not necessarily include personal interactions with characters or the sense that the characters are the ones in charge. The experience reported by authors also sounds a bit like automatic writing (i.e., when writers report being unaware of what they are writing), but automatic writers often do not recall what they have written and might not recognize it when shown the passage.[11]

Whereas effortlessness is the hallmark of both flow and automatic writing, autonomous characters can be difficult. In the examples provided thus far, the authors have been impressed by or at least agree with what the characters have to say, but often the character and the author disagree about the direction of the story and the character's role in it. Proust is reported to have answered a reader who complained that the character Swann had become ridiculous by replying that Swann reached this state in spite of Proust's intention as author.[12] Similarly, John Fowles interrupted the narrative of *The French Lieutenant's Woman* in Chapter 7 to alert the reader that his characters were no longer following his directions.[13]

Sometimes, deals have to be struck. In a radio interview, Sara Paretsky described a conflict with her recurring character, V. I. Warshawski, about a storyline in the novel *Hard Time*.[14] The plot required V. I. to spend four weeks in prison where she was beaten, humiliated, served contaminated food, sliced with a razor, sexually harassed, and shot with an electric weapon. V. I. didn't want to do it. In the interview, Paretsky recalled that she had to bargain with her character in order to get compliance. In the final step of the negotiation, Paretsky promised to give V. I. true love in the next book in exchange for going to prison in the current one.

For some authors, the characters arrive fully formed from the beginning and are resistant to any sort of alteration. When J. K. Rowling, the author of the Harry Potter books, was asked in a National Public Radio interview why she made her main character a boy, she answered that she had tried, but failed, to make him a girl.

> He was very real to me as a boy, and to put him in a dress would have felt like Harry in drag... I never write and say, "OK, now I need this sort of character." My characters come to me in this sort of mysterious process that no one really understands, they just pop up.[15]

In some works of fiction, the autonomy of the imagined characters is what the authors write about as part of the plot, as in Pirandello's famous play *Six Characters in Search of an Author*,[16] Stephen King's *The Dark Half*,[17] Ursula Hegi's *Intrusions*,[18] and many more examples. More rarely, characters are reported to move from the world of the novel to have a physical presence in the author's world or to voice unsolicited advice about matters concerning the author's real life. Francine de Plessis Gray described her characters as sleeping in her bed and sometimes waking her up to ask about her plans for their future.[19] Alice Walker reported having lived for a year with her characters Celie and Shug while writing the novel *The Color Purple*.

> Just as summer was ending, one or more of my characters—Celie, Shug, Albert, Sofia, or Harpo—would come for a visit. We would sit wherever I was, and talk. They were very obliging, engaging, and jolly. They were, of course, at the end of their story but were telling it to me from the beginning. Things that made me sad, often made them laugh. Oh, we got through that; don't pull such a long face, they'd say.[20]

When fictional characters comment on the author's personal life, narrate the story, and/or argue with the author about the plot, they are being experienced as independent agents with their own thoughts, feelings, and actions. Similarly, when imaginary friends surprise, fight with, and/or disobey their child creators, they seem to have a mind of their own. Marjorie and her colleagues Sara Hodges and Adele Kohanyi dubbed these experiences as the "illusion of independent agency."[21]

The Illusion of Independent Agency

Psychologists who work in the area of perception note that although illusions tend to be special cases that occur under restricted conditions, they often are revealing about entire systems. For example, when the moon is over the horizon it appears to be much larger than when it is at its zenith.[22] Perception psychologists are interested in the moon illusion because it tells them about the way our visual system integrates information about distance and retina size in judgments and perception of distal size. The other interesting thing about the moon illusion and many others—including the illusion of independent agency—is that they are "impenetrable." An impenetrable illusion is one in which the person experiencing it knows the true state of affairs and in no way believes that the illusion corresponds to reality (e.g., authors know that they are the ones composing the story), but they still experience the illusion (e.g., authors feel like they are passively taking dictation from a character or simply writing what they observe in their mind's eye). We think that the illusion of independent agency is a conceptual illusion that is revealing about the nature of how some people experience fantasy.

The illusion of independent agency is not an obscure phenomenon with no counterparts outside the world of imaginary characters. In fact, the report of autonomous characters is the tip of the iceberg in terms of experiences in which one's actions or thoughts do not seem under our conscious control. In his fascinating book *The Illusion of Conscious Agency*, psychologist Daniel Wegner described a host of such "automatisms" in which people are not aware of producing their actions or thoughts (e.g., automatic writing, Ouija board spelling, channeling, hypnosis, sensation from phantom limbs).[23] He believed these phenomena are related to interactions with imaginary friends, autonomous fictional characters, and several clinical conditions ranging from rare and unusual syndromes (e.g., *alien hand syndrome* in which one's hand operates with a mind of its own, as immortalized in *Dr. Strangelove*) to more common types of dissociation (e.g., arriving at a destination with no memory of having driven there).

In a more recent discussion of automatisms, Jim Davies included dreams, hallucinations, and tulpas (i.e., a Tibetan thought-form method in which mental images of humans or animals are manifested in a physical form and animated such that they are taken to be real by others).[24] The phenomenon of hearing voices has also received considerable attention in this literature. In *Muses, Madmen and Prophets*, Daniel Smith reviewed the historical examples of people who heard voices, including Joan of Arc and Socrates.[25] In some of his examples, the voices are symptoms of mental illness, but for many others, they appeared to be a source of creative inspiration. Smith argues that we need to move beyond the assumption of pathology to develop interpretations of automatisms that work for healthy minds as well as troubled ones. Charles Fernyhough has also written extensively about hearing voices, thoroughly documenting the experience in people who are not mentally ill.[26] We recommend the books by Wegner, Smith, and Fernyhough for readers who want more information about the many different forms of automatisms and the circumstances under which they occur. Meanwhile, we return to the parallels between descriptions of autonomous characters collected from fiction writers and children's accounts of their imaginary friends.

Beyond Anecdotes

In Chapter 2, we established that children experiencing imaginary friends as having minds of their own is a relatively common phenomenon, but how prevalent is the experience of autonomy in fictional characters for authors? What are the circumstances that lead to this experience? Do writers who vary in skill and experience also vary in their reports of the illusion? To answer these questions, we needed to move beyond the collection of individual anecdotes, compelling though they may be. Assessing frequency required interviewing a large sample of fiction writers in a systematic way about their creative process.

Marjorie, Sara Hodges, and Adele Kohanyi began with a newspaper advertisement seeking the help of adults who had been writing fiction for at least five years.[27] The 50 fiction writers who responded varied considerably in their experience and success, ranging from an award-winning author of several published novels, who supported himself entirely by writing, to individuals who identified themselves as fiction writers but had not published or received payment for any of their work. The writers filled out questionnaires and were interviewed about the characters in their work, starting with general questions (e.g., Do you feel there were different stages in the development of your character?), and moving to more specific questions about autonomy (e.g., How much control do you feel you have over what your character does and says?).

We thought the questions about autonomy might sound strange, but everyone immediately knew what we were asking about and shared their experiences. Of the 50 writers, 46 (92%) reported some degree of autonomy in their characters, and some provided vivid examples of characters who not only had taken over the narrative but also resisted the writer's attempts to control the story. A few characters were even experienced as leaving the pages of the stories to inhabit the writers' everyday worlds (e.g., "... suddenly, I felt the presence of two of the novels' more unusual characters behind me. I had the sense that if I turned around they would actually be there on the sidewalk behind me").

More recently, Foxwell and colleagues[28] conducted an extensive study in which 181 professional writers (12% of the writers who were invited to participate) were asked similar types of questions. About 61% of the authors described characters who had independent agency, with substantial variation in how this independence was manifested (e.g., hearing voices, sensing physical presence, character dictating story). Taken together with our study, these results establish that autonomous characters are a common experience for adult fiction writers. But why are some imagined characters autonomous and not others? And why do some writers have this experience and not others?

Expertise and the Illusion of Independent Agency

Not all children report autonomy in their imaginary friends. In fact, for some children having an imaginary friend under one's thumb is exactly what they seem to like about the fantasy. Under what conditions do imagined characters become autonomous, and what does autonomy mean for the understanding or enjoyment of the fantasy experience? One possibility is that the illusion might be partly related to the automatization that comes with acquiring expertise in performing a task. Experts of all kinds become increasingly efficient with practice until they operate at least to some extent without conscious guidance.[29] When a person first starts to operate within a domain—driving a car, playing chess, or making medical diagnoses—judgments and behaviors come slowly with lots of conscious, effortful thinking and reasoning. For example, the demands of operating a car (e.g., attending to traffic lights, changing lanes) might make it difficult or even dangerous for the novice driver to participate in a conversation with a passenger at rush hour. With increased expertise, however, the process of operating the car becomes automatized, freeing the driver's conscious attentional capacity for other tasks. It becomes possible to listen to music or have a conversation (but not text!) while continuing to drive safely.

Someone who pretends a lot—a child who regularly plays with an imaginary friend or an adult who day after day thinks about the world of a novel—is developing expertise. Perhaps the process of imagining the friend or the fictional world becomes automatized until it is no longer consciously experienced. The fantasy characters present themselves automatically. Their words and actions begin to be perceived, listened to, and recorded rather than consciously created. Autonomy in characters might even make them more exciting imaginary friends or more compelling characters in works of fiction. As André Gide puts it,

> The poor novelist constructs his characters; he controls them and makes them speak. The true novelist listens to them and watches them function; he eavesdrops on them even before he knows them. It is only according to what he hears them say that he begins to understand who they are.[30]

Is the expertise hypothesis supported by evidence? Determining exactly how much time a child has spent interacting with an imaginary friend is tricky, and unfortunately, our study of fiction writers did not include a good measure of expertise. We did find a trend for the 17 published writers to report greater levels of the illusion of independent agency than the unpublished writers, but factors other than expertise (e.g., higher levels of empathy)[31] could have accounted for this result.[32] Marjorie decided to follow up by consulting fiction writers whose expertise with their characters was undeniable—successful authors who had published several books with recurring characters. Perhaps authors who have years of experience writing about the same characters might have particularly compelling or noteworthy accounts of the illusion of independent agency. Would their descriptions of their relationships with their characters have parallels or be helpful in understanding what children experience with autonomous imaginary friends?

Authors with Recurring Characters

The first challenge in launching a study of accomplished people is the recruitment of participants. For example, in Csikszentmihalyi's large-scale study of eminent creators, only a third of the individuals he contacted agreed to be interviewed about their lives and creative process. Most either did not respond or declined to participate. Similarly, Marjorie's expert author study had a low rate of positive responses. But the five authors (out of 20) who agreed to be interviewed were an elite group. Three were known primarily for their detective series (Sue Grafton, P. D. James, and Tony Hillerman), one for a fantasy/science fiction series (Philip Pullman), and one for magical realism (Ursula Hegi), although all of them had written other kinds of books. The fictional characters in these authors' books had captured the attention and affection of thousands or even millions of fans. What do the creators of such beloved characters have to say about them? If expertise with a character contributes to the illusion of independent agency, the accounts of these authors could be particularly informative.

In addition to the difficulty of finding authors who were willing to participate, conducting the study brought other challenges. The preparation required for each interview was daunting. Marjorie's process was to send out a small number of requests and then to start reading the books (the ones she had not already read) by those authors. Mostly, there were declines or no responses, so after a while she would abandon that group and go on to the next set of requests. When an author did agree to participate, she read the remaining novels as fast as possible to be ready for whenever the interview would fit into the author's busy schedule.

Although the authors in this study were similar in having years of experience with their characters, they varied in their attitudes about themselves as writers and their relationships with their characters. Some believed the creative process was sort of magical, and others were careful to describe themselves as ordinary people and writing as just another job. They also varied in their experience with the illusion of independent agency, ranging from almost none to vivid examples.

Given the well-established variability in imaginary friends, we should not have been surprised by the diversity in how the authors described their characters and process. Perhaps we expected the descriptions to fit more neatly into boxes because their creators were adults who could explain them better than preschoolers. But the interviews with the expert authors provided a course correction for research investigating adult versions of imaginary friends. The goal of identifying characteristic features of the author/character relationship as a function of expertise reflected an overly simplistic view of what authors experience. Relationships—even imaginary ones—are influenced by a complex array of factors. By the time the fifth interview was complete, Marjorie realized that capturing the diversity of the experiences of fiction writers would require a huge study with authors from different genres of writing who varied in their own personalities, as well as the personalities of their characters. Still, the five interviews provide a glimpse of the complexity of relationships with fictional characters and an expanded understanding of the ways the illusion of independent agency infuses the creative process. Here are some excerpts.

Sue Grafton

Sue Grafton (1940–2017) was the award-winning author of 25 detective novels featuring Kinsey Millhone, a private detective who lives on the edge of solvency and is always worrying about her next paycheck. Grafton has explicitly referred to Kinsey as her imaginary friend, and in the interview, Grafton touched on almost every aspect of the illusion of independent agency in describing her relationship with Kinsey.

On Physical Presence of Character, Conflict over Plot

There are certain passages where I can just feel her over my shoulder. Usually in trying to encourage me to do something quite tacky. I go, "I cannot do that" … some of the time she is just out of control. I'm having to whang her, beat her down, or I will write it to satisfy her and then I go back and take it out.

On Disagreements with Character

And I think ok we'll do this and that and the other. And she will be saying to me, "How can I do that? You know this makes no sense whatsoever." So, she and I will sort of argue and she always gets to win. Well, you know it is her life and she knows what she would do and even though it might be convenient for me for her to discover the fatal clue. She is just saying, "I wouldn't look under there. It wouldn't even occur to me." So, then I have to back off and find some other way to make the story point or make the story work in that regard.

But she is capable of pouting. I mean people ask me if I intend to write another series character. I'm thinking, I would never live through that. Ms. Millhone would be on me. You know she's not interested in sharing the stage center with anybody.

On Writing Becoming like Dictation

There is the mother in *F is for Fugitive* who has diabetes and she is just so self-dramatizing and she's so manipulative. What I loved about her was that every time she had a scene she would totally take over. She was so excited to be on camera and I could just about not wrestle the center of attention away from her. So, what you really look for in life are those characters that are so powerful that they just get in there and do the job for you. And then you sit and take dictation which is much easier than thinking it all up by yourself.

On Having an Independent Existence

> I didn't know anything about her husbands. I just knew that she had married them. So, when I wrote *E is for Evidence*, I learned who her second husband was. And when I wrote *O is for Outlaw*, I learned about the first husband.... And she is kind of stingy to tell you the truth. But I think family issues are so thorny. Nothing gets resolved with a simple heart felt chat. So, she is working through some stuff and I am just having to be patient about it.... But again it (Kinsey's life) is not something I am privy to. So, I just disregard that. I am just hoping that she will cooperate in the times when I am in touch, you know. So, I just try to mind my own business aside from that.

Overall, Grafton's account of her relationship with Kinsey was very like having an imaginary friend who had a mind of her own. Kinsey was experienced as a separate entity with her own life, who interacted with Grafton in and out of the fictional world of the novels. In other interviews, Grafton has expressed gratitude to Kinsey, not only for being a friend, but also for being a benefactor who brought her fame and fortune. Grafton's account was consistent with the idea that author/character relationships can function like adult versions of children's imaginary friendships. However, Kinsey Millhone turned out to be the only imaginary friend that was described by this group of five authors.

Philip Pullman

Philip Pullman (1946–) is an award-winning British author of over 30 books, including the *His Dark Materials* trilogy: *The Golden Compass* (aka *Northern Lights* in the United Kingdom), *The Subtle Knife*, and *The Amber Spyglass*. The main protagonist in the trilogy is Lyra Belaqua, a 12-year-old girl who lives in a universe that is parallel to our own. Pullman's account of his relationships with Lyra and his other characters was much less like having imaginary friends than in the Grafton interview. He was emotionally attached to at least some of them (especially Lee Scorsby), but in many cases, the relationships seemed more professional than personal. In some respects, he was like the director of a movie, but Pullman pointed out that the movie director metaphor wasn't quite right either, because his experience included dictation from the characters:

> And it is partly dictation. Because I can hear what they are saying.
> So, coming back to the point that you began with—is it like being dictated to or is it like seeing a movie? It is a bit of both but the easy stuff is the dialogue because I am given the words—I hear it. Yeah, that's right. I hear what they are saying.

Taking dictation from characters is an aspect of the illusion of independent agency that some authors experience as mysterious, but Pullman has a matter-of-fact attitude about the job of writing fiction and was at pains to dispel any magical ideas about the creative process:

> This is a job. I start when I pick up my pen and I stop when I put it down. Then I do other things. I have to write letters; I have to go shopping; I have to do this and that. . . . I have to put curtains up. You know. So the idea of the creative artist lost in a world of his own imagination, strange eccentric person. No, it is not like that at all. This is a job.

The illusion of independent agency often suggests an effortlessness as the author listens and watches what the characters say and do. Most of what Pullman described was different:

> There is a lot of sitting and thinking and a lot of sitting and tapping your pencil on the table and swinging back in your chair and wondering what the hell to write next because you can't think of what to write next. . . . How do you get inspiration, where do you get your ideas from? . . . That isn't the point. The point is, how do you write without ideas? That is the real question. Because for most of the time we are without ideas.

Nevertheless, as the interview went on, there were more descriptions of the illusion of independent agency.

On Characters Taking Over the Narrative

> I didn't know how Lyra was going to get out of that fix when she was in the palace of the Bear King. She thought of the way out, I didn't. But equally, Will did the same thing in *The Amber Spyglass* when he defeats Iorek Byrnison. He challenges him to fight a combat and manages to beat him without actually having to fight. I didn't know how he would do that. He thought of it and I didn't. I just wrote down what he did.

On the Independent Existence of Characters

> Ok, well now for me the experience of becoming acquainted with a character that I am going to write about is rather like making the acquaintance of someone in real life. They do present themselves to me, in my mind's eye, of course, in my mind's ear. But with characters that are fully established already. . . . It's as if the characters are already alive in some sort of dimension and I just meet them or they come to me. They enter my mind. Now this is an awkward kind of thing for me to believe because I don't

believe there is another dimension.... So I have to sort of struggle to reconcile my midway explicit beliefs with the experience I have. But they do seem to come to me as if they are fully fleshed out characters already existing.

On Conflict with Character

If I want a character to do something there are different ways of approaching them. Some of them are very approachable. Lee Scoresby would do anything I asked him to do. Mrs. Coulter would not. I wanted her to spend a bit of time in the cave for example, at the beginning of *The Amber Spyglass*, so I would have to sort of negotiate with her. Almost bring her a bunch of roses and say, "Look Mrs. Coulter, I wonder if you would mind. I've got this scene in mind for a cave. It's a very nice cave. You would like it there, you know. It's a very important scene and we need you in it. Would you mind very much?"

Pullman's interview was helpful in dispelling a one-size-fits-all view of author/character relationships. The characters in his novels were not experienced as personal friends. In addition, Pullman brought up another type of imagined character that is intrinsic to the creative process: the "narrator" who is not one of characters in the story (as in first person narration), but a character who has access to all the minds of the characters who are in the story.

Pullman's interest in the narrator began in childhood when he became attached to the characters in his favorite books and wanted to tell their stories. His observations about the narrator's voice underscores the multifaceted ways in which we create and interact with imaginary others. Not all of the characters that authors create are protagonists in the story. In addition to the narrator, other characters invade the process of writing, facilitating or sometimes standing in the way of the work. Sue Grafton talked about "She who writes" and "Shadow," characters who facilitated her creative process. For some writers, an inner critic becomes an elaborated character. For example, Gail Godwin (author of *The Odd Woman, Violet Clay, A Mother and Two Daughters*, and many other works of fiction) envisioned her inner critic as the "Watcher at the Gate"—a thin man in his 50s with bushy eyebrows and a little moustache who was always ready to point out the flaws, the mistakes, and to suggest that she start over.[33]

P. D. James

P. D. James (1920–2014) was a celebrated British author who, among many other awards, was named Officer of the Order of the British Empire. She is best known for her mystery writing, including 14 books featuring Adam Dalgliesh, a brilliant, poetry-loving Scotland Yard detective who was the focus of the interview. From her account, James was clearly emotionally attached to Dalgliesh, but he was not her imaginary friend. Instead of interacting with him, James described *becoming* Dalgliesh. He was actually more like a pretend identity—a character that a person role-plays for an extended period of time (see Chapter 2). The experience of being inside Dalgliesh and looking through his eyes was so strong that James was vague when asked about his physical appearance. She explained that she did not see him directly face to face:

> Because I think I am so inside him, it's rather like not seeing oneself very clearly.
> . . . when I am writing I enter the mind of the character I am dealing with at the time. I'm inside him all the time . . . when I am writing, I am, that person. Actually, I feel like that person and I see like that person, and I speak like that person.

Foxwell and colleagues also found that some authors (22%) experienced the events of the story as if they shared a body with the character and were seeing the world through their eyes.[34] In their interviews, this experience was mixed with the illusion of independent agency. There were also elements of the illusion of independent agency in what James described, but that type of experience did not dominate the interview as it had with Grafton. Here are some examples.

On Being Surprised by Characters

> You decide what your characters are going to do and yet in a very mysterious way sometimes they can behave in rather surprising ways. I don't mean that they behave entirely out of character, but it is perfectly possible to be rather surprised by a character. Be surprised by what a character says or does or the character's reaction.

On Independent Existence—Life of Their Own

> It is almost as if the whole book and the people already exist in some limbo outside myself and it is my business, by a long process of thought and effort, to get in touch with them and put them down on paper.
> And I can remember when I was writing the book, waking up one morning and it was almost as if the character was standing by the bed saying, "That's where I went." And I knew at once that it was exactly right. . . . And

this can happen quite often. It seems as if these people do exist and you are getting in touch with them instead of making them up.

In her autobiography, James wrote about the independent existence of characters.

> And during the writing the character will reveal himself or herself more clearly, will display unexpected quirks of personality and will sometimes act in a way I neither planned nor expected.[35]

Overall, P. D. James' relationship with Adam Dalgliesh was unlike what was described by Sue Grafton or Philip Pullman. However, she was not the only author who inhabited her character.

Ursula Hegi

Ursula Hegi (1946–) is an award-winning author of 10 novels, including several with recurring characters such as Trudi Montag, the central protagonist in Hegi's best-known book, *Stones from the River* (1994).[36] Like P. D. James, Hegi's experience of writing involves a period of getting to know the character until she is inside—and then seeing through the character's eyes. *All* the interviews included elements of this process, but for Hegi, like P. D. James, this experience was the predominant one. When asked about her relationship with a character, she corrected Marjorie, saying, "No, I am the character":

> I mean, for me to write from the perspective of a gay 14-year-old, I need to become that boy at that moment, okay. For me to write from the point of view of a dwarf woman, I need to be her size, at that moment. I need to feel her rage, her joy, her bliss, her humiliation, and you know, I will sit at my desk laughing or crying or cursing, because in order to write about those feelings, I need to experience them.

To the extent that Hegi described the illusion of independent agency, it did not include having a personal relationship with the character. However, the characters' independence was reflected in her comments about their lives outside the story and their physical presence.

On Independent Existence—Life of Their Own

> It was almost as if, from the time I finished the book to the time of that interview, as if during that year, the character had kept developing, so when she sort of, you know, asserted herself that day, she was at a different level of development than where I had left her off.

On Physical Presence of Character

> The character had a very, very strong presence, so strong that at one point when my husband, Gordon, and I were driving from the state of Oregon to Washington, we were along Hood River where it's very windy—you know, the Columbia Gorge it's called—and her presence was so strong that he could feel it.
>
> I mean, we've joked about characters living with us in the house.
>
> The characters have moved in. They follow me around, even crowd my family at the dinner table.

Questions about control did not make a lot of sense to Hegi. She sometimes experienced characters asserting themselves (e.g., Trudy Moretag "demanding her own story" after being a minor character in *Floating in My Mother's Palm*). But when asked about losing control of what the character did, Hegi reported that she would never try to control a character:

> I mean I hate control anyhow and . . . to me control in writing would mean fitting characters into certain situations. I really, I follow them. You know, I have to become every one of them.

Overall, Hegi was more explicit about surrendering control to her characters than the other authors. Her novels might also be described as particularly focused on character, suggesting the possibility that genre affects how characters are experienced. Fiction can be categorized in different ways (e.g., mysteries, romance, science fiction, fantasy),[37] but one basic and commonly made distinction involves the emphasis placed on narrative plot versus character development. Although both plot and character development are always important, in some works of fiction, particular attention is given to the twists and turns of a plot that has to be carefully mapped out for things to add up in a specific way. A novel with such a puzzle-like structure does not allow a lot of freedom for a character to take charge. If a character becomes autonomous in this type of writing, we might expect the illusion of independent agency to feature more conflict between the author and character. According to P. D. James, detective stories are plot driven to the point that characters cannot completely take over:

> For in my kind of fiction, of course, no character can completely escape his author. I can't have a murderer deciding that he would prefer to be an innocent victim.[38]

Novels that are more stream of consciousness or that have a greater emphasis on the exploration of character might be different. An author might be more receptive to out-of-the-blue ideas that seem to originate with the character. The emphasis on plot versus character also varies in children's descriptions of their imaginary friends. For some children, describing the adventures of their imaginary friends is the central activity (e.g., taking the Lunar Express to the Moon), whereas other children are more focused on how their friend's empathetic support helps them process the events in the children's own lives. However, the distinction between plot-driven and character-driven novels (or imaginary friends) is not clear-cut, and the next interview suggested that it is far from the whole story.

Tony Hillerman

Tony Hillerman (1925–2008) is best known for 15 mystery novels featuring Joe Leaphorn, a Navajo Nation police officer, as the main character. Hillerman received many awards during his long career but was most proud of being named Special Friend of the Dineh (the Navajo people) in 1987 by the Navajo Nation. For Hillerman, writing novels provided a vehicle for thinking and learning about Native American culture and history. An important part of his work was to educate both himself and his readers. This function of storytelling—the exploration of real-life interests—was also present in many children's accounts of their imaginary friends and paracosms (e.g., the significance of Swiss Army knives in the fictional culture of Abixia as discussed in Chapter 10).

The illusion of independent agency was pretty much absent from Hillerman's reflections about his writing process. It often seemed like Marjorie was asking the wrong questions. For example, when she asked if he considered his novels to be driven primarily by plot or by character, the answer was neither: "Well, let me put it this way. When I start a book it's very important to me to know where geographically." Again and again in the interview, he returned to geography, setting, or landscape as the source of his inspiration. "I like to remember the setting—where it is going to happen."

The closest that Hillerman came to the illusion of independent agency was when he was asked if his characters ever had an opinion about the plot:

> I even have characters who absolutely in my mind won't go along and do what I want them to do.
>
> Once in a while I lecture at writing courses and I tell students that—I warn them that—sometimes characters don't turn out, sort of takeover in a way. It sounds pretentious to say that, but it does happen.

But as he went on to give examples, the processes he described seemed more like the author realizing that he wanted the plot to go differently because of his developing ideas about the character, rather than the character making suggestions or demands. When asked about emotional attachment to his characters, he answered by relating them to real people he had known. For example, Hillerman liked the person who had inspired the character of Leaphorn and so assumed he would like Leaphorn too. He mentioned that he felt bad when he had to kill Emma, Leaphorn's wife, for the sake of the plot in one of the novels, but he gently discouraged Marjorie from making too much of that:

> This is, you know, your writing. You've also got six kids and when I was writing that one, let's see, I was working for the university, part time job. I don't think I was, maybe I was teaching already. But anyway, you know, you've got financial problems and all sorts of other problems. . . . So, you've got a lot of other things on your mind. So, you finally, you sort of sometimes say, "Oh well, I gotta get this book finished." And you don't really let it torture you too much.

Hillerman's plots required careful construction, but the occasional conflict over plot lines that was clear in Grafton's and Pullman's interviews was absent. Maybe one reason was that Leaphorn is a quiet and patient character—quite unlike feisty Kinsey Millhone or difficult Mrs. Coulter. As Pullman suggested, the personality of the character affects the relationship with the author. Characters are more or less difficult or more or less compliant; some are willing to go along with an author's ideas and some are not. The personality of the author is also important to consider. Based on the 45-minute interview, Tony Hillerman seemed a lot like Leaphorn—a wise individual who would not be quick to anger or conflict with anyone, real or imaginary. Hillerman's interview clearly indicated that the personalities of the author and the character likely also play a role in how the creative process is experienced.

Shedding Light on the Childhood Experience of Having an Imaginary Friend

As interesting as fiction writing itself can be, the main goal of the work with authors was to better understand children's relationships with their imaginary friends. But interviewing authors did not turn out to be a shortcut for learning about imaginary friends. With one exception, the relationships between the authors and their characters—even ones who were featured in several books—did not seem much like imaginary friends. In addition, only Philip Pullman remembered having imaginary friends in childhood.[39] Mostly he did not recall any of their details, except for the ones based on characters he met in books, whom he thought of as a type of imaginary friend. We have also encountered imaginary friends that were inspired by characters children heard about in books. These characters start out in a book narrative but then move into the child's life to become a personal friend. Pullman believes that many children may seek out the characters in literature, not to identify with, but to befriend:

> Fiction gives a shape and a voice and a name to imaginary companions, if you like. Or fiction provides us with friends. This is where I think we often go wrong when we use the word identify—"children need someone they can identify with." Well, I

don't think that is what happens. I don't think we read a story of Robin Hood and say I am Robin Hood. I am doing this and I am doing that. What we do when we read a story of Robin Hood is—we want to be us still but in the story. . . . Cause you don't want to lose your own character, you see. If you identify with somebody else it means that you are leaving yourself behind. You don't want to do that. We want to be ourselves still. But we want to be valued by the characters in the story. Perhaps more than our real friends value us. So we want to be an important member of Robin Hood's gang or whatever it is.

In summary, describing the relationship between author and character is challenging because not all fiction writing is the same genre or involves the same process. Authors write in different narrative voices, and novels vary on many dimensions including the extent to which they are driven by character versus plot, making the experience of one writer unlike that of another. In addition, the relationship between the author and character is likely to be partly a function of their individual personalities. Finally, the process of an individual author might vary across projects, as described by Jane Smiley:

> I had experienced every form of literary creation I had ever heard of—patient construction (*A Thousand Acres*), joyous composition (*Moo, Horse Heaven*), the grip of inspiration that seems to come from elsewhere (*The Greenlanders*), steady accumulation (*Duplicate Keys*), systematic putting together (*Barn Blind*), word-intoxicated buzz (*The Age of Grief*), even disinterested dedication (*The All-True Travels and Adventures of Liddie Newton*).[40]

One lesson from the interviews with the five expert authors is that the characters created for novels do not routinely function as an author's imaginary friends. Nevertheless, the reflections of the five authors did have some parallels with the accounts of children. Imaginary friends, like the characters in novels, sometimes arrive fully formed and are resistant to change. Like the narratives created for novels, children's storytelling often incorporates real-life interests into the exploits of their imaginary friends, who are sometimes are experienced as having minds of their own. And like children with pretend identities, some adult authors inhabit their characters. More generally, many adults and young children share a strong motivation to create imaginary characters and to enjoy telling stories about them.

Summary

The goal of this chapter was to explore the possibility that research with adult authors might shed light on children's descriptions of their imaginary friends. In particular, we were interested in the accounts of both children and adult authors who experienced their imagined characters as having some amount of autonomy. The main finding from the author interviews was that the illusion of independent agency can be part of the phenomenology for pretenders of all ages, but it is not a necessary feature of sustained storytelling. After interviewing 50 fiction writers and five expert authors, we have a renewed respect for the idiosyncratic and complex process whereby storytellers invent and develop their characters. Although the illusion of independent agency occurs in adult fiction writing and childhood imaginary friends, care must be taken to avoid overinterpreting superficial similarities.

The research with the five expert authors was motivated by the idea that authors who had published several books with the same main character might be particularly likely to have imagined personal relationships with their characters because they had been writing about them for so long. In all five interviews, the nature of the author–character relationship shifted from time to time and book to book, but only one of the writers (Sue Grafton) had the sort of personal, interactive relationship with a character that we would describe as an imaginary friendship. Philip Pullman seemed somewhat like the director of a film in which his characters (sometimes uncooperatively) were acting. Ursula Hegi and P. D. James became their characters as they wrote, seeing and understanding the world through their character's eyes and minds. Tony Hillerman did little of that. Our conclusion is that while the illusion of independent agency might be enhanced for some authors by extensive practice, it varies in the extent to which it occurs for any author, regardless of expertise.

Children also vary in the extent to which they report independent agency in their imaginary friends, but the fact that this illusion occurs *at all* in young children is interesting, given its seemingly complex mix of automatic and controlled processes. However, the capacity to experience the illusion of independent agency appears to be a feature of human consciousness that develops early—a cognitive illusion that is experienced throughout life in various contexts. In the next chapter we include more discussion of autonomous imaginary friends, along with other themes that have emerged in our review of research investigating children's imaginary friends.

Notes

1. Freud, S. (1908/1983). Creative writers and daydreaming. In E. Kurzweil & W. Phillips (Ed.), *Literature and Psychoanalysis* (pp. 19-28). Columbia University Press. See p. 19. https://doi.org/10.7312/kurz91842-003.
2. Ibid.
3. Watkins, M. (1990). *Invisible guests: The development of imaginal dialogues*. Siego Press.
4. Examining the experiences of actors might also be instructive, but according to Kogan (2002), writers and actors are engaged in strikingly different activities, with the actors primarily interpreting rather than creating a character. This distinction between the interpretation and creation of a role is one of degree and certainly there are exceptions. Actors add to a character and make it their own. Some actors have become inextricably linked with a particular character (e.g., Leonard Nimoy and Spock), yet one still might argue that it is their unique interpretation of the character that has received the recognition.

Kogan, N. (2002). Careers in the performing arts. A psychological perspective. *Creativity Research Journal, 14*, 1–16.
5. Watkins, M. (1990). *Invisible guests: The development of imaginal dialogues*. Siego Press.
6. Stoney, B. (1974). *Enid Blyton: A biography* (pp. 206–207). Hodder.
7. Curry, A. (2018). Worlds of Ursula K. Le Guin [TV series episode]. *American Masters*. Season 33, Episode 9. PBS.
8. Siegel, R. K. (1992). *Fire in the brain: Clinical tales of hallucinations*. Penguin Books, p. 163.
9. Csikszentmihalyi, M. (1996). *Creativity: Flow and the psychology of discovery and invention*. HarperCollins.
10. Perry, S. K. (1999). *Writing in flow: Keys to enhanced creativity*. Writer's Digest.
11. Wegner, D. M. (2002). *The illusion of conscious agency*. The MIT Press.
12. Becker, Allen W. (1959). Ellen Glasgow and the Southern literary tradition. *Modern Fiction Studies, 5*(4), 295–304.
13. This was not a worry for Fowles because he believed that "it is only when our characters and events begin to disobey us that they begin to live."
    Fowles, J. (1969). *The French Lieutenant's woman*: Little, Brown & Company, pp. 96–97.
14. Paretsky, S. (1999). *Hard Time*. Delacourt Press.
15. Rowling, J. K. (1999, October 20). Radio interview. *The Diane Rehm show*. NPR.
16. Pirandello, L. (1921). *Six characters in search of an author*. English translation by E. Storer (1922) E.P. Dutton & Co.
17. King, S. (1989). *The dark half*. Viking Press.
18. Hegi, U. (1997). *Intrusions*. Simon & Schuster.
19. Watkins, M. (1990). *Invisible guests: The development of imaginal dialogues*, p. 359.
20. Walker, A. (1983). *In search of our mothers' gardens*. Harcourt Brace Jovanovich, p. 359.
21. Taylor, M., Hodges, S. D., & Kohanyi, A. (2003). The illusion of independent agency: Do adult fiction writers experience their characters as having minds of their own? *Imagination, Cognition and Personality, 22*, 361–380.
22. Holway, A. H., & Boring, E. G. (1940). The moon illusion and the angle of regard. *The American Journal of Psychology, 53*(1), 109–116.
23. Wegner, D. M. (2002). *The illusion of conscious agency*.
24. Davies, J. (2023). Explaining the illusion of independent agency in imagined persons with a theory of practice. *Philosophical Psychology, 36*(2), 337–355. https://www.tandfonline.com/doi/full/10.1080/09515089.2022.2043265
25. Smith, D. B. (2007). *Muses, madmen, and prophets: Rethinking the history, science, and meaning of auditory hallucination*. Penguin.
26. Fernyhough, C. (2016). *The voices within: The history and science of how we talk to ourselves*. Basic Books.
27. Taylor, M., Hodges, S. D., & Kohanyi, A. (2003). The illusion of independent agency: Do adult fiction writers experience their characters as having minds of their own?
28. Foxwell, J., Alderson-Day, B., Fernyhough, C., & Woods, A. (2020). "I've learned I need to treat my characters like people": Varieties of agency and interaction in writers' experiences of their characters' Voices. *Consciousness and Cognition, 79*, 102901.
    Jones, S. R., & Fernyhough, C. (2007). Thought as action: Inner speech, self-monitoring, and auditory verbal hallucinations. *Consciousness and Cognition, 16*(2), 391–399.
29. Dreyfus, H. L., & Dreyfus, S. E. (1986). *Mind over machine*. The Free Press.

30. Gide, A., cited in Chatman, S. B. (1978). *Story and discourse*. Cornell University Press, p. 38.
31. Davies, J. (2023). Explaining the illusion of independent agency in imagined persons with a theory of practice. *Philosophical Psychology*.
32. Foxwell et al.'s participants were professional writers attending the Edinburgh International Book Festival, but the authors did not report whether the illusion of independent agency was more prevalent with the relatively more successful writers.
    Foxwell, J., Alderson-Day, B., Fernyhough, C., & Woods, A. (2020). "I've learned I need to treat my characters like people": Varieties of agency and interaction in writers' experiences of their characters' voices.
33. Godwin, G. (1995). Rituals and readiness: Getting ready to write. In N. Baldwin & D. Osen (Eds.), *The writing life: A collection of essays and interviews* (pp. 3–13). Random House.
34. Foxwell, J., Alderson-Day, B., Fernyhough, C., & Woods, A. (2020). "I've learned I need to treat my characters like people": Varieties of agency and interaction in writers' experiences of their characters' voices.
35. James, P. D. (1999). *Time to be in earnest: A fragment of autobiography*. Faber & Faber, p. 116.
36. Hegi, U. (1994). *Stones from the river*. Poseidon Press.
37. Smiley, J. (2005). *13 ways of looking at the novel*. Alfred A. Knopf.
38. James, P. D. (1999). *Time to be earnest: A fragment of autobiography*, p. 116.
39. Forty percent of the 50 writers in our study remembered having imaginary friends as children, which we initially thought was a high proportion for a retrospective study, but more recent research suggests that this proportion is within the bounds of what might be expected with adults. In both our study and in Fernyhough et al., having a childhood imaginary friend was not related to the current report of experiencing the illusion of independent agency in fiction writing.
    Fernyhough, C., Watson, A., Bernini, M., Moseley, P., & Alderson-Day, B. (2019). Imaginary companions, inner speech, and auditory hallucinations: What are the relations? *Frontiers in Psychology, 10*, p. 1665.
40. Smiley, J. (2005). *13 ways of looking at the novel*, p. 5.

Chapter 14
Final Thoughts

Fantasy in the Lives of Children and Adults

> The Brain—is wider than the Sky— / For—put them side by side— / The one the other will contain / With ease—and you—beside—
>
> **Emily Dickinson, c. 1862**

Imaginary friends are only one of many forms that fantasy takes during early childhood, but for us they have special appeal. First of all, the breathtaking diversity of imaginary friends bears witness to the richness of children's fantasy lives. Imaginary friends come in all shapes and sizes, all ages, genders, and species. They vary as much as the children who create them, defying the attempts of researchers to make generalizations about what imaginary friends are like and what it means to have one. The phenomenon is also rife with interesting contradictions. Imaginary friends are exotic, but common. They seem to be the products of special minds, but researchers have struggled to identify any substantial differences between children who have them and children who do not. Parents are pushed to extremes of both pride and concern by their children's friendships with imaginary beings, applauding the creativity evidenced by their child's inventiveness until some line is crossed, and they begin to wonder about their child's mental health. The children themselves love their imaginary friends dearly, but many don't miss or even remember them after they are gone. Parents often feel nostalgic for ones that have disappeared, but become worried if they stay around too long. Lots of grist for the psychologist mill. In what follows, we reflect on some of the points made elsewhere in this book and add some final thoughts.

On Being the Parent of a Child Who Has an Imaginary Friend

What are parents supposed to make of all of this? One recurrent theme in this book is that the invention of an imaginary friend should not—in and of itself—be interpreted as a symptom of emotional or interpersonal problems. In fact, children who create imaginary friends tend to be sociable individuals who enjoy the company of others and are somewhat advanced in social understanding. We have included clinical case studies because they demonstrate the beneficial role of fantasy in helping children cope with traumatic events, but it is important to keep in mind that the creation of an imaginary friend is best interpreted as a positive sign of mental health and creativity.

When is there legitimate cause for concern? Parents often say that it is fine to be reassured that imaginary friends are *usually* a healthy, relatively common variation of the normal play behavior of young children. However, they don't really care about the general phenomenon; they are focused on the specific case of their own child. Maybe your child's behavior seems more extreme than the examples we have discussed, or the characteristics of your child's imaginary friend strike you as stranger than any of the ones we have described. The phenomenon of having an imaginary friend is so varied that many parents are not going to find the counterpart of their child's pretend friend in the pages of this book. At what point does it make sense to worry about a child's absorption in play with a fantasy friend?

To answer this question, we would need some other information: Does the child have any real-life friends? Does the child have trouble sleeping, show nervous habits, or seem depressed? The answers to these questions would help determine if there was cause for concern. A child who shows signs of problems or experiences trauma might become motivated to create an imaginary friend. But note—a parent would be worried about a child who had no friends or was unhappy, whether or not they had started to play with an imaginary friend. Actually, we would be more concerned about a lonely, unpopular child who did not have an imaginary friend or a child whose play showed the monotony and grimness that raises red flags for child therapists. The presence of the imaginary friend indicates that the child is at least trying to cope with unhappiness. And the imaginary friend is helpful to the parent as well as to the child. Parents can learn a lot about what their child is going through by asking about the pretend friend and paying attention to parallels between imaginary events involving the friend and the child's real-life concerns.

Parents also wonder about their own influence over whether or not a child creates an imaginary friend. There are significant cultural variations in the support of and prevailing attitudes about children's fantasy behaviors, including cultures in which imaginary friends are barely tolerated or even outright discouraged. If we look more narrowly within the context of the family, encouragement of fantasy behavior also varies considerably and has some effect on the probability of children having imaginary friends. Conditions that are conducive for imaginary friends include having supportive adults, some props, time, and space.[1] Children whose lives are fully scheduled or who have very little time by themselves are less likely to invent pretend friends. Christopher Milne points out the importance of the conditions that promoted his own childhood fantasies:

> ... if we wanted to go to the Forest we went on foot. And so did others: only those who could walk to the Forest went there. This meant that when we got there, we

had the Forest almost entirely to ourselves. And this, in turn, made us feel that it was our Forest and so made it possible for an imaginary world—Pooh's world—to be born within the real world. Pooh could never have stumped a Forest that was littered with picnic parties playing their transistor radios.[2]

In addition to the practical questions about how to interpret and deal with imaginary friends in one's household, the phenomenon raises a variety of more general questions about child development. At the top of the list is children's understanding of the distinction between fantasy and reality. Anyone who has observed a child playing and laughing with a pretend friend might wonder if the child believed the friend were real. The answer is no. With a few rare exceptions, children seem very clear about the pretend status of the imaginary friends that they have created for themselves. And more generally, children actually do surprisingly well at sorting out all the mixing of various types of fantasy with real-world experiences and knowledge that they encounter.[3]

In our view, children's understanding of the various distinctions between fantasy and reality is an example of childhood wizardry, right up there with children's remarkable ability to acquire their first language.[4] Yes, children in many cultures might place lost teeth under their pillows for the Tooth Fairy to exchange for money, hang up their stockings on Christmas Eve for Santa Claus to fill, and look forward to eating the chocolate eggs left by the Easter Bunny. But children are not the originators of these cultural myths; they are told about them in the same way as they are told about characters and events that are meant to be understood as real or to really have happened (e.g., the way they are told about dinosaurs or stories from the Bible).[5] In addition, parents take concrete steps to blur the fantasy–reality boundary by leaving traces of the characters' actions. A focus on children's mistaken beliefs about Santa Claus and his kind can result in adults seriously underestimating children's understanding of fantasy. When children react emotionally to fantasy, their behavior also might suggest that they have not clearly grasped the reality of the situation. And there is no question that young children have strong emotional responses to fantasy material. They become terrified while engaging in a game of pretense involving monsters. They deeply love their imaginary friends. But throughout life, fantasy evokes strong emotion even when there is no confusion about it all being just pretend. For example, the strong emotional reactions of adults to fictional narratives suggests that caution is warranted when interpreting children's behavior. Confusion about what is real and what is pretend might not be what underlies the child's emotional involvement, any more than adult tears at a sad movie are indicators of a lost grip on reality. On the other hand, it is possible that children and adults differ in how they interpret the experience of emotion elicited by fantasy material. A strong emotional response to fantasy might be confusing for children and result in their being less sure about what is real. In any case, the emotional response itself should not be taken as clear evidence that children have a problem distinguishing fantasy from reality. When children begin to fear the monster of their own invention, parents might be tempted to remind them that it isn't real, but a more effective strategy might be to suggest a change (e.g., it is just a baby monster). The monster's reality status is not the point.

How much should a parent enter into play with imaginary friends? Children enjoy sharing their imaginary friends with others, and parents can gain insight about their children by monitoring the ongoing events in the lives of the imaginary friends. Ask about the pretend friend and pay attention to parallels between imaginary events involving the friend and the child's real-life concerns. Think of the imaginary friend as providing a window on your child's thoughts and feelings. One note of caution is that the parents should have a supporting role in this play, rather than trying to direct the activities of the imaginary friend. Some of the children's pleasure is in their mastery of their friend. Relinquishing control to the parent strips the fantasy of its most important appeal, at least for some children. In this type of play, follow your child's lead (within limits)[6] and enjoy where it takes you.

On Being in Control of a Fantasy

Fantasy experiences vary considerably in how much control is exercised by the children themselves. Confusions about fantasy and reality are most prevalent in contexts where other people present the fantasy to children as compared with fantasy that children dream up for themselves. In cultural myths, storybooks, television, movies, video games, and magic shows, fantasy is ready-made for children. In interactions with artificially intelligent agents, the responses of the agent have been programmed, and although they might be capable of adapting to the child's input, the child is not the author of the agent's behavior or communications. In parasocial relationships, there is never complete control.

In contrast, children make up their imaginary friends, and the creative control that children exercise over them might be what makes imaginary friends such excellent companions. They can be depended upon to provide whatever the child needs or wants at a particular moment in time. We also believe that the control that children have over the characteristics, behavior, and communications of their imaginary friends is at the heart of why children are so clear about their friend's pretend status. When children are the ones in control of a fantasy, they know what is going on. However, there is tension between our claim that creative control is fundamental to the experience of having an imaginary friend, while also reporting that imaginary friends are often described as badly behaved or otherwise experienced as having a mind of their own. We believe that in some cases a difficult imaginary friend might reflect a child's way to process bad behaviors—so they actually are intentionally imagined that way and thus under the child's control. But there are also imaginary friends that are experienced as independent and argumentative to the point of causing the child to be frustrated or annoyed. We don't believe such cases are a cause for concern. They typically do not seem to be truly distressing to children and do not appear to be accompanied by symptoms of problems such as poor reality monitoring. Although the autonomy of an imaginary friend is easiest to detect when it results in bad behavior that the child complains about, there are positive examples of independent behavior as well.[7] And loss of control is not the whole story. In the cases we have encountered, the imaginary friend is experienced as autonomous on occasion rather than all the time.[8]

The perceived independence of some imaginary friends caught our attention early on and inspired Marjorie and her colleagues' research with adult fiction writers.[9] Like fiction writers, children often use imaginary friends as vehicles for telling stories to their parents and other family members. And like children who have imaginary friends with minds of their own, some fiction writers experience their characters as having their own independent agendas.

One might assume that the creator of a fantasy controls the way it unfolds. But once set in motion, fantasies often develop in a dynamic fashion. At times, novelists resist the imaginary characters' contributions, but they also report enjoying the experience of surrendering to a runaway fantasy and seeing where it takes them.

We have speculated that the illusion of independent agency—our name for perceived loss of control of an imaginary character—might characterize intense involvement in fantasy, whether the pretender is an adult or a child. For some children, well-practiced interactions with an imaginary friend might promote the conditions under which components of the creative process become automatic. If so, the feeling of being the author of the friend's contributions to the interaction might be diminished. Maybe part of becoming an expert pretender is learning to relinquish control of a fantasy and allowing ourselves to be surprised by it. There are puzzles over these experiences of autonomy and control of fantasy that need to be worked out, but we suspect that an understanding of children's behaviors, and the processes underlying this type of imaginative activity, can be informed by the perspective gained from the study of adult fantasy. More specifically, the insights of adult fiction writers reflecting on their creative process might help us better understand why some imaginary friends come and go as they please and don't always behave as the children wish.

On Deciding What Is Real

In 1971, Big Bird made friends with a large elephant-like creature named Snuffleupagus. Everyone on Sesame Street (and the viewing audience) assumed he was an imaginary friend because no one but Big Bird ever saw him. However—unlike the children in our studies—Big Bird insisted that Snuffleupagus was real and kept attempting to arrange for a meeting with the other residents of Sesame Street so that they would stop calling him imaginary. But Big Bird's strategy didn't work because Snuffleupagus always came up with an excuse to run off just before the others could see him (e.g., he would suddenly decide to go home to comb his hair so he would look nice for Big Bird's friends). Big Bird started wondering if maybe Snuffleupagus *was* imaginary. For some reason, he thought he couldn't play with him anymore if that were the case. Snuffleupagus reluctantly agreed, saying that he didn't feel imaginary, but that if everyone else said he was, it must be so. However, when Big Bird saw Snuffleupagus's real tears, he reasoned that if the tears were real, then Snuffleupagus must be real too and they could be friends after all. After 14 years (1971–1985) of this plot line, the writers of *Sesame Street* had become concerned about their portrayal of adults not believing what Big Bird told them. They changed course and Snuffleupagus was outed as real. Gordon, Susan, Bob, Maria, and Luis all met Big Bird's *real* friend, Snuffleupagus, in an episode that brought tears to the eyes of Carol Spinney and Jerry Nelson, Big Bird's and Snuffleupagus's longtime puppeteers (and maybe some viewers).[10]

This is a true story about the reality status of the possibly imaginary friend of a beloved fictional character. Snuffleupagus transitions from being a fictional imaginary friend of a real fictional character to being a real fictional character, himself. And when Snuffleupagus is outed as a real fictional character (instead of an imaginary one), the humans (real ones) who pretend to be the fictional characters shed real tears of happiness over this development in a fictional plot line. Wow.

All those fuzzy lines beg the question that keeps coming up for us: What makes something real? And why do we keep asking that question? Is that even the right question to be asking? Does the child believe the robotic dog that talks back in a seemingly contingent way is "real?" Is the parasocial relationship between an adult and a celebrity who is followed on social media a real relationship? The examples from AI and other technologies are why scientists and journalists are now arguing that it is getting harder to separate which relationships are "real" and which relationships are "imaginary."[11] With the accelerating advancement of generative AI tools such as ChatGPT, it seems dated to us to be talking about *the* distinction between fantasy and reality as if there is a clear, well-defined boundary.[12] Douglas Hofstadter predicts that "We're approaching the stage when we're going to have a hard time saying that this machine is totally unconscious. We're going to have to grant it some degree of consciousness, some degree of aliveness."[13] How will the next generation cope with such a complex mix of fantasy and reality in their lives? Given how successful children are in accepting and living with the current blending of fantasy and reality, we suspect that they will do just fine. It is the rest of us that might be bewildered.

Hart and Zellars argue against the focus on the question of whether or not an entity is "real," suggesting that we should instead "determine the legitimacy and value of these experiences based on the quality of the phenomenon, the information provided, and the impact it has on one's life. How we name them is not as important as the quality of their impact."[14] A child who knows that her pretend friend is not "real" might become angry when an adult points that out and thus dismisses an imaginary friend as a second-rate companion because it is pretend. The child understands that the love is real. One adolescent explained that she had fully understood that her childhood imaginary friend "was not actually there," but that did not make her any less real. Maybe the reality status of an entity or one's relationship with the entity matters less than the extent to which the relationship can influence thoughts, feelings, attitudes, and behaviors.

While not all friendships, be they real or imaginary, have the depth and stability to become significant in our lives, do at least some imaginary friends evolve into an important source of real-world support? Note that we are not asking if children think their imaginary friends are real. The evidence clearly indicates that even preschool children are well aware that they are pretend.[15] Their pretend status is often convenient, allowing imaginary friends to bear the brunt of a child's anger, be blamed for mishaps, and provide an especially private audience for secrets. The question is whether self-generated imaginary friendships provide some of the same benefits associated with high-quality friendships with real children. We believe they do. Like living and breathing friends, imaginary ones can provide love and support and serve as sounding boards. They can also be challenging, annoying, and difficult, but ultimately, they enrich our lives.

On the Role of Imagination in Adult Life

In the past, it was believed that the extraordinary imagination of young children was something that they would outgrow—that the fantasy worlds of childhood revealed a lack of coherence that gradually was resolved as thinking became more adapted to reality.[16] But we believe that this view downplays the role of fantasy in development and overlooks the pervasive role of imagination in the lived experience of adults. We think about the past, imagine the future, and become absorbed in the fictional narratives presented in books, movies, theater, and TV shows. We silently talk to ourselves, playing out social interactions, rehearsing upcoming conversations, or improving upon ones that happened in the past.[17] We hear the voice of loved ones who have died.[18] Music plays in our head with the lyrics connecting our thoughts to experiences and people. We forget our surroundings as we mull over world events, scientific puzzles, and fictional narratives. Our stream of consciousness drifts along, with a chance encounter setting off a host of reminiscences or a random occurrence reminding us of upcoming goals, plans, past friends, family members, and pets. As Caughey reminds us,

> We do not live only in the objective world of external objects and activities. On the contrary, much of our experience is inner experience. Each day we pass through multiple realities—we phase in and out, back and forth, between the actual world and imaginary realms.[19]

With the growing appreciation of the role that imagination plays in everyday adult cognitive, social, and emotional experiences, the developmental story of imagination is shifting to acquisition and enrichment rather than decline. In addition, the scope of imagination research has broadened to include a wide range of investigations.

With our imaginations, we mentally transcend time, place, and/or circumstance to think about what might have been, plan and anticipate the future, create fictional worlds, and consider remote and close alternatives to actual experiences.[20] Such thoughts shape our emotional reactions and causal explanations and thus are integral to everyday thinking rather than occasional distractions from it.[21]

Imaginary friends are particularly linked with storytelling, a universal and lifelong human activity that is believed to promote insight into behaviors, contribute to empathy, extend our experience beyond personal circumstance, and help us find meaning in life.[22] The extension of experience that is possible from stories is not limited to scenarios that we might someday experience in real life. Science fiction presents narratives that shine light on everyday assumptions—changing our perspectives in ways that can deepen our understanding of ourselves and our world. Evolutionary social scientists Dudgar Dubourg and Nicolas Baumard[23] ask why authors, film producers, and others devote themselves so much to the creation of nonexistent worlds and why their efforts are so massively successful—resulting in top-grossing movies (e.g., *Star Wars*), bestselling novels (e.g., *Lord of the Rings*), and highly-rated TV series (e.g., *Game of Thrones*). Their answer is that "imaginary worlds tap into exploratory preferences which have evolved in a wide range of species to propel individuals toward new environments."[24] It is our inner explorer that made us wait so eagerly for the next installment of *Game of Thrones*. Fantasy is not just a form of entertainment or a means of escape. Imagination builds a bridge between the known and the unknown; it enables us to ponder, play with, and generate new possibilities—to go beyond the information given, beyond the facts as they exist, in order to create new ways of seeing the world and planning for the future.

Although children come to mind when we think about individuals with great imaginations, the imagination is a powerful tool that is available to all of us throughout life. Even interacting with an imaginary friend—an activity strongly associated with the preschool years—can be similar to adult behavior, both cognitively and emotionally. Progress in understanding the development of imaginative abilities will come as a result of studying such phenomena in young children and consequently looking for analogs in adult behavior and vice versa.

Summary

Typically developing children start to show clear evidence of their growing imaginations when they begin to pretend in the second year of life. For some, pretend play quickly becomes one of the dominant activities of their waking hours. How wonderful that this capacity is available so early on to help children process life events, achieve mastery of their emotions, enrich their social understanding, and develop their communication abilities! Their pretending begins with simple acts like saying "snake" while twisting a rope up mother's arm or "drinking" from an empty cup with a knowing smile but rapidly becomes complex and often highly imaginative, outstripping by far any capacity for pretense observed in other species.[25] A 5-year-old girl holds long conversations with an invisible flying dolphin hovering outside her bedroom window; a 6-year-old boy refers to a tree house as a spaceship and describes a series of ventures into the stars; a 10-year-old invents an imaginary world populated by soldier cats.

Parents, psychologists, and other adults sometimes have questioned the importance of early pretending and, in our opinion, underestimated the continued role of fantasy in later life. More specifically, there has been a tendency to dismiss imaginary friends, relegating them to the category of amusing childhood anecdotes and mementos, along with bedtime rituals, charming mispronunciations, and security blankets. But imaginary friends are more than nostalgic artifacts of childhood. They are early evidence of the fundamental and lifelong human capacity to contemplate fictional worlds, consider alternatives to the actual experiences of our lives, and derive companionship from imaginary others.

Notes

1. Singer, D. G., & Singer, J. L. (1990). *The house of make-believe: Children's play and developing imagination*. Harvard University Press.
2. Milne, C. (1974). *The enchanted places*. Eyre Methuen Ltd., p. 61.
3. Woolley, J. (1997). Thinking about fantasy: Are children fundamentally different thinkers and believers from adults? *Child Development, 68*, 991–1011.
4. Susan Carey famously described young children as "word learning wizards."
   Carey, S. (1985). Are children fundamentally different kinds of thinkers and learners than adults? *Thinking and Learning Skills, 2*, 485–517.
5. Harris, P. L. (2000). *The work of the imagination*. Basil Blackwell.
6. Parents should feel free to rein it in when they feel the need just as they would with any other play. So talking to your imaginary friend while attending a concert might not be ok, but neither is shouting during the performance.
7. Hoff, E. (2005a). A friend living inside me: The forms and functions of imaginary companions. *Imagination, Cognition and Personality, 24*, 151–189.
8. Taylor, M., Carlson, S, M., & Shawber, A. B. (2007). Autonomy and control in children's interactions with imaginary companions. In I. Roth (Ed.), *Imaginative minds* (pp. 81–100). British Academy and Oxford University Press.
9. Taylor, M., Hodges, S. D., & Kohanyi, A. (2003). The illusion of independent agency: Do adult fiction writers experience their characters as having minds of their own? *Imagination, Cognition and Personality, 22*, 361–380.
10. Borgenicht, D. (1998). *Sesame Street unpaved: Scripts stories and songs*. Hyperion, pp. 38–41.
11. Hoffner, C. A., & Bond, B. J. (2022). Parasocial relationships, social media, & well-being. *Current Opinion in Psychology, 45*, 101306.
    Yuan, S., & Lou, C. (2020). How social media influencers foster relationships with followers: The roles of source credibility and fairness in parasocial relationship and product interest. *Journal of Interactive Advertising, 20*(2), 133–147.

12. When we started writing this book, it did not occur to us that we might need to include a statement that the text was written by two humans and not a generative AI tool.
13. Brooks, D. (July 13, 2023). Human beings are soon going to be eclipsed. *The New York Times.* https://www.nytimes.com/2023/07/13/opinion/ai-chatgpt-consciousness-hofstadter.html
14. Hart, T., & Zellars, E. E. (2006). When imaginary companions are sources of wisdom. *Encounter: Education for Meaning and Social Justice, 19*(1), 6–15, see p. 10.
15. Taylor, M., & Mottweiler, C. M. (2008). Imaginary companions: Pretending they are real but knowing they are not. *American Journal of Play, 1,* 47–54.
16. Piaget, J. (1962). *Play, dreams, and imitation in childhood.* Norton.
17. Honeycutt, J. M. (2003). *Imagined interactions: Daydreaming about communication.* Hampton.
18. Klass, D., Silverman, P. R., & Nickman, S. L. (Eds.). *Continuing bonds: New understanding of grief.* Taylor & Francis.
19. Caughey, J. L. (1984). *Imaginary social worlds.* University of Nebraska Press, p. 241.
20. Harris, P. L. (2000). *The work of the imagination.*
    Suddendorf, T., & Corballis, M. C. (2007). The evolution of foresight: What is mental time travel and is it unique to humans? *Behavioral and Brain Sciences, 30,* 299–351.
    Taylor, M. (2013). Imagination. In P. Zelazo (Ed.), *Oxford handbook of child development: Body and mind* (Vol. 1, pp. 791–831). New York: Oxford University Press.
21. Riggs, K. J., & Beck, S. R. (2007). Thinking developmentally about counterfactual possibilities. *Behavioural and Brain Sciences, 30,* 463.
22. Bruner, J. (1986). *Actual minds, possible worlds.* Harvard University Press.
    Mar, R. A., & Oatley, K. (2008). The function of fiction is the abstraction and simulation of social experience. *Perspectives on Psychological Science, 3,* 173–192.
    Zunshine, L. (2006). *Why we read fiction: Theory of mind and the novel.* Ohio State University Press.
23. Dubourg, D., & Baumard, N. (2021). Why imaginary worlds? The psychological foundations and cultural evolution of fictions with imaginary worlds. *Behavioral and Brain Sciences,* 1–52. https://doi.org/10.1017/S0140525X21000923 hal-03419898
24. Ibid., p. 1.
25. Mitchell, R. M. (Ed.). (2002). *Pretense in animals and humans.* Cambridge University Press.

References

Acredolo, L. P., Goodwyn, S. W., & Fulmer, A. H. (1995). *Why some children create imaginary companions: Clues from infant and toddler play preferences* [Paper presentation]. Biennial Meeting of the Society for Research in Child Development, Indianapolis, IN.

Adam, A., & Sizemore, B. (2013). Parasocial romance: A social exchange perspective. *Interpersona: An International Journal on Personal Relationships, 7*(1), 12–25.

Adamo, S. M. G. (2004). An adolescent and his imaginary companions: From quasi-delusional constructs to creative imagination. *Journal of Child Psychotherapy, 30,* 275–295.

Adams, K., Stanford, E., & Singh, H. (2022). Reconceptualizing imaginary friends: Interdisciplinary approaches for understanding invisible companions. *Journal of Childhood Studies, 47,* 32–49.

Aguiar, N. A., & Taylor, M. (2015). Children's concepts of the social affordances of a virtual dog and a stuffed dog. *Cognitive Development, 34,* 16–27.

Aguiar, N. R. (2021). A paradigm for assessing adults' and children's concepts of artificially intelligent virtual characters. *Human Behavior and Emerging Technologies, 3*(4), 618–634.

Aguiar, N. R., Mottweiler, C. M., Taylor, M., & Fisher, P. (2017). The imaginary companions created by children who have lived in foster care. *Imagination, Cognition and Personality, 36*(4), 340–355.

Aguiar, N. R., Richards, M. N., Bond, B. J., Brunick, K. L., & Calvert, S. L. (2019). Parents' perceptions of their children's parasocial relationships: The recontact study. *Imagination, Cognition and Personality, 38*(3), 221–249. https://doi.org/10.1177/0276236618771537

Aguiar, N. R., Richards, M. N., Bond, B. J., Putnam, M. M., & Calvert, S. L. (2019). Children's parasocial breakups with media characters from the perspective of the parent. *Imagination, Cognition and Personality, 38*(3), 193–220. https://doi.org/10.1177/0276236618809902

Albee, E. (1962). *Who's afraid of Virginia Woolf?* Atheneum.

Aleman A., Nieuwenstein M. R., Böcker, K. B. E., & de Hán, E. H. F. (2000). Music training and mental imagery ability. *Neuropsychologia, 38*(12), 1664–1668.

Ames, L. B., & Learned, J. (1946). Imaginary companions and related phenomena. *Journal of Genetic Psychology, 69,* 147–167.

Anderson, N. T., Vander Hook, P., & Vander Hook, S. (1996). *Spiritual protection for your children: Helping your children and family find their identity, freedom and security in Christ.* Regal Books.

Armah, A., & Landers-Potts, M. (2021). A review of imaginary companions and their implications for development. *Imagination, Cognition and Personality, 41*(1), 31–53.

Arnold, J. (1986, March 11). High jinks: O'Hare may handle more flights but none as crazy as the New York-to-Miami run. *Chicago Tribune,* p. 1.

Associated Press. (2016, November 18). Meet the next Mozart, an 11-year-old who just wrote her first opera. *Washington Post.* https://www.washingtonpost.com/lifestyle/kidspost/meet-the-next-mozart-an-11-year-old-girl-who-just-wrote-her-first-opera/2016/11/18/93876bf0-ada7-11e6-8b45-f8e493f06fcd_story.html

Auerbach, N. (2015, March 25). Kentucky's Karl-Anthony Towns fueled by criticism, "Karlito." *USA Today.* https://www.usatoday.com/story/sports/ncaab/2015/03/24/kentucky-basketball-karl-anthony-towns-ncaa-tournament/70380424/

Auter, P. J., & Palmgreen, P. (2000). Development and validation of a parasocial interaction measure: The audience-persona interaction scale. *Communication Research Reports, 17*(1), 79–89.

Bagwell, C. L., & Schmidt, M. E. (2013). *Friendships in childhood and adolescence*. Guilford Press.

Bairdain, E. F. (1959). Psychological characteristics of adolescents who have had imaginary companions. *Dissertation Abstracts International, 29*, 747.

Barnes, J. (1985). *Flaubert's parrot*. Alfred A. Knopf.

Barnes, J. (2012). Fiction, imagination and social cognition: Insights from autism. *Poetics, 40*, 299–316.

Baron-Cohen, S. (1987). Autism and symbolic play. *British Journal of Developmental Psychology, 5*, 139–148.

Barry, D. (1998, February 6). Briton demands Pooh bear's release. *The New York Times*. Section, B, p. 3. https://www.nytimes.com/1998/02/06/nyregion/pooh-cornered-blair-cedes-bear.html

Bass, H. (1983). The development of an adult's imaginary companion. *Psychoanalytic Review, 70*(4), 519–533.

Becker, A. W. (1959). Ellen Glasgow and the Southern literary tradition. *Modern Fiction Studies, 5*(4), 295–304.

Bender, L., & Vogel, B. F. (1941). Imaginary companions of children. *American Journal of Orthopsychiatry, 11*, 56–65.

Benson, R. M., & Pryor, D. B. (1973). When friends fall out: Developmental interference with the function of some imaginary companions. *Journal of the American Psychoanalytic Association, 21*, 457–468.

Bloom, P. (2010). *How pleasure works: The new science of why we like what we like*. W. W. Norton & Co.

Bloom, P. (2024, March 25). Small potatoes, be right back. *Substack*. https://smallpotatoes.paulbloom.net/p/be-right-back'

Bond, B. J., & Calvert, S. L. (2014). A model and measure of US parents' perceptions of young children's parasocial relationships. *Journal of Children and Media, 8*, 286–304. https://doi.org/10.1080/17482798.2014.890948

Borgenicht, D. (1998). *Sesame Street unpaved: Scripts stories and songs*. Hyperion.

Botsman, R. (2017, October 7). Co-parenting with Alexa. *The New York Times*. https://www.nytimes.com/2017/10/07/opinion/sunday/children-alexa-echo-robots.html?searchResultPosition=5

Bouldin, P. (2006). An investigation of the fantasy predisposition and fantasy style of children with imaginary companions. *The Journal of Genetic Psychology, 167*(1), 17–29.

Bouldin, P., & Pratt, C. (1999). Characteristics of preschool and school-age children with imaginary companions. *The Journal of Genetic Psychology, 160*(4), 397–410.

Bouldin, P., & Pratt, C. (2001). The ability of children with imaginary companions to differentiate between fantasy and reality. *British Journal of Developmental Psychology, 19*, 99–114.

Bouldin, P., Bavin, E. L., & Pratt, C. (2002). An investigation of the verbal abilities of children with imaginary companions. *First Language, 22*(3), 249–264.

Bourchier, A., & Davis, A. (2000). Individual and developmental differences in children's understanding of the fantasy-reality distinction. *British Journal of Developmental Psychology, 18*(3), 353–368.

Bretherton, I. (1989). Pretense: The form and function of make-believe play. *Developmental Review, 9*, 383–401.

Bretherton, I., & Beeghley, M. (1982). Talking about internal states: The acquisition of an explicit theory of mind. *Developmental Psychology, 18*, 906–921.

Brinhthaupt, T. M., & Dove, C. T. (2012). Differences in self-talk frequency as a function of age, only-child, and imaginary companion status. *Journal of Research in Personality, 46*, 326–333.

Brooks, A. C. (2023, April 6). Parasocial relationships are just imaginary friends for adults: If you get too invested in a fake friendship, your real ones might suffer. *The Atlantic.* https://www.theatlantic.com/family/archive/2023/04/parasocial-relationships-imaginary-connections-fans-celebrities/673645/

Brooks, D. (July 13, 2023). Human beings are soon going to be eclipsed. *The New York Times.* https://www.nytimes.com/2023/07/13/opinion/ai-chatgpt-consciousness-hofstadter.html

Brooks, M., & Knowles, D. (1982). Parents' views of children's imaginary companions. *Child Welfare, 61*, 25–33.

Brooks, N. R. (1997). Goodbye to an imaginary friend. *Los Angeles Times.* https://www.latimes.com/archives/la-xpm-1997-01-19-ls-20055-story.html.

Broomfield, N. (Director). (1998). *Kurt & Courtney* [Film]. Capital Films.

Bruner, J. (1986). *Actual minds, possible worlds.* Harvard University Press.

Buevas, M. (2015). *Confessions of an imaginary friend: You are only as invisible as you feel.* Puffin Books.

Burlingham, D., & Freud, A. (1944). *Infants without families.* George Allen & Unwin.

Calvert, S. L., Putnam, M. M., Aguiar, N. R., Ryan, R. M., Wright, C. A., Liu, Y. H. A., & Barba, E. (2020). Young children's mathematical learning from intelligent characters. *Child Development, 91*(5), 1491–1508. https://doi.org/10.1111/cdev.13341

Calvert, S. L., & Valkenburg, P. M. (2013). The influence of television, video games, and the internet on children's creativity. In M. Taylor (Ed.), *The Oxford handbook of the development of imagination* (pp. 438–450). Oxford University Press.

Carballo, R. (2023, December 11). Using A.I. to talk to the dead. *The New York Times.* https://www.nytimes.com/2023/12/11/technology/ai-chatbots-dead-relatives.html

Carey, S. (1985). Are children fundamentally different kinds of thinkers and learners than adults? *Thinking and Learning Skills, 2*, 485–517.

Carlson, S. M., & Davis, A. C. (2005). *Executive function and pretense in preschool children* [Poster presentation]. Annual meeting of the Jean Piaget Society, Vancouver, BC.

Carlson, S. M., & White, R. E. (2013). Executive function, pretend play, and imagination. In M. Taylor (Ed.), *The Oxford handbook of the development of imagination* (pp. 161–174). Oxford University Press.

Carlson, S. M., & White, R. E., & Davis-Unger, A. C. (2014). Evidence for a relation between executive function and pretense representation in preschool children. *Cognitive Development, 29*, 1–16.

Carlson, S. M., Tahiroglu, D., & Taylor. M. (2008). Links between dissociation and role play in a non-clinical sample of preschool children. *Journal of Trauma and Dissociation, 9*, 149–171.

Carlson, S. M., Taylor, M., & Levin, G. R. (1998). The influence of culture on pretend play: The case of Mennonite children. *Merrill Palmer Quarterly, 44*, 538–565.

Carlson, S. M., Zelazo, P. D., & Faja, S. (2013). Executive function. In P. Zelazo (Ed.), *The Oxford handbook of developmental psychology: Vol. 1. Body and mind* (pp. 706–743). Oxford University Press.

Carson, S. H., Peterson, J. B., & Higgins, D. M. (2003). Decreased latent inhibition is associated with increased creative achievement in high-functioning individuals. *Journal of Personality and Social Psychology, 85*, 499–506.

Cataldo, I., Lepri, B., Neoh, M. J. Y., & Esposito, G. (2021). Social media usage and development of psychiatric disorders in childhood and adolescence: A review. *Frontiers in Psychiatry, 11,* 508595.

Caughey, J. L. (1984). *Imaginary social worlds.* University of Nebraska Press.

Chase, M. (1944). *Harvey.* Dramatists Play Service.

Chatman, S. B. (1978). *Story and discourse.* Cornell University Press.

Chicoine B. (2006). Self-talk, imaginary friends, and fantasy life. In D. McGuire & B. Chicoine (Eds.), *Mental wellness in adults with Down syndrome: A guide to emotional and behavioral strengths and challenges* (pp. 136–146). Woodbine House, Inc.

Christie, A. (1977). *Agatha Christie: An Autobiography.* Dodd, Mead & Co.

Chukovsky, K. (1925/1968). *From two to five.* University of California Press.

Clark, C. D. (1995). *Flights of fancy, leaps of faith: Children's myths in contemporary America.* Chicago: University of Chicago Press.

Clark, C. D. (1998). Childhood imagination in the face of chronic illness. In J. de Rivers & T. R. Sarbin (Eds.), *Believed-in imaginings: The narrative construction of reality* (pp. 87–100). American Psychological Association.

Clark, C. D. (2003). *In sickness and in play: Children coping with chronic illness.* Rutgers University Press.

Coetzee, H., & Shute, R. (2003). "I run faster than him because I have faster shoes": Perceptions of competence and gender role stereotyping in children's imaginary friends. *Child Study Journal, 33*(4), 257–272.

Cohen, D., & MacKeith, S. A. (1991). *The development of imagination: The private worlds of childhood.* Routledge.

Cole, T., & Leets, L. (1999). Attachment styles and intimate television viewing: Insecurely forming relationships in a parasocial way. *Journal of Social and Personal Relationships, 16,* 495–511.

Couple. (1991, October). Fantastic voyages. *Sesame Street Magazine.*

Csikszentmihalyi, M. (1996). *Creativity: Flow and the psychology of discovery and invention.* HarperCollins.

Curry, A. (2018). (Director). Worlds of Ursula K. Le Guin [TV series episode]. *American Masters.* Season 33, Episode 9. PBS.

Daniel, E. S., Jr., Crawford Jackson, E. C., & Westerman, D. K. (2018). The influence of social media influencers: Understanding online vaping communities and parasocial interaction through the lens of Taylor's six-segment strategy wheel. *Journal of Interactive Advertising, 18*(2), 96–109.

Dannenbaum, S., & Kinnier, R. (2009). Imaginal relationships with the dead: Applications for psychotherapy. *Journal of Humanistic Psychology, 49,* 100–113.

Davies, J. (2023). Explaining the illusion of independent agency in imagined persons with a theory of practice. *Philosophical Psychology, 36*(2), 337–355.

Davis, P. E., King, N., Meins, E., & Fernyhough, C. (2023). "When my mummy and daddy aren't looking at me when I do my maths she helps me"; Children can be taught to create imaginary companions: A new method of studying imagination. *Infant and Child Development, 32*(2), e2390.

Davies, P. E., Simon, H., Meins, E., & Robins, D. L., (2018). Imaginary companions in children with autism spectrum disorder, *Journal of Autism and Developmental Disorders, 48,* 2790–2799.

Davis, P. E., Slater, J., Marshall, D., & Robins, D. L. (2023). Autistic children who create imaginary companions: Evidence of social benefits. *Autism, 27*(1), 244–252.

Dawkins. R. (January/February 1995). Putting away childish things. *Skeptical Inquirer, 19*(1), 31–36.

De Figueiredo, M. (2024, March 22). Our last, impossible conversation. *The New York Times*. https://www.nytimes.com/2024/03/22/style/modern-love-ai-our-last-impossible-conversation.html

Dibble, J. L., Hartmann, T., & Rosaen, S. F. (2016). Parasocial interaction and parasocial relationship: Conceptual clarification and a critical assessment of measures. *Human Communication Research, 42*(1), 21–44. https://doi.org/10.1111/hcre.12063

Dibble, J. L., & Rosaen, S. F. (2011). Parasocial interaction as more than friendship: Evidence for parasocial interactions with disliked media figures. *Journal of Media Psychology: Theories, Methods, and Applications, 23*(3), 122. https://doi.org/10.1027/1864-1105/a000044

Dierker, L. C., Davis, K. F., & Sanders, B. (1995). The imaginary companion phenomenon: An analysis of personality correlates and developmental antecedents. *Dissociation: Progress in the Dissociative Disorders, 8*(4), 220–228.

DiLalla, L. F., & Watson, M. W. (1988). Differentiation of fantasy and reality: Preschoolers' reactions to interruptions in their play. *Developmental Psychology, 24*, 286–291.

Docter, P. (2015). *Inside out* [Film]. Walt Disney Studios.

Dorr, A. (1983). No shortcuts to judging reality. In J. Bryant & D. R. Anderson (Eds.), *Children's understanding of television: Research on attention and comprehension* (pp. 199–220). Academic Press.

Dreyfus, H. L., & Dreyfus, S. E. (1986). *Mind over machine*. The Free Press.

Dubourg, D., & Baumard, N. (2022). Why imaginary worlds? The psychological foundations and cultural evolution of fictions with imaginary worlds. *Behavioral and Brain Sciences*,1-52. https://doi.org/10.1017/S0140525X21000923 hal-03419898

Dunn, J., & Hughes, C. (2001). "I got some swords and you're dead!": Violent fantasy, antisocial behavior, friendship, and moral sensibility in young children. *Child Development, 72*(2), 491–505.

Farver, J. M., & Howes, C. (1993). Cultural differences in American and Mexican mother-child pretend play. *Merrill-Palmer Quarterly, 39*, 344–358.

Fernyhough, C. (2016). *The voices within: The history and science of how we talk to ourselves*. Basic Books.

Fernyhough, C., Bland, K., Meins, E., & Coltheart, M. (2007). Imaginary companions and young children's responses to ambiguous auditory stimuli: Implications for typical and atypical development. *Journal of Child Psychology and Psychiatry, 48*(11), 1094–1101.

Fernyhough, C., Watson, A., Bernini, M., Moseley, P., & Alderson-Day, B. (2019). Imaginary companions, inner speech, and auditory hallucinations: What are the relations? *Frontiers in Psychology, 10*, 1665. https://doi.org/10.3389/fpsyg.2019.01665

Field, T., De Stephano, L., & Koewler, J. H. (1982). Fantasy play of toddlers and preschoolers. *Developmental Psychology, 18*, 503–508.

Fincher, D. (1999). *Fight club* [Film]. 20th Century Studios.

Finkelstein, S., Yarzebinski, E., Vaughn, C., & Cassell, J. (2013). Modeling ethnicity into technology: Using virtual agents to understand sociolinguistic variation. *Proceedings of NWA, 42*, 17–20.

Firth, L., Alderson-Day, B., Woods, N., & Fernyhough, C. (2015). Imaginary companions in childhood: Relations to imagination skills and autobiographical memory in adults. *Creativity Research Journal, 27*, 308–313. https://doi.org/10.1080/10400419.2015.1087240

Fisher, P. A., Burraston, B., & Pears, K. (2005). The early intervention foster care program: Permanent placement outcomes from a randomized trial. *Child Maltreatment, 10*(1), 61–71. https://doi.org/10.1177/1077559504271561

Fisher, P. A., Gunnar, M. R., Dozier, M., Bruce, J., & Pears, K. C. (2006). Effects of therapeutic interventions for foster children on behavioral problems, caregiver attachment, and stress regulatory neural systems. *Annals of the New York Academy of Sciences, 1094*(1), 215–225.

Flavell, J. H., Flavell, E. R., & Green, F. L. (1987). Young children's knowledge about the apparent-real and pretend-real distinctions. *Developmental Psychology, 23*, 816–822.

Flavell, J. H., Flavell, E. R., Green, F. L., & Korfmacher, J. E. (1990). Do young children think of television images as pictures or real objects? *Journal of Broadcasting and Electronic Media, 34*, 399–419.

Fowles, J. (1969). *The French Lieutenant's woman*. Little, Brown & Company.

Foxwell, J., Alderson-Day, B., Fernyhough, C., & Woods, A. (2020). "I've learned I need to treat my characters like people": Varieties of agency and interaction in writers' experiences of their characters' voices. *Consciousness and Cognition, 79*, 102901.

Fraiberg, S. H. (1959). *The magic years*. Charles Scribner's Sons.

Frank, A. (2003). *The diary of Anne Frank: The revised critical edition*. Doubleday Books.

Freud, A. (1966). A short history of child analysis. *The Psychoanalytic Study of the Child, 21*(1), 7–14.

Freud, S. (1908/1983). Creative writers and daydreaming. In E. Kurzweil & W. Phillips (Ed.), *Literature and Psychoanalysis* (pp. 19-28). Columbia University Press. https://doi.org/10.7312/kurz91842-003

Friedman, B., Kahn Jr. P. H., & Hagman, J. (2003). Hardware companions? What online AIBO discussion forums reveal about the human-robotic relationship. In G. Cockton & P. Korhonen (Eds.), *CHI '03: Proceedings of the SIGCHI conference on human factors in computing systems* (pp. 273–280). Association for Computing Machinery. https://doi.org/10.1145/642611.642660

Frost, B. J. (Writer) & Stern, T. (Director). (2017). *He-man* (Season 1, episode 3) [TV series episode]. In B. Volk-Weiss, T. Stern, A. Carkeet, & E. Zane (Executive Producers), *The toys that made us*. The Nacelle Company, Netflix.

Ganea, P. A., Pickard, M. B., & DeLoache, J. S. (2008). Transfer between picture books and the real world by very young children. *Journal of Cognition and Development, 9*(1), 46–66.

Gaskins, S. (2013). Pretend play as culturally constructed activity. In M. Taylor (Ed.), *The Oxford handbook of the development of imagination* (pp. 224–250). Oxford University Press.

Gaskins, S., Haight, W., & Lancy, D. F. (2007). The cultural construction of play. In A. Göncü & S. Gaskins (Eds.), *Play and development* (pp. 184–207). Psychology Press.

Gerrig, R. J. (1993). *Experiencing narrative worlds: On the psychological activities of reading*. Yale University Press.

Gibbs, S. (2015, November 26). Hackers can hijack Wi-Fi Hello Barbie to spy on your children. *The Guardian*. https://www.theguardian.com/technology/2015/nov/26/hackers-can-hijack-wi-fi-hello-barbie-to-spy-on-your-children

Giles, D. C. (2002). Parasocial interaction: A review of the literature and a model for future research. *Media Psychology, 4*(3), 279–305. https://doi.org/10.1207/S1532785XMEP0403_04

Giménez-Dasí, M., Pons, F., & Bender, P. K. (2016). Imaginary companions, theory of mind and emotion understanding in young children. *European Early Childhood Education Research Journal, 24*(2), 186–197.

Gleason, T. (2004). Imaginary companions and peer acceptance. *International Journal of Behavioral Development, 28*(3), 204–209.

Gleason, T. (2007). Murray: The stuffed bunny. In S. Turkle (Ed.), *Evocative objects: Things we think with* (pp. 171–177). The MIT Press.

Gleason, T., & White, R. (2005, April). Talking to a tiger: Children's day-to-day interactions with their imaginary companions [Paper presentation]. Biennial meeting of the Society for Research in Child Development, Atlanta.

Gleason, T. R. (2002). Social provisions of real and imaginary relationships in early childhood. *Developmental Psychology, 38,* 979–992.

Gleason, T. R. (2004). Imaginary companions: An evaluation of parents as reporters. *Infant and Child Development: An International Journal of Research and Practice, 13*(3), 199–215.

Gleason, T. R. (2013). Imaginary relationships. In M. Taylor (Ed.), *The Oxford handbook of the development of imagination* (pp. 251-271). New York: Oxford University Press. https://doi.org/10.1093/oxfordhb/9780195395761.013.0017

Gleason, T. R., & Hohmann, L. M. (2006). Concepts of real and imaginary friendships in early childhood. *Social Development, 15*(1), 128–144.

Gleason, T. R., Jarudi, R. N., & Cheek, J. M. (2003). Imagination, personality, and imaginary companions. *Social Behavior and Personality: An International Journal, 31*(7), 721–737.

Gleason, T. R., & Kalpidou, M. (2014). Imaginary companions and young children's coping and competence. *Social Development, 23*(4), 820–839.

Gleason, T. R., Sebanc, A. M., & Hartup, W. W. (2000). Imaginary companions of preschool children. *Developmental Psychology, 36,* 419–428.

Gleason, T. R., Theran, S. A., & Newberg, E. M. (2017). Parasocial Interactions and relationships in early adolescence. *Frontiers in Psychology, 8,* 1–11. https://doi.org/10.3389/fpsyg.2017.00255

Glenn, S. M., & Cunningham, C. C. (2000). Parents' reports of young people with Down syndrome talking out loud to themselves. *Mental Retardation, 38*(6), 498–505.

Godwin, G. (1995). Rituals and readiness: Getting ready to write. In N. Baldwin & D. Osen (Eds.), *The writing life: A collection of essays and interviews* (pp. 3–13). Random House.

Gola, A. A., Richards, M. N., Lauricella, A. R., & Calvert, S. L. (2013). Building meaningful parasocial relationships between toddlers and media characters to teach early mathematical skills. *Media Psychology, 16*(4), 390–411. https://doi.org/10.1080/15213269.2013.783774

Goldstein, T. R. (2009). The pleasure of unadulterated sadness: Experiencing sorrow in fiction, nonfiction and "in person". *Psychology of Aesthetics, Creativity, and the Arts, 3,* 232–237.

Goldstein, T. R., & Woolley, J. (2016). Ho! Ho! Who? Parent promotion of belief in and live encounters with Santa Claus. *Cognitive Development, 39,* 113–127.

Golomb, C., & Galasso, L. (1995). Make believe and reality: Explorations of the imaginary realm. *Developmental Psychology, 31,* 800–810.

Golomb, C., & Kuersten, R. (1996). On the transition from pretence play to reality: What are the rules of the game? *British Journal of Developmental Psychology, 14,* 203–217.

Gopnik, A. (2002, September 30). Bumping into Mr. Ravioli. *The New Yorker,* 80–84. https://www.newyorker.com/magazine/2002/09/30/bumping-into-mr-ravioli

Gopnik, A. (2009). *The philosophical baby.* Farrar, Straus, & Giroux.

Gottman, J. M., & Parker, J. G. (Eds.) (1986). *Conversations of friends: Speculations on affective development.* Cambridge University Press.

Grandin, T. (1996). *Thinking in pictures.* Vintage.

Graziano, M. S. A. (2010). *God, soul, mind, brain.* Leapfrog Press.

Greene, D. (Host). (2018, May 30). Weezer gives in to fans and covers Toto's "Africa." [Audio radio episode]. *Morning Edition.* NPR. https://www.npr.org/2018/05/30/615388548/weezer-gives-in-to-fans-and-covers-totos-africa

Gribbon, B. (Director). (2010). *Born schizophrenic: January's story* [Film]. Homerun Entertainment.

Grose, J. (2021, May 5). When grown-ups have imaginary friends: "Parasocial relationships" explain why you think influencers are your pals. *The New York Times.* https://www.nytimes.com/2021/05/05/parenting/influencers-social-media-relationships.html?searchResultPosition=1

Guilford, J. P. (1967). The nature of human intelligence. McGraw-Hill.

Gupta, A., & Desai, N. G. (2006). Pathological fantasy friend phenomenon. *International Journal of Psychiatry in Clinical Practice, 10*(2), 149-151. https://doi.org/10.1080/13651500600578961

Halpern A. R. (1988). Mental scanning in auditory imagery for songs, *Journal of Experimental Psychology: Learning, Memory, and Cognition, 14*(3), 434-443.

Hamlin, J. K., Wynn, K., & Bloom, P. (2007). Social evaluation by preverbal infants. *Nature, 450*, 557-560.

Hamlin, J. K., Wynn, K., & Bloom, P. (2010). Three-month-olds show a negativity bias in their social evaluations. *Developmental Science, 13*, 923-929.

Haraldsson, E., Fowler, P. C., & Periyannapillai, V. (2000). Psychological characteristics of children who speak of a previous life: A further field study on Sri Lanka. *Transcultural Psychiatry, 37*, 525-544.

Harner, L. (1975). Yesterday and tomorrow: Development of early understanding of the terms. *Developmental Psychology, 11*(6), 864-865.

Harriman, P. L. (1937). Some imaginary companions of older subjects. *The American Journal of Orthopsychiatry, 7*, 368-370.

Harris, P. L. (2000). *The work of the imagination*. Basil Blackwell.

Harris, P. L. (2012). *Trusting what you have been told: How children learn from others*. Belknap Press/Harvard University Press.

Harris, P. L. (2013). Fairy tales, history and religion. In M. Taylor (Ed.), *The Oxford handbook of the development of imagination* (pp. 31-41). Oxford University Press.

Harris, P. L. (2021). Early constraints on the imagination: The realism of young children. *Child Development, 92*(2), 466-483.

Harris, P. L., Brown, E., Marriott, C., Whittall, S., & Harmer, S. (1991). Monsters, ghosts and witches: Testing the limits of the fantasy-reality distinction in young children. *British Journal of Developmental Psychology, 9*, 105-123.

Harris, P. L., & Kavanaugh, R. D. (1993). Young children's understanding of pretense. *Monographs of the Society for Research in Child Development, 58*(1), i-107.

Harris, P. L., Kavanaugh, R. D., & Meredith, M. C. (1994). Young children's comprehension of pretend episodes: The integration of successive actions. *Child Development, 65*, 16-30.

Harris, P. L., Pasquini, E. S., Duke, S., Asscher, J. J., & Pons, F. (2006). Germs and angels: The role of testimony in young children's ontology. *Developmental Science, 9*(1), 76-96.

Hart, T., & Zellars, E. E. (2006). When imaginary companions are sources of wisdom. *Encounter: Education for Meaning and Social Justice, 19*(1), 6-15.

Harter, S., & Chao, C. (1992). The role of competence in children's creation of imaginary friends. *Merrill-Palmer Quarterly, 38*, 350-363.

Healy, D. (2005). *Attention deficit hyperactivity disorder and creativity: An investigation into their relationship* [Dissertation]. University of Canterbury, New Zealand.

Heath, S. B. (1983). *Ways with words: Language, life, and work in communities and classrooms*. Cambridge University Press.

Hegi, U. (1994). *Stones from the River*. Poseidon Press.

Hegi, U. (1997). *Intrusions*. Simon & Schuster.

Heider, F., & Simmel, M. (1944). An experimental study of apparent behavior. *American Journal of Psychology, 57*, 243-259.

Heise, D. R. (1988). Delusions and the construction of reality. In T. F. Oltmanns & B. A. Maher (Eds.), *Delusional beliefs* (pp. 259-272). Wiley.

Hirsch-Pasek, K., Golinkoff, R., Berk, L., & Singer, D. (2009). *A mandate for playful learning in preschool: Presenting the evidence*. Oxford University Press.

Hoff, E. (2005a). A friend living inside me: The forms and functions of imaginary companions, *Imagination, Cognition and Personality, 24*, 151-189.

Hoff, E. (2005b). Imaginary companions, creativity, and self-image in middle childhood. *Creativity Research Journal, 17*, 167–180.

Hoffman, A., Owen, D., & Calvert, S. L. (2021). Parent reports of children's parasocial relationships with conversational agents: Trusted voices in children's lives. *Human Behavior and Emerging Technologies, 3*(4), 606–617.

Hoffner, C. (2008). Parasocial and online social relationships. In S. L. Calvert & B. J. Wilson (Eds.), *The handbook of children, media, and development* (pp. 309–333). Wiley-Blackwell.

Hoffner, C. A., & Bond, B. J. (2022). Parasocial relationships, social media, & well-being. *Current Opinion in Psychology, 45*, 101306.

Holway, A. H., & Boring, E. G. (1940). The moon illusion and the angle of regard. *The American Journal of Psychology, 53*(1), 109–116.

Honeycutt, J. M. (2003). *Imagined interactions: Daydreaming about communication*. Hampton.

Honeycutt, J. M. (2020). Imagined interactions and inner speech. *Imagination, Cognition and Personality, 39*(4), 386–396.

Hood, B. M., & Bloom, P. (2008). Children prefer certain individuals over perfect duplicates. *Cognition, 106*, 455–462.

Horton, D., & Richard Wohl, R. (1956). Mass communication and para-social interaction: Observations on intimacy at a distance. *Psychiatry, 19*(3), 215–229.

Hostetler, J. A., & Huntington, G. E. (1971). *Children in Amish Society: Socialization and Community Education*. Holt, Rinehart and Winston, Inc.

Huolman, M., & Peltonen, K. (2022). Dissociative features related to imaginary companions in the assessment of childhood adversity and dissociation: A pilot study. *European Journal of Trauma & Dissociation, 6*(4), 100295.

Hurlock, E. B., & Burnstein, M. (1932). The imaginary playmate: A questionnaire study. *Journal of Genetic Psychology, 41*, 380–391.

Huurre, T., & Aro, H. (2000). The psychological well-being of Finnish adolescents with visual impairments versus those with chronic conditions and no disabilities. *Journal of Visual Impairment & Blindness, 94*, 625–637.

Imafuku, M., & Seto, A. (2022). Cognitive basis of drawing in young children: Relationships with language and imaginary companions. *Early Child Development and Care, 192*(13), 2059–2065.

Imperiale, N. (1992, September 30). Imaginary pals say a lot about kids. *Orlando Sentinel Tribune*, P. E1.

Jackson, C., & Yi, J. (2019, October 24). *Less than half of Americans believe ghosts are real. Vast majority of parents eat their child's Halloween candy*. Ipsos. https://www.ipsos.com/en-us/news-polls/halloween-2019

Jackson, P. (1994). *Heavenly creatures* [Film]. Miramax.

Jalongo, M. R. (1984). Imaginary companions in children's lives and literature. *Childhood Education, 60*, 166–171.

James, P. D. (1999). *Time to be earnest: A fragment of autobiography*. Random House Group.

Jersild, A. T., Markey, F. V., & Jersild, C. L. (1933). Children's fears, dreams, wishes, daydreams, likes, dislikes, pleasant and unpleasant memories. *Child Development, 12*, xi–172.

Jipson, J. L., & Gelman, S. A. (2007). Robots and rodents: Children's inferences about living and nonliving kinds. *Child Development, 78*(6), 1675–1688.

Johnson, C., & Harris, P. L. (1994). Magic: Special but not excluded. *British Journal of Developmental Psychology, 12*, 35–51.

Jones, S. R., & Fernyhough, C. (2007). Thought as action: Inner speech, self-monitoring, and auditory verbal hallucinations. *Consciousness and Cognition, 16*(2), 391–399.

Kahlo, F. (1995). *The diary of Frida Kahlo: An intimate self-portrait.* (Introduction by Carlos Fuentes, essay by Sarah Lowe). Harry N. Abrams, Inc.

Kahn, P. H., Jr. Friedman, B., Perez-Granados, D. N., & Freier, N. G. (2006). Robotic pets in the lives of preschool children. *Interaction Studies, 7,* 405–436.

Kahn, P. H. Jr., Gary, H. E., & Shen, S. (2013). Children's social relationships with current and near-future robots. *Child Development Perspectives, 7,* 32–37.

Kahn, Jr. P. H., Kanda, T., Ishiguro, I., Hiroshi, F., Nathan, G., Severson, R. L., Gill, B. T., Ruchert, J. H., & Shen, S. (2012). "Robovie, you'll have to go into the closet now": Children's social and moral relationships with a humanoid robot. *Developmental Psychology, 48,* 303–314.

Kalyan-Masih, V. (1986). Imaginary play companions: Characteristics and functions. *International Journal of Early Childhood, 18*(1), 30-40.

Kalyan Masih, V. (1978). Imaginary companions of children. In R. B. R. Weizmann, P. J. Levinson, & P. A. Taylor (Eds.), *Piagetian theory and its implications for the helping professions.* University of Southern California.

Kambhampaty, A. P. (2021, October 28). Many Americans say that they believe in ghosts. Do you? Beliefs in paranormal phenomena may be a way of grappling with the unknown. *The New York Times.* https://www.nytimes.com/2021/10/28/style/do-you-believe-in-ghosts.html

Kang, S., Dove, S., Ebright, H., Morales, S., & Kim, H. (2021). Does virtual reality affect behavioral intention? Testing engagement processes in a K-Pop video on YouTube. *Computers in Human Behavior, 123,* 106875.

Kapitány, R., Nelson, N., Burdett, E. R., & Goldstein, T. R. (2020). The child's pantheon: Children's hierarchical belief structure in real and non-real figures. *PLOS ONE, 15*(6), e0234142.

Karmiloff-Smith, A. (1990). Constraints on representational change: Evidence from children's drawing. *Cognition, 34,* 57–83. https://doi.org/10.1016/0010-0277(90)90031-E

Kastenbaum, R., & Fox, L. (2008). Do imaginary companions die? An exploratory study. *OMEGA-Journal of Death and Dying, 56*(2), 123–152.

Kavanaugh, R., & Taylor, M. (April, 1997). *Adult correlates of childhood fantasy.* Poster presented at the Biennial Meeting of the Society for Research in Child Development, Washington, DC.

Kaye, M. (1990). *The real tooth fairy.* Harcourt, Brace, & Co.

King, S. (1989). *The dark half.* Viking Press.

Klass, D. (2006). Continuing conversation about continuing bonds. *Death Studies, 30*(9), 843–858.

Klass, D., Silverman, P. R., & Nickman, S. L. (Eds.). (2014). *Continuing bonds: New understanding of grief.* Taylor & Francis.

Klinger, E., Henning, V. R., & Janssen, J. M. (2009). Fantasy-proneness dimensionalized: Dissociative component is related to psychopathology, daydreaming is not. *Journal of Research in Personality, 43,* 506–510.

Kluft, R. P. (1984). Treatment of multiple personality disorder: A study of 33 cases. *Psychiatric Clinics of North America, 7,* 9–29.

Koenig, M. A., & Harris, P. L. (2005). Preschoolers mistrust ignorant and inaccurate speakers. *Child Development, 76*(6), 1261–1277.

Koenig, M. A., & Harris, P. L. (2007). The basis of epistemic trust: Reliable testimony or reliable sources? *Episteme, 4*(3), 264–284.

Kogan, N. (2002). Careers in the performing arts. A psychological perspective. *Creativity Research Journal, 14,* 1–16.

Kosslyn, S. M., Margolis, J. A., Barrett, A. M., Goldknopf, E. J., & Daly, P. F. (1990). Age differences in imagery abilities. *Child Development*, *61*(4), 995–1010.

Kottmeyer, M. (1996). Fairies. In G. Stein (Ed.), *The Encyclopedia of the Paranormal* (pp. 265–271). Prometheus Books.

Kozhevnikov M., Hegarty M., & Mayer R. E. (2002). Revising the visualizer-verbalizer dimension: Evidence for two types of visualizers. *Cognition and Instruction*, *20*(1), 47–77.

Kresovich, A., & Noar, S. M. (2020). The power of celebrity health events: Meta-analysis of the relationship between audience involvement and behavioral intentions. *Journal of Health Communication*, *25*(6), 501–513.

Kushnir, J., & Sadeh, A. (2012). Assessment of brief interventions for nighttime fears in preschool children. *European Journal of Pediatrics*, *171*, 67–75.

Latham, C., & Sakol, J. L. (1988). *The Royals*: Congdon & Weed.

Lauricella, A. R., Gola, A. A. H., & Calvert, S. L. (2011). Toddlers' learning from socially meaningful video characters. *Media Psychology*, *14*, 216–232. https://doi.org/10.1080/15213269.2011.573465

Lazurus, A. (1984). *In the mind's eye: The power of imagery for personal enrichment*. Guilford Press.

Legal & General. (2023). *A million imaginary friends*. Legal & General. https://www.legalandgeneral.com/insurance/life-insurance/imaginary-friends/

Legorreta, M. D. (1999). *Relación entre amigos imaginarios, tipo psicológico y creatividad artística (on the relationship between imaginary companions, psychological type and artistic creativity)*, [Doctoral dissertation] Universidad Iberoamericana.

Legorreta, M. D. (2002). Differences in Mexican and American parents; interpretations of chilkdren's imaginary companions. Unpublished data. University of Oregon, Eugene OR.

Lequerica A., Rapport L., Bradley N. A., Telmer K., Whitman R. D. (2002). Subjective and objective assessment methods of mental imagery control: Construct validation of self-report measures. *Journal of Clinical and Experimental Neuropsychology*, *24*(8), 1103–1116.

Leslie, A. M. (1987). Pretense and representation: The origins of theory of mind." *Psychological Review*, *94*, 412–426.

Lewis, C. (1871). *Through the looking glass*. Macmillan.

Lewis, C. S. (1955). *Surprised by joy: The shape of my early life*. Harcourt, Brace & Co.

Li, H., Boguszewski, K., & Lillard, A. S. (2015). Can that really happen? Children's knowledge about the reality status of fantastical events in television. *Journal of Experimental Child Psychology*, *139*, 99–114.

Lillard, A. (1994). Making sense of pretense. In C. Lewis & P. Mitchell (Eds.), *Children's early understanding of mind* (pp. 211–234). Lawrence Erlbaum.

Lillard, A. S. (2013). Playful learning and Montessori education. *Namta Journal*, *38*(2), 137–174.

Lillard, A. S., & Kavanaugh, R. D. (2014). The contribution of symbolic skills to the development of an explicit theory of mind. *Child Development*, *85*(4), 1535–1551.

Lillard, A. S., Lerner, M. D., Hopkins, E. J., Dore, R. A., Smith, E. D., & Palmquist, C. M. (2013). The impact of pretend play on children's development: A review of the evidence. *Psychological Bulletin*, *139*(1), 1–34. https://doi.org/10.1037/a0029321

Lillard, A. S., & Taggart, J. (2018). Pretend play and fantasy: What if Montessori was right? *Child Development Perspectives*, *6*, 1–6.

Lim, J. S., Choe, M. J., Zhang, J., & Noh, G. Y. (2020). The role of wishful identification, emotional engagement, and parasocial relationships in repeated viewing of live-streaming games: A social cognitive theory perspective. *Computers in Human Behavior*, *108*, 106327.

Lin, Q., Fu, H., Wan, Y., Zhou, N., & Xu, H. (2018). Chinese children's imaginary companions: Relations with peer relationships and social competence. *International Journal of Psychology, 53*(5), 388–396.

Lin, Q., Zhang, R., Zhang, Y., & Zhou, N. (2022). Did Chinese children with imaginary companions attribute more agencies to non-human items?: Evidences from behavioral cues and appearance characteristics. *Frontiers in Psychology, 13,* 1–9. https://doi.org/10.3389/fpsyg.2022.899047

Lin, Q., Zhou, N., & Fu, H. (2020). Prevalence of imaginary companions among Chinese children aged 4 to 6 years. *Social Behavior and Personality: An International Journal, 48*(3), 1–11.

Lin, Q., Zhou, N., Wan, Y., & Fu, H. (2020). Relationship between Chinese children's imaginary companions and their understanding of second-order false beliefs and emotions. *International Journal of Psychology, 55*(1), 98–105.

Lindsey, R. (1988, July 24). Promises to keep. *The New York Times Magazine,* pp. 23–24.

Liu, D., Wellman, H. M., Tardif, T., & Sabbagh, M. A. (2008). Theory of mind development in Chinese children: A meta-analysis of false-belief understanding across cultures and languages. *Developmental Psychology, 44*(2), 523–531.

Lloyd, B., & Goodwin, R. (1995). Let's pretend: Casting the characters and setting the scene. *British Journal of Developmental Psychology, 13*(3), 261–270.

Lovinger, S. L. (1983). Multiple personality: A theoretical view. *Psychotherapy: Theory, Research & Practice, 20*(4), 425–434. https://doi.org/10.1037/h0088503

Lynn, S. J., Pintar, J., & Rhue, J. W. (2013). Fantasy proneness, dissociation, and narrative construction. In S. Krippner & S. M. Powers (Eds.), *Broken images, broken selves* (pp. 274–302). Brunner/Mazel.

Machtlinger, V. J. (1976). Psychoanalytic theory: Pre-oedipal and oedipal phases with special reference to the father. In M. E. Lamb (Ed.), *The role of the father in child development* (pp. 277–305). Wiley.

Majors, K. (2013). Children's perceptions of their imaginary companions and the purposes they serve: An exploratory study in the United Kingdom. *Childhood, 20,* 550–565. https://doi.org/10.1177/0907568213476899

Manguel, A., & Guadalupi, G. (1980). *The dictionary of imaginary places.* Macmillan.

Mannering, A. M., & Taylor, M. (2009). Cross-modality correlations in the imagery of adults and 5-year-old children. *Imagination, Cognition, and Personality, 28,* 207–238.

Manosevitz, M., Fling, S., & Prentice, N. M. (1977). Imaginary companions in young children: Relationships with intelligence, creativity and waiting ability. *Journal of Child Psychology and Psychiatry, 18,* 73–78.

Manosevitz, M., Prentice, N. M., & Wilson, F. (1973). Individual and family correlates of imaginary companions in preschool children. *Developmental Psychology, 8,* 72–79.

Mar, R. A., & Oatley, K. (2008). The function of fiction is the abstraction and simulation of social experience. *Perspectives on Psychological Science, 3*(3), 173–192.

Mares, M. L., & Acosta, E. (2008). Be kind to three-legged dogs: Children's literal interpretations of television's metaphorical messages about tolerance. *Media Psychology, 11,* 377–399.

Martindale, C. (1999). Biological basis of creativity. In R. Sternberg (Ed)., *Handbook of creativity* (pp. 137–152). Cambridge University Press.

Mathur, R., & Smith, M. C. (2008). An investigation of imaginary companions in an ethnic and grade diverse sample. *Imagination, Cognition and Personality, 27*(4), 313–336.

Mauro, J. (1991). *The friend that only I can see: A longitudinal investigation of children's imaginary companions* [Doctoral dissertation]. University of Oregon.

McAnally, H. M., Forsyth, B. J., Taylor, M., & Reese, E. (2020). Imaginary companions in childhood: What can prospective longitudinal research tell us about their fate by adolescence? *The Journal of Creative Behavior, 55*, 276–283. https://doi.org/10.1002/jocb.468

McCurdy, H. G., & Follett, H. (1966). *Barbara: The unconscious autobiography of a child genius.* The University of North Carolina Press.

McInnis, M. A., Pierucci, J. M. & Gilpin, A. T. (2013). Investigating valence and autonomy in children's relationships with imaginary companions. *International Journal of Developmental Science, 7*, 151–159. https://doi.org/10.3233/DEV-130123

McLewin, L. A., & Muller, R. T. (2006). Childhood trauma, imaginary companions, and the development of pathological dissociation. *Aggression and Violent Behavior, 11*, 531–545. https://doi.org/10.1016/j.avb.2006.02.001

Mead, M. (1930). *Growing up in New Guinea.* William Morrow.

Mills, A. (2003). Are children with imaginary playmates and children said to remember previous lives cross-culturally comparable categories? *Transcultural Psychiatry, 40*, 62–90.

Milne, A. A. (1926). *Winnie-the-Pooh.* Methuen & Co.

Milne, C. (1974). *The enchanted places.* Eyre Methuen Ltd.

Miner, J. L. (2004). Parental attitudes toward pretend play and imaginary companions in preschool children [Unpublished honors thesis]. University of Oregon.

Mitchell, R. W. (Ed.) (2002). *Pretense in animals and humans.* Cambridge University Press.

Montanez, A. (2022, November 4). *Wilson, the volleyball that kept Tom Hanks company in "Castaway," just sold for over $85,000.* Robb Report. https://robbreport.com/lifestyle/news/wilson-volleyball-auction-1234769064/

Moriguchi, Y., Kanakogi, Y., Todo, N., Okumura, Y., Shinohara, I., & Itakura, S. (2016). Goal attribution toward non-human objects during infancy predicts imaginary companion status during preschool years. *Frontiers in Psychology, 7*, 221–229. https://doi.org/10.3389/fpsyg.2016.00221

Moriguchi, Y., Shinohara, I., & Ishibashi, M. (2016). Agent perception in children with and without imaginary companions. *Infant and Child Development, 25*(6), 550–564.

Moriguchi, Y., & Todo, N. (2018). Prevalence of imaginary companions in Japanese children: A meta-analysis. *Merrill-Palmer Quarterly, 64*, 459–482. https://doi.org/10.13110/merrpalmquar1982.64.4.0459

Morison, P., & Gardner, H. (1978). Dragons and dinosaurs: On distinguishing the realms of reality and fantasy. *Child Development, 49*, 642–648.

Morris, B. (1990). Dovima, a regal model of the 50s is dead at 63. *The New York Times*, p. 31. https://www.nytimes.com/1990/05/05/obituaries/dovima-a-regal-model-of-the-50-s-is-dead-at-63.html

Motoshima, Y., Shinohara, I., Todo, N., & Moriguchi, Y. (2014). Parental behaviour and children's creation of imaginary companions: A longitudinal study. *European Journal of Developmental Psychology, 11*(6), 716–727.

Mottweiler, C. M., & Taylor, M. (2014). Elaborated role play and creativity in preschool age children. *Journal of Aesthetics, Creativity and the Arts, 8*, 277–286.

Murphy, L. B. (1965). *The widening world of childhood: Paths toward mastery.* Basic Books.

Myrick, J. G., & Erlichman, S. (2020). How audience involvement and social norms foster vulnerability to celebrity-based dietary misinformation. *Psychology of Popular Media, 9*(3), 367.

Nagera, H. (1969). The imaginary companion: Its significance for ego development and conflict resolution. *The Psychoanalytic Study of the Child, 24*, 165–196. https://doi.org/10.1080/00797308.1969.11822691

Nelson, D. (2008). *My son Marshall, my son Eminem.* Phoenix Books, Inc.

Newman, J. (2014, October 17). To Siri, with love. *The New York Times.* https://www.nytimes.com/2014/10/19/fashion/how-apples-siri-became-one-autistic-boys-bff.html

Newport, F., & Strausberg, M. (2001, June 8). Americans' belief in psychic and paranormal phenomena is up over the last decade. Gallup. https://news.gallup.com/poll/4483/americans-belief-psychic-paranormal-phenomena-over-last-decade.aspx

Newson, J., & Newson, E. (1968). *Four years old in an urban community.* George Allen & Unwin Ltd.

Newson, J., & Newson, E. (1976). *Seven years old in an urban environment.* George Allen & Unwin Ltd.

Ng, B. (2021, December 17). Did you see what Big Bird tweeted? Social media is fueling our "parasocial relationships" with TV characters. *The New York Times.* https://www.nytimes.com/2021/12/17/style/sesame-street-social-media-parasocial-relationships.html?searchResultPosition=3

Niu, S., Bartolome, A., Mai, C., & Ha, N. B. (2021, May). # StayHome# WithMe: How do YouTubers help with COVID-19 loneliness? In Y. Yoshifumi & A. Quigley (Eds.) *Proceedings of the 2021 CHI conference on human factors in computing systems* (pp. 1–15). Assocation for Comuputing Machinery.

O'Connor, K. J. (1991). *The play therapy primer.* Wiley.

Opie, I., & Opie, P. (1959). *The lore and language of school children.* Oxford University Press.

Paley, V. G. (2004). *A child's work: The importance of fantasy play.* University of Chicago Press.

Paretsky, S. (1999). *Hard Time.* Delacourt Press.

Parker, J. G., & Asher, S. R. (1993). Friendship and friendship quality in middle childhood: Links with peer group acceptance and feelings of loneliness and social dissatisfaction. *Developmental Psychology, 29,* 611–621.

Partington, J. T., & Grant, C. (1984). Imaginary playmates and other useful fantasies. In *Play in Animals and Humans* (pp. 217–240). Basil Blackwell.

Pearson, D., Rouse, H., Doswell, S., Ainsworth, C., Dawson, O., Simms, K., Edwards, L., & Faulconbridge, J. (2001). Prevalence of imaginary companions in normal child population. *Child: Care, Health and Development, 27,* 12–22. https://doi.org/10.1046/j.1365-2214.2001.00167.x

Perner, J., Leekam, S. R., & Wimmer, H. (1987). Three-year-olds' difficulty understanding false beliefs: Representational limitation, lack of knowledge or pragmatic misunderstanding. *British Journal of Developmental Psychology, 5,* 125–137.

Perry, S. K. (1999). *Writing in flow: Keys to enhanced creativity.* Writer's Digest.

Piaget, J. (1923/73). *Language and thought of the child. Concept of the mind.* Routledge Classics.

Piaget, J. (1929). *The child's conception of the world.* Routledge and Kegan Paul.

Piaget, J. (1962). *Play, dreams, and imitation in childhood.* Norton.

Pirandello, L. (1921). *Six characters in search of an author.* English translation by E. Storer (1922). E.P. Dutton & Co.

Prentice, N. M., & Gordon, D. (1986). Santa Claus and the Tooth Fairy for the Jewish child and parent. *Journal of Genetic Psychology, 148,* 139–151.

Prentice, N. M., Manosevitz, M., & Hubbs, L. (1978). Imaginary figures of early childhood: Santa Claus, Easter Bunny and the Tooth Fairy. *American Journal of Orthopsychiatry, 48,* 618–628.

Putnam, F. W. (1989). *Diagnosis and treatment of multiple personality disorder.* Guilford Press.

Quarforth, J. M. (1979). Children's understanding of the nature of television characters. *Journal of Communication, 29,* 210–218.

Rachford, F. E. (1949). *The Brontës' web of childhood.* Columbia University Press.

Redekop, C. (1989). *Mennonite society.* Johns Hopkins University Press.

Renee, R. & Bonis, J. (2023, April 26). Parasocial relationship pitfalls (No. 5) [Audio podcast episode]. In *Doxxed The Podcast*. (RSS.com). https://rss.com/podcasts/doxxedthepodcast/910459/

Richards, M. N., & Calvert, S. L. (2016). Parent versus child report of young children's parasocial relationships in the United States. *Journal of Children and Media, 10*, 462–480. https://doi.org/10.1080/17482798.2016.1157502

Richards, M. N., & Calvert, S. L. (2017). Measuring young U.S. children's parasocial relationships: Toward the creation of a child self-report survey. *Journal of Children and Media, 11*, 229–240. https://doi.org/10.1080/17482798.2017.1304969

Richert, R. A., Shawber, A. B., Hoffman, R. I., & Taylor, M. (2009). Learning from real and fantasy characters in preschool and kindergarten. *Cognition and Development, 10*, 41–66.

Richert, R. A., & Smith, E. I. (2011). Preschoolers' quarantining of fantasy stories. *Child Development, 82*(4), 1106–1119.

Rideout, V., & Robb, M. B. (2020). *The Common Sense census: Media use by kids age zero to eight, 2020*. Common Sense Media. https://www.commonsensemedia.org/sites/default/files/research/report/2020_zero_to_eight_census_final_web.pdf

Riggs, K. J., & Beck, S. R. (2007). Thinking developmentally about counterfactual possibilities. *Behavioural and Brain Sciences, 30*, 463–463.

Robinson, M. (2016, May 17). *A teen actor from "Game of Thrones" has been getting death threats from viewers*. Business Insider. https://www.businessinsider.com/olly-actor-game-of-thrones-death-threats-2016-5

Roby, A. C., & Kidd, E. (2008). The referential communication skills of children with imaginary companions. *Developmental Science, 11*, 531–540.

Root-Bernstein, M. (2014). *Inventing imaginary worlds: From childhood play to adult creativity across the arts and sciences*. Rowman & Littlefield Publishers.

Root-Bernstein, M. (2021). Creating imaginary worlds across the lifespan. In S. W. Russ, J. D. Hoffmann, & J. C. Kaufman (Eds.), *The Cambridge handbook of lifespan development of creativity* (pp. 327–350). Cambridge University Press.

Root-Bernstein, M., & Root-Bernstein, R. (2006). Imaginary worldplay in childhood and maturity and its impact on adult creativity. *Creativity Research Journal, 18*(4), 405–425.

Rosengren, K. S., Johnson, C., & Harris, P. L. (Eds.). (2000). *Imagining the impossible: The development of magical, scientific, and religious thinking in contemporary society*. Cambridge University Press.

Rosengren, K. S., Kalish, C. W., Hickling, A. K., & Gelman, S. A. (1994). Exploring the relation between preschool children's magical beliefs and causal thinking. *British Journal of Developmental Psychology, 12*, 69–82.

Roth, I. (2007). Autism and the imaginative mind. In I. Roth (Ed.), *Imaginative minds* (277–306). Oxford University Press.

Roudane, M. C. (1990). *Who's afraid of Virginia Woolf?: Necessary fictions, terrifying realities*. Twayne Publishers.

Rowling, J. K. (October 20, 1999). Radio interview. *The Diane Rehm show*. NPR.

Ruben, E., French, J., Lee, H. J., Aguiar, N. R., Richert, R., & Gleason, T. (2023, March). *Let it go: Media influences on imaginary companions in early childhood* [Poster presentation]. Biennial Meeting of the Society for Research in Child Development, Salt Lake City, UT.

Rubin, A. M., Perse, E. M., & Powell, R. A. (1985). Loneliness, parasocial interaction, and local television news viewing. *Human Communication Research, 12*, 155–180. https://doi.org/10.1111/j.1468-2958.1985.tb00071.x

Rubin, S. S., & Shechory-Stahl, M. (2013). The continuing bonds of bereaved parents: A ten-year follow-up study with the two-track model of bereavement. *OMEGA - Journal of Death and Dying, 66*(4), 365–384. https://doi.org/10.2190/OM.66.4.f

Rubio, M., & Waterson, E. (Eds.) (1985). *The selected journals of L. M. Montgomery, Vol 1: 1889–1910.* Oxford University Press.

Sakol, J. & Latham, C. (1988). *The Royals.* Congdon & Weed.

Sadeh, A., Hen-Gal, S., & Tikotzky, L. (2008). Young children's reactions to war-related stress: A survey and assessment of an innovative intervention. *Pediatrics, 121,* 46–53.

Salinger, J. D. (1953). *Nine stories.* Little, Brown, & Co.

Samuels, A., & Taylor, M. (1994). Children's ability to distinguish fantasy events from real-life events. *British Journal of Developmental Psychology, 12,* 417–427.

Sanders, B. (1992). The imaginary companion experience in multiple personality disorder. *Dissociation, 5,* 159–162.

Sawa, T., Oae, H., Abiru, T., Ogawa, T., & Takahashi, T. (2004). Role of imaginary companion in promoting the psychotherapeutic process. *Psychiatry and Clinical Neurosciences, 58*(2), 145–151.

Sayfan, L., & Lagattuta, K. H. (2009). Scaring the monster away: What children know about managing fears of real and imaginary creatures. *Child Development, 80*(6), 1756–1774.

Scarlett, W. G., & Wolf, D. (1979). When it's only make-believe: The construction of a boundary between fantasy and reality in storytelling. In E. Winner, & H. Gardner (Eds.), *New directions for child development: Fact, fiction and fantasy in childhood* (pp. 29–40). Jossey-Bass.

Schaefer, C. E. (1969). Imaginary companions and creative adolescents. *Developmental Psychology, 1,* 747–749.

Scheibe, C. (1987). *Developmental differences in children's reasoning about Santa Claus and other fantasy characters* [Doctoral dissertation]. Cornell University.

Schlesinger, M. A., Flynn, R. M., & Richert, R. A. (2016). US preschoolers' trust of and learning from media characters. *Journal of Children and Media, 10*(3), 321–340. https://doi.org/10.1080/17482798.2016.1162184

Schramm, H., & Hartmann, T. (2008). The PSI-process scales. A new measure to assess the intensity and breadth of parasocial processes. *Communications: The European Journal of Communication Research, 33,* 385–401. https://doi.org/10.1515/COMM.2008.025

Seiffge-Krenke, I. (1993). Close friendship and imaginary companions in adolescence. In B. Laursen (Ed.), *Close friendships in adolescence* (pp. 73–87). Jossey-Bass.

Seuss, Dr. (1957). *The cat in the hat.* Random House.

Seuss, Dr. (1974). *There's a wocket in my pocket.* Random House.

Severson, R. L., & Carlson, S. M. (2010). Behaving as or behaving as if? Children's conceptions of personified robots and the emergence of a new ontological category. *Neural Networks, 23,* 1099–1103.

Sharon, T., & Woolley, J. D. (2004). Do monsters dream? Young children's understanding of the fantasy/reality distinction. *British Journal of Developmental Psychology, 22*(2), 293–310.

Shook, J. J., Vaughn, M. G., Litschge, C., Kolivoski, K., & Schelbe, L. (2009). The importance of friends among foster youth aging out of care: Cluster profiles of deviant peer associations. *Children and Youth Services Review, 31,* 284–291. https://doi.org/10.1016/j.childyouth.2008.07.024

Shtarkman, R. (2022, April 24). The puppet from Israel helps Ukrainian kids cope with unspeakable trauma. *Haaretz.* https://www.haaretz.com/israel-news/2022-04-24/ty-article-magazine/a-doll-from-israel-helps-ukrainian-children-cope-with-unspeakable-trauma/00000180-5bee-de8c-a1aa-dbee4c070000

Shtulman, A., & Carey, S. (2007). Improbable or impossible? How children reason about extraordinary events. *Child Development, 78,* 1015–1032.

Siegel, R. K. (1992). *Fire in the brain: Clinical tales of hallucination.* Penguin Books USA Inc.

Silberg, J. L. (2021). *The child survivor: Healing developmental trauma and dissociation.* Routledge.

Singer, D. G. (1993). *Playing for their lives: Helping troubled children through play therapy.* The Free Press.

Singer, D. G., & Lenahan, M. L. (1976). Imagination content in dreams of deaf children. *American Annals of the Deaf, 121*(1), 44–48.

Singer, D. G., & Singer, J. L. (1990). *The house of make-believe: Children's play and developing imagination.* Harvard University Press.

Singer, D. G., & Singer, J. L. (2005). *Imagination and play in the electronic age.* Harvard University Press.

Singer, D. G., & Singer, J. L. (Eds.). (2012). *Handbook of children and the media.* Sage Publications Inc.

Singer, J. L. (1961). Imagination and waiting ability in young children. *Journal of Personality, 29,* 396–413.

Singer, J. L., & Singer, D. G. (1981). *Television, imagination, and aggression: A study of preschoolers.* Erlbaum.

Singer, J. L., & Streiner, B. F. (1966). Imaginative content in the dreams and fantasy play of blind and sighted children. *Perceptual and Motor Skills, 22,* 475–482.

Smilansky, S. (1968). *The effects of sociodramatic play on disadvantaged preschool children.* John Wiley & Sons.

Smiley, J. (2005). *13 ways of looking at the novel.* Alfred A. Knopf.

Smith, D. B. (2007). *Muses, madmen, and prophets: Rethinking the history, science, and meaning of auditory hallucination.* Penguin.

Smith, M. C. (2019). Imaginary companions of blind, deaf, and typically developing school children. *Imagination, Cognition and Personality, 38*(3), 290–314.

Spock, B. (1974). *Bringing up children in a difficult time.* The Bodley Head.

Stoney, B. (1974). *Enid Blyton: A biography.* Hodder.

Subbotsky, E. V. (1993). *Foundations of the mind.* Harvard University Press.

Suddendorf, T., & Corballis, M. C. (2007). The evolution of foresight: What is mental time travel and is it unique to humans? *Behavioral and Brain Sciences, 30,* 299–351.

Sugarman, S. (2013). *An investigation into parents' attitudes to their children having imaginary companions.* [Doctoral dissertation.] University of London.

Sutton-Smith, B. (2001). *The ambiguity of play.* Harvard University Press.

Svendsen, M. (1934). Children's imaginary companions. *Archives of Neurology and Psychiatry, 2,* 985–999.

Tahiroglu, D., Mannering, A. M., & Taylor, M. (2011). Visual and auditory imagery associated with children's imaginary companions. *Imagination, Cognition and Personality, 31,* 99–112.

Tahiroglu, D., & Taylor, M. (2019). Anthropomorphism, social understanding, and imaginary companions. *British Journal of Developmental Psychology, 37,* 284–299. doi.org/10.1111/bjdp.12272.

Tammet, D. (2006). *Born on a blue day: Inside the extraordinary mind of an autistic savant.* Free Press.

Taylor, B., & Howell, R. J. (1973). The ability of three-, four-, and five-year-old children to distinguish fantasy from reality. *Journal of Genetic Psychology, 122,* 315–318.

Taylor, M. (1997). The role of creative control and culture in children's fantasy/reality judgments. *Child Development, 68,* 1015–1017.

Taylor, M. (2013). Imagination. In P. Zelazo (Ed.), *Oxford handbook of child development: Body and mind* (Vol. 1, pp. 791–831). Oxford University Press.

Taylor, M., & Carlson, S. M. (1997). The relation between individual differences in fantasy and theory of mind. *Child Development, 68,* 436–455.

Taylor, M., Carlson, S. M., Maring, B. L., Gerow, L., & Charley, C. (2004). The characteristics and correlates of high fantasy in school-aged children: Imaginary companions, impersonation and social understanding. *Developmental Psychology, 40,* 1173–1187.

Taylor, M., Carlson, S. M., & Shawber, A. B. (2007). Autonomy and control in children's interactions with imaginary companions. In I. Roth (Ed.), *Imaginative minds* (pp. 81–100). British Academy and Oxford University Press.

Taylor, M., Cartwright, B. S., & Carlson, S. M. (1993). A developmental investigation of children's imaginary companions. *Developmental Psychology, 29*(2), 276–285.

Taylor, M., Lussier, G. L., & Maring, B. L. (2003). The distinction between lying and pretending. *Journal of Cognition and Development, 4*(3), 299–323.

Taylor, M., Hodges, S. D., & Kohanyi, A. (2003). The illusion of independent agency: Do adult fiction writers experience their characters as having minds of their own? *Imagination, Cognition and Personality, 22,* 361–380.

Taylor, M., Hulette, A. C., & Dishion, T. J. (2010). Longitudinal outcomes of young high-risk adolescents with imaginary companions. *Developmental Psychology, 46,* 1632–1636.

Taylor, M., & Mottweiler, C. M. (2008). Imaginary companions: Pretending they are real but knowing they are not. *American Journal of Play, 1,* 47–54.

Taylor, M., Mottweiler, C. M., Aguiar, N. R., Naylor, E. R., & Levernier, J. G. (2018). Paracosms: The imaginary worlds of middle childhood. *Child Development, 91,* 164–178. https://doi.org/10.1111/cdev.13162

Taylor, M., Mottweiler, C. M., Naylor E., & Levernier, J. (2015). Imaginary worlds in middle childhood: A qualitative study of two pairs of coordinated paracosms. *Creativity Research Journal, 27,* 167–174.

Taylor, M., Sachet, A. B., Mannering, A. M., & Maring, B. L. (2013). The assessment of elaborated role-play in young children: Invisible friends, personified objects and pretend identities. *Social Development, 22,* 75–93.

Taylor, M., Shawber, A. B., & Mannering, A. M. (2009). Children's imaginary companions: What is it like to have an invisible friend? In K. Markman, W. Klein, & J. Suhr (Eds.), *The handbook of imagination and mental simulation* (pp. 211–224). Psychology Press.

Taylor, P. (1999). *Private domain: An autobiography.* University of Pittsburgh Press.

Terr, L. (1990). *Too scared to cry: Psychic trauma in childhood.* Basic Books.

Tolbert, A. N., & Drogos, K. L. (2019). Tweens' wishful identification and parasocial relationships with YouTubers. *Frontiers in Psychology, 10,* 1–15.

Tolkien, J. R. R. (1947). On fairy stories. In C. Tolkien (Ed.), *Essays presented to Charles Williams* (pp. 38–89). Oxford University Press.

Toto. (1982). Africa. On *Toto IV* [Album]. Columbia Records.

Trionfi, G., & Reese, E. (2009). A good story: Children with imaginary companions create richer narratives. *Child Development, 80,* 1301–1313.

Trujillo, K., Lewis, D. O., Yeager, C. A., & Gidlow, B. (1996). Imaginary companions of school boys and boys with Dissociative Identity Disorder/Multiple Personality Disorder: A normal to pathological continuum. *Child and Adolescent Psychiatric Clinics of North America, 5,* 375–391.

Turkle, S., Taggart, W., Kidd, C. D., & Dasté, O. (2006). Relational artifacts with children and elders: The complexities of cybercompanionship. *Connection Science, 18,* 347–361. https://doi.org/10.1080/09540090600868912

Turner, M. (1996). *The literary mind.* Oxford University Press.

Ustinov, P. (1977). *Dear me.* Penguin.

van Allsburg, C. (1985). *The polar express.* Houghton Mifflin.

References

Volpe, A. (July 30, 2019). Why kids invent imaginary friends. *The Atlantic*. https://www.theatlantic.com/family/archive/2019/07/why-do-kids-have-imaginary-friends/594919/
Vostrovsky, C. (1895). A study of imaginary companions. *Education, 15*, 383–398.
Vygotsky, L. S. (1978). *Mind in society*. Harvard University Press.
Walker, A. (1983). *In search of our mothers' gardens*. Harcourt Brace Jivanovich.
Walton, K. L. (1990). *Mimesis as make-believe*. Harvard University Press.
Warfield, F. (1948). *Cotton in my ears*. The Viking Press.
Watkins, M. (1990). *Invisible guests: The development of imaginal dialogues*. Siego Press.
Watterson, B. (1995). *The Calvin and Hobbes tenth anniversary book*. Andrews and McMeel.
Waytz, A., Epley, N., & Cacioppo, J. T. (2010). Social cognition unbound: Insights into anthropomorphism and dehumanization. *Current Directions in Psychological Science, 19*, 58–62.
Weaver, L. H. (1982). Forbidden fancies: A child's vision of Mennonite plainness. *Journal of Ethnic Studies, 11*, 51–59.
Weezer. (2018). Africa [Cover of Toto original song]. On *The teal album* [Album]. Crush Music & Atlantic Records.
Wegner, D. M. (2002). *The illusion of conscious agency*. The MIT Press.
Wellman, H. M., Cross, D., & Watson, J. (2001). Meta-analysis of theory of mind development: The truth about false belief. *Child Development, 72*, 655–684. https:/doi.org/10.1111/1467-8624.00304
Wellman, H. M., & Estes, D. (1986). Early understanding of mental entities: A reexamination of childhood realism. *Child Development, 57*, 910–923.
White, H. A., & Shah, P. (2006). Uninhibited imaginations: Creativity in adults with attention-deficit/hyperactivity disorder. *Personality and Individual Differences, 40*(6), 1121–1131.
White, J., & Allers, C. T. (1994). Play therapy with abused children: A review of the literature. *Journal of Counselling and Development, 72*, 390–394.
White, R. E., Prager, E. O., Schaefer, C., Kross, E., Duckworth, A. L., & Carlson, S. M. (2017). The "Batman Effect": Improving perseverance in young children. *Child Development, 88*, 1563–1571.
Wickes, F. G. (1927). *The inner world of childhood*. D. Appleton & Company.
Wigger, J. B. (2019). *Invisible companions: Encounters with imaginary friends, gods, ancestors, and angels*. Stanford University Press.
Willey, L. H. (2014). *Pretending to be normal: Living with Asperger's syndrome (autism spectrum disorder)* (Expand. ed.). Jessica Kingsley Publishers.
Williams, D. (1994). *Nobody nowhere: The extraordinary autobiography of an autistic*. Avon.
Williams, M. (1975). *The velveteen rabbit*. Avon Books.
Wilson, S. C., & Barber, T. X. (1981). *Vivid fantasy and hallucinatory abilities in the life histories of excellent hypnotic subjects ("somnambules"): Preliminary report with female subjects*. In E. Klinger (Ed.), *Imagery, vol 2: Concepts, results, and applications* (pp. 341–387), Plenum Press.
Wimmer, H., & Perner, J. (1983). Beliefs about beliefs: Representation and constraining function of wrong beliefs in young children's understanding of deception. *Cognition, 13*, 103–128.
Wingfield, R. C. (1948). Bernreuter personality ratings of college students who recall having had imaginary companions during childhood. *Journal of Child Psychiatry, 1*, 190–194.
Winnicott, D. W. (1953). Transitional objects and transitional phenomena. *International Journal of Psychoanalysis, 34*, 89–97.
Woolley, J. (1997). Thinking about fantasy: Are children fundamentally different thinkers and believers from adults? *Child Development, 68*, 991–1011.

Woolley, J. D., Boerger, E. A., Markman, A. B. (2004). A visit from the Candy Witch: Factors influencing young children's belief in a novel fantastical being. *Developmental Science, 7*, 456–468.

Woolley, J. D., & Cox, V. (2007). Development of beliefs about storybook reality. *Developmental Science, 10*, 681–693.

Woolley, J. D., & E. Ghossainy, M. (2013). Revisiting the fantasy-reality distinction: Children as naïve skeptics. *Child Development, 84*(5), 1496–1510.

Woolley, J. D., & Phelps, K. E. (1994). Young children's practical reasoning about imagination. *British Journal of Developmental Psychology, 12*, 53–67.

Woolley, J. D., & Wellman, H. M. (1993). Origin and truth: Young children's understanding of imaginary mental representations. *Child Development, 64*, 1–17.

Wright, J. C., Huston, A. C., Reitz, A. L., & Piemyat, S. (1994). Young children's perceptions of television reality: Determinants and developmental differences. *Developmental Psychology, 30*, 229–239.

Wullschlager, J. (1996). *Inventing Wonderland*. The Free Press.

Yamaguchi, M., & Moriguchi, Y. (2022). Did children interact with their personified objects during the COVID-19 pandemic? *Imagination, Cognition and Personality, 41*(3), 354–367.

Yamaguchi, M., Okanda, M., Moriguchi, Y., & Itakura, S. (2023). Young adults with imaginary companions: The role of anthropomorphism, loneliness, and perceived stress. *Personality and Individual Differences, 207*, 112159.

Yarrow, P., & Lipton, L. (1963). Puff (the magic dragon) [Song recoded by Peter, Paul, and Mary on *Moving*]. Warner Bros.

Yawkey, T. D., & Yawkey, M. L. (1983, June 29). *Assessing young children for imaginativeness through oral reporting: Preliminary results* [Paper presentation]. International Conference on Play and Play Environments: Research and its Application to Play Settings, Austin, TX.

Yazıcı Arıcı, E., Keskin, H. K., Papadakis, S., & Kalogiannakis, M. (2022). Evaluation of children's discourses regarding imaginary companion: The case of Türkiye. *Sustainability, 14*, 16608. https://doi.org/10.3390/su142416608

Yuan, S., & Lou, C. (2020). How social media influencers foster relationships with followers: The roles of source credibility and fairness in parasocial relationship and product interest. *Journal of Interactive Advertising, 20*(2), 133–147.

Zarei, T., Pourshahbaz, A., & Poshtmashhadi, M. (2021). Childhood imaginary companion and schizotypy in adolescents and adults. *Journal of Anomalous Experience and Cognition, 2*(1), 166–189.

Zemeckis, R. (Director). (2000). *Cast Away* [Film]. 20th Century Fox.

Zhang, Y.Q., Pei, M. J., Chen, X. L., & Zhang, W. R. (2014). The impact of imaginary companions on 5 to 6 years old children's emotion understanding. *Journal of Tongling Vocational College, 9*, 66–69.

Zhao, R., Papangelis, A., & Cassell, J. (2014). Towards a dyadic computational model of rapport management for human-virtual agent interaction. In G. Goos (Ed.) *International Conference on Intelligent Virtual Agents* (pp. 514–527). Springer International Publishing.

Zolotow, C. (1961). *The three funny friends*. Harper & Row.

Zunshine, L. (2006). *Why we read fiction: Theory of mind and the novel*. Ohio State University Press.

Index

For the benefit of digital users, indexed terms that span two pages (e.g., 52–53) may, on occasion, appear on only one of those pages.

Tables and figures are indicated by an italic *t* and *f* following the paragraph ID.

A

Abiru, T., 112–113
Abstract Patterns Task, 57
Abuse, 111–113
Acredolo, L. P., 52
Actors, 134, 231–232 n4
Adam, A., 83
Adjustment to preschool, 158–159
Adolescents, 95, 115–116, 176, 189, 213
Adults, 197, *see also* Fiction writers
    Reactions to imaginary friends, 1, 4, 76–77, 153, 154–155, 197–198, 234
    Who have imaginary friends, 11, 151, 200–201
Advice to parents, 27, 97–98, 138, 234–237, 242 n6
Age
    Of child, 76–77, 154–155, 159–160, 197
    Of imaginary friends, 18–19
Aguiar, N. R., 19–21, 113–115, 174, 182–185, 185*f*
AIBO, 39–40
Ainsworth, C., 113, 154–155
Albee, E., 197–198
Alderson-Day, B., 200–201
Alexa, 179, 186, 190
Alien Hand Syndrome, 217
Ames, L. B., 26, 33, 47–48
Anderson, N. T., 78
Anderson-Day, B., 218, 225
Animals
    Invisible, 19
    Stuffed animals, *see* Personified objects
Anne of Green Gables, 197, 201
Anthropomorphism, 40–42
Artificial intelligence, 179, 183–186, 190, 210–211 n18
Asthma, 119
Atlantic, The, 72, 188
Attention Deficit Disorder, 54, 110–111
Authors, *see* Fiction writers
Autism spectrum disorder, 56

Autobiographies, 201–202
Automatic writing, 215, 217

B

Babies, *see* Infants
Bad/uncooperative behavior of imaginary friends, 21–25, 22*t*
Barba, E., 182–183, 185
Barber, T. X., 211 n20
Barbie, 40, 186–187
Barnes, J., 197
Batman Effect, 27
Baumard, N., 241
Bender, L., 102
Bender, P. K., 50
Benson, R. M., 30–31, 153–154
Bergen, E., 215
Bergen, G., 215
Bernini, M., 200–201
Bing Bong from *Inside Out*, 93
Birth of a sibling, 71
Birth order, 70–71, 81
Bland, K., 60
Blind children, 101–102
Bloom, P., 38–39, 197, 210–211 n18
Blyton, E., 214
Boerger, E. A., 133
Bond, B. J., 189–190
Bouldin, P., 52, 55–56
Bretherton, I., 25
Brontë, A., 164
Brontë, B., 164
Brontë, C., 164, 165*f*
Brontë, E., 164
Brooks, A. C., 74
Brooks, M., 74
Brooks, N. R., 148–149
Brown, E., 136–137
Bruner, J., 103
Buevas, M., 162 n31

C

Cacioppo, J. T., 41
Calvert, S. L., 182–183, 185–186
Calvin and Hobbes, 30–31, 158
Candy Witch, 133
Carballo, R., 210–211 n18
Carey, S., 242 n4
Carlson, S. M., 4, 27, 50–51, 53–54, 55–56, 62 n9, 79–80, 118, 151–154, 175–176, 193 n24
Carroll, L., 128, 164
Cartwright, B. S., 151–154
Cassell, J., 183
Cast Away, 41
Cat in the Hat, The, 92
Caughey, J. L., 188–189, 240
Celebrities, 11, 179–180, 188
Channeling, 215
Characteristics of children with imaginary friends, 47
Charley, C., 188–189, 240
Chase, M., 197–198
ChatGPT, 239
Child Behavior Checklist, 62 n11
Child Dissociative Checklist, 118
Child's Play, 40
China, 81
Christie, A., 11, 202–205, 209
Christmas, *see* Santa Claus
Christopher Robin, 15–16, 42
Chucky, 40
Chukovsky, K., 73–76
Clark, C. D., 77–78, 110, 131–132
Clements, S., 22–23
Cobain, K., 202
Cohen, D., 173–174
Color Purple, The, 216
Coltheart, M., 60
Communication
  With imaginary friends, 18–19
  With other people, 96–98
  By phone, 24
Competence, 99–100
Complaints by child about imaginary friend, 21–25
Confessions of an Imaginary Friend, 158
Contingent responding, 182–183, 184–187
Coping, 10, 110
Continuing bonds, 200, 210–211 n18
Coppola, F. F., 95
Covid-19, 71
Creative control, 43, 141–142, 147 n74, 187–188, 237–238
Creativity, 54, 57–59, 167, 174, 219–220
Csikszentmihalyi, M., 199, 219–220

Cultural myths, 77–78, 130–133, 143 n28
Culture, 9

D

Dasté, O., 39–40
Davies, J., 217
Davis, A. C., 54
Davis, P. E., 56, 72–73, 126–127 n45
Dawson, O., 113, 154–155
Deaf children, 101–102
Death, of imaginary friend, 156–158
Deficit Hypothesis, 95
Definition of imaginary friend, 2, 25–26, 28, 30–31, 83
Descriptions of imaginary friends, 1, 4, 5–6, 99–101, 114t
  Of invisible friends, 16–21, 19t
  Of personified objects, 31–32, 34t, 35
Deutscher, A., 165
Devil, 78–79
Diabetes, 119
Diaries, 95, 106 n25, 110, 201–202
Dickens, C., 134
Dickinson, E., 234
Dictionary of Imaginary Places, 164
Digital media, 60–61, 69 n109, 134–135
DiLalla, L. F., 136
Disappearance of imaginary friend, 150
Dishion, T. J., 115–116
Dishonesty, *see* Lying
Dissociation, 118
Dissociative Identity Disorder, 117–119
Diversity of imaginary friends, *see* Variation in imaginary friends
Dolls, *see* Personified objects
Dominican Republic, 84
Dora the Explorer, 181–183, 185
Dore, R. A., 71
Doswell, S., 113, 154–155
Down Syndrome, 55
Dovima, 160
Doyle, Sir A. C., 210 n8
Drawings, 5f, 17f, 18f, 58–59, 172f, 176
Drogos, K. L., 180
Dubourg, D., 241
Dr. Strangelove, 217
Dr. Seuss, 21, 92
Dungeons and Dragons, 197

E

Easter Bunny, 129, 130–131, 236–237
Edwards, L., 113, 154–155
Elwood Dowd from *Harvey*, 197–198
Eminem, 19–21
Emotions, 50, 149, 154, 189–190, 235, 236–237

Enemies, imaginary, 22–23
Epley, N., 41
Evangeline, 197
Executive function, 53–55
Expertise, 218–219, 233 n32

F

Fairies, 198, 210 n8
False belief, 49–51, 64 n28
Family structure, 9, 70–71
Fans, 180, 188–224
Fantasy proneness/orientation, 52–53, 132–133, 200, 211 n20
Fantasy/reality distinction, 10, 53, 76, 129–130, 142 n4, 236–237, 238–240
  In pretend play, 135–138
  For imaginary friends, 138–141
Farver, J. M., 84–85
Fate of imaginary friends, 10–11
Faulconbridge, J., 113, 154–155
Fear, 98–99
  Of animals, 99
  Of the dark, 23, 98
  Of drain, 96–97
  Of puddles, 98
  Of ghosts, 98
Fernyhough, C., 60, 72–73, 126–127 n45, 200–201, 217–218, 225
Fictional characters, 12, 19–21, 182–183, 185–186, 214–216
Fiction writers, 12, 197, 213, 238
Fight Club, 197–198
Fisher, P. A., 113–115, 174
Flaubert, G., 42
Fling, S., 54
Flow, 215
Flynn, R. M., 182
Follett, B., 164
Forsyth, B. J., 148
Foster care, 113–115, 114*t*
Foster's Home for Imaginary Friends, 158
Fowles, J., 215
Fox, L., 151, 157
Foxwell, J., 218, 225
Fraiberg, S. H., 99
Frank, A., 106 n25, 110
French, J., 19–21
French Lieutenant's Woman, The, 215
Freud, A., 99
Freud, S., 213
Friedman, B., 39–40
Friendship, 92, 104, 188
  high quality, 1, 240
  Number of real-life friends, 89 n57, 95, 155–156
Fu, H., 81

Fulmer, A. H., 52
Function of imaginary friends, 10
  As a response to trauma, 110
  For communication, 96–98
  For fun and companionship, 92
  For storytelling, 96
  To avoid blame, 102–104
  To conquer fears, 98–99
  To ease loneliness, 95–96
  To feel competent, 99–100
  To make up for limitations, 100–101
  To process lived experience, 103–104
Fundamentalist Christians, 77–80

G

Game of Thrones, 188–189, 241
Gary, H. E., 193 n24
Gaskins, S., 85
Gelman, S. A., 193 n24
Gender differences, 51–52, 99–100, 173
Genre of fiction, 227–228, 230
Gerow, L., 51, 53, 62 n9
Ghosts, 98, 139, 198–199
Gide, A., 219
Gilpin, A. T., 23
Giménez-Dasí, M., 50
Gleason, T. R., 4, 17–18, 19–21, 31, 33, 35, 72, 94, 95, 122, 180
God, 77–78, 89 n44
Godfather, The, 95
Godwin, G., 224
Gola, A. A. H., 182
Goldstein, T. R., 138
Golomb, C., 98, 138
Gopnik, Adam, 23–24
Gopnik, Alison, 54–55
Gottman, J. M., 98
Grafton, S., 219–220, 221–222, 224, 226, 229, 231
Grandin, T., 56
Graziano, M. S. A., 36–37

H

Hagman, J., 39–40
Halloween, 133
Hallucinations, 60, 198, 217
Hanks, T., 41
Harmer, S., 136–137
Harris, P. L., 25–26, 50, 71–72, 77–78, 103, 135–137
Harry Potter, 179, 197, 215–216
Hart, T., 239–240
Hartup, W. W., 33, 35
Harvey, 197–198
Healy, D., 54
Hearing voices, 217

H

Heath, S. B., 75
Heavenly Creatures, 175–176
Heider, F., 41
Hegi, U., 216, 219–220, 226–228, 231
Hen-Gal, S., 121–123
Henning, V. R., 211 n20
High risk sample, 115–116
High season of imaginative play, 7–8
Hillerman, T., 219–220, 228–229, 231
Hodges, S. D., 216, 218, 238
Hohmann, L. M., 94
Hopkins, E. J., 71
Hoff, E., 57, 99, 102–104, 114–115, 167
Hoffner, C., 189–190
Hofstadter, D., 239
Hood, B. M., 38–39
Howes, C., 84–85
Huggy Puppy Intervention, 121–123, 126–127 n45
Hulette, A. C., 115–116

I

Illusion, 216–217
Illusion of independent agency, 12, 216–219, 238
Imafuku, M., 58–59
Imaginary identity, *see* Pretend identity
Imaginary world, *see* Paracosm
Imagined interaction, 240
Impersonation, *see* Pretend identity
Inconsistency in descriptions, 3–4
India, 83, 166, 174–175
Infants, 51–52, 64 n32, n35, 82
Inhibitory control, 27, 53–55, 175–176
Intelligence, 55–56
Interviews
  With adults, 5–7
  With children, 3, 13 n10, 151–152, 213
  With parents, 3–5, 13 n10, 94
Invisible imaginary friends, 8–9, 15
  Based on real people, 17–18

J

Jalongo, M. R., 104
James, P. D., 219–220, 224–227, 231
Janssen, J. M., 211 n20
Japan, 71, 81–82
Jehovah's Witnesses, 77
Jipson, J. L., 193 n24
Johnson, C., 137
Juba, D., 160
Jumbled Speech Task, 60

K

Kahlo, F., 202, 203*f*
Kahn, P. H., Jr., 39–40, 193 n24
Kalogiannakis, M., 82–83
Kalpidou, M., 122
Karmiloff-Smith, A., 58–59
Kastenbaum, R., 151, 157
Kavanaugh, R. D., 50, 136
Kaye, M., 132
Kenya, 84
Keskin, H. K., 82–83
Kidd, C. D., 39–40
King, N., 72–73, 126–127 n45
Knowles, D., 74
Koenig, M. A., 135
Kogan, N., 231–232 n4
Kohanyi, A., 216, 218, 238
Kottmayer, M., 210 n8
Kuersten, R., 98, 138
Kushnir, J., 122

L

Lauricella, A. R., 182
Lazurus, A., 98–99
Learned, J., 26, 33, 47–48
Lee, H. J., 19–21
Legorreta, D., 84–85
Le Guin, U., 214–215
Lenahan, M. L., 101
Lerner, M. D., 71
Leslie, A. M., 135–136
Levin, G. R., 79
Lewis, C. S., 164, 174–176
Lillard, A. S., 50, 71
Limitations, *see* Restrictions
Lin, Q., 81
Little Nell from *The Old Curiosity Shop*, 134
Loneliness, 67 n81, 95–96
Longfellow, H. W., 197
Love, 1, 72, 139, 149, 184, 234
Liu, Y. H. A., 182–183, 185
Loss of interest in imaginary friends, 150–151
Lussier, G. L., 75–76
Lying, 75–76, 84–85
Lynn, S. J., 200

M

MacKeith, S. A., 166–167, 173–175
Majors, K., 100–101, 104
Malawi, 84
Mannering, A. M., 49, 56, 59, 139–141
Manosevitz, M., 49, 54
March of the Penguins, The, 134
Markman, A. B., 133
Maring, B. L., 49, 51, 53, 62 n9, 75–76
Marriott, C., 136–137
Mathur, R., 95
Mauro, J., 48–49, 50, 55–56, 92, 155–156
Media characters, 11, 19–21

Mennonites, 79–80
Mental illness, 116–117, 197–198
Mental imagery, 16–17, 59–60
Mexico, 84–85
McAnally, H. M., 148
McInnis, M. A., 23
Mead, M., 85
Megan, 40
Meins, E., 56, 60, 72–73, 126–127 n45
Mexico, 84–85, 202
Middle Earth, 164
Mills, A., 83–84
Milne, A. A., 15–16, 25, 149
Milne, C., 149, 235
Miner, J. L., 74–75
Miracle on 34th Street, 131
Mister Rogers' Neighborhood, 96–97, 184
Moana, 15–16
Montgomery, L. M., 201–202
Montessori, M., 87 n13
Moriguchi, Y., 51, 71, 81–82
Moseley, P., 200–201
Motoshima, Y., 51, 82
Mottweiler, C. M., 57, 58–59, 113–115, 174
Movies
  Emotional reactions to, 137–138, 236–237
  Portrayals of imaginary friends, 40–41, 93, 155, 175–176, 197–198
Multiple personalities, *see* Dissociative Identity Disorder
Murphy, L. B., 120
Mysterious Stranger, The, 22–23

N
Nagera, H., 111
Narrative, 133–135, *see* storytelling
Nepal, 84
Newberg, E. M., 180
Newson, E., 22–23, 30, 76–77, 97, 102–103, 130, 155–156, 159–160
Newson, J., 22–23, 30, 76–77, 97, 102–103, 130, 155–156, 159–160
New York Times, 134, 188
Nietzsche, F., 164

O
Oae, H., 112–113
Ogawa, T., 112–113
Only children, 70–71
Owen, D., 186

P
Paley, V. G., 25
Palmquist, C. M., 71
Papadakis, S., 82–83
Papangelis, A., 183

Paracosms, 11, 163
Paranormal, 199, 210 n8
Parasocial relationship, 11, 179
Parents, *see* Interviews, with parents
  Attachment to imaginary friends, 42, 72, 148–149
  Encouragement, 73–74, 235
  Participation/interference, 35, 153–154
  Reactions to imaginary friends, 1, 4, 8, 71, 74, 88 n24, 128
  Reactions to pretend identities, 26–27
  Reaction to paracosms, 163–164
Paretsky, S., 215
Past lives, 83
Peabody Picture Vocabulary Test, 55–56
Penguin Picture stories, 57
Pearson, D., 113, 134, 154–155
Perspective taking, 49–51, 55–56
Personality, 47–48, 62 n5
  Big Five Factors, 48, 62 n9
Personified objects, 9
  Disadvantages, 36, 128, 149–150
  How they differ from invisible friends, 31–33, 35, 81–82, 89 n57, 94
  Replacement, 36–38–39, 45 n18
  Role of parents, 36
Peter Pan, 133–134
Peter, Paul and Mary, 148
Physical problems, 119–120
Piaget, J., 41, 97, 100–101, 130
Pierucci, J. M., 23
Pinocchio, 133–134
Pintar, J., 200
Pirandello, 216
Polar Express, The, 131
Pons, F., 50
Prager, E. O., 27
Pratt, C., 52, 55–56
Prentice, N. M., 49, 54
Pretend identity, 8–9, 25–27, 51, 53, 180, 224–225
Pretend play, 1–2, 7, 12, 26, 53–54, 56, 71, 74–75, 79–80, 85, 119, 124 n12, 213
  Comprehension of, 80, 129, 135–138
  Negative themes, 74–75
  Pretend actions, 136
Princess Margaret, 102–103
Problems with early studies, 47–48
Proust, M., 215
Pryor, D. B., 30–31, 153–154
Puff (the magic dragon), 148
Pullman, P., 219–220, 222–224, 226, 229, 231
Putnam, M. M., 182–183, 185

R
Real life themes, 25, 71–72, 81, 157–158, 173–174, 228, 230

Real life friends, 94
Real Tooth Fairy, The, 132
Reciprocity in friendship, 94, 187, 213–214
Reese, E., 57–58, 148
Relationship type, 35, 81, 94, 113–114
Religion, 77–80, 84, 198
Replacement of imaginary friend, 16, 36–39, 45 n18, 151–153
Research methods, 7–8, 13 n10, 32, 115–116, 168
Resilience, 10
Restrictions in children's lives, 100–102
Retrospective reports, 2, 5–7, 201–202
Rhue, J. W., 200
Richert, R. A., 19–21, 182
Robins, D. L., 56
Robots, 39–41, 193 n24
Role play, 25–26, 50
Root-Bernstein, M., 164, 167, 173
Root-Bernstein, R., 167, 173
Rouse, H., 113, 154–155
Rowling, J. K., 214–216
Ruben, E., 19–21
Russia, 76
Ryan, R. M., 182–183, 185

S
Sachet, A. B., 49
Sadeh, A., 121–123
Salinger, J. D., 151
Sanders, B., 117–118, 124 n12, 211 n20
Santa Claus, 77, 89 n44, 130–131, 167–168, 236–237
Santa Clause, The, 131
Satan, 22–23, 77–78
Saturday Night Live, 72
Sawa, T., 112–113
Scapegoat, 102–104
Scary imaginary friends, 21–25, 28 n12
Scary pretend play, 136–138
Schaefer, C. E., 27, 57
Schizophrenia, 116
Schlesinger, M. A., 182
Sebanc, A. M., 33, 35
Seiffge-Krenke, I., 95
Self-esteem, 99, 103
Sesame Street, 72, 134, 182, 238–239
Seto, A., 58–59
Severson, R. L., 193 n24
Sharon, T., 53
Shawber, A. B., 139–141
Shinohara, I., 51, 82
Shyness, 48–49, 63 n13
Siblings, *see* Family structure
Siegel, R. K., 160, 215
Silberg, J. L., 118

Silvey, R., 163–164, 166–167, 173–175
Simmel, M., 41
Simms, K., 113, 154–155
Simon, H., 56
Simulation, 50
Singer, D. G., 22–23, 25, 30, 49, 53–54, 61, 71, 73, 77, 96–98, 101, 110–111, 120–121, 144 n30
Singer, J. L., 22–23, 25, 30, 49, 53–54, 61, 71, 73, 77, 96–98, 144 n30
Singh, H., 83
Single parent families, *see* Family structure
Siri, 186
Snuffleupagus, 238–239
Social media influencers, 180, 189–190
Social robots, *see* Robots
Social understanding, *see* Theory of mind
Society for Creative Anachronism, 197
Socioeconomic status, 74–75, 115–116, 174
Sources of information about imaginary friends, 2
  Multiple sources of information, 7–8
Special abilities of imaginary friends, 2
Spirits, 83–85
Spiritual warfare, 78
Splitting, 116–117
Smiley, J., 230
Smith, D. B., 217
Smith, E. D., 71
Smith, M. C., 95, 101–102
Spock, B., 129–130
Stanford, E., 83
Stereotype of children with imaginary friends, 9, 48–49, 58t
Stevenson, R. L., 164
Storybooks, 133–135, 155, 229
Storytelling, 12, 57–58, 58t, 75, 96, 97t, 170–172, 176, 205, 228, 241
Stuffed animals, *see* Personified objects
Subbotsky, E. V., 22–23
Sugarman, S., 76–77
Summoning the imaginary friend, 18–19, 19t
Svendsen, M., 2, 30, 47

T
Tacet, G., 206–209, 208f
Taggart, W., 39–40
Tahiroglu, D., 41, 60, 82–83, 118
Takahashi, T., 112–113
Tammet, D., 56, 156–157
Taylor, M., 4, 41, 49–51, 53, 55–57, 58–60, 62 n9; 75–76, 78–79, 112–116, 118, 139–141, 148, 151–154, 158–159, 174, 183–184, 200–201, 214, 216, 218–220, 238
Taylor, P., 11, 202, 205–209, 208f
Television, 60–61, 133–135, 144 n30, 144–145 n37, 179, 181, 188–189, 197

Temperament, 47–49, 62 n5, 62–63 n12
Terr, L., 116–117, 119
Testimony, 134–135
Theran, S. A., 180
Theory of mind, 49–51, 56, 81
Therapy, 98–99, 110–112, 116–117, 120–121, 153–154
Tinkerbell, 133–134
Todo, N., 51, 81–82
Tolbert, A. N., 180
Tolkien, J. R. R., 164
Tooth Fairy, 129, 130–132, 236–237
Torrance's Thinking Creatively with Pictures, 57
Towns, K. A., 199–200
Trauma, 111–113, 116–117, 119, 120–123
Transitional object, 31–32
Three Funny Friends, The, 155
Tikotzky, L., 121–123
Trionfi, G., 57–58
Tulpa, 217
Turkey/Türkiye, 82–83
Turkle, S., 39–40
Twain, Mark, 22–23

U

Uncle Wiggily in Connecticut, 151
Unusual Uses Test, 57, 175–176
Ustinov, P., 26–27

V

van Allsburg, C., 131
Vander Hook, P., 78
Vander Hook, S., 78
Variation in imaginary friends, 15–16, 19, 27–28, 60, 234
Velveteen Rabbit, The, 138
Verbal ability, 55–56
Virtual characters, 183–184, 185–186
Vogel, B. F., 102
Volpe, A., 72

W

Waiting ability, 53–54

Walker, A., 216
War, 120–123
War of the Worlds, 145 n38
Warfield, F., 101, 156–157
Watch Tower, The, 77
Watkins, M., 214
Watson, A., 200–201
Watson, M. W., 136
Watterson, B., 30–31, 158
Waytz, A., 41
Weaver, L. H., 79
Wechsler Intelligence Scale, 47
  Block Design subtest, 55–56
Wegner, D. M., 217
Who's Afraid of Virginia Woolf?, 197–198
White, R. E., 27, 175–176
Whittall, S., 136–137
Wickes, F. G., 23
Wigger, J. B., 84–85, 99
Willey, L. H., 56
Wilson from *Castaway,* 41
Wilson, F., 49
Wilson, S. C., 211 n20
Winnie the Pooh, 15–16, 25–26, 42, 149, 235
Woods, A., 218, 225
Woolley, J., 53, 133
Wonderland, 164, 171*t*
Wellman, H. M., 182–183, 185
Wright, C. A., 182–183, 185

X

X, 190

Y

Yamaguchi, M., 71
Yazıcı Arıcı, E., 82–83

Z

Zellars, E. E., 239–240
Zhao, R., 183
Zhou, N., 81
Zolotow, C., 155